Rogue States and U.S. Foreign Policy

Rogue States and U.S. Foreign Policy

Containment after the Cold War

Robert S. Litwak

W Published by *The Woodrow Wilson Center Press*
Distributed by The Johns Hopkins University Press

EDITORIAL OFFICES

The Woodrow Wilson Center Press
One Woodrow Wilson Plaza
1300 Pennsylvania Avenue, N.W.
Washington, D.C. 20004-3027
Telephone 202-691-4010
www.wilsoncenter.org

ORDER FROM

The Johns Hopkins University Press
P.O. Box 50370
Baltimore, Maryland 21211
Telephone 1-800-537-5487
www.press.jhu.edu

2 4 6 8 9 7 5 3 1

Library of Congress Cataloging-in-Publication Data

Litwak, Robert.
    Rogue states and U.S. foreign policy : containment after the Cold War /
Robert S. Litwak.
        p. cm
    Includes bibliographical references and index.
    ISBN 0-943875-97-8 (pbk. : acid-free paper) — ISBN 0-943875-98-6 (hc :
acid-free paper)
    1. Aggression (International law) 2. Intervention (International law) 3. United
States—Foreign relations—1993– 4. Belligerency. I. Title: Rogue states and United
States foreign policy. II. Title.
KZ6374.L58 1999
327.73—dc21
                                                                    99-050562

*To my wife, Liz, for her steadfast
support in this as in everything else*

Contents

Abbreviations

CIA	Central Intelligence Agency
COCOM	Coordinating Committee for Multilateral Export Controls
CWC	Chemical Weapons Convention
DCI	Defense Counterproliferation Initiative
DPRK	Democratic People's Republic of Korea (North Korea)
EU	European Union
G-7	Group of Seven
IAEA	International Atomic Energy Agency
ILSA	Iran-Libya Sanctions Act
KEDO	Korean Peninsula Energy Development Organization
LWR	light-water reactor
MFN	most-favored-nation
MRC	major regional conflict
MTCR	Missile Technology Control Regime
NATO	North Atlantic Treaty Organization
NMD	national missile defense
NPT	Nonproliferation Treaty
NSC	National Security Council
PDD	Presidential Decision Directive
ROK	Republic of Korea (South Korea)
UN	United Nations
UNSCOM	United Nations Special Commission
UNSCR	United Nations Security Council Resolution
WMD	weapons of mass destruction

Preface

Since the end of the Cold War, one of the main objectives of American foreign policy has been the containment of "rogue" or "outlaw" states. Senior U.S. policy-makers have asserted that these countries—North Korea, Iran, Iraq, and Libya—constitute a distinct category of states. The term "rogue state" has been much in the news. During the February 1998 impasse with Iraqi president Saddam Hussein over UN arms inspections, President Clinton warned that "in the next century, the community of nations may see more and more the very kind of threat Iraq poses now—a *rogue state* with weapons of mass destruction, ready to use them or provide them to terrorists, drug traffickers or organized criminals. . . ."[1] While in Japan in November 1998, President Clinton told a Tokyo television audience that "in your children's lifetime, you will have to worry more about chemical and biological weapons put in the hands of terrorists as well as *rogue states.*"[2] Speaker of the House Dennis Hastert likewise highlighted the threat of "the *rogue state* that aims a deadly missile at one of our cities" in his inaugural speech to Congress.[3] National Security Adviser Sandy Berger justified the further development of a national missile defense system to provide "effective protection against the emerging long-range missile threat from *rogue states.*"[4] As evidenced in these recent statements, the term "rogue state" or its synonym, "outlaw state," is gaining acceptance in our foreign policy debate through usage by American officials from the president down. The policies that arise from this concept, however, have been highly contentious—particularly with America's closest allies in Europe and with Japan and Canada.

The purpose of this book is not to advance any particular policy—for example, whether U.S. policy should seek to topple Saddam Hussein or simply contain him, or whether the new political alignment in Teheran warrants a change in policy toward Iran. Rather the focus of this book is on a key premise underpinning such analysis: namely, the assertion that those countries designated as "rogues" and "outlaws" by the U.S. administration constitute a distinct *class* of states in the post–Cold War international system. This proposition raises three sets of questions:

First, what is a rogue state? What are the main characteristics attributed to it? Is it a useful category of international relations or a counterproductive political epithet?

Second, how has the concept been translated into American policy during the post–Cold War era? What is the U.S. strategy toward rogue states?

And third, has the strategy been effective in terms of achieving U.S. objectives? In short, are the means and ends of American policy in sync?

The central argument of this book is that the rogue state designation—that is, demonizing a disparate group of states—significantly distorts policy-making. It perpetuates the false dichotomy that sets up containment and engagement as mutually exclusive strategies. Thus, the United States is actively *containing* rogue states such as Iran while *engaging* others (such as Syria, Pakistan, and China) that exhibit some of the same behavior, though not to the same degree. America's post–Cold War foreign policy debate has revolved around the question of whether to contain or to engage. The question is emblematic of the problem. U.S. policy-makers need to break out of this false dichotomy. Foreign policy is made along a continuum of choice. Policies should be fashioned to address the particular circumstances in each country rather than grouping countries under generic categories such as "rogue state." This targeted approach—what former National Security Adviser Zbigniew Brzezinski and others have called "differentiated containment"—requires a repertoire of strategies that combines incentives with penalties as appropriate. This shift—from the generic to the specific—would promote more effective policies to achieve what Stanford political scientist Alexander George has called the "resocialization" of these problem countries back into the mainstream of international politics. Such an approach would better relate the means and ends of American policy. This book will contribute to that policy debate by helping to improve the framework for analysis and decision.

This book was conceived while I was an executive fellow of the United States Institute of Peace (USIP). I am deeply grateful to Dick Solomon, the USIP's president, and Joe Klaits, its fellowship director, for the extraordinary opportunity that this fellowship provided me to work on the National Security Council staff for a year and then to spend six months as a residential fellow at the institute. I would also like express my thanks to the USIP's collegial staff and fellows, particularly Sally Blair, John Crist, and Fen Hampson.

I continued this project at the Woodrow Wilson International Center for Scholars, where I organized two workshops on this topic in close collaboration with Bruce Jentleson, now director of the Terry Sanford Institute of Public Policy at Duke University. I am greatly indebted to Bruce for his valuable advice in the development of this project. I have also benefited greatly from the Wilson Center's ongoing "Nonproliferation Forum" series, which I co-organize with Zachary Davis of the Congressional Research Service and Michael Vaden of the Wilson Center's Division of International Studies, and which is supported by the W. Alton Jones Foundation's Secure World Program, run by George Perkovich. Special thanks go as well to Sam Wells, the Wilson Center's associate director, and my Division of International Studies' colleagues for their help in bringing this project to fruition.

Both at the USIP and at the Wilson Center, I was extraordinarily fortunate to have the help of outstanding research assistants in gathering documentary materials and editing draft chapters: Heather Hughes, Monika Borbely, Jason McKellar, Jennie Quick, Clair Twigg, Jessica Powers, Kate Sawyer, and Dean Caras. Many colleagues and friends were kind enough to read all or part of the manuscript: James Morris, Shaul Bakhash, Haleh Esfandiari, Amatzia Baram, Phebe Marr, Daniel Poneman, Cengiz Candar, Ivo Daalder, Robert Hathaway, and Mitchell Reiss. I am grateful to Joseph Brinley and Carol Walker at the Woodrow Wilson Center Press and to the copyeditor, Traci Nagle, for their expert advice and for shepherding this book through production.

Finally, I would like to thank my parents for their constant encouragement. This book is dedicated to my wife, Liz, for her steadfast support in this as in everything else.

NOTES

[1] Text of President Clinton's remarks to the Joint Chiefs of Staff and Pentagon staff, reported in the *New York Times*, February 18, 1998, p. A9. Emphasis added here and in those quotations cited below.

[2] The White House, Office of the Press Secretary, "A Conversation with President Clinton, Tokyo Broadcasting Systems, Tokyo, Japan, November 19, 1998."

[3] Remarks of Speaker Dennis Hastert, House of Representatives, January 6, 1999 (http://thomas.loc.gov).

[4] Letter from National Security Adviser Samuel R. Berger to Senator Carl Levin, Ranking Minority Member, Senate Armed Services Committee, February 3, 1999.

Introduction

"Our policy must face the reality of recalcitrant and outlaw states that not only choose to remain outside the family [of nations] but also assault its basic values."
—Anthony Lake, 1994[1]

"Happy families are all alike; every unhappy family is unhappy in its own way."
—Leo Tolstoy, *Anna Karenina*, 1878

Since the end of the Cold War, American policy-makers have struggled to formulate a coherent, overarching strategy to guide U.S. diplomacy in the uncharted waters of this new era. Their inability to develop a present-day counterpart to diplomat George Kennan's containment doctrine is less a failure of analysis and creativity (as critics contend) than testimony to what former secretary of state Henry Kissinger has called the "infinite complexity" of the post–Cold War international system.[2] All of the major elements of the international environment are in a simultaneous state of flux. With the demise of the Soviet Union, the chief characteristic of the new era is the absence of great-power competition carrying the significant risk of conflict. The United States emerged from the Cold War as "the sole superpower"—the only state capable of projecting its military power globally. And yet, in terms of the distribution of *other* categories of power—political and economic—the post–Cold War system is increasingly multipolar and the United States but one of several major powers vying to shape the international milieu. Overall, this emerging post–Cold War international order is characterized by greater diversity and less hierarchy.

Initial euphoria about the end of the Cold War was reinforced by the allied coalition's stunning victory in the Gulf War. The demise of the Soviet bloc fostered a sense of Western triumphalism over the East, while the Gulf War created unrealistic expectations about the possibilities of a United Nations–based, U.S.-led collective security system to maintain the post–Cold War peace. Within a few years after the Gulf War, however,

1

rhetoric about a "New World Order" was quickly dropped by the Bush administration as euphoria gave way to sobering realities in the Balkans, the former Soviet bloc, Somalia, and elsewhere. At home, amid mounting domestic problems, doubts arose about whether Congress and the public would support (or fund) a continuing American global role. President Bush spoke about the emergence of a post–Cold War international system organized around the twin principles of democratization and market economics—and forcefully argued that the United States had a unique responsibility to foster its further development. This conviction later found expression in the Clinton administration's strategy of "engagement and enlargement."[3] Many view the effort to forge a stable international order through the export of Western-style democracy as a revival of Wilsonian universalism. The objective of democratic enlargement has been advanced by the Clinton administration within the context of a radically transformed security environment. For the first time in two generations, the United States no longer confronts a global strategic and ideological adversary seeking to reshape the international system. Today, the sources of disorder—notably ethnic nationalism and the breakdown of order *within* states—are more diffuse and their tangible impact on American interests is less obvious.

A major challenge to the post–Cold War order stems from what President Clinton has described as "rogue states [that] pose a serious danger to regional stability in many corners of the globe."[4] During his administration, President Bush had similarly highlighted the danger of "renegade regimes."[5] The most detailed articulation of the emerging rogue state policy was made by Anthony Lake, President Clinton's national security adviser, in a controversial *Foreign Affairs* article published in early 1994. In that piece, "Confronting Backlash States," Lake argued that "as the sole superpower, the United States has a special responsibility for developing a strategy to neutralize, contain, and through selective pressure, perhaps eventually transform these backlash states into constructive members of the international community." Although best known for its elaboration of the policy of "dual containment" toward Iraq and Iran, the article also laid out the administration's general approach for dealing with those regimes (North Korea, Libya, and Cuba were also specifically cited) grouped under the rubric of backlash or rogue states. Lake argued that these regimes—with their authoritarian ruling cliques, their "aggressive and defiant" behavior, their "chronic inability to engage constructively with the outside world," and their pursuit of weapons of mass destruction (WMD)—made clear "their recalcitrant commitment to remain on the wrong side of history." Having successfully contained Soviet power during the Cold War, the United States "now faces a less formidable challenge in containing [this] band of outlaws." The article concluded with an acknowledgment to Kennan, whose 1947 essay in *Foreign Affairs* had "made the case for containment of an outlaw empire."[6] The Lake article, in turn, was an effort by the Clinton administration to articulate a post–Cold War containment doctrine to meet the challenge of rogue states. Secretary of State Madeleine Albright told members of the Council on Foreign Relations in September 1997 that "dealing with the rogue states is one of the great challenges of our time . . . because they are there with the sole purpose of destroying the system." She argued that rogue states constitute one of four distinct categories of countries in the post–Cold War international system (the other three being advanced industrial states, emerging democracies, and failed states).[7]

The term "rogue state" is an American political rubric without standing in international law that has gained currency since the end of the Cold War. The Clinton administration's rogue state policy—which comprises the *criteria* by which states are included in (or excluded from) this category, the determination of policy *objectives*, and the selection of appropriate *strategies* and policy *instruments*—has been a significant source of contention with the European, Canadian, and Japanese governments, as well as with the U.S. Congress. During the Cold War, American administrations from Truman to Bush were able to build and sustain a broad consensus both at home and abroad about the containment of Soviet power. No such consensus currently exists with respect to rogue states.

Indeed, in a number of instances, the United States and its European, Canadian, and Japanese allies are pursuing quite different approaches—even as their respective leaderships avow similar objectives. These policy divergences do not, by and large, stem from differences over the extent to which rogue states constitute a threat to their neighbors and Western interests (although U.S. allies believe Washington is inclined to exaggerate the magnitude of their threat). Rather, they arise from different assessments about the effectiveness of inducements or penalties in changing rogue states' behavior. Domestic political and commercial interests also play a significant role in shaping these contending approaches. The impact of domestic factors on the development of policy toward rogue states has been particularly evident in the case of the United States. Indeed, some critics contend that the Clinton administration's determined pursuit of comprehensive containment (while eschewing any meaningful effort at engagement) is largely the product of domestic politics.

These differences of perspective and policy have been manifested most sharply in the case of Iran. The Clinton administration, citing the Teheran regime's efforts to acquire WMD and its sponsorship of terrorism abroad, tightened U.S. economic sanctions as part of a comprehensive containment strategy in 1995. By contrast, the European Union (EU) pursued limited engagement with Iran through its policy of "critical dialogue" in order to moderate Iranian behavior. Both sides have traded charges that the other's policy toward Iran is ineffectual.[8] In the aftermath of the March 1996 suicide bombings in Israel by the Iranian-supported Palestinian terrorist group Hamas, the United States raised the rhetorical and policy stakes. President Clinton invited nations that were resisting the U.S. embargo of the Teheran regime to "look in the mirror" and ask themselves how they can conduct normal trade relations with a state that sponsors or supports terrorism.[9] Senator Alfonse D'Amato (R-N.Y.), with the Clinton administration's belated support, sponsored a bill, which became law in August 1996, sanctioning foreign commercial entities that engage in trade or investment in Iran's energy sector. The bill contained an amendment offered by Senator Edward Kennedy (D-Mass.) that would extend these same extraterritorial sanctions against foreign firms doing business in Libya. The threatened use of "secondary boycotts" to force foreign compliance with U.S. sanctions prompted a sharp reaction from European officials, who promised appropriate retaliation.[10] One critic of the Iran-Libya Sanctions Act (ILSA), as the August 1996 legislation was called, quipped that, if implemented, it would change the political dynamic from "the United States and the world versus Iran" to "Iran and the world versus the United States." The *Washington Post* editorialized, "Too often . . . U.S. allies are content to allow the United States to take the lead in disciplining the world's rogue states. . . . [While] there is something troubling in the unilateralism [of the pending legislation,] the Europeans and Japanese owe more than complaints about potential U.S. bullying. . . . The burden is now on them to join with the United States or come up with a better way."[11] In the wake of the 1996 presidential election, the Clinton administration moved to defuse tensions with the Europeans over the extraterritorial sanctions provisions contained in the ILSA. Following the summit meeting of the G-8 group of nations (the former G-7 plus Russia) in May 1998, President Clinton issued a waiver of ILSA sanctions for an oil and natural gas project in Iran involving French, Russian, and Malaysian energy companies. Although the Clinton administration continued its public opposition to foreign investment in the Iranian economy, the move came at a time when Washington was reconsidering its Iran policy in the wake of the overwhelming victory of former minister of culture Mohammed Khatami over a radically anti-American opponent in the May 1997 Iranian presidential election.

A similar political controversy erupted between the Clinton administration and U.S. allies with respect to Cuba—a state whose inclusion in the administration's roster of rogue states is largely driven by U.S. domestic politics (notably the substantial political clout of the Cuban émigré community). Following the downing of two American civilian aircraft off the Cuban coast in late February 1996, the Clinton administration, which had previously resisted moves to tighten the thirty-five-year-old U.S. embargo on Cuba, reached swift agreement with congressional negotiators on a new package sponsored by Senator Jesse Helms (R-N.C.) and Representative Dan Burton (R-Ind.). The Cuban Liberty and Democratic Solidarity Act, commonly referred to as the Helms-Burton Act and signed by President Clinton in mid-March 1996, contains a contentious provision that would permit Cuban exiles to sue foreign companies using expropriated property in Cuba and bar those firms' executives entry visas to the United States. Administration officials, downplaying the potential negative impact on allied relations, note that the Helms-Burton Act permits the president to waive these extraterritorial sanctions for unlimited six-month intervals if he determines the delay is "necessary to the national interest" and likely to "expedite a transition to democracy in Cuba."[12] Critics of the legislation argued that, rather than hastening Fidel Castro's downfall, as proponents claimed, it would feed into the Cuban leader's domestic propaganda by permitting him to blame the country's economic plight on Washington.[13]

U.S policy toward rogue states—whether pursued multilaterally (Iraq and Libya) or unilaterally (Iran and Cuba)—has been that of comprehensive containment and isolation. Depending on the target country, the objective is to precipitate a change either in regime or in behavior. The sole exception to this pattern of containment and isolation has been North Korea (the Democratic People's Republic of Korea, or DPRK). In that case, the Clinton administration—because of the acute danger posed by Pyongyang's mature nuclear program, the forward deployment of the DPRK's sizable conventional forces along the demilitarized zone with South Korea, and serious concerns about the stability of the regime following the death of Kim Il Sung—opted to integrate a significant engagement component into its overall approach. The primary mechanism for engagement with North Korea has been the U.S.–North Korea Agreed Framework, concluded in Geneva in October 1994 after fifteen months of intensive negotiations. The core provision of the agreement commits North Korea to freeze activity at and eventually dismantle its existing graphite-moderated nuclear reactors and related facilities in return for the provision of two proliferation-resistant light-water reactors (LWRs) by a U.S.-led international consortium. Beyond the nuclear question, the Agreed Framework provided for the exchange of liaison offices and paved the way for diplomatic engagement with the Pyongyang regime on other "issues of concern" (e.g., sales of North Korean ballistic missiles to other countries). Since the conclusion of the Agreed Framework, the domestic crisis in North Korea has deepened to the point where General John Shalikashvili, former chair of the Joint Chiefs of Staff, observed that "we are now in a period where most who watch the area would say it's either going to implode or explode—we're just not quite sure when it's going to happen."[14] The United States's complex and subtle dialogue with North Korea raises key questions—most immediately, whether the U.S. move toward engagement will prove successful in moderating Pyongyang's behavior in the short to medium term while facilitating the regime's nonviolent reunification (the so-called soft landing) with South Korea in the long term; and, more broadly, whether the North Korean case holds relevant lessons for the management of relations with other rogue states.

Throughout history, some states have always been dissatisfied with the status quo and (to varying degrees) have rejected the norms of international order. This condition of international affairs—far from being the aberration—is to be expected. Political scientist Alexander George has framed the contemporary debate about rogue states in a broader historical and analytical context:

Outlaw states and their rogue leaders refuse to accept and abide by some of the most important norms and practices of the international system. Such states may seek to dominate and reshape the system to their own liking, and they may aim at global or regional hegemony. . . . [T]here exists no clear and commonly accepted definition of an outlaw or rogue state. These concepts have no standing in international law, and the United Nations works imperfectly to single out such offenders and deal with them. In fact, members of the international community may disagree among themselves whether the behavior of a state justifies its being regarded as an outlaw and treated as a pariah. . . . Much of the task of recognizing and coping with outlaws . . . is undertaken by individual states, usually one or more of the Great Powers, which have a stake in preserving the system that they have helped to create and that they subscribe to, as well as in protecting interests threatened or damaged by an outlaw. At the same time, it should be recognized that efforts by one or more states to cope with outlaws do not always win agreement and support from other states; resocialization of the rogue leader then becomes all the more difficult.[15]

In the post–Cold War era, the rogue state challenge comes not from a great power like Nazi Germany or Stalin's Soviet Union seeking to re-shape or overturn the existing international order. Rather, it arises from a disparate group of isolated states—North Korea, Iran, Iraq, and Libya—which threaten stability (and important Western interests) within their region, but whose ability to affect the system as a whole is marginal. Another notable feature of the contemporary debate, which will be ex-plored below, is that the criterion for rogue state status has significantly shifted over the last two decades. Until the late 1970s, the term "pariah" or "rogue" was used to describe regimes whose *internal* system or behav-ior toward its own people was viewed as abhorrent: Idi Amin's Uganda, Pol Pot's Cambodia, South Africa under apartheid. After 1979, with the advent of the State Department's annual report on state-sponsored ter-rorism, the criterion for rogue state status shifted from internal to exter-nal behavior. This shift was given further impetus during the Bush presi-dency as the Soviet threat receded and the Gulf War highlighted the problem of radical states with regional hegemonic ambitions and in pur-suit or possession of WMD.

Lake's *Foreign Affairs* article on "backlash states" alluded to "their re-calcitrant commitment to remain on the wrong side of history"—that is, their resistance to the wave of democratic enlargement and the move to-ward market economies. This factor, however, does not account for their inclusion in the small group of countries under the rogue state rubric. Bucking the tide of democratization is not the issue per se. If that were the criterion, the listing of rogue states would be more expansive and include countries from Nigeria to Saudi Arabia to Burma. Stripping away Clinton administration rhetoric, the key criteria of external behavior that confer rogue state status relate to traditional national security concerns: the pur-suit of WMD, the use of terrorism as an instrument of state policy, and the perceived threat to Western interests in key regions (i.e., Northeast Asia and the Persian Gulf). Although the rogue state rubric has been used by the Clinton and Bush administrations for purposes of political mobi-lization, the concept did not originate in the Pentagon as part of a search for new enemies to justify post–Cold War defense budgets.[16] However one judges the efficacy of the Clinton administration's strategy toward rogue states, the designation is rooted in tangible external behavior of concern (with the notable exception of Cuba, where the primary deter-minant is U.S. domestic politics). The policy has fostered charges of inconsistency and selectivity; critics point out that several states engaged in demonstrably rogue behavior (e.g., Syria) have been excluded from the list for political reasons. In a similar vein, Russian officials have bristled at Washington's strident opposition to any Russian nuclear commerce with Iran even as the United States proceeds with the transfer of two LWRs to the DPRK under the Agreed Framework. Finally, the fact that the majority of states under the rogue state rubric are Islamic has fueled criticism in the Middle East that the policy is being used by Washington as a politically convenient device to cast Islamic states pursuing policies contrary to U.S. interests as the new post–Cold War threat.

These issues raise fundamental questions about the means and ends of American post–Cold War foreign policy. "War," the Prussian military strategist Carl von Clausewitz stated, "has its own language but not its own logic."[17] The metaphor applies equally to the realm of diplomacy. It underscores the central challenge confronting foreign-policy makers of relating means to ends—of selecting strategies and instruments appropriate to one's political objectives. The contemporary debate about foreign policy is notable for its polarization. It is a polarization, however, less about the ends of foreign policy (though many have questioned the Clinton administration's priorities) than about its means. To contain or engage? That has been the recurring question across a range of foreign policy issues extending well beyond that of rogue states. As *New York Times* columnist Thomas Friedman has observed, " 'Hawks' and 'doves' are out. All anyone wants to know is whether you are an 'embargoer' or an 'embracer'—whether you think the way to deal with Bosnia, Haiti, Iraq or Cuba is by embargoing them into better behavior or embracing them with trade and tourism until they evolve into good citizens."[18] This either-or dichotomy may be useful in mobilizing political support for a policy behind a slogan, but it can undercut an administration's ability to pursue discriminating policies across a range of ostensibly like cases. Foreign policy options should be conceived not as a dichotomy, but as a continuum of choice. Policies should be fashioned to address the particularities of individual cases rather than grouping them under generic categories. These issues have been highlighted by the ongoing debate about U.S. policy toward rogue states.

The Clinton administration's rogue state policy takes a disparate group of states—North Korea, Iran, Iraq, Libya, and Cuba—and essentially demonizes them for purposes of political mobilization. A Clinton administration official conceded that unless the United States appears "completely maniacal" about Iran and the other rogue states in multilateral forums, such as the G-8, the Europeans and Japanese will take no meaningful actions to address behavior of concern. In historical terms, this demonization strategy can be viewed as the latest manifestation of the traditional impulse in U.S. foreign policy to depict international relations as a moral struggle between forces of good and evil (e.g., the Truman Doctrine's depiction of the Cold War as a clash between "alternative ways of life," President Reagan's characterization of the Soviet Union as an "evil empire," etc.). The question, however, is not whether the regimes in question are odious or not (they are). Rather, the key issue—and the central focus of this study—is whether the administration's strategy and choice of instruments will best promote its avowed objectives, that is, what George has described as the "resocialization" of the rogue state into the international community (through either regime change or behavior moderation).[19]

While the administration has talked of pursuing a differentiated policy toward rogue states, the political dynamic has, in practice, pushed it toward a one-size-fits-all strategy of containment and isolation. The one exception, as noted above, is North Korea, for which the Clinton administration, by necessity, integrated a significant engagement component into its containment strategy in order to address the pressing danger posed by the DPRK's mature nuclear program. That exception, however, underscores the problematic nature of the overall approach—that once a state has been relegated to the "rogue state" category, it is politically difficult to pursue any policy other than containment and isolation. In the North Korean case, congressional critics accused the Clinton administration of "appeasement" because the Agreed Framework incorporated a major policy inducement that seemingly rewarded North Korean noncompliance with its nonproliferation obligations. In addition, there were continuing doubts, fueled by North Korean actions (examined in Chapter 6), about whether the Pyongyang regime had indeed given up its nuclear aspirations.

The inability to distinguish adequately between cases and to tailor policies to specific circumstances is one liability of the rogue state policy as currently conceived and implemented. A related problem is the difficulty of moving a state out of the "rogue state" category as the process of resocialization unfolds or events otherwise warrant. Such a change in policy toward a rogue state, particularly after a prolonged period of castigation and the mobilization of public support by the administration for a hard-line policy of containment and isolation, requires deft skills of political negotiation and is likely to generate stiff domestic opposition. The

Clinton administration is currently engaged in dialogue with the North Korean regime on several negotiating fronts—the implementation of the Agreed Framework, food aid, missile proliferation, and the replacement of the 1953 armistice agreement with a peace treaty. In support of these diplomatic moves, the administration has sought to change the atmosphere of the relationship through more subdued rhetoric. In a January 1996 speech, for example, Secretary of State Warren Christopher quietly dropped North Korea from the list of pariah states as a gesture to ease relations.[20] Although North Korea remains on various U.S. export control lists, the change in official language complements administration efforts to normalize relations. At a time of deep crisis in the DPRK, the United States is, in effect, offering the Pyongyang regime an alternative to the dead end of autarchy in return for the moderation of DPRK behavior over the medium term. Both the administration and the Seoul leadership view this new engagement strategy as helping to forestall a potentially cataclysmic collapse in the North while establishing some of the prerequisites for long-term, peaceful reunification.

In negotiating the transition from containment and isolation to a mixed strategy incorporating an engagement component, policy-makers will invariably run up against the inertia of past policy and mind-sets. In the case of North Korea, the Clinton administration's domestic critics have characterized the shift toward engagement as a misguided policy of appeasement that is propping up a rogue regime on the verge of collapse.[21] This attitude, though understandable given the track record of the Pyongyang regime, manifests a misreading of Kennan's containment doctrine and reinforces the false containment-engagement dichotomy. As historian John Lewis Gaddis observes,

[A key element] in Kennan's strategy had been to try to bring about changes, over time, in the Soviet concept of international relations: to convince Russian leaders that their interests could be best served by learning to live with a diverse world than by trying to remake it in their image. Kennan had rejected both war and appeasement as means of accomplishing this; it could be done, he thought, through a long-term process of what might be called "behavior modification"— responding positively to whatever conciliatory initiatives emanated from the Kremlin, while firmly countering those that were not. . . . Kennan took the position that modifying Soviet behavior required *both* positive and negative reinforcement: it was as important to reward the Kremlin for conciliatory gestures as it was to resist aggressive ones. This meant being prepared to engage in such negotiations as seemed likely to produce mutually acceptable results.[22]

Kennan's concept of containment, in short, included the possibility of conditioned engagement as part of a long-term strategy (in conjunction with the playing out of the Soviet system's internal contradictions) to transform the Soviet Union from a revolutionary power into an orthodox great power. Viewed within this context, the Clinton administration's approach toward North Korea (through such instruments as the Agreed Framework) is wholly consistent with Kennan's containment doctrine. It is also an example of what George describes as a strategy of "conditional reciprocity—demanding meaningful changes in policy and behavior in return for each concession or benefit."[23]

The discussion has so far introduced the problems of implementation *within* the "rogue state" category—that is, the difficulties in developing a differentiated approach toward a disparate group of cases and in moving a state out of the category once relegated to it. Policy-makers also face the challenge of effectively dealing with those states engaging in rogue behavior that lie *outside* the category. This again highlights the analytically soft nature of the rogue state concept and the criticisms of selective implementation. The Clinton administration has grappled with the problem of rogue behavior by such non-rogue states as Syria, Pakistan, India, and China. The difficulty here is the mirror image of that described above in incorporating an engagement component into the containment strategy toward rogue states. In these cases, the administration's public commitment to an engagement strategy complicates its ability to take negative actions (perceived as running contrary to engagement) in response to behavior of concern. For example, in defending the administration's decision to transfer conventional arms to Pakistan following reports that it had received sensitive equipment for making nuclear weapons from China, a senior U.S. official stated, "The basic issue is how we influence Pakistan. Our strong view is that Pakistan is more likely to remain on a course that will serve American national interests if we remain engaged."[24] Likewise Syria, notwithstanding its continued support for terrorism and pursuit of WMD, has been assiduously courted by the United States to induce President Hafiz al-Assad to adopt a more forthcoming stance toward the Middle East peace process.

The problems of conceptualization and implementation identified above raise serious questions about the efficacy of the rogue state policy that has emerged since the end of the Cold War. By lumping a small, disparate group of states under the rogue state rubric, it has put the United States at odds with its closest allies. Criticizing the policy's political selectivity, French journalist Eric Rouleau argues, "The notion that there are rogue states has no equivalent in the French political vocabulary and continues to be a source of puzzlement. In European eyes, Washington's criteria for categorizing good and bad states would, if applied rigorously, significantly lengthen the list of the latter."[25] The rogue state policy also reinforces the American tendency to frame policy choices in terms of the false containment-engagement dichotomy. In so doing, the generic rogue state approach (with its sole emphasis on containment and isolation) hamstrings the ability of decision-makers to pursue discriminating strategies tailored to the particular circumstances of individual cases. It creates a political dynamic in which the United States is seen to be containing rogue states while engaging others (e.g., Syria and China) regardless of their behavior. The challenge is to break out of this dichotomized approach and to develop a repertoire of strategies to address problems across a continuum of state behavior. Such a strategy of "differentiated containment," fashioned to address the complexities and diversity of the post–Cold War era, would be more in keeping with Kennan's original formulation.[26]

In concluding this overview of the major themes and questions that this book addresses, a brief description of its structure and the analytical approach to be employed would be useful. Part I, comprising the first three chapters, focuses on the development of the rogue state strategy. Chapter 1 frames the rogue state issue within the context of American post–Cold War foreign policy. It focuses on three key elements of this evolving strategy within which the rogue state debate is embedded: conceptions of the post–Cold War international order, the reorientation of American defense policy from global containment to regionalism, and the development of a post–Cold War nonproliferation policy aimed at Third World states seeking to acquire WMD. This examination leads, in turn, to a detailed consideration in Chapter 2 of the rogue state policy—its conceptual origins, the criteria by which a state is deemed rogue, and the process by which this concept was transformed into policy. This analysis of the origins and development of the U.S. rogue state strategy is followed in Chapter 3 by a critique of that policy and an examination of alternative strategies in light of its perceived liabilities. This chapter, building on the earlier analysis, will make the case for jettisoning the generic rogue state approach in favor of a repertoire of targeted strategies under the "differentiated containment" rubric. The chapter will attempt to flesh out analytically the typology of alternative strategies that the United States might employ in meeting the challenge posed by those states currently under the rogue rubric. This spectrum of policy choice ranges from an explicit policy of rollback to comprehensive containment and isolation, to mixed strategies (combining containment and engagement).

The context and analytical framework in the earlier chapters lays the basis for the examination of U.S. policy toward three rogue states—Iraq, Iran, and North Korea—that follows in Part II. The purpose of these case studies is not to provide a detailed history, but instead to use the contemporary history of these states to illustrate the themes of this study—specifically, the critique that it presents of the rogue state concept and policy. In doing so, the focus of analysis will be on the formulation and implementation of U.S. policy in three particular contexts: Iraq in the aftermath of the Gulf War; Iran during the period leading up to and following the election of President Khatami in 1997; and the U.S.–North Korean Agreed Framework.

Employing George's method of structured, focused comparison, Part II (Chapters 4–6) will identify the key determinants or causal patterns that account for variance between the three cases.[27] The cases were selected because of their similarities as well as their significant differences. These states share three important characteristics: first, they have active programs to acquire WMD; second, they are on the State Department's list of state sponsors of terrorism; and third, they are the potential threats motivating Pentagon force and contingency planning for "major regional conflicts" (MRCs).[28] In selecting these cases, the study will not focus in detail on Libya, a smaller state that does not pose the same magnitude of regional threat, or Cuba, whose addition to the rogue state roster was largely driven by U.S. domestic politics.

While sharing these characteristics, the cases display a striking variance in strategy, instruments, and objectives. In the Iraqi case, U.S. strategy is containment and isolation, pursued multilaterally through economic sanctions (among other measures), with the aim of toppling Saddam Hussein or, at a minimum, keeping the Iraqi leader "in his box." For Iran, the U.S. strategy is, again, containment and isolation, but it is being pursued unilaterally by Washington with the avowed objective of moderating the Teheran regime's external behavior. It should be noted that the objectives referred to above are long-term. In the case of North Korea, the United States is pursuing a mixed strategy (containment with limited engagement through the Agreed Framework) in pursuit of a long-term objective of promoting a regime change and peaceful Korean reunification. As will be discussed in Chapter 3, objectives may be multiple and vary significantly over time. For example, U.S. policy may aim to change the Iraqi regime in the long term; in the short-to-medium term, however, it is focused on preventing renewed Iraqi aggression against its neighbors and rolling back Baghdad's programs to acquire WMD.

In keeping with the comparative case approach, each country chapter will address a common set of questions:

U.S. Policy toward the Case Country

- What is the U.S. policy objective toward the target country? Has it been consistent or has it changed over time? What policy instruments have been employed to achieve this goal?
- What has been the relative mix of foreign policy interest-based motivations and domestic political pressures on U.S. policy formulation?
- Does U.S. policy enjoy the political support of key regional and international actors? Is an alternative strategy being pursued or advocated by others?
- To what extent has U.S. policy been successful in achieving its stated objective (acknowledging that other factors beyond the actions of Washington may affect the outcome)?

Domestic Politics and Foreign Policy in the Case Country

- How is the historical record of U.S. relations with the case country viewed? How does this historical legacy affect current relations and policy formation?
- What does the case country hope to achieve in its relations with the United States and other external actors? Have those objectives changed over time and, if so, what factors account for the change?
- Is foreign policy, and in particular relations with the United States, an issue of contention within the leadership of the case country? What is the range of views among different interest groups with respect to relations with the United States? How do any differences of view within the leadership affect policy outcomes?[29]

The Conclusion will summarize the findings of the study and address how the U.S. policy debate can move beyond counterproductive political hyperbole (demonization) and the false containment-engagement dichotomy. A central question, one that has come up repeatedly in the context of Iran and Cuba, revolves around the issue of engagement—specifically, the conditions under which an engagement component should be integrated into an overall containment strategy. Under what conditions can some degree of engagement with a regime facilitate its transformation and a "soft landing"? The North Korean case points to two major factors underlying the initiation of dialogue between the two sides: domestic crisis in the target country and the perception of an imminent national security threat to the United States. Alternatively, when is containment and isolation (with the eschewal of engagement) the appropriate choice in strategy to promote a regime change? Limited engagement may make sense with North Korea, but not with Iraq. The efficacy of a strategy must also be weighed in terms of its costs. When should the United States be prepared to go it alone? Is the negative impact on alliance relations of unilateral U.S. measures (such as "secondary boycotts") worth the increased pressure that it brings on the target state? In addressing these issues, this book seeks to contribute to the development of a more differentiated, better-targeted approach to the challenge of rogue state behavior.

NOTES

[1] Anthony Lake, "Confronting Backlash States," *Foreign Affairs* 73, no. 2 (March/April 1994), p. 45.

[2] Kissinger, address to United States Institute of Peace conference "Managing Chaos," December 1, 1994, reported in *Peace Watch* 1, no. 2 (February 1995), p. 7.

[3] See President William J. Clinton, *A National Security Strategy of Engagement and Enlargement* (Washington, DC: White House, February 1995).

[4] Ibid., p. i. In public and academic discourse, the terms "rogue," "backlash," "pariah," and "outlaw" in referring to a state are used interchangeably and, as will be discussed in Chapter 2, are synonymous. Of the three, "rogue state" enjoys somewhat greater currency and will be employed in this study for consistency. For other pertinent books on this topic see Michael Klare, *Rogue States and Nuclear Outlaws: America's Search for a New Foreign Policy* (New York: Hill and Wang, 1995), and Raymond Tanter, *Rogue Regimes: Terrorism and Proliferation* (New York: St. Martin's Griffin, 1999).

[5] See, for example, his address to the Aspen Institute on August 2, 1990 (the day after Iraq invaded Kuwait), in *Public Papers of the Presidents: George Bush, 1990* (Washington, DC: U.S. Government Printing Office, 1991), p. 1092.

[6] Lake, "Confronting Backlash States," pp. 45–46, 55.

[7] Department of State, Office of the Spokesman, "Secretary of State Madeleine K. Albright Address before the Council on Foreign Relations, September 30, 1997" (http://secretary.state.gov/www/statements/9770930).

[8] For example, EU officials have privately criticized the American "obsession" with Iran, and a U.S. congressional staffer quipped that the Europeans "can't even get the hit on Salman Rushdie lifted."

[9] "After the Terrorism Meeting" (editorial), *Washington Post*, March 17, 1996, p. C6.

[10] In an interview President Jacques Chirac of France said, "The European Union will retaliate if the D'Amato bill becomes law. And I do not want that off the record." See Jim Hoagland, "A Sudden Romance with Europe," *Washington Post*, May 5, 1996, p. C7.

[11] "Loner" (editorial), *Washington Post*, May 12, 1996, p. C8.

[12] Helen Dewar, "Clinton, Hill Agree on Cuba Sanctions," *Washington Post*, February 29, 1996, p. A4.

[13] See, for example, "Helping Castro" (editorial), *Financial Times*, March 7, 1996, p. 13.

[14] Quoted in Mary Jordan, "Speculation Grows on Demise of N. Korea," *Washington Post*, April 6, 1996, p. A11.

[15] Alexander L. George, *Bridging the Gap: Theory and Practice in Foreign Policy* (Washington, DC: United States Institute of Peace Press, 1993), p. 49.

[16] The argument that the Pentagon promoted the rogue state threat as a justification for Cold War levels of military spending is made by Michael Klare in *Rogue States and Nuclear Outlaws*.

[17] Cited in Bernard Brodie, *War and Politics* (London: Cassell, 1973), p. 1.

[18] Thomas L. Friedman, "A Diplomatic Question: Embargo or Embrace?" *New York Times*, September 4, 1994, section 4, p. 4.

[19] See George, *Bridging the Gap*, chapter 4.

[20] Michael S. Lelyveld, "US Removes North Korea from List of 'Pariah States,' " *Journal of Commerce*, February 2, 1996, p. 1. A Clinton administration official said the goal was to have Pyongyang become a "more responsible member of the international community."

[21] Senator Robert Dole (R.-Kans.), while not advocating the jettisoning of the Agreed Framework, accused the Clinton administration of appeasement in its dealings with North Korea. During the 1996 presidential election campaign, he called on the administration to halt its bilateral talks on North Korea's missile proliferation, an effort he likened to "discussing religious tolerance with the Hezbollah." See R. Jeffrey Smith, "Dole Attacks Clinton for Asia Policy Failure," *Washington Post*, May 10, 1996, p. A34.

[22] John Lewis Gaddis, *Strategies of Containment: A Critical Appraisal of Postwar American National Security Policy* (Oxford: Oxford University Press, 1982), p. 71.

[23] George, *Bridging the Gap*, pp. 50–51.

[24] Quoted in R. Jeffrey Smith, "U.S. to Send Arms to Pakistan Despite Nuclear Deal," *International Herald Tribune*, March 21, 1996, p. 4.

[25] Eric Rouleau, "America's Unyielding Policy toward Iraq: The View from France," *Foreign Affairs* 74, no. 1 (January/February 1995), p. 59. I would like to thank Gregory D. Koblentz for bringing this and other pertinent citations to my attention; see his "Resocializing 'Rogue' States: The Case of North Korea" (B.A. thesis, Department of Political Science, Brown University, 1996).

[26] The strategy of "differentiated containment" toward Iran and Iraq has been advanced by Zbigniew Brzezinski, Brent Scowcroft, and Richard Murphy as an alternative to "dual containment"; see Brzezinski, Scowcroft, and Murphy, "Differentiated Containment," *Foreign Affairs* 76, no. 3 (May/June 1997), pp. 20–30.

[27] See Alexander L. George, "Case Studies and Theory Development: The Method of Structured, Focused Comparison," in Paul Gordon Lauren, ed., *Diplomacy: New Approaches in History, Theory, and Policy* (New York: Free Press, 1979), pp. 43–68.

[28] Department of Defense (DOD), *Report on the Bottom-Up Review* (Washington, DC: DOD, October 1993), pp. 14–22.

[29] I would like to thank Bruce Jentleson for his help in developing these questions, which were used in a workshop that we co-organized, "U.S. Policy toward 'Rogue States'—Strategies, Instruments, and Objectives," at the Woodrow Wilson International Center for Scholars on May 13, 1997.

I

Policy Development

1

The Post–Cold War Context

CONCEPTS OF INTERNATIONAL ORDER

It is a telling sign of our collective confusion about the "post–Cold War era" that we are able to characterize the current period of international relations only in terms of what preceded it. Policy-makers continue to grapple with what former president George Bush referred to as "the vision thing." In assessing U.S. policy toward rogue states, it is necessary to begin with a brief exploration of American thinking about the nature of the post–Cold War order, for it is within the context of that conception of international order that the rogue state challenge has been framed.

The Bush administration's initial attempt to articulate such a vision at the end of the Cold War coincided, significantly, with the outbreak of a hot war in the Persian Gulf region. In his 1991 State of the Union address, President Bush asserted that "what is at stake is more than one small country; it is a big idea: a new world order, where diverse nations are drawn together in common cause to achieve the universal aspirations of mankind—peace and security, freedom and the rule of law. . . . The world can . . . seize this opportunity to fulfill the long-held promise of a new world order, where brutality will go unrewarded and aggression will meet collective resistance."[1] Bush's concept of a "new world order" reflected the widespread sense of Western triumphalism that accompanied the end of the Cold War. Many saw the stunning (and unanticipated) chain of events in 1989–91, from the fall of the Berlin Wall to the disintegration of the Soviet Union, as validating the moral superiority and universal applicability of the Western model of political pluralism and market economics. Although Bush's rhetoric did tap these political sentiments, the most striking aspect of his "new world order" design was its emphasis on collective security rooted in international law.[2] The prominence of this

19

feature, however, was less a consequence of the end of the Cold War than the administration's successful effort in marshaling a broad international coalition to expel Iraqi forces from Kuwait. This, of course, raised the question of the extent to which one could plan for post–Cold War contingencies on the basis of the Desert Storm experience.[3]

Analysts were quick to point out the exceptional nature of the Gulf War and that such circumstances were unlikely to arise elsewhere. The response of the United Nations (UN) to the Iraqi invasion was based on one of the first principles of international order—that proscribing interstate aggression (or, as one observer baldly put it, that one state should not be permitted to murder another). While grounded on this principle, the response of the United States and other coalition members was also powerfully motivated by the tangible vital interests at stake in this oil-rich region. Desert Storm thus resulted from a rare conjunction of principle and interest in the face of unambiguous aggression. Bush administration rhetoric, perhaps reflecting American discomfort with an interests-based foreign policy, tended to emphasize the lofty ideals for which the war was being waged and on which the administration sought to forge a "new world order" in its aftermath. Harvard political scientist Joseph Nye observed that "the problem for the Bush administration was that it thought and acted like Nixon, but borrowed the rhetoric of Wilson and Carter."[4] The history of American diplomacy reflects the interplay, and often the tension, between the contending realist and liberal conceptions of international order exemplified in the foreign policies of Nixon and Wilson, respectively. In the wake of the Gulf War, the American debate about the "new world order" highlighted the tension between the realist and liberal conceptions within the context of two important issues.[5]

The first is the tension between unilateralism and multilateralism. Although the Desert Storm victory was hailed by the Bush administration as heralding a new era of collective security, this vision of a neo-Wilsonian liberal international order was sharply disputed. In a trenchant critique published in *Foreign Affairs*, conservative columnist Charles Krauthammer asserted that the Gulf War was an exercise in "pseudo-multilateralism": without the United States "leading and prodding, bribing and blackmailing, no one would have stirred. . . . The world would have written off Kuwait the way the last body pledged to collective security, the League of Nations, wrote off Abyssinia." Krauthammer urged the Bush administration to seize "the unipolar moment" and "unashamedly lay down the rules of world order and be prepared to en-

force them."[6] This line of argument, rooted in the realist tradition, eschewed both the liberal internationalism of Bush's "new world order"
and the neo-isolationism of those who called for significant American dis-
engagement from world affairs with the end of the Cold War. The issue
of unilateralism versus multilateralism subsequently arose in connection
with the policy debate over American participation in UN-sponsored
peacekeeping operations in Somalia, Bosnia, and elsewhere. It also
emerged in the context of U.S. economic sanctions against rogue states
(notably Iran and Cuba) and whether Washington should continue with
unilateral sanctions in the face of European and Japanese resistance.
Those advocating a unilateralist foreign policy supported America's continuing international engagement, but on American terms and in accord
with U.S. interests. The self-confident tone of this post–Cold War debate
about America's global role contrasted strikingly with that of the late
1980s, when historian Paul Kennedy's best-selling book, *The Rise and
Fall of the Great Powers*, had proposed that the United States was entering a period of long-term decline relative to other major powers.[7]

The question of unilateralism versus multilateralism points to a second
area of tension in U.S. post–Cold War policy—that surrounding the definition of American interests. Bush's grand design was sharply criticized
for potentially creating a set of open-ended American commitments
around the globe under the banner of collective security. In *The Imperial Temptation*, foreign policy specialists Robert Tucker and David Hendrickson called for a rejection of a *"pax universalis"*:

If put into practice [it] would extend an American security guarantee to virtually
the entire world. In pursuit of this vision of a new world order, the nation is to exercise a police power which confers the right to prevent states of the developing
world from acquiring certain weapons, and which imposes the duty to guarantee
the territorial integrity of the members of the international community. . . . This
kind of universalism is the bane of American foreign policy in the twentieth century. If history has taught us anything, it is precisely the contrary of the lesson
drawn by those who urge us to be the world's policeman. It is that peace is normally divisible and that conflicts, whatever their origin, are normally of merely local or regional significance. To convert a lesson drawn from America's experience
with the totalitarian great powers of this century into a general rule applicable to
smaller powers is an altogether misleading basis for national security policy.[8]

During the Cold War, the global extension of containment had led to
the blurring of distinctions between vital and peripheral interests and
thereby fostered an approach that former secretary of state Henry Kissinger described as "undifferentiated globalism." What drove this process,
in large measure, was the ideological nature of the Cold War. This ideo-

logical character transformed the stakes of the U.S.-Soviet competition and made it more than just a traditional great power rivalry: ideology contributed to the Cold War's virulence and created a framework in which interests were conceived and expressed in universal terms—hence the Truman Doctrine's characterization of the Cold War as a "clash between alternative ways of life." For nearly half a century this strategic and ideological cleavage between East and West defined international relations, often with distorting consequences. Critics of the "new world order" argued that the Bush administration, through its advocacy of a neo-Wilsonian system of collective security that failed to distinguish between vital and peripheral interests, was creating "the functional equivalent of global containment."[9]

No sooner had Desert Storm successfully concluded than the Bush administration faced a new crisis, as the remnants of Saddam Hussein's army regrouped to crush insurgent Kurds in northern Iraq and Shiites in the south. Ironically, it was this rebellion—which threatened to splinter the Iraqi state—rather than the war to liberate Kuwait itself that was to prove paradigmatic of the post–Cold War period. In the Kurdish and Shiite uprising, the Bush administration faced an ethnic-sectarian conflict that pitted aspirations for national self-determination against the integrity of an existing state structure. While mobilizing international support for refugee relief and the creation of military exclusion zones for Iraqi forces, the Bush administration was careful not to undermine the existence of Iraq as a unitary state. The administration's concern, reportedly shared by Turkey and Saudi Arabia, was that the breakup of the Iraqi state would yield an inherently unstable regional order. The type of conflict manifested in the Kurdish and Shiite uprising—what might be called a clash between "the nation" and "the state"—presented a dilemma to U.S. policy-makers and, again, reflected the competing pulls of liberal and realist conceptions of international order in American diplomacy. The same considerations arose in connection with the collapse of the Soviet Union and the demise of the former Yugoslavia—that is, whether the realization of one norm (national self-determination) would promote the erosion of another (the maintenance of a stable international order).

Within months of the Desert Storm victory, as the Bush administration confronted a range of difficult foreign policy problems from Yugoslavia to Somalia, the postwar euphoria began to fade and commentators made disparaging references to the "new world *dis*order." This characterization brought to mind Deputy Secretary of State Lawrence Eagleburger's 1989 observation that many would soon be nostalgic for the clarity of the

Cold War. In the face of this more chaotic international environment and an American public less supportive of an activist overseas role, the Bush administration quietly dropped references to the "new world order" and went into the 1992 presidential election campaign emphasizing its past accomplishments rather than its vision of America's future international role.[10] This shift both stemmed from the campaign's understandable focus on domestic economic matters as the country struggled to pull out of recession and attested to the difficulties of forging a new domestic consensus for a post–Cold War foreign policy.

In an effort to distinguish himself from President Bush, candidate Bill Clinton criticized the administration's supposed "coddling" of dictators from Baghdad to Beijing, as well as its ineffectual response to Serbian aggression in Bosnia and its forced repatriation of Haitian refugees. This criticism in the heat of a presidential campaign presaged the dilemmas that the Clinton administration itself would subsequently face in dealing with such thorny issues as "humanitarian intervention" and most-favored-nation (MFN) trade status for China. The differences that emerged between Bush and Clinton were less about the objectives of foreign policy than the appropriate mix and application of means to achieve those ends. Indeed, on most of the big issues, such as relations with Russia and the North American Free Trade Agreement (NAFTA), the candidates' views were largely in accord. Clinton's principal criticism of Bush's presidency was that he had excessively focused on international diplomacy as pressing domestic issues festered. In contrast, President Clinton assumed office in January 1993 with an ambitious domestic agenda, but it was less clear where he wanted to take American foreign policy. Early setbacks in Somalia and Haiti—dramatically symbolized by images of an American soldier's corpse being dragged through the streets of Mogadishu and a U.S. military supply ship being turned back by a government-sponsored mob in Port-au-Prince—fostered the perception (in the words of two *New York Times* correspondents) that the Clinton administration was "floundering, reacting rather than imposing American leadership on world events. The President was not ready or able to articulate the structure of American foreign policy or explain its themes to a confused global constituency."[11]

After a shaky first year, this perception began to change as the Clinton administration overcame its early organizational disarray and became more focused. In part, this process entailed a pragmatic shift from some of its 1992 campaign positions and early rhetoric. On China, for example, the administration backed off the linkage that it had earlier advocated between MFN trade status and Beijing's human rights record. Likewise, notwithstanding its previous stress on humanitarian intervention, the Clinton administration refused to deploy American military forces to halt genocidal violence in Rwanda on the grounds that no vital American interests were at stake. In addition to these pragmatic shifts (or what some of the administration's disillusioned supporters considered a betrayal of principle), the president assumed a more publicly visible role in the foreign policy arena and became his administration's own chief spokesperson.[12] The administration scored foreign policy successes in the Middle East, Haiti, and North Korea, while leading the international effort to extend the nuclear Nonproliferation Treaty (NPT) indefinitely. President Clinton, through his advocacy of NAFTA and export promotion, created a strong linkage between his domestic economic and foreign policy agendas.

Running through the Clinton administration's approach to discrete policy issues has been an overarching conception of the post–Cold War international order—a conception embodied in its "strategy of engagement and enlargement." Underlying this strategy is the liberal, neo-Wilsonian belief in democratization as the key to a stable (and just) international order. As President Clinton argued in his 1994 State of the Union address: "Ultimately, the best strategy to ensure our security and to build a durable peace is to support the advance of democracy elsewhere. Democracies don't attack each other, they make better trading partners and partners in diplomacy."[13] In a major address at Johns Hopkins University in September 1993, National Security Adviser Anthony Lake stated, "Throughout the Cold War, we contained a global threat to market democracies; now we should seek to enlarge their reach. . . . The successor to a doctrine of containment must be a strategy of enlargement—enlargement of the world's free community of market democracies."[14] Many observers questioned how this general foreign policy orientation, which echoed much of the Bush administration's earlier rhetoric, would translate into particular policies. How would support for democratization as a policy objective fare when set against powerful competing interests, such as commercial relations with China?[15] In an effort to explain and build domestic support for its foreign policy (as well as to comply with a congressional mandate), the Clinton administration published national security reports, titled *A National Security Strategy of Engagement and Enlargement*, in July 1994 and February 1995.

The Clinton administration's "strategy of engagement and enlargement" is particularly pertinent to this discussion framing the rogue state issue within the context of American thinking about the post–Cold War international order. In its articulation and implementation, the policy again highlights the ongoing tension in American foreign policy between liberal and realist conceptions of international order. A key difference between these competing schools of international relations theory revolves around the issue of legitimacy. Does the legitimacy of the international system derive from how states organize themselves internally (i.e., their domestic structures) or from agreed understandings about the power relationship between states? To liberal thinkers and practitioners from Immanuel Kant to Woodrow Wilson, the criterion of legitimacy is rooted in the domestic structure—hence the notion that international peace can best be ensured through the global proliferation of democracies (as reflected in Clinton's observation that "democracies don't attack each other"). In contrast, realists, such as Kissinger, argue that legitimacy derives not from the domestic order but from the international framework. In *A World Restored*, Kissinger's study of the Congress of Vienna, he wrote that "stability has commonly resulted not from a quest for peace but from a generally accepted legitimacy. 'Legitimacy' as here used should not be confused with justice." Kissinger warned against confusing stability and justice precisely because the latter arises from a state's domestic structure (the society's mores and organizing principles) and is therefore intrinsically "parochial" and absolute.[16] Linking the two may result in the fomentation of a "revolutionary" situation as an individual state attempts to identify the legitimizing principle of the international system with a concept of justice derived from its domestic structure. In recent years, the competing pulls of realism and liberalism have been reflected in the pendular swings of U.S. foreign policy.[17] During the period of superpower détente in the early 1970s, Kissinger discovered that it was not possible to sustain domestic support for a policy of realpolitik divorced from American core values; Jimmy Carter subsequently encountered the opposite problem of liberal idealism running up against the power realities of an increasingly assertive Soviet Union.

In his address at Johns Hopkins, Lake explicitly rooted the Clinton administration's "strategy of engagement and enlargement" in the Wilsonian tradition of American statecraft. He observed that "although [Wilson's] moralism sometimes weakened his argument, he understood that our own security is shaped by *the character of foreign regimes*. Indeed, most Presidents who followed, Republicans and Democrats alike, understood we must promote democracy and market economics in the world— because it protects our interests and security and because it reflects values that are both American and universal."[18] This formulation is wholly consistent with the liberal concept of international relations, in which the legitimacy of the system derives from the *internal* organization of its members. Lake went on to address the continuing challenge posed by authoritarian forces resisting the tide of democratic change. And yet, in Lake's advancement of the rogue state concept (both in his Johns Hopkins speech and his subsequent *Foreign Affairs* article), the key determinant accounting for a state's inclusion in this category is not its (nondemocratic) internal character per se. (If that were the case, the list would be much longer and would include a number of U.S. allies in the Third World.) Rather, rogue state status (with the notable exception of Cuba) derives from destabilizing *external* behavior—the pursuit of weapons of mass destruction (WMD), support for international terrorism, and threats to American interests in key regions. Lake, drawing a link between a state's domestic structure and its foreign policy behavior, argued that nondemocratic systems are the most prone to contravene important international norms. But the key point in this context is that the behavioral criteria for inclusion in the "rogue state" category have been external rather than internal. Although the Clinton administration's "strategy of engagement and enlargement" is liberal Wilsonian in orientation, the key determinants of its rogue state policy are realist. Thus, Iraq is labeled a rogue state not as a result of Saddam Hussein's brutal internal rule (witness the muted international response to his 1988 use of chemical weapons against Iraq's Kurdish population), but because of his aggressive foreign policy culminating in the invasion of Kuwait. North Korea, Iran, and Libya are likewise categorized not because of "the character of [their] regimes" but because of their pursuit of WMD and their use of international terrorism as an instrument of state policy. This question of the criteria by which a state is deemed to be rogue will be examined in greater detail in the next chapter.

DEFENSE STRATEGY AND THE USE OF FORCE

The preceding discussion focused on American conceptions of the post–Cold War international order to establish the broader foreign policy context within which the Bush and Clinton administrations' rogue state policy has been conceived and implemented. This section will address the related question of American military power—and the contentious issue of adjusting U.S. military doctrine and capabilities to meet the radically altered conditions of the post–Cold War era. The centerpiece of this process of reorientation and restructuring has been the shift from a strategy of global containment focused on the Soviet Union to a regional strategy designed to meet the challenge of rogue states in the Persian Gulf and Northeast Asia. On one level, the post–Cold War defense debate has been a fairly mechanistic discussion about force structure, missions, budgets, and interservice rivalries. But at the heart of this debate has been the more fundamental question about the *ends* for which American military *means* should be harnessed. This issue relates not only to potential threats posed by rogue states in regions of vital interest, but also to cases of "humanitarian intervention" where there is great human suffering but American interests are less tangibly at stake.

The shift in American military strategy from globalism to regionalism can be traced to the early Bush administration, as official Washington gradually came to accept Soviet leader Mikhail Gorbachev as a genuine reformer and the Soviet threat began visibly to recede. During the Cold War, U.S. military strategy did, of course, have regional components, but they were formulated largely within the context of an overarching global containment doctrine focused on the Soviet Union and its allies. The tendency to frame regional strategy in these terms was particularly evident in the late 1970s and early 1980s—a period marked by sharp U.S.-Soviet competition in the Third World from Nicaragua to Angola to the Horn of Africa. This geographically extended rivalry was one of the primary factors underlying the demise of the détente forged during the Nixon-Kissinger period. The regional dimension of global containment was further accentuated after the December 1979 Soviet invasion of Afghanistan. This unprecedented action outside the Warsaw Pact prompted the enunciation of the Carter Doctrine (affirming the American commitment to defend the Persian Gulf region from external attack) and raised fears that a U.S.-Soviet conflict might break out through inadvertent involvement and escalation in a peripheral region on the model of 1914. In particular, the Afghan invasion led to a renewed focus by Pentagon contingency planners on the scenario of a Soviet military move against Iran. A major planning assumption in this exercise was that a force sufficient to deal with this contingency (the political plausibility of which was hotly disputed) could equally address "lesser" contingencies involving local actors threatening regional order or the internal stability of key U.S. allies.

The tendency to frame regional strategy (notably in the case of the Persian Gulf) within the context of global containment began to change during 1988–89 under the influence of two developments. The first, of course, was the beginning of the end of the Cold War. When Bush assumed office, the Soviet Union, far from pushing for access to warmwater ports and threatening Iran, was on the diplomatic fast track to extricating itself from Afghanistan. Undersecretary of Defense Paul Wolfowitz subsequently observed, "One result of the new era in superpower relations is that . . . regional conflicts can now be treated more independently of the East-West context."[19] A second important factor influencing the recasting of American military strategy was the end of the Iran-Iraq War, a conflict that had featured the use of chemical weapons and ballistic missiles. Together, these changes in the security environment fostered a new approach in which regional strategy was developed in its own terms, not as a function of a possible extraregional threat. In addition, they led to a concerted focus by defense planners on the potential threat posed by a small group of Third World states armed with WMD and their means of delivery.

The Bush administration's "New Defense Strategy" was publicly presented in a major presidential speech at the Aspen Institute on August 2, 1990. That address, delivered the day after Saddam Hussein's move into Kuwait, provided an overview of the administration's plans to reorient American strategy from global containment to regional defense with a non-Soviet focus. It marked the culmination of a review process within the Pentagon that had been driven by such dramatic developments as the fall of the Berlin Wall and the revolutions of 1989 in Eastern Europe. The shift in American military strategy from globalism to regionalism was accompanied by a 25 percent reduction in the size of the U.S. force structure. The Bush administration's plan for restructuring American military forces and reorienting them to post–Cold War missions was further detailed by Secretary of Defense Dick Cheney in the aftermath of the Gulf War.[20]

The post–Cold War defense debate, which began with the collapse of the Berlin Wall and continued through Desert Storm into the early Clinton administration, was dominated by two central issues. The first, noted above, is that of the force structure required to meet the plausible threats that might arise in a transformed external environment. During the Cold War, defense planners had faced the bottom-line question—how much is enough?—within the context of a bipartisan consensus about the nature of the Soviet threat and the means necessary to meet it. By contrast, the post–Cold War era is distinguished precisely by its complexity and lack of clarity about the nature and significance of threats to American interests. The second issue follows from that of force structure—namely, the conditions under which U.S. military power will be exercised in response to contingencies ranging from regional conflict to humanitarian intervention.

The Bush administration's sustained effort from 1989 onward to reorient U.S. defense strategy from global containment to regionalism culminated in the publication of Cheney's *Regional Defense Strategy* in January 1993.[21] This document laid out the administration's assessment of the strategic environment and the spectrum of potential threats to U.S. interests. Its analysis further elaborated the rationale underpinning the administration's decision (backed by the Joint Chiefs of Staff) to maintain a "Base Force" three-quarters the size of that which existed during the Cold War, when the United States faced a global adversary. The *Regional Defense Strategy*, although sharply criticized by some for not going far enough in its downsizing of U.S. forces, was likened by others to NSC-68 because, like that seminal 1950 policy statement, the Cheney document was fashioned at a time of great flux and sought to lay out a strategic road map for a new era of international relations. Given the rapid and unforeseen pace of events, General Colin Powell, then chair of the Joint Chiefs of Staff and the principal architect of the Base Force plan, acknowledged that there was a certain intuitive aspect to this process. The decision to implement only a 25 percent force reduction did not stem solely from an assessment of the forces required to meet plausible contingencies—notably, regional challenges in Korea and the Persian Gulf. It also derived from a general sense (again, challenged by some outside defense analysts) that this was the force size necessary for the United States to maintain its superpower status. Indeed, one could argue that even if the Gulf War had not occurred the force structures recommended by Cheney and Powell would have been virtually identical.

One of the key issues of contention to emerge from the *Regional Defense Strategy* that went to the heart of the debate about force structure was whether the United States should maintain the capabilities to meet more than one Desert Storm–type contingency at the same time (e.g., simultaneous crises in the Persian Gulf and Korea). The Cheney document had argued that "when the United States is engaged . . . in a substantial regional crisis . . . potential aggressors in other areas may be tempted to exploit our preoccupation. Under these circumstances, our forces must remain able to deter or to respond rapidly to other crises. . . ." The Base Force strategy thus called for capabilities sufficient to wage two major regional conflicts (MRCs) simultaneously, either as part of a coalition or, if necessary, unilaterally.[22] The debate over this issue extended into the Clinton administration and was a central focus of the "Bottom-Up Review" (BUR) of U.S. defense requirements initiated by Secretary of Defense Les Aspin. Aspin, former chair of the House Armed Services Committee, had been critical of the Cheney-Powell Base Force concept, arguing that it appeared more a response to bureaucratic imperatives inside the Pentagon than to changes in the strategic environment. This attitude, coupled with the 1992 Clinton campaign's pledge to trim the defense budget further, prompted Aspin's decision to reassess U.S. defense requirements from the "bottom up."

Aspin shared the doubts of Bush administration critics who had questioned the political plausibility of the two-MRC strategy—that is, the possibility that the United States would find itself engaged in two Desert Storm–type conflicts simultaneously. In keeping with Aspin's desire to develop a better threats-based determination of force requirements, the BUR considered a range of contingencies. The two contingencies that received greatest attention "envisioned aggression by a remilitarized Iraq against Kuwait and Saudi Arabia, and by North Korea against the Republic of Korea."[23] (It is striking that Iran did not figure prominently in the scenarios that provided the basis for the BUR's conclusions.) The study's options regarding the future structure of U.S. armed forces flowed from the analysis of possible contingencies. One of those options, reportedly supported by Aspin early in the BUR process, would have yielded a force structure with a one-MRC capability. In the event that the United States found itself engaged in two regional theaters simultaneously the strategy would have been to fight one conflict while mounting a holding action in the other. This "win-hold-win" approach was premised on the political implausibility of two simultaneous MRCs and the fact that no potential aggressor in the near term (a shattered Iraq, a weak Iran, and a stagnating North Korea) possessed capabilities comparable to that of Iraq prior to Desert Storm. The option foundered, however, on two political grounds.

First, the South Koreans reportedly inquired whether, in this scenario, their theater was the one to be placed "on hold" while the United States was engaged in an MRC elsewhere (presumably the Persian Gulf).[24] Second, the "win-hold-win" option encountered staunch opposition from the Joint Chiefs of Staff at a time when relations between the administration and the military were already strained over the issue of gays in the armed forces, as well as proposed defense budget cuts. When it was finally published in October 1993, the BUR endorsed a force structure that was, in Powell's words, the "lineal ancestor" of the Bush administration's Base Force strategy and concluded that such a force would provide the capabilities necessary "to fight and win two major regional conflicts that occur *nearly simultaneously.*" The two-MRC strategy was explicitly aimed at "rogue leaders set on regional domination through military aggression while simultaneously pursuing nuclear, biological, and chemical weapons capabilities."[25] This two-theater approach was reaffirmed by Secretary of Defense William Cohen in the Quadrennial Defense Review issued in May 1997.[26]

Running in tandem with this debate over force structure and strategy has been another focused on the *conditions* under which the United States will employ military power in the post–Cold War era. This issue arose in the Bush administration in connection with the December 1989 intervention in Panama to oust dictator Manuel Noriega (in what one observer referred to as the first American intervention since 1945 undertaken without explicit reference to the Cold War). The debate over the use of force emerged again after the Gulf War when the rhetoric of Bush's "new world order" (notwithstanding efforts by administration officials to dampen expectations) pointed to a more activist American policy in support of a UN-based system of collective security. In December 1992, President Bush authorized the deployment of American forces in Somalia on a mission of humanitarian intervention to avert mass starvation. This type of intervention, where American strategic interests were not directly threatened, presaged the difficult choices that the Clinton administration faced after January 1993 in Somalia, the former Yugoslavia, Rwanda, and Haiti. The use-of-force issue came up most prominently in these cases of humanitarian intervention and conflicts *within* states. But the administration also faced the challenge of integrating force and diplomacy in other contexts pertinent to this study (notably Iraq and North Korea) where significant American interests were indisputably at stake.

Even with the end of the Cold War, American thinking about the use of force remains powerfully influenced by the Vietnam experience—and the perceived lessons of that conflict. The first major post-Vietnam pronouncement on the use of force (which came, significantly, in the wake of the disastrous deployment of American marines in Lebanon) was made by Secretary of Defense Caspar Weinberger in November 1984. Weinberger outlined a set of criteria to determine whether and how U.S. military power should be employed. These general guidelines (e.g., "we should have clearly defined political and military objectives") were intended to avoid the errors of conceptualization and implementation that had led to the Vietnam debacle.[27] The lessons of Vietnam—encapsulated in the so-called Weinberger Doctrine—guided the Bush administration's conduct of the Gulf War. The conceptual link between Weinberger and Bush was provided by Powell, who had been Weinberger's chief military aide when those criteria for the use of force were developed. In the aftermath of Desert Storm, as the Bush administration faced difficult choices on Kurdistan and Bosnia, Powell articulated what was essentially an up-dated reformulation of the Weinberger Doctrine. His concept of "decisive force" was the centerpiece of the administration's January 1992 *National Military Strategy*: "Once a decision for military action has been made, half measures and confused objectives extract a severe price in the form of a protracted conflict which can cause needless waste of human lives and material resources, a divided nation, and defeat. Therefore, one of the essential elements of our national military strategy is the ability to rapidly assemble the forces needed to win—the concept of applying *decisive force* to overwhelm our adversaries and thereby terminate conflicts swiftly and with a minimum loss of life."[28] The Gulf War was *the* archetypal case suited to the doctrine of decisive force. Saddam Hussein's invasion of Kuwait violated a fundamental norm of international behavior, vital American interests were at stake, the objective (reversing the invasion) was clear and attainable, the Bush administration had strong domestic and international backing, and the U.S. military was authorized to bring all available capabilities to bear short of nuclear weapons. If the Gulf War was a pure contingency, those that the United States has faced since (and which are far more characteristic of the post–Cold War era) have been anything but clear-cut. In Bosnia, Somalia, Haiti, Rwanda, and elsewhere, American objectives have been limited and the interests at stake have been less than vital. These types of contingencies have largely shaped the debate about the use of force during the Clinton administration. During the 1999 Kosovo crisis, critics charged that the Clinton administration's gradual escalation of the air war and its reluctance to commit ground forces marked a retreat from the Powell-Weinberger line of decisive force to the incrementalism of the Vietnam era. Secretary of State Madeleine Albright, among others, pushed for the use of force in more flexible ways to achieve limited ends.[29]

   The administration's early rhetoric suggested a greater propensity to become involved in internal conflicts and to do so multilaterally under the auspices of the United Nations. The increased willingness to contemplate intervention in internal conflicts (i.e., to focus on the domestic order of states) was wholly consistent with the administration's conception of international order as manifested in its "strategy of engagement and enlargement." The necessity of acting in concert with others, particularly America's North Atlantic Treaty Organization (NATO) allies, was depicted as a fiscal necessity in an era of dwindling budgets. During 1993, congressional criticism of this approach—characterized by then UN Ambassador Albright as "assertive multilateralism"—centered on the deteriorating situation in Somalia and the problem of "mission creep" (i.e., from humanitarian intervention to "nation-building"). In the face of this criticism and public reluctance to become involved in internal conflicts, the administration began to back away from its earlier rhetoric. This shift (or what the administration preferred to characterize as a "clarification") occurred even prior to the disastrous episode in Mogadishu involving American special forces in early October 1993. In his September 1993 address to the UN General Assembly, President Clinton baldly stated, "The United Nations simply cannot become engaged in every one of the world's conflicts. If the American people are to say yes to UN peacekeeping, the United Nations must know when to say no."[30] The debate about the use of force in general, and American participation in UN peacekeeping/ peacemaking operations in particular, culminated in May 1994 with the completion of a major interagency review and the issuance of Presidential Decision Directive (PDD) 25. The public presentation of PDD-25 marked what one observer has called the administration's "new realism" and signified that multilateral peace operations were not to be the centerpiece of its foreign and defense policy.[31] In addition to bowing to congressional and public attitudes, PDD-25 was also powerfully influenced by the reluctance of the Joint Chiefs of Staff to become involved in missions that deviated from the criteria in Powell's concept of "decisive force."

While multilateral peace operations dominated the use-of-force debate, other contingencies persisted involving rogue states where American interests were vitally engaged and the action undertaken (or contemplated) by the Clinton administration entailed the *limited* use of force for purposes of deterrence or compellence. These included the continued enforcement of the UN-sanctioned "no-fly zone" over Iraq, the June 1993 bombing of an Iraqi intelligence facility in retaliation for the attempted assassination of former President Bush during a visit to Kuwait, and the consideration of preventive strikes against North Korean nuclear facilities in response to the Pyongyang regime's refusal to submit those facilities to inspections by the International Atomic Energy Agency (IAEA) and its moves toward weaponization. With respect to these types of contingencies involving major regional adversaries, Lake stated that the American public would support the use of force "if classic interests like security in Europe or Asia or the Middle East are in question." This was an implicit acknowledgment that such domestic support would be difficult to sustain for the use of force in other cases (such as humanitarian intervention and internal conflict) where American "vital interests" were not demonstrably at stake.[32]

NONPROLIFERATION POLICY

A recurrent theme of this chapter is that the charting of American post–Cold War strategy has been strongly influenced by the fact that the end of the Cold War coincided with the Gulf War. In the area of nonproliferation, this conjunction has had paradoxical implications. On the one hand, the transformation of the U.S.-Soviet relationship has made possible rapid progress in the area of "vertical" proliferation—that is, in the nuclear arms race between the superpowers. Thus, following the breakup of the Soviet Union, President Clinton and Russian president Boris Yeltsin reached agreement on the second Strategic Arms Reduction Treaty (START II), which, when ratified and implemented, will lead to deep reductions in the two sides' strategic nuclear arsenals. During the Cold War, arms control negotiations to cap and reduce levels of strategic nuclear weapons had been the centerpiece of the bilateral relationship. With the Cold War's end, the political center of gravity of the U.S.-Russian relationship has shifted to a new bilateral agenda dominated by a wide range of initiatives relating to Russia's democratization and its transition to a market economy. Ironically, at the precise moment in history when serious reductions have finally become possible, the political transformation underlying that possibility has made arms control less central and seemingly less urgent.

On the other hand, as the vertical arms spiral between the superpowers is being reversed, the Gulf War and the revelations about Iraq that came to light in its aftermath have highlighted the problem of "horizontal" proliferation—that is, efforts by additional states (beyond the five nuclear powers acknowledged in the NPT) to acquire WMD and their means of delivery. Without question, the key condition of the post–Cold War era that has altered the traditional nonproliferation equation is the increased availability of fissile material. In the past, the major technological brake on an aspiring nuclear power was the difficulty of fabricating the necessary highly enriched uranium (HEU). (Prior to the Gulf War, Saddam Hussein spent some $8 billion on all conceivable enrichment approaches to produce the kilograms of HEU necessary for a weapon.) In the post–Cold War era, with tons of ineffectively secured HEU and plutonium in the Soviet successor states, a Saddam Hussein can attempt to circumvent lax controls through bribes and other covert actions to obtain the fissile material for a weapons program without even bothering to build enrichment facilities. This change arising out of the collapse of the Soviet Union has fundamentally altered the old terms of debate about nonproliferation that focused on denying countries like Iraq the necessary technological capabilities to produce nuclear weapons.

The Gulf War culminated a decade of increasing international concern about the spread of unconventional weapons to aspiring regional powers. Iraq was but the most extreme example of this trend because its acquisition of unconventional capabilities was linked to an expansionist foreign policy. During the Iran-Iraq War (1980–88), the Saddam Hussein regime flouted international norms of warfare through its indiscriminate missile attacks on Iranian cities and, most grievously, its battlefield employment of chemical weapons.[33] The United States failed to vigorously condemn these acts (which included the use of chemical weapons against Iraq's own Kurdish population) because of the Reagan administration's "tilt" toward Iraq and its belief in the efficacy of an engagement strategy to moderate Baghdad's behavior.

In addition to Iraq, other countries of proliferation concern in the 1980s included Iran, North Korea, Libya, Syria, Egypt, Israel, Pakistan, India, South Africa, Brazil, Argentina, and Taiwan. In the nuclear area, for example, former South African president F. W. de Klerk publicly confirmed in 1993 what many had suspected—namely, that South Africa during the 1980s had developed a limited nuclear weapons capability.[34] With respect to chemical weapons, Iraq was not the only country to use these unconventional weapons in combat; in 1987, when Libyan forces faced defeat at the hands of Chadian troops after the Libyans violated their shared border, Muammar Qaddafi ordered his forces to use chemical weapons against the defending Chadians.[35] Increased concern about the horizontal proliferation of nuclear, chemical, and biological capabilities coincided with the wider availability, either through indigenous production or import, of ballistic missiles. To cite but a few prominent examples from that period, Saudi Arabia reportedly received intermediate-range ballistic missiles from China in 1988, Argentina (with technical and financial support from Egypt and Iraq, respectively) worked after 1984 to perfect an extended-range version of its Condor missile, and North Korea produced advanced Scud missiles with a range of 500 kilometers. The spread of ballistic missiles threatened to extend the geographical scope of regional crises and to provide incentives for a regional power to strike preemptively against an adversary similarly armed with ballistic missiles during a crisis. Most ominously, these systems provided platforms for the potential use of unconventional weapons.[36] In February 1989, William Webster, director of the Central Intelligence Agency (CIA), stated that at least ten countries were developing biological weapons; in May 1989, he further revealed that at least fifteen developing countries would be capable of producing ballistic missiles by 2000. In his September 1989 address to the UN General Assembly, President Bush stated that more than twenty nations possessed chemical weapons or the capability to produce them.[37]

Following the Gulf War, the Bush administration proposed additional export control measures to strengthen the key institutional underpinnings of the international nonproliferation regime—institutions that included the Missile Technology Control Regime (MTCR), the Australia Group, the Nuclear Suppliers Group, and the IAEA. These proposals on the international level were complemented by a stiffening of U.S. national export control regulations. The Bush administration's Enhanced Proliferation Control Initiative of December 1990 covered dual-use technologies relevant to the production of chemical and biological weapons and ballistic missiles. From Congress, both prior to and after the Gulf War, came a number of nonproliferation measures, including the Missile Technology Control Act of 1990, the Chemical and Biological Weapon Control and Warfare Elimination Act of 1991, and the Iran-Iraq Arms Non-Proliferation Act of 1992.[38] Some of this legislation placed significant congressional reporting requirements on the executive branch regarding compliance. Such requirements were partly motivated by congressional questions about the vigilance and effectiveness of past administrations' nonproliferation efforts. This concern was heightened by the postwar revelations about Iraq's across-the-board drive to acquire nuclear, chemical, and biological weapons, and the view held by some critics that these efforts had been facilitated by a permissive export control regime and the tendency of Western governments to look the other way out of political and commercial expediency.

The troubling discoveries about Iraq's unconventional weapons programs came from the United Nations Special Commission (UNSCOM), which was established pursuant to UN Security Council Resolution 687 to oversee the destruction of Iraq's WMD and ballistic missile capabilities. The magnitude of the Iraqi WMD program, as it became known after 1991, was striking in both its breadth and its depth. UNSCOM and IAEA officials uncovered efforts by Iraqi scientists to use every known uranium-enrichment technique to produce fissile material for nuclear weapons. In May 1994, UNSCOM announced that over a two-year period all known Iraqi chemical munitions, agents, and precursors had been destroyed: this encompassed more than 27,000 chemical-filled bombs, rockets, and artillery shells; 30 chemical warheads for Scud missiles; 500 tons of mustard and nerve agents; and thousands of tons of precursor chemicals. UNSCOM inspections also revealed an extensive Iraqi program to produce and weaponize biological agents; the Iraqi regime finally admitted in August 1995 to having produced 90,000 liters of botulinum toxin and 8,300 liters of anthrax and having developed the capability to deliver these biological weapons by Scud missiles and aerial bombs. A particularly disturbing aspect of the Iraqi biological weapons program is that some of the pertinent technologies (ostensibly acquired by the Iraqis for legitimate agricultural and biomedical purposes) were not on export control lists; thus, for example, Iraq was able to procure tons of biological growth medium, an amount that went far beyond any legitimate civilian use.[39]

Given the Iraqi experience and the concerns that it raised about other Third World states potentially seeking to acquire WMD and ballistic missile capabilities, the Clinton administration came to office in January 1993 with the avowed goal of elevating nonproliferation as a U.S. foreign policy objective. Within the National Security Council (NSC), this commitment was symbolized by the creation of a new and separate Directorate for Nonproliferation and Export Controls. The NSC oversaw an intensive interagency review process that yielded PDD-13, detailing the administration's nonproliferation goals and overall approach. The essential elements of PDD-13 were unveiled by President Clinton in his September 1993 address to the UN General Assembly. Citing the Iraqi experience, President Clinton stated,

One of our most urgent priorities must be attacking the proliferation of weapons of mass destruction, whether they are nuclear, chemical, or biological, and the ballistic missiles that can rain down on populations hundreds of miles away. We know this is not an idle problem. All of us are still haunted by the pictures of Kurdish women and children cut down by poison gas. We saw Scud missiles dropped during the Gulf War that would have been far graver in their consequences if they had carried nuclear weapons. . . . More than a score of nations likely possess such weapons, and their number threatens to grow. These weapons destabilize entire regions. They could turn a local conflict into a global human and environmental catastrophe. . . . I have made nonproliferation one of our Nation's highest priorities. We intend to weave it more deeply into the fabric of all our relationships with the world's nations and institutions.[40]

Among the objectives specified in PDD-13's comprehensive statement of the Clinton administration's nonproliferation policy were the following: indefinite extension of the NPT and ratification of the Chemical Weapons Convention (CWC); reduction of proliferation threats in "regions of tension" such as the Korean peninsula, the Middle East, and South Asia; development of long-term options for fissile material disposition and security (both in the United States and abroad), as well as discouragement of plutonium use; negotiation of a multilateral convention prohibiting the production of HEU for military purposes; strengthening the IAEA's ability to detect clandestine nuclear activities; and reform of U.S. export controls for dual-use technologies.[41]

The most acute nonproliferation challenge facing the Clinton administration was that posed by North Korea's suspected nuclear facilities and evidence that Pyongyang was engaged in covert activities to develop nuclear weapons. This crisis escalated significantly in March 1993, within weeks of President Clinton's inauguration, when the Pyongyang regime announced that it was withdrawing from the NPT and would no longer permit IAEA inspectors to monitor its nuclear facilities. This decision led to an intensive series of U.S.–North Korean negotiations over the next fifteen months that yielded the Agreed Framework of October 1994. In addition to the North Korean crisis, the Clinton administration also became embroiled in a serious nonproliferation dispute with China concerning the reported export of M-11 missile components to Pakistan. The issue of Chinese missile exports to countries of concern (also including Syria, Algeria, Iran, and Iraq) had ostensibly been resolved during the Bush administration when Secretary of State James Baker received Chinese assurances that it would abide by MTCR guidelines if the United States waived economic sanctions for past behavior. Evidence about the M-11 transfer to Pakistan prompted the Clinton administration to impose new economic sanctions on China in August 1993. This step did not, however, affect the administration's subsequent decision in May 1994 to extend unconditionally MFN trading status to China. Because of the enormous commercial interests at stake, as well as the belief that compliant Chinese behavior can be achieved through continued engagement, the Clinton administration decided not to link MFN status to nonproliferation (or human rights) issues.

The Clinton administration's nonproliferation strategy focused on two interrelated sets of issues—first, strengthening the international nonproliferation regime through NPT extension, CWC ratification, the creation of a successor organization to the Coordinating Committee for Multilateral Export Controls (COCOM), etc.; and second, resolving, or at least ameliorating, nonproliferation problems in specific countries or regions. The latter included the North Korean and Chinese issues cited above, as well as other initiatives ranging from fissile material security in the former Soviet Union to missile proliferation in South Asia, to a regional arms control and nonproliferation dialogue in the Middle East. The generic issue of rogue states and the nonproliferation challenges posed by them arose in three specific policy contexts—the controversy surrounding the Defense Counterproliferation Initiative (DCI), the debate about the feasibility and necessity of ballistic missile defense, and the establishment of the Wassenaar Arrangement as a multilateral export control organization to succeed COCOM.

The DCI had its roots in the Gulf War experience, when U.S. and coalition forces were threatened by, and in turn targeted, Iraqi unconventional weapons. When Aspin enunciated the DCI at the National Academy of Sciences in December 1993, he highlighted the changes in the post–Cold War security environment that prompted it—notably the specter of "a handful of nuclear devices in the hands of *rogue states* or even terrorist groups." Aspin stated that "at the heart of the Defense Counterproliferation Initiative . . . is a drive to develop new military capabilities to deal with this new threat."[42] The DCI included proposed changes in procurement (e.g., improved non-nuclear munitions to target underground installations), intelligence gathering, and military doctrine. Critics charged that the initiative was merely a repackaging of existing Defense Department capabilities and programs that was motivated, in large part, by a bureaucratic interest in mobilizing support for continued congressional funding of these activities. However one judges the motivation underlying the DCI, the manner in which it was publicly enunciated did generate considerable confusion and alarm.

The confusion stemmed from an initial lack of clarity in whether the DCI was being advanced as a component of, or an alternative to, traditional nonproliferation policy. This issue was clarified in February 1994 when the NSC issued a memorandum on "Agreed Definitions" that characterized counterproliferation as "the activities of the Department of Defense across the full range of U.S. efforts to combat proliferation, including diplomacy, arms control, export controls, and intelligence collection and analysis, with particular responsibility for assuring that U.S. forces can be protected should they confront an adversary armed with weapons of mass destruction or missiles."[43] Both this NSC memorandum and the May 1995 report of the interagency Counterproliferation Program Review Committee, chaired by Deputy Secretary of Defense John Deutch, underscored that the counterproliferation initiative was firmly embedded within a comprehensive nonproliferation policy.[44] The confusion that stemmed from Aspin's December 1993 speech was coupled with alarm overseas that the DCI augured the possibility of unilateral and preemptive American military strikes against suspected targets producing or housing WMD in the Third World. The initiative, of course, was not formulated in a political vacuum; its political perception, particularly in foreign governments and research institutes, was shaped by rhetoric about America's role as the "the sole superpower" and the unfolding nuclear crisis in North Korea.[45] In addition to clarifying the meaning of counterproliferation during the first half of 1994, administration officials also worked to assuage these foreign fears about the initiative by emphasizing both the DCI's deterrent character and the U.S. commitment to addressing the problem of unconventional weapons multilaterally through the international nonproliferation regime.

Just as the Gulf War experience gave impetus to the DCI, so too did it fuel renewed attention on the issue of ballistic missile defense. The threat to American and allied forces posed by rogue states in regional theaters had been dramatically underscored by Saddam Hussein's large-scale use of Scud missiles against targets ranging geographically from Israel to Saudi Arabia. The initial euphoria about the effectiveness of the Patriot anti–ballistic missile system in dealing with the Iraqi Scud capability gave way to a more modest assessment of its performance in the war's aftermath.[46] In contrast to the Bush administration, which had scaled back but essentially maintained the Reagan administration's commitment to national missile defense (NMD), the Clinton administration focused its efforts (and budget share) on land-based theater defense programs, such as upgraded Patriot and "theater high-altitude area defense" systems.

A major source of contention between the Republican-led Congress and the Clinton administration—one that became an issue in the 1996 presidential campaign—was whether the United States should develop a comprehensive NMD by 2003 to counter the threat posed by rogue states seeking to acquire or produce long-range ballistic missiles. In advocating legislation that would require the Clinton administration to work toward such a system, Senator Thad Cochran (R-Miss.) argued, "START II . . . cannot and does not intend to take a single missile or mass-destruction weapon out of the hands of countries such as North Korea, Iran and Libya. The Defend America Act calls for defenses against the limited arsenals existing and sought by such rogue states."[47] Secretary of Defense William Perry argued that while basic research for an NMD should continue (at a proposed funding level of $500 million), priority should remain on fielding a next-generation Patriot to protect U.S. forces against short-range, conventional threats from regional adversaries.

The point of contention in this continuing debate about ballistic missile defense is the timeline when rogue states might acquire long-range ballistic missiles. A 1995 National Intelligence Estimate, leaked to the press, concluded that no hostile nation capable of building a nuclear weapon would be able to threaten the continental United States for fifteen years. Republican charges that White House pressure had politically skewed the intelligence community's finding led to the creation of an independent panel of experts, chaired by former CIA director Robert Gates, which found no such evidence of political interference.[48] A follow-on commission, chaired by former secretary of defense Donald Rumsfeld, concluded in July 1998 that the American intelligence community's estimates were overly optimistic. The Rumsfeld Commission concluded that a rogue state could develop and deploy an intercontinental ballistic missile (ICBM) within as little as five years (ten, in the case of Iraq).[49] On the issue of ballistic missile defense, the Clinton administration attempted to position itself between the Republican Congress, pushing for an early deployment of an NMD, and arms-control advocates, who argued that any move in that direction would undermine the Anti–Ballistic Missile (ABM) Treaty. The administration originally supported a modest research program for an NMD while seeking to defer a decision to deploy until 2003 at the earliest.[50] In response to the Rumsfeld Commission report and the August 1998 testing of a long-range missile by North Korea, Cohen announced plans to accelerate the development of a limited NMD capability "focused primarily on countering rogue nation threats. . . ."[51]

In an April 1996 speech on nuclear proliferation, then Secretary of Defense Perry spoke about the "here-and-now threat" of Scud missiles and the "future threat that a rogue state, that may be impossible to deter, will obtain ICBMs that can reach the United States."[52] Secretary Perry's reference to "undeterrable rogue states" is striking. It suggests that rogue states such as North Korea, Iran, and Iraq are potentially prone to irrational behavior and that the normal rules of deterrence (as it were) may not hold in American interactions with them.[53] This attitude, if translated into policy, has two implications. First, the imputation of irrationality—that, for example, an adversary cannot be deterred—makes it difficult to formulate an appropriate foreign policy response. Second, it debases the value of the American deterrent by conceding that it may not, in fact, deter a rogue state from using WMD. The most recent experience with Iraq during the Gulf War indicates the contrary. Saddam Hussein may have been ruthlessly expansionist, but he did not act irrationally. When Baker met Iraqi foreign minister Tariq Aziz in January 1991 just prior to the outbreak of hostilities, he reportedly told Aziz, "God forbid . . . chemical weapons are used against our forces—the American people would demand revenge, and we have the means to implement this." The Iraqi leadership told UN officials in 1995 that they interpreted Baker's statement as a threat to retaliate with nuclear weapons if Iraq used chemical or other unconventional weapons against American and coalition forces.[54] The issue here is not the desirability of ballistic missile defense, but rather, whether U.S. policy should be premised on the assumption that certain regimes are irrational and, therefore, "undeterrable." The characteristics of rogue states will be addressed in Chapter 2.

A final aspect of nonproliferation policy bearing on the general issue of rogue states is that of export control reform. In March 1994, COCOM, the multilateral export control regime established in 1949 to control the transfer of dual-use products and technologies to Eastern-bloc states, was formally ended. As with NATO and other Cold War institutions, the political cement of COCOM was the Soviet threat. The absence of such a central, commonly perceived threat complicated American efforts to forge an effective successor organization to COCOM. In negotiations with its former COCOM partners, the Clinton administration, citing the lessons of Iraq, pushed unsuccessfully for the designation of Iran, Iraq, North Korea, and Libya as "states of concern." In December 1995, twenty-eight governments agreed to establish the Wassenaar Arrangement on Export Controls for Conventional Arms and Dual-Use Goods and Technologies.[55] When the Wassenaar Arrangement was formally established in July 1996, the number of charter members had grown to thirty-three and included the Russian Federation, the former target of the COCOM regime. At that time, American officials emphasized the fact that a COCOM successor organization was in existence and that, as in previous experiences with the MTCR and the Australia Group, it provided an institutional structure that could be built on and, it was hoped, strengthened. With respect to the most contentious issue in the Wassenaar negotiations—exports to rogue states—French and Russian officials stressed that the written framework does not designate, nor proscribe transfers to, "states of serious concern." This view was bluntly asserted by one Russian official during the negotiations: "Iran is our partner. It *was* our partner, it *is* our partner, it *will be* our partner."[56] Likewise, German negotiators asserted that transfers by German firms to civilian end users in Iran were consistent with the Wassenaar framework. The Wassenaar experience points to the difficulty that the Clinton administration has encountered in making its rogue state policy multilateral—and is emblematic of the challenge that the United States has faced in shaping an effective post–Cold War policy.

NOTES

[1] *Public Papers of the Presidents: George Bush, 1991* (Washington, DC: U.S. Government Printing Office [GPO], 1992), pp. 74, 78.

[2] For example, in testimony before the House Foreign Affairs Committee, Secretary of State James Baker stated, "The United Nations has played a historic role in the Gulf crisis, one that is close to fulfilling the vision of its founders. The Security Council's twelve resolutions . . . symbolized the unity of the international community against Iraq's aggression and established the principle of collective security as a cornerstone of the post–Cold War era." See *Congressional Record: House*, February 6, 1991, p. H928.

[3] For a sanguine analysis of the prospects for collective security that draws on international relations theory see Andrew Bennett and Joseph Lepgold, "Reinventing Collective Security after the Cold War and Gulf Conflict," *Political Science Quarterly* 108, no. 2 (Spring 1993), pp. 213–37.

[4] Joseph S. Nye, "What New World Order?" *Foreign Affairs* 71, no. 2 (Spring 1992), p. 84. Nye succinctly characterizes the difference between realist and liberal conceptions of international order: "Realists, in the tradition of Richard Nixon and Henry Kissinger, see international politics occurring among sovereign states balancing each others' power. World order is the product of a stable distribution of power among the major states. Liberals, in the tradition of Woodrow Wilson and Jimmy Carter, look at relations among peoples as well as states. They see order arising from broad values like democracy and human rights, as well as from international law and institutions such as the United Nations."

[5] For a more detailed treatment of the American post–Cold War foreign policy debate see Wyn Q. Bowen and David H. Dunn, *American Security Policy in the 1990s: Beyond Containment* (Aldershot, England: Dartmouth Publishing, 1996), chapter 1, and Richard A. Melanson, *American Foreign Policy Since the Vietnam War: The Search for Consensus from Nixon to Clinton* (Armonk, NY: M. E. Sharpe, 1996), pp. 210–41.

[6] Charles Krauthammer, "The Unipolar Moment," *Foreign Affairs* 70, no. 1 (special issue, "America and the World 1990/91"), pp. 25, 33.

[7] Paul M. Kennedy, *The Rise and Fall of the Great Powers* (New York: Random House, 1988).

[8] Robert W. Tucker and David C. Hendrickson, *The Imperial Temptation: The New World Order and America's Purpose* (New York: Council on Foreign Relations Press, 1992), pp. 202, 207.

[9] Ibid., p. 203.

[10] Presidential aide David Gergen stated that the Bush White House feared "that the public debate over a new world order was spinning beyond control." Quoted in Melanson, *American Foreign Policy*, p. 221.

[11] Steven Erlanger and David E. Sanger, "The Clinton Record: Foreign Policy—On Global Stage, Clinton's Pragmatic Turn," *New York Times*, July 29, 1996, p. A1.

[12] Ibid., p. A16.

[13] *Weekly Compilation of Presidential Documents* 30, no. 4 (January 31, 1994), p. 154.

[14] Anthony Lake, "From Containment to Enlargement," *Dispatch* (U.S. Department of State) 4, no. 39 (September 27, 1993), pp. 658–64.

[15] President Clinton's commitment to democratization was symbolized by his creation of a specific directorate within the NSC devoted to that issue and a proposed 60 percent increase in the budget of the National Endowment for Democracy. Thomas Carothers of the Carnegie Endowment for International Peace noted the Clinton ad-

ministration's gradual de-emphasis of democratization over time and observed, "With the single exception of Haiti, Clinton has not, relative to Bush, substantially increased the U.S. emphasis on democracy promotion in any country or region." Quoted in Judith Miller, "At Hour of Triumph, Democracy Recedes as the Global Ideal," *New York Times*, February 18, 1996, p. E1.

[16] Henry Kissinger, *A World Restored: The Politics of Conservatism in a Revolutionary Era* (London: Victor Gollancz, 1977), pp. 1, 328. See also Philip Windsor, "Henry Kissinger's Scholarly Contribution," *British Journal of International Studies* 1, no. 1 (April 1975), p. 27.

[17] For an excellent discussion of the liberal and realist traditions see Stephen M. Walt, "International Relations: One World, Many Theories," *Foreign Policy* 110 (Spring 1998), pp. 29–46. The liberal tradition associated with Wilson focuses on the *domestic order* of states and views democratic states as being "inherently more peaceful than authoritarian states." But, as Walt notes, there is also an international strand of liberal thought which argues that "international institutions such as the International Energy Agency and the International Monetary Fund could overcome selfish state behavior by encouraging states to forego immediate gains for the greater benefits of enduring cooperation" (p. 32).

[18] Lake, "From Containment to Enlargement" (emphasis added).

[19] Paul Wolfowitz, "The New Defense Strategy," in Graham Allison and Gregory F. Treverton, eds., *Rethinking America's Security: Beyond Cold War to New World Order* (New York: Norton, 1992), p. 178.

[20] See, for example, Department of Defense (DOD), *Annual Report to the President and the Congress* (Washington, DC: DOD, February 1992).

[21] DOD, *Defense Strategy for the 1990s: The Regional Defense Strategy* (Washington, DC: DOD, January 1993).

[22] Ibid., pp. 15–16.

[23] DOD, *Report on the Bottom-Up Review* (Washington, DC: DOD, October 1993), p. 14.

[24] Colin Powell with Joseph E. Persico, *My American Journey* (New York: Random House, 1995), p. 579.

[25] DOD, *Report on the Bottom-Up Review*, pp. 1, 19. For a critique of the Bottom-up Review's two-MRC strategy and force structure recommendations see Michael O'Hanlon, *Defense Planning for the Late 1990s: Beyond the Desert Storm Framework* (Washington, DC: Brookings Institution, 1995), pp. 42–78. A certain artificial quality marked the two-MRC debate in that, even after the Reagan buildup, the United States did not have a true two-theater capability. The Gulf War stretched U.S. logistical and other important capabilities to their limits; if challenged on the Korean Peninsula at the same time, it is highly questionable whether the United States could have mounted a Desert Storm equivalent.

[26] Secretary Cohen stated, "We intend to maintain a robust presence in key regions of the world. . . . We need the capability to fight and win major theater wars in two places. It signals our resolve to friends and foes alike." Quoted in "Pentagon Plan on Shaping the Military Is under Fire," *New York Times*, May 15, 1997, p. A28. In December 1997, however, the National Defense Panel, chartered by Congress, recommended that the Department of Defense develop a "transformation strategy" for the next century with an emphasis on the defense of the U.S. "homeland" against attack by unconventional weapons. While endorsing the two-MRC strategy for the time being, the panel described it as a "low-probability scenario" that soon would be outdated. The panel further endorsed the Clinton administration's decision to deploy an NMD system until the nature of future threats is better understood. Reported in Associated Press, "Panel to Urge Pentagon to Shift toward Defense of U.S. Cities," *New York Times*, November 30, 1997, p. A30.

[27] For a comprehensive treatment of this topic see Richard N. Haass, *Intervention: The Use of American Military Force in the Post–Cold War World* (Washington: Carnegie Endowment for International Peace, 1994).

[28] Cited in Ivo Daalder, "The United States and Military Intervention in Internal Conflict," in Michael E. Brown, ed., *The International Dimensions of Internal Conflict* (Cambridge, MA: MIT Press, 1996), p. 470 (emphasis added).

[29] Eric Schmitt, "The Powell Doctrine Is Looking Pretty Good Again," *New York Times*, April 4, 1999, section 4, p. 5. Commenting on the NATO air war against the Serbs in Kosovo, Senator John McCain (R-Ariz.) commented, "This only affirms the Powell Doctrine. This is more reminiscent of the gradual escalation and bombing pauses that characterized the Vietnam War."

[30] *Public Papers of the Presidents: William J. Clinton, 1993* (Washington, DC: GPO, 1991), p. 1617.

[31] For a detailed analysis of the evolution of the Clinton administration's peace-keeping policy and PDD-25 see Ivo Daalder, "Knowing when to Say No: The Development of U.S. Peacekeeping Policy in the 1990s," in William Durch, ed., *UN Peacekeeping, American Policy, and the Uncivil Wars of the 1990s* (New York: St. Martin's, 1995), pp. 35–68.

[32] See Melanson, *American Foreign Policy*, p. 265, for excerpts of Lake's October 1994 address at Harvard University and commentary.

[33] Iran retaliated against Iraqi missile attacks in kind, though to a lesser degree (estimated by one expert at one-third the number of missiles launched by Iraq). Reports that Iran used chemical weapons on a limited basis in retaliation for Iraqi gas attacks have not been verified.

[34] For the most authoritative account of the development and eventual dismantling of the South African nuclear program see Mitchell Reiss, *Bridled Ambition: Why Countries Constrain Their Nuclear Capabilities* (Washington, DC: Woodrow Wilson Center Press, 1995), pp. 7–44.

[35] DOD, Office of the Secretary of Defense, *Proliferation: Threat and Response* (Washington, DC: GPO, April 1996), p. 25.

[36] See Martin Navias, *Ballistic Missile Proliferation in the Third World*, Adelphi Papers no. 252 (London: International Institute for Strategic Studies, Summer 1990).

[37] Quoted in Bowen and Dunn, *American Security Policy in the 1990s*, p. 119.

[38] Ibid., pp. 120–21.

[39] DOD, Office of the Secretary of Defense, *Proliferation: Threat and Response*, pp. 20–21.

[40] *Public Papers of the Presidents: William J. Clinton, 1993* (Washington, DC: GPO, 1994), p. 1615.

[41] White House, Office of the Press Secretary, "Nonproliferation and Export Control: Fact Sheet," September 28, 1993.

[42] Remarks by Secretary of Defense Les Aspin at the National Academy of Sciences Committee on International Security and Arms Control, December 7, 1993, published in U.S. Senate, Committee on Governmental Affairs, "Nuclear Proliferation Factbook" (103rd Cong., 2nd sess., 1994), pp. 198, 203 (emphasis added).

[43] Daniel Poneman, "National Security Council Memorandum: Agreed Definitions," February 18, 1994, published in "Nuclear Proliferation Factbook," p. 205.

[44] See Counterproliferation Program Review Committee, "Report on Activities and Programs for Countering Proliferation" (aka the "Deutch Report"), May 1994.

[45] An October 1994 workshop at the Woodrow Wilson International Center for Scholars that involved both senior Clinton administration officials and foreign experts on nonproliferation concluded, "The original presentation of the DCI created a host of unnecessary questions and misunderstandings abroad. . . . [I]nitial fears that the DCI was aimed at the unilateral and preemptive use of U.S. military force to strike

at targets in the developing world were largely misplaced. . . ." See Mitchell Reiss and Harald Muller, eds., *International Perspectives on Counterproliferation,* Division of International Studies Working Paper no. 99 (Washington, DC: Woodrow Wilson International Center for Scholars, January 1995), executive summary.

[46] The U.S. Army estimated that only 25 percent of the Patriot missiles destroyed their targets. See Bowen and Dunn, *American Security Policy in the 1990s,* p. 129.

[47] Thad Cochran, "Unready for Rogue Threats," *Washington Post,* May 8, 1996.

[48] Tim Weiner, "Panel Rejects Charges Study Politicized Atom Threat," *New York Times,* December 5, 1996, p. A17.

[49] Eric Schmitt, "Panel Says U.S. Faces Risk of a Surprise Missile Attack," *New York Times,* July 16, 1998, p. A24. In a letter to Senator James M. Inhofe (R-Okla.) dated August 24, 1998, General Henry H. Shelton, chair of the Joint Chiefs of Staff, stated (contrary to the conclusion of the Rumsfeld Commission) that the United States would have a strategic warning of at least three years to deploy a defensive system in order to counter an ICBM threat from a rogue state.

[50] For a succinct review of Clinton administration policy see the summary of the "Nuclear Roundtable" meeting with Robert Bell, special assistant to the president and senior director for defense policy and arms control at the NSC, Henry L. Stimson Center, March 18, 1996.

[51] DOD, Office of Public Affairs, *DoD News Briefing,* January 20, 1999.

[52] "Remarks of Secretary of Defense William Perry at George Washington University," Federal News Service transcript, April 25, 1996, p.1.

[53] The issue of "undeterrable" states is discussed in Janne Nolan and Mark Strauss, "The Rogues' Gallery," *Brown Journal of World Affairs* 4, no. 1 (Winter/Spring 1997), pp. 32–36.

[54] Cited in National Defense University (NDU), Institute for National Strategic Studies, *Strategic Assessment 1996: Instruments of U.S. Power* (Washington, DC: NDU Press, 1996), p. 203.

[55] Wassenaar is the town outside The Hague where five rounds of negotiations took place during 1994–95.

[56] Quoted in Natalie J. Goldring, "Wassenaar Arrangement in Limbo," *British-American Security Information Council [BASIC] Reports,* no. 52, May 13, 1996 (emphasis in original).

2

U.S. Strategy toward Rogue States (1): Origins and Development

ORIGINS OF THE ROGUE STATE CONCEPT AND POLICY

Throughout history, dissatisfied states—whether revolutionary or revanchist—have rejected international norms and the status quo. This is a normal condition of international relations. Designing effective strategies to deal with such states is a traditional challenge that great powers have faced to maintain the stability of the international system. The post–Cold War era stands in contrast to earlier historical periods when an expansionist great power, such as Nazi Germany or the Soviet Union, threatened to overthrow the existing international order. The contemporary focus of concern is on relatively marginalized states that threaten the stability of their immediate region but not the international system as a whole. Indeed, in one case, North Korea, the country of concern evidences many of the attributes of a "failed state."

Although American policy-makers have used the term "rogue state" in recent years to describe regimes that flout international norms, it is striking to note that the concept has no standing in international law. Rather, as Alexander George has observed, it is a political category employed by one or more great powers with a stake in the maintenance and orderly working of the international system.[1] In current usage, the rogue state designation reflects, specifically, the policy preferences of the United States as the post–Cold War era's preeminent power. Critics of the rogue state concept argue that the term is analytically soft and highly subjective; or, put more bluntly, that it is simply shorthand for a small group of states threatening American interests in key regions. Given the absence of objective criteria rooted in international law, it is not surprising that sharp differences have emerged between the United States and other countries (including its closest allies) over the implementation of its rogue state policy. To be sure, many abroad (as well as in the United States) have questioned the logic of a policy that relegates Cuba to this demonized category while conspicuously omitting a state like Syria, which is on the State Department's own terrorist list and has active programs for the development of weapons of mass destruction (WMD).

The Syrian case underscores the political (as opposed to legal) basis of the concept. The exclusion of Syria from the roster of rogue states has a political rationale that stems from its importance to the Middle East peace process. During its first term, the Clinton administration actively engaged the Damascus regime in an unsuccessful effort to draw it into a comprehensive peace settlement with Israel. Despite a disturbing pattern of behavior not unlike that of Iran, Syria was not designated a rogue state because so doing would have made such overtures politically difficult, if not impossible. The administration would instead have been pushed toward the adoption of a strategy of comprehensive containment and isolation, as with Iran and Iraq. Indeed, critics of this courting of Syria—an engagement strategy tangibly symbolized during the first Clinton administration by Secretary of State Warren Christopher's twenty-five-odd visits to Damascus in four years—have argued for precisely such a toughening in U.S. policy.[2] The political selectivity and glaring inconsistencies manifested in the case of Syria raise serious questions about the utility of the rogue state approach. Proponents of the rogue state policy argue that its primary utility is as a mobilization strategy to build political support both domestically and overseas for tough measures to counter the behavior of states like Iran, Iraq, Libya, and North Korea that threaten important American interests. As discussed in Chapter 3, this asserted value of the rogue state policy for mobilization purposes must be judged in terms of its effectiveness in promoting American objectives (e.g., behavior modification) and its costs (notably with America's allies). The salient point, further explored below, is that the rogue state concept arose not from an international legal tradition, but from American political culture and the distinctive approach to international relations derived from it.

The preceding chapter on the nature of the post–Cold War system included an examination of the contending conceptions of international order that have influenced U.S. policy formulation. That discussion highlighted the competing pulls of realism and liberalism in American diplomacy. This traditional tension continues to play out in the post–Cold War era across a range of policy issues from the expansion of the North Atlantic Treaty Organization (NATO) to humanitarian intervention. It has also strongly influenced the debate about rogue states—how such states are identified and the development of strategies to deal with them. Building on and extending the analysis of Chapter 1, the basic issue is whether rogue state or pariah status derives from a regime's *domestic* behavior (i.e., how it treats its own people) or from *external* actions that violate important norms (such as territorial aggression or the use of terrorism).

The liberal and realist schools of political thought offer contrasting perspectives on this question that reflect their underlying assumptions about the conditions of international order. Liberal political theorists and policy practitioners have argued that the key to the central issue in international relations—how to secure peace—lies in the internal organization of states. That view, manifested in the proposition that "democracies don't fight one another," is at the heart of the Clinton administration's "strategy of engagement and enlargement." By contrast, the realist school, best exemplified in the post–World War II era by the Nixon-Kissinger foreign policy and whose intellectual roots trace back to Thucydides and Thomas Hobbes, is premised on the core assumption that international order derives from a stable distribution of power between states. Although U.S. diplomatic history has evidenced periodic shifts between realism and liberalism—recall the pendular swing from Nixon to Carter in the 1970s—these changes have been of emphasis, not of one school totally supplanting the other. Both traditions have continually influenced the making of American foreign policy, albeit to varying degrees depending on the administration. The competing pulls of liberalism and realism have fostered distinct approaches to rogue states, with the former emphasizing internal factors and the latter, external behavior.

The contemporary rogue state category can be viewed as an offshoot of the realist tradition of U.S. diplomacy in that it is linked not to the internal organization or national character of those states, but to three criteria of external behavior: first and foremost, the pursuit of weapons of mass destruction; second, the use of international terrorism as an instrument of state policy; and third, a foreign policy orientation that threatens U.S. allies or important American interests in key regions. The focus of this chapter is on the conceptual origins and evolution of the rogue state policy. Of particular note in this context is the shifting use of external and internal criteria for defining such states during the Cold War and post–Cold War periods.

Prior to 1980, the term "rogue" (as well as "pariah" and "outlaw") in referring to a state was not used widely by either academic analysts or policy practitioners. To the extent such terms were used, it was in reference to states whose brutal internal repression placed them "beyond the pale." Thus, in a characteristic use of the rogue state concept prior to 1980, the *Washington Post* editorialized, "How does the international community deal with rogue regimes, those that under the color of national sovereignty commit unspeakable crimes against their own citizens? We have in mind not the mass deprivation of rights practiced by police states everywhere but the virtual genocide perpetrated by such regimes as Pol Pot's Cambodia and Idi Amin's Uganda."[3] This April 1979 editorial captured the dilemma of competing international norms—the principle of national sovereignty safeguarding states' right against outside interference in their internal affairs versus standards of human rights to protect individual citizens within states. This tension translates into now-familiar terms of debate—witness the Beijing regime's sharp rebuff of U.S. efforts to promote human rights in China. The international community's unified condemnation of the 1990 Iraqi invasion of Kuwait indicates the strong, and understandable, attachment of states to the principle of national sovereignty. The international response to the Kuwaiti invasion stands in sharp contrast to that following the 1978 Vietnamese intervention in Cambodia to drive Pol Pot from power and the 1979 incursion of Tanzanian troops into Uganda in support of anti-Amin forces. The difference in international response stems from the pariah status of the leaders whose countries were the targets of the intervention. In those instances, the international community turned a blind eye to the violation of one international norm—the inviolability of state borders and national sovereignty—in the face of the systematic violation of another through brutal repression and genocide. Pol Pot's Cambodia and Idi Amin's Uganda were the archetypal examples of the rogue, outlaw, or pariah state during the pre-1980 period. They were so considered because of their horrific records of *internal* behavior, not because they posed a threat to their neighbors or engaged in other forms of *external* behavior that undermined international stability. Indeed, it is testimony to their pariah status that the international community virtually acquiesced to interventions by neighboring states to unseat their ruling regimes.

The concept of the rogue state based on internal criteria of behavior, and thus rooted in the liberal tradition of American political thought, was prevalent during the pre-1980 period. During the late 1970s, however, the term "pariah state" was employed by policy analysts in a secondary context to describe a small set of diplomatically isolated states—notably Israel, South Africa, Taiwan, and South Korea—that were attracted to the nuclear option as a response to their perceived security dilemma. According to political scientist Robert Harkavy, these states shared several characteristics: they were pro-Western in political orientation but isolated from the numerically larger Soviet and Third World political blocs; the legitimacy of their regimes or national status within their defined borders was challenged by one or more powerful adversaries; and they were states reliant largely on a single source of conventional arms, and thus were highly vulnerable in a crisis to cutoffs of spare parts or denials of resupply.[4] Harkavy concluded that in view of "the pariah states' security situations, it should not be surprising that each would at least consider the acquisition of nuclear weapons as an equalizer. Each pariah has given strong signals—or is the subject of widespread rumors—in regard to an intent to produce nuclear weapons."[5]

In light of this trend, political scientist Richard Betts, writing at the start of the Carter administration, argued that an effective U.S. nonproliferation policy needed to take into account the security incentives that these "pariah states" had in acquiring nuclear weapons. He noted the strong reluctance of President Carter to face up to the contradiction between an "extreme commitment to nonproliferation and his other policy goals" (e.g., curtailing U.S. conventional arms sales). Betts concluded that the Carter administration should develop a mix of nonproliferation options, including security measures addressed to the sources of these states' insecurity, to prevent the "pariahs" from going nuclear. "Let Peking decide whether it prefers a non-nuclear Taiwan, still guaranteed against invasion by the United States, or an abandoned Taiwan with a nuclear crash program."[6] In the case of another "pariah," South Africa, an authoritative recent study indicates that the Pretoria regime's perception of a deteriorating regional situation in the 1970s (notably the rise of pro-Soviet regimes in Angola and Mozambique) was the major factor underlying its decision to embark on a nuclear weapons program. South African strategy emphasized not the immediate military utility of nuclear weapons, but rather their value as a political instrument. It is highly revealing that South Africa moved to dismantle its nuclear weapons and join the Nonproliferation Treaty (NPT) in 1989–90, when the international conditions that had motivated its nuclear program during the 1970s disappeared with the end of the Cold War.[7]

This secondary usage of the term "pariah state" during the late 1970s did not gain currency outside academic policy circles. In contrast to the current use of "rogue state," the term was not used by the Carter administration to describe these states because their marginalization and diplomatic isolation was instigated by the Soviet and Third World blocs. Indeed, several of them (Taiwan, South Korea, and Israel) were close U.S. allies, while others (South Africa) were not viewed as a threat to important American interests. This use of the term "pariah state" by academic analysts in the late 1970s to describe nuclear threshold states is particularly noteworthy in that it presaged the conceptual and policy changes of the 1980s by focusing on external as opposed to internal behavioral criteria. As detailed below, the current definition of the term "rogue state" took root in the 1980s and is explicitly linked to threatening external behavior, such as the pursuit of WMD and the use of terrorism as an instrument of state policy. In the 1990s, states that violate their citizens' human rights and engage in other forms of unacceptable internal behavior (e.g., Burma and Nigeria) are the targets of U.S. criticism and, in some instances, unilateral economic sanctions. They are not, however, politically demonized and targeted for strong international action by the American administration with the same energy and commitment as the roster of officially designated rogue states.[8]

In addition to anticipating this important shift from internal to external behavioral criteria of definition, the discussion of pariah states in connection with nuclear proliferation in the late 1970s was also significant because of its focus on the security motivations that those threshold states had in acquiring nuclear weapons. In so doing, it underscored the need to develop a mix of policy instruments as part of an overall nonproliferation strategy that takes those motivations into account. This issue has clear relevance in the transformed international environment of the 1990s, as the United States attempts to deal with a different group of potential proliferators, a subset of which has been characterized by the Clinton administration as rogue states. For example, in devising a policy to counter Iran's clandestine nuclear and chemical weapons program, American policy-makers should acknowledge the core security motivation underlying the Teheran regime's efforts to acquire unconventional weapons: namely, the fact that Iran was itself the victim of Iraqi poison gas attacks during the Iran-Iraq War. In light of that history, an American official privately conceded that he could well understand why an Iranian military planner, looking across the border at a weakened but defiant Saddam Hussein, would want nuclear weapons as an ultimate security guarantee. An American policy that goes no further than denying Iran technology and military capabilities without addressing the security motivation underlying the Teheran regime's pursuit of unconventional weapons is unlikely to succeed. This important question—that is, devis-

ing the appropriate mix of policy instruments (incorporating inducements as well as penalties) to achieve U.S. objectives—will be examined
further below.

The immediate origins of the contemporary rogue state policy can be
traced to the inauguration by the State Department of its "terrorist list" of
countries officially designated by the secretary of state under the Export
Administration Act of 1979.[9] This step marked a heightened U.S. focus on
the problem of state-sponsored terrorism that continued under the Reagan
administration. In a major speech to the American Bar Association in July
1985, President Reagan identified Iran, Libya, North Korea, Cuba, and
Nicaragua as "outlaw governments who are sponsoring international terrorism against our nation. . . . Most of the terrorists . . . are being trained,
financed, and indirectly controlled by a core group of radical and totalitarian governments—a new international version of Murder Incorporated."[10] Secretary of State George Shultz, who made the issue of state-
sponsored terrorism a recurring theme of his public diplomacy, argued,
"States that support and sponsor terrorist actions have managed to co-opt
and manipulate the terrorist phenomenon in pursuit of their own strategic
goals. It is not a coincidence that most acts of terrorism occur in areas of
importance to the West. . . ."[11] This strong American rhetoric was backed
up by tough action. In April 1986, for example, U.S. military aircraft
struck targets in Libya in retaliation for the Muammar Qaddafi regime's
alleged role in the bombing of a Berlin discotheque frequented by American military personnel. Reagan administration officials subsequently attributed Libyan quiescence after the raid to its deterrent effect. During
the 1980s, support of international terrorism, particularly that targeted
against important American interests, became a key defining characteristic of the outlaw (later rogue) state. As earlier noted, this period marked
the shift from internal to external behavior as the criteria of "outlaw" status. Thus, the pariahs of the 1970s (e.g., Pol Pot and Idi Amin) were supplanted by new ones, notably Khomeini and Qaddafi, whose "outlaw"
status stemmed not from the unacceptable treatment of their own civilian
populations but from foreign policy behavior that threatened American
interests.

Like the current rogue state policy, the State Department's terrorist list
generated charges of political expediency and inconsistency soon after its
inauguration. The particularly glaring focal point of this criticism was
the 1982 decision to drop Iraq from the list of states supporting international terrorism. This move, which was highly contentious within the
U.S. government (pitting the Defense Department against the State De-

partment), reflected the Reagan administration's decision to pursue an engagement strategy toward Iraq to cultivate better relations. It occurred at a time when the Baghdad regime was threatened with defeat in the war that it had initiated with Iran in 1980. As political scientist Bruce Jentleson has persuasively argued, the driving strategic logic behind the administration's "tilt" was captured in the old axiom, "the enemy of my enemy is my friend."[12] Although the action was defended in terms of maintaining a balance of power in the Persian Gulf region and preventing Iranian hegemony, it was also shaped within a political context of American antipathy toward Iran in the wake of the hostage crisis. The continued exclusion of Iraq from the terrorist list after 1982 flew in the face of contrary evidence, such as Iraq's providing sanctuary to Abu Nidal and other terrorist groups. The Reagan administration's flawed strategy toward Iraq was premised on both the perceived need to enter into strategic cooperation with Iraq to counter Iran and the political assessment that Iraqi behavior could be moderated through engagement. This policy of engagement was continued by the Bush administration into 1990 and, in fact, had no moderating effect on Saddam Hussein's behavior (witness his continued support of terrorism and use of chemical weapons against Iranian troops and Iraq's own Kurdish population). It also fostered a permissive multilateral export control regime that permitted Iraq, through open and covert procurement practices, to assemble its astounding arsenal of conventional and unconventional weapons.

In addition to state support for international terrorism, the second key criterion leading to outlaw or rogue designation was the pursuit of WMD. This did not, however, emerge as a defining characteristic until 1989, as the Cold War was entering its final phase and the receding Soviet threat began to be supplanted by others in U.S. defense planning. During the 1980s, the issue of horizontal proliferation of WMD capabilities to Third World states did receive considerable attention. But many of the states of concern were either American allies or countries with which the United States enjoyed close relations, such as Argentina, Brazil, South Korea, and Israel. Indeed, the state that received probably the greatest public attention because of its nuclear weapons program was Pakistan—which was permitting the Afghan mujahideen to operate from its territory and serving as a conduit for American military assistance under the Reagan Doctrine to this anti-Soviet insurgency movement. In defending the Reagan administration's engagement policy toward Pakistan, Assistant Secretary of State Richard Murphy stated, "We believe that our continuing economic assistance to Pakistan not only underpins our extremely important interests by allowing Pakistan to stand up to Soviet pressure through Afghanistan but also serves to encourage Pakistani nuclear restraint and to undercut any perceived security need for a national nuclear deterrent."[13] Under the 1985 Pressler Amendment, the president was required to certify annually to Congress that Pakistan did not possess a nuclear weapon.[14] Although the Pakistani case was a major focus of congressional attention, Iraq had by far the worst record of actual behavior with respect to WMD acquisition and use. The United States condemned specific Iraqi actions (such as the March 1988 gassing of the Kurdish town of Halabja), but this did not lead to a reassessment of the overall American approach to Saddam Hussein's Iraq.[15] Actual Iraqi WMD use received less attention than did the suspected Libyan chemical weapons factory at Rabta.

Political scientist Michael Klare, tracing the rise of what he refers to as the American "Rogue Doctrine," notes that by the late 1980s U.S. officials began to link the terrorism and WMD issues in the context of certain Third World states. In his January 1989 Senate confirmation hearings, secretary of state–designate James Baker explicitly did so, stating that "chemical warheads and ballistic missiles have fallen into the hands of governments with proven records of aggression and terrorism."[16] During the Reagan-Bush years, external behavior flouting international norms (i.e., regional aggression, sponsorship or support of terrorism, and the pursuit of WMD capabilities) came to define "outlaw" status. This emerging rogue state policy gained further political momentum, and indeed official status as American policy, during the Clinton administration when National Security Adviser Anthony Lake argued that countries exhibiting this external behavior constituted a class of states.

In reviewing the historical record of the 1980s, the most striking incongruity is that the country that would later be held up as the archetypal rogue state—Iraq—was being courted, not sanctioned, by the Reagan and Bush administrations as part of what later proved to be a flawed engagement strategy toward the Baghdad regime. In fact, Iraq, which was dropped from the State Department's terrorist list in 1982, was not placed back on it until a month after the August 1990 invasion of Kuwait. Iraq, however, was not the only case in which the Reagan and Bush administrations' own criteria of international "outlaw" status were ignored in pursuit of an ill-conceived political gambit to cultivate better relations with a radical regime. In 1985–86, the Reagan administration also initiated a political opening to Iran—another country on the terrorist list that had held fifty-two American hostages for more than a year and had been implicated in the October 1983 bombing of the U.S. Marine Corps' barrack in Beirut. The currency of this dialogue—a political fiasco that became the Iran-Contra scandal—was American arms that the Teheran regime sorely needed in its ongoing war with Iraq. The underlying rationale for what General Colin Powell characterized as National Security Adviser Robert MacFarlane's "bid for Kissingerian immortality" was both long-term (a geostrategic move to court a major state on the Soviet Union's southern periphery) and immediate (trading American arms for the Khomeini regime's assistance in securing the release of U.S. hostages in Lebanon).[17]

   In terms of the evolution of the rogue state concept and policy, the 1980s were a crucial formative period in that those years witnessed the emergence of the core criteria, rooted in external behavior, that would later come to define what the Clinton administration characterized as a category of states. At the same time, the failed initiatives toward Iran and Iraq defied the Reagan and Bush administrations' own hard-line policy toward "outlaw" states and generated criticisms (notably during the congressional hearings on the Iran-Contra scandal) of hypocrisy and naïveté in the pursuit of political expediency. As will be seen, the Clinton administration's rogue state policy would similarly encounter charges of political selectivity as it attempted to translate a problematic concept into diplomatic practice.

THE CLINTON ADMINISTRATION

Although the criteria determining rogue status emerged during the 1980s, the policy gained political impetus with the end of the Cold War. This epochal development coincided with another event that would define the new era—the Gulf War. Opinion polls indicated that among the various rationales offered by the Bush administration for the war (e.g., the economic threat posed by Iraqi control of Persian Gulf oil supplies, the moral and legal injunction against interstate aggression) the one that most resonated with the American public was concern about a nuclear-armed Iraq.[18] Since the last war often governs policy-makers' thinking about the next one, it is not surprising that Iraq became the archetype for U.S. defense planners in the wake of Desert Storm. The Bush administration highlighted specific countries of concern, such as Iran, Libya, North Korea, and, of course, Iraq (which was being stripped of its WMD capabilities under the mandate of the United Nations [UN]). But in publicly framing these issues, the Bush administration did not characterize them as a category of state under the rogue rubric. This continued into the first year of the Clinton administration, after a presidential election in which foreign policy issues received scant attention.[19]

The Clinton administration's rogue state policy arose in a curious fashion. The occasion for its emergence was the administration's enunciation of a strategy of "dual containment" toward Iran and Iraq. A specific policy aimed at two radical regimes in a region of vital interest to the United States thus became the vehicle for the articulation of a general policy that grouped a disparate set of countries under the rogue state banner. The application of the "dual containment" strategy toward Iraq and Iran will be examined in detail in Part II. Given the link between the dual containment and rogue state policies, a brief overview of the development of the former would provide the necessary context for a consideration of the latter.

Dual containment was a policy born of frustration. Since the withdrawal of British forces from the Persian Gulf in 1971, the United States had taken on responsibility as the security guarantor of the region. In pursuit of this objective, Washington had followed a balancing strategy aimed at preventing any local power from achieving regional hegemony. During the Nixon-Kissinger years and continuing into the Carter administration, this strategy had entailed a tilt toward the Shah's Iran. Under the Nixon Doctrine, Iran and Saudi Arabia purchased American arms (recycling petrodollars in the process) and became the "twin pillars" of U.S. security policy in the Gulf. With its substantial arsenal, sizable population, and pro-American orientation, Iran was viewed by successive U.S. administrations during the 1970s as the security manager of the Persian Gulf region. This devolution of responsibility was a reflection both of Iran's rise and the realities of American post-Vietnam retrenchment in the Third World. The principal target of this regional strategy in the Gulf was Iraq, which was politically allied with the Soviet Union through their 1972 Treaty of Friendship. This pattern of regional alignments prevailed until the 1979 Iranian Revolution and the advent of a virulently anti-American regime in Teheran. During the 1980s, American policy flipped political polarity. In 1982, the Reagan administration initiated its famous "tilt" toward Iraq, dropping the Baghdad regime from the State Department's terrorist list and making it eligible for American export credits. The move was undertaken at a time when Iraq was faring poorly in the war that it had started with Iran in September 1980. U.S. claims of neutrality were belied by covert military assistance (i.e., permitting third-party transfers of American-licensed equipment) and limited intelligence-sharing. This tilt toward Iraq was complemented by a concerted American effort under the so-called Operation Staunch to deny Iran arms through an international embargo.[20] In mid-1985, however, the Reagan administration contravened its own policy by providing U.S. arms to Iran (via Israel) in return for cash (which was then covertly funneled to the Nicaraguan resistance) and the Teheran regime's assistance in freeing American hostages in Lebanon. When the Iran-Contra scandal became public in November 1986, the Reagan administration had nothing tangible to show from this initiative and the fiasco exposed it to charges of hypocrisy from European allies that Washington had strongly pressed to limit their dealings with Iran.[21]

In the wake of the Iran-Contra affair, U.S. policy reverted to its previous tilt toward Iraq. This change was reflected in the Reagan administration's 1987 decision to reflag Kuwaiti oil tankers and provide them protection against Iranian naval and air attacks. In Washington, the Iranian threat to shipping in the northern Gulf provoked discussion of military options, including a proposal (advocated by then Representative Aspin) to mine Iranian harbors. The adoption of a more bellicose U.S. stance toward Iran was accompanied in mid-1987 by a tough diplomatic line in the United Nations to compel Iran to accept a cease-fire or face mandatory sanctions. When Iran subsequently accepted a cease-fire with Iraq under duress (likened by Khomeini to drinking poison), there was a widespread perception in the Gulf region that American support for Iraq had been a significant factor. The eight-year Iran-Iraq War left the Baghdad regime financially strapped and exhausted but also the dominant military power in the region. This conjunction of financial need, military dominance, and Saddam Hussein's proclivity to strategic miscalculation led to the Iraqi invasion of Kuwait within two years of the cease-fire with Iran. During the period between the end of the Iran-Iraq War in 1988 and the Iraqi invasion of Kuwait in 1990, the Bush administration, even in the face of an increasingly bellicose and provocative stance from Saddam Hussein, remained committed to its engagement policy toward Iraq. This course of events was motivated by the belief that continuing engagement could lead to the moderation of Iraqi behavior and that the Baghdad regime would for the foreseeable future be preoccupied internally with the formidable tasks of postwar reconstruction. The Bush administration's engagement policy came to an abrupt halt with the Iraqi invasion of Kuwait in August 1990 and the ensuing Gulf War of January–February 1991.

The Clinton administration's policy of "dual containment" was essentially a continuation of the comprehensive containment policy that the

Bush administration had pursued toward Iran and Iraq after the Gulf War. After a decade of frustration (notably the failed engagement policy toward Iraq and the "Irangate" fiasco), U.S. policy-makers eschewed the notion that Washington could play off one regional power against the other to maintain balance and stability. The enunciation of the dual containment policy came in a major address by Martin Indyk, senior director for Near East and South Asian Affairs at the National Security Council (NSC), at the Washington Institute for Near East Policy on May 19, 1993. In that speech, Indyk stated,

The Clinton Administration's policy of "dual containment" of Iraq and Iran derives in the first instance from an assessment that the current Iraqi and Iranian regimes are both hostile to American interests in the region. Accordingly, we do not accept the argument that we should continue the old balance of power game, building up one to balance the other. We reject that approach not only because its bankruptcy was demonstrated in Iraq's invasion of Kuwait. We reject it because of a clear-headed assessment of the antagonism that both regimes harbor towards the United States and its allies in the region. And we reject it because we don't need to rely on one to balance the other.[22]

Although the "dual containment" rubric created a linkage that later became a persistent source of confusion and contention, Indyk noted the significant difference in American objectives between the two cases. In the Iraqi case, he stated, "Our purpose is deliberate: it is to establish clearly and unequivocally that the current regime in Iraq is a criminal regime, beyond the pale of international society and, in our judgment, irredeemable."[23] The speech did not explicitly state that the U.S. objective was a regime change; it repeated an earlier formulation that Washington sought full Iraqi compliance with UN Security Council resolutions, on the assumption that Saddam Hussein could not meet those requirements while remaining in power. This constituted an implicit policy of rollback. In the case of Iran, by contrast, the focus of the dual containment speech was on objectionable Iranian *external* behavior—its sponsorship of terrorism and support for radical groups seeking to undermine the Arab-Israeli peace process, its efforts "to subvert friendly governments" in the Gulf region, and its sustained effort to acquire WMD. Indyk stated that the Clinton administration was "not opposed to Islamic government in Iran. . . . We do not seek a confrontation but we will not normalize [relations] with Iran until and unless Iran's policies change, across the board."[24] He also called for multilateral support for sanctions against Iran, arguing that the failure to do so would have an adverse impact on the regional balance of power: "Iran does not yet face the kind of international regime that has been imposed on Iraq. A structural imbalance therefore exists between the measures available to contain Iraq and Iran. To the extent that the international community, as a result, succeeds in containing Iraq but fails to contain Iran, it will have inadvertently allowed the balance of power in the Gulf to have tilted in favor of Iran, with very dangerous consequences. That imbalance therefore argues for a more energetic effort to contain Iran and modify its behavior even as we maintain the sanctions regime against Iraq."[25]

In the months following Indyk's dual containment speech, it was unclear whether this NSC initiative enjoyed support across the administration, particularly at the State Department. At a hearing of the House Foreign Affairs Committee in July 1993, Assistant Secretary of State for Near Eastern Affairs Edward Djerijian declined to characterize U.S. Gulf policy as dual containment, while repeating and elaborating on much that had been in the Indyk speech. This evident reluctance in using the term stemmed from the widespread perception, despite efforts to the contrary, that dual containment meant the pursuit of identical containment strategies toward these two rogue states. The rumor of an NSC-State rift over dual containment prompted Indyk to clarify publicly that his previous statements had been cleared by the State Department and constituted the Clinton administration's official policy toward the Gulf region.[26]

The new line received an authoritative boost from National Security Adviser Lake in the spring 1994 issue of *Foreign Affairs*. The primary purpose of the article was to elaborate on the dual containment strategy that Indyk had unveiled in his May 1993 speech. At the same time, however, it went beyond the specific issue of U.S. policy toward Iran and Iraq to assert that these countries, along with others evidencing specific behavioral attributes, constituted a generic category of "backlash" or "rogue" states in the emerging post–Cold War order:

Our policy must face the reality of recalcitrant and outlaw states that not only choose to remain outside the family [of nations] but also assault its basic values. There are few "backlash" states: Cuba, North Korea, Iran, Iraq and Libya. For now they lack the resources of a superpower, which would enable them to seriously threaten the democratic order being created around them. Nevertheless, their behavior is often aggressive and defiant. The ties between them are growing as they seek to thwart or quarantine themselves from a global trend to which they seem incapable of adapting.

These backlash states have some common characteristics. Ruled by cliques that control power though coercion, they suppress human rights and promote radical ideologies. While their political systems vary, their leaders share a common antipathy toward popular participation that might undermine the existing regimes. These nations exhibit a chronic inability to engage constructively with the outside world. . . . They are often on the defensive, increasingly criticized and targeted with sanctions in international forums. Finally, they share a siege mentality. Accordingly, they are embarked on ambitious and costly military programs—especially in weapons of mass destruction (WMD) and missile delivery systems—in a misguided quest for a great equalizer to protect their regimes or advance their purposes abroad.[27]

The debate that followed the publication of the Lake article focused primarily on the efficacy of dual containment as a strategy, not on the merits of using the "backlash" or rogue rubric to designate a category of states that included Iran and Iraq. For example, the accompanying rejoinder to Lake's article in *Foreign Affairs*, written by political scientist Gregory Gause, was entitled "The Illogic of Dual Containment." Gause argued that "the major flaw in dual containment is the contention that Iran and Iraq can be contained simultaneously." Neither regional power can be contained without the cooperation of the other. Likewise, as demonstrated in the Iraqi invasion of Iran in September 1980, instability and weakness in one invites intervention by the other. He also argued that by isolating both, dual containment could have the unintended consequence of pushing the Teheran and Baghdad regimes into a tactical alliance against the United States and its regional allies.[28] Finally, Gause advocated an alternative strategy that would "view the question of Iraq, the pivot around which the geopolitics of the gulf will turn, as an issue for regional consultation, and potentially cooperation."[29] This strategy would entail the initiation of a dialogue with the Teheran regime on the grounds that Iran poses a less severe threat than Iraq presents and that Iranian cooperation will be necessary in bringing about a regime change in Baghdad. This alternative of pursuing differentiated strategies toward Iran and Iraq would be a recurring theme in the debate about dual containment.

Although the Lake article did break new ground in articulating the administration's thinking about this new, post–Cold War category of rogue states, the bulk of the article was devoted to the issue of dual containment. At one point in his discussion of "the challenge from Teheran," Lake, referring indirectly to political scientist Samuel Huntington's influential 1993 *Foreign Affairs* article, asserted, "The American quarrel with Iran should not be construed as a 'clash of civilizations' or opposition to Iran as a theocratic state. Washington does not take issue with the 'Islamic' dimension of the Islamic Republic of Iran."[30] This line prompted speculation that dual containment was cast in the broader context of containing "backlash states" to insulate the Clinton administration from criticism that its policy was anti-Islamic.

The Lake article remains the Clinton administration's most detailed articulation of its rogue state policy. Since 1994, the term has been used widely by both government officials and policy analysts. It has become an established term in the American political lexicon. One of the earliest instances of its usage came in January 1994, prior to the publication of the Lake article, when President Clinton warned a Brussels audience that "growing missile capabilities are bringing more of Europe into the range of rogue states such as Iran and Libya."[31] The administration's emerging rogue state policy was consistent with and complementary to its overarching grand strategy encapsulated in the slogan "engagement and enlargement." Foreign policy expert Michael Nacht observes that the administration has offered "a vision of four-tiered structure in contemporary world politics":

The first level contains the democratic and market economy states, all of which have a stake in the current international system; the second includes states such as the former Soviet Union and possibly China that seek, at least to some degree, to join the first tier; the third is a small collection of "rogue states," including Iran, Iraq, Libya, and North Korea, that oppose the current system; and the final group encompasses the "failed states" such as Bosnia and Somalia that have lost the fundamental elements of sovereignty. As a general proposition, the administration is committed to moving (to the extent feasible) all the states in tiers two through four into tier one.[32]

In conceptual and historical terms, the Clinton administration's rogue state policy is noteworthy in two respects. First, as discussed in Chapter 1, the intellectual bedrock of the administration's "engagement and enlargement" strategy is the liberal Wilsonian conception that the key to forging a post–Cold War peace is the global extension of democratic political systems. The emphasis here is on the domestic order—that is, how states are constituted internally. The underlying assumption of this school of international relations is that democratic states do not wage war against one another; the proliferation of democracies, in short, extends the zone of peace. The striking aspect of the rogue state concept, as previously noted, is that it is rooted not in the authoritarian, antidemocratic nature of their regimes, but in their external behavior. The concept is a reflection more of the realist than of the liberal political tradition of American diplomacy. Although Lake's article laying out the "backlash state" argument made reference to the odious nature of these regimes, the core considerations that place them into this demonized category are how they relate to the outside world—their support of international terrorism, their pursuit of WMD, their challenge to the regional political order, and so forth. If the criteria triggering the designation as a rogue state were grounded in terms of the domestic order—how a regime treats its own people—the rogue state list would be much longer and would include a number of American allies in the Third World.

Second, the rogue state approach is a product of America's unique political culture. It reflects the traditional Manichean streak of American diplomacy in which international affairs is cast as a struggle between forces of good and evil. This deeply rooted belief is at the core of what sociologist Robert Bellah describes as America's "civil religion."[33] In the post–World War II period, this characteristic contributed to the Cold War's virulence (and, indeed, had a mirror image in Soviet communism's own millennial propaganda); thus, the Truman Doctrine cast the U.S-Soviet competition not in traditional balance-of-power terms, but as an all-out clash between "alternative ways of life." With the end of the Cold War and the demise of the former "evil empire," the rogue states have become the objects of American demonology. This approach to foreign policy stands in contrast to that of others, such as America's European allies, who view international relations as a competition more between interests than between values (hence former French president Charles de Gaulle's oft-quoted observation that states do not have friends, just interests). In large part, it explains why Washington's approach to dealing with countries of concern such as Iran has often put the United States at odds with its close allies. Regimes that the United States views as "beyond the pale" are engaged by others who argue that "critical dialogue" will yield better results in terms of ameliorating their objectionable external behavior. The emergence of the rogue state policy as a central component of U.S. post–Cold War strategy should be seen as a product of a deeply rooted American political culture. The Clinton administration has demonized the rogue states as part of its political strategy to mobilize broad domestic support for tough action against them. In addition, the policy has received political impetus from influential domestic constituencies that advocate strong measures against specific states under the Clinton administration's rogue state rubric (e.g., the Cuban émigré community for Cuba, the families of the victims of the bombing of Pan Am flight 103 for Libya, the American-Israel Public Affairs Committee [AIPAC] for Iran). This linkage between foreign policy and domestic politics is a key determinant of the administration's rogue state policy.

Following the publication of the Lake's article in spring 1994, the term "rogue state" gained wide currency. It was frequently used by senior Clinton administration officials, including the president, in describing the range of security challenges (e.g., ethnic conflict, terrorism) facing the United States in the post–Cold War era. The administration invoked the term to mobilize domestic and international support for major multilateral arms control measures; it forcefully argued that the international community's extension of the NPT in May 1995 and the Senate's ratification of the Chemical Weapons Convention in April 1997 would reinforce the international norm against proliferation and make it more difficult as a practical matter for rogue states to acquire WMD because of these treaties' export control regimes. In Congress, proponents of a national missile defense system have argued that this program is necessary to defend the country against possible long-range ballistic missile attack by a rogue state early in the twenty-first century. These examples reflect the growing acceptance of the rogue state rubric as a term of reference in the American policy debate. The purpose of this study is not to take issue with particular policy issues, such as the desirability of ballistic missile defense. Rather, it is to highlight the policy distortions that stem from this artificial lumping of disparate states and hinder the ability to realize the discrete U.S. objectives with respect to these countries individually.

As previously noted, the Clinton administration's rogue state policy was an outgrowth of its "dual containment" strategy toward Iran and Iraq. Lake's elaboration of the dual containment strategy in *Foreign Affairs* became the occasion for the enunciation of this more general policy framework encompassing additional states (specifically, North Korea, Libya, and Cuba). The policy toward Iran and Iraq—comprehensive containment and isolation—set the policy tone and pattern for the others. The United States pursued this policy multilaterally with its close allies in the cases of Iraq and Libya, and unilaterally vis-à-vis Iran and Cuba. It did so despite the fact that American objectives with respect to these regimes varied significantly: for Iran, the avowed U.S. objective has been the moderation of objectionable Iranian behavior; in the case of Iraq, the goal (notwithstanding earlier State Department euphemisms about merely seeking Baghdad's compliance with Security Council resolutions) is to oust Saddam Hussein from power. The sole exception to this pattern of comprehensive containment and isolation, of course, has been North Korea. As will be examined in detail in Chapter 6, the North Korean case was the major point of departure in which the Clinton administration integrated a limited engagement component into its containment strategy (through the October 1994 Agreed Framework) to address the pressing danger of Pyongyang's advanced nuclear weapons program.

The primary instrument of the Clinton administration's rogue state policy has been economic sanctions to ratchet up the pressure on these radical regimes. They have proved a blunt instrument of questionable effectiveness in furthering U.S. policy objectives—whether in compelling a change in behavior (e.g., Iran) or promoting a regime change (e.g., Iraq and Libya). During the administration's first term, the White House adopted a series of measures to strengthen the U.S. sanctions regime against rogue states at the urging and occasional instigation of the Congress. Two key pieces of legislation by which this was accomplished were, first, the Cuban Liberty and Democratic Solidarity Act of March 1996, commonly referred to as the Helms-Burton Act after its congressional sponsors, Senator Jesse Helms (R-N.C.) and Representative Dan Burton (R-Ind.); and second, the Iran-Libya Sanctions Act (ILSA) of July 1996, sponsored by Senator Alfonse D'Amato (R-N.Y.). Both acts include provisions for the United States to impose "secondary" or extraterritorial sanctions against foreign commercial entities doing business with these rogue states. These congressional initiatives transformed the politics of the rogue state issue by shifting the terms of debate—that is, from pressuring the targeted regimes in Teheran, Tripoli, and Havana to punishing businesses based in London, Paris, and Frankfurt. In the process, it exposed probably the most significant rift in the transatlantic relationship since the end of the Cold War. The International Institute for Strategic Studies' *Strategic Survey* aptly characterized the controversy: "It would be misleading to conclude . . . that the transatlantic dispute over rogue states is simply a difference in analysis, and that the respective positions on the issue could be just as easily reversed. In fact, the U.S. and European positions have just as much to do with their own domestic politics, economic interests and political cultures as with a genuine policy dispute."[34]

The inclusion of Cuba on the Clinton administration's roster of rogue states has been particularly contentious and anomalous. Even if one accepts the rogue state concept on its own terms, the Cuban case does not fit the criteria.[35] Indeed, the Clinton administration itself has only episodically included Cuba in its rogue state list. For example, while included in Lake's article, Cuba was not part of the core group (comprising Iran, Iraq, Libya, and North Korea) for which the United States sought the strictest possible export controls in the international negotiations leading to the creation of the Wassenaar Arrangement.

The inclusion of Cuba was largely driven by American domestic politics. When the Helms-Burton Act was signed into law by the president, observers were quick to point to the impending presidential election and the importance of Florida and New Jersey, with their sizable Cuban-American populations and forty electoral votes. The administration's eventual embrace of the Helms-Burton Act, in fact, marked a reversal from its prior policy orientation toward Cuba, which had held open the possibility for dialogue and engagement as a means of positively influencing that country's internal evolution. In April 1995, for example, the Clinton administration indicated its willingness to respond to economic reforms in advance of desired political reforms by Fidel Castro: "We are prepared to reduce sanctions in carefully calibrated ways in response to significant, irreversible change in Cuba," Assistant Secretary of State Wendy Sherman told a House committee.[36] This policy trend was abruptly reversed in late February 1996 when Cuba downed two civilian aircraft manned by Cuban-American émigrés over its territory. That event fundamentally altered the politics of the Cuban sanctions issue in Washington. Thereafter, the administration worked with Congress to craft tougher sanctions.[37] In that negotiating process, the White House was able to ensure that the Helms-Burton Act included a waiver provision to maintain the president's flexibility; the waiver was a tacit signal to U.S. allies of the administration's intent to limit the bill's political fallout. (This fueled congressional criticism that the administration was trying to have its Cuban policy both ways.) The Canadian, Mexican, and European governments declared the act's extraterritorial sanctions illegal and passed laws of their own allowing their companies to retaliate if the United States invoked sanctions. The danger that this dispute might escalate further was highlighted when the European Union (EU) threatened to seek legal recourse in the World Trade Organization.

The transatlantic dispute over Cuba paled in significance and degree of acrimony to that over Iran. The Clinton administration's dual containment policy was an indicator of its antipathy toward the Teheran regime. The fact that the policy's avowed objective was to change Iranian behavior rather than the regime itself (as with Iraq) was less a statement of Washington's preference than its recognition of the reality of the Islamic Republic's political durability. The administration's hard-line approach was reportedly led by Christopher, who had been the Carter's administration's negotiator in the 1979–81 hostage crisis. Unlike Cuba, Iran fit the administration's rogue state criteria—it used terrorism as an instrument of state policy, was illicitly attempting to develop WMD, and threatened the stability of neighboring regimes in a region of vital interest to the United States. In contrast to the American policy of comprehensive containment and isolation, the EU sought to moderate Iranian policy through "critical dialogue" and trade. The Europeans claimed that the United States exaggerated the Iranian threat and that its policy of expanding commercial relations offered a way to give Iran a stake in the international economy and thereby foster its resocialization (to use George's term). The Clinton administration and congressional leaders condemned this as a policy, rationalized on mercantilist grounds, that was all carrot and no stick.

Early in its first term, the Clinton administration had signaled a U.S. willingness to pay an economic price for its hard-line policy by rejecting proposals to permit the sale of Boeing 737 aircraft and American-made heavy trucks to Iran. The Europeans, however, pointed to a loophole in the law that permitted U.S. oil companies to purchase Iranian oil and sell it in non-American markets; this inconsistency, in effect, made the United States one of Iran's largest trade partners. On April 30, 1995, President Clinton closed this loophole and declared a total ban on U.S. economic relations with Iran. The decision scuttled a deal signed a month earlier between the U.S. oil company Conoco and Iran for offshore oil exploration.[38] Two other developments shaped the context of Clinton's pronouncement: the January 1995 announcement of a $1 billion deal between Russia and Iran for the purchase of civil nuclear reactors, and Palestinian terrorist attacks in Israel in March 1995 that were hailed (if not sanctioned, as some claimed) by the Teheran leadership. Defending the administration's decision, Christopher portrayed Iran as an "outlaw state" and urged American allies to follow Washington's lead. Administration officials argued that its tough action raised U.S. credibility on the issue and permitted President Clinton to press Russian president Boris Yeltsin (albeit to no avail) at their May 1995 summit meeting to forego his government's nuclear deal with Iran. A telling sign of American diplomatic isolation over policy toward Iran was the fact that the Clinton administration did not seriously consider raising the issue of economic sanctions in a multilateral forum, such as the Security Council.

The Clinton administration's policy toward Iran was not only motivated by external developments, such as Middle East terrorism and Russian nuclear commerce. As with Cuba, it was also powerfully influenced by U.S. domestic politics. The decision to impose a total trade embargo came amid congressional calls for still-stronger action, including the imposition of secondary sanctions on foreign companies doing business in Iran. This congressional pressure steadily increased during 1995–96 as American allies rejected Washington's hard-line approach in favor of continued "critical dialogue" with the Teheran regime. Attempting to head off new legislation, a senior Clinton administration official argued, "It's one thing to lead by example. But to try to impose a secondary boycott on others who won't go along is totally counterproductive and harms other interests as well."[39] When it appeared that new legislation sponsored by D'Amato (with the strong lobbying of AIPAC) would be overwhelmingly approved by Congress in 1996, the administration adapted its tactics: it entered into negotiations with the key congressional actors to limit the scope of any new legislation to just the energy sector and to include a waiver provision to maintain presidential flexibility. As these negotiations entered their final phase, the scope of the proposed sanctions legislation was expanded to include Libya. Senator Edward Kennedy (D-Mass.) sponsored this amendment to the D'Amato bill in response to a plea from the families of victims of Pan Am flight 103 to punish Libya for its complicity in the bombing and, specifically, to compel the Qaddafi regime to turn over two Libyan suspects for trial.[40] (Multilateral sanctions through the Security Council affected only air travel to and from Libya.) The ILSA received overwhelming congressional approval and was signed into law by President Clinton on August 5, 1996. The law requires the president to impose sanctions on foreign firms that invest $40 million (reduced to $20 million in August 1997) or more in the Iranian or Libyan oil and natural gas industries. As with the earlier passage of the Helms-Burton Act, the EU and other allies condemned the ILSA as an illegal extraterritorial extension of American sanctions law and threatened retaliation.

As the transatlantic dispute over Iran escalated during 1995–96, the Clinton administration struggled to maintain allied support for the other leg of its "dual containment" policy: the comprehensive containment and isolation of Iraq through multilateral sanctions. Since those sanctions were imposed on Iraq during the Gulf War by the Security Council, where the United States holds a veto, the Clinton administration has been able to forestall efforts by France and Russia to weaken or lift them. Unlike Iran, no one has advocated "critical dialogue" and engagement with Iraq (notwithstanding visits to Baghdad by European oil and construction companies to position themselves for the post-sanctions era). But concerns have been raised about the dire impact of sanctions on the Iraqi people and the unexpected political durability of Saddam Hussein more than eight years after his regime's decisive defeat in the Gulf War. These concerns, in turn, have raised questions about the efficacy of the American strategy and, in particular, about what one administration official referred to as the "endgame": how to achieve the Clinton administration's avowed goal (reaffirmed by Secretary of State Madeleine Albright in a March 1997 speech) of bringing about a change in the Iraqi regime. As examined in Chapter 4, the absence of an "endgame" in U.S. strategy has heightened the political fissures within the allied coalition (and the broader Security Council consensus) that have existed since the Bush administration forged it in 1990–91. Saddam Hussein has proved adept at exploiting these fissures; the October–November 1997 crisis instigated by Saddam Hussein's expulsion of United Nations Special Commission (UNSCOM) inspection teams highlighted the sharp division in the Security Council between the United States and Britain, on the one hand, and Russia and France, on the other, with the latter two prominently opposing the Clinton administration's threatened use of force to resolve the crisis.

During the first year of the Clinton administration's second term, its rogue state strategy came under mounting pressures that called into question its coherence and efficacy. Most prominent among these concerns was the growing view in the policy community that "dual containment" was a strategic dead end. A 1997 Council on Foreign Relations task force concluded, "U.S. policy toward the states of the Persian Gulf is at an impasse. Maintenance of the policy known as dual containment concerning Iraq and Iran is producing uneven results, not all of them positive from the point of view of either U.S. interests or those of our friends among the Gulf states."[41] In drawing this conclusion, the Council's task force advocated that dual containment be supplanted by a strategy of "differentiated containment" better targeted to these countries' particular circumstances and the varying U.S. objectives toward them (i.e., behavior modification versus regime change).

Events in 1997 underscored these differences and punctuated this and other calls for a rethinking of U.S. strategy in the Persian Gulf. Perhaps the most significant of these developments was the election of Iranian president Mohammed Khatami over his hard-line, radically anti-Western opponent in May 1997. The impact of this "interesting development" (as President Clinton termed the electoral outcome) on Iranian foreign policy remains an open question; but the fact of the election itself, even if contested among candidates politically vetted by the clerical regime, holds out the possibility of change. Iraq, by contrast, remains a totalitarian state in which political discourse is nonexistent: a liberally interpreted law that makes insulting the president a capital offense gives new meaning to the term "cult of personality." Moreover, as evidenced in his continued defiance of the UN arms inspection regime, Saddam Hussein remains committed to the acquisition of WMD as a means of furthering his goal of regional dominance. Thus, developments during 1997 pointed to potentially significant differences between Iraq and Iran that argued for discrete strategies as an alternative to dual containment.

One notable, if qualified, area of success for U.S. policy was in its relations with North Korea. During 1996–97, the U.S.–North Korean Agreed Framework, with its structure of reciprocal steps, continued to be successfully implemented. The construction of two proliferation-resistant light-water nuclear reactors in return for the shutdown of North Korea's existing nuclear facilities occurred even as the Pyongyang regime's domestic economic crisis deepened. Although North Korea was designated by the Clinton administration as a rogue state, the Agreed Framework marked a significant departure from the policy's default strategy of comprehensive containment and isolation. As examined in Chapter 6, the integration of a limited engagement component into the U.S. containment strategy toward North Korea was necessitated by the imminent danger of its mature nuclear program and the absence of better alternatives (including military options). The administration's ability to negotiate this shift was hampered by its designation of North Korea as a rogue state, as congressional critics condemned this limited engagement as tantamount to appeasement. The Clinton administration's mixed record of success with North Korea, Iran, and Iraq highlights the deficiencies of generic approaches to strategy, such as that stemming from the rogue state concept. As examined in the next chapter, it points to the need for the development of a repertoire of strategies of "differentiated containment"—what George refers to as "actor-specific models"—to address the distinct challenges posed by this diverse group of states.

NOTES

[1] Alexander L. George, *Bridging the Gap: Theory and Practice in Foreign Policy* (Washington, DC: United States Institute of Peace Press, 1993), pp. 48–49.

[2] For a detailed discussion of this case see U.S. House, Committee on International Relations, "Syria: Peace Partner or Rogue Regime?" (104th Cong., 2nd sess., 1996).

[3] "Rogue Regime" (editorial), *Washington Post*, April 3, 1979, p. A18.

[4] Robert Harkavy, "Pariah States and Nuclear Proliferation," *International Organization* 35, no. 1 (Winter 1981), pp. 136ff.

[5] Robert E. Harkavy, "The Pariah State Syndrome," *Orbis* 21, no. 3 (Fall 1977), p. 640. Political scientist George Quester uses the term "outlaw states" in discussing the same phenomenon in *What's New on Nuclear Non-Proliferation* (Aspen, CO: Aspen Institute for Humanistic Studies, 1975); cited in Harkavy, "Pariah State Syn-

drome," p. 624. In a 1971 study, Yehezkel Dror, an Israeli analyst, warned of the danger posed by radical "crazy states," such as Libya, and argued that Western policy should aim "to hinder emerging crazy states from developing a significant external-action capability" (i.e., to deny them the ability to project force or acquire unconventional weapons); see Dror, *Crazy States: A Counterconventional Strategic Problem* (Lexington, MA: D.C. Heath, 1971), p. 77.

6 Richard K. Betts, "Paranoids, Pygmies, Pariahs and Nonproliferation," *Foreign Policy* 26 (Spring 1977), pp. 182–83.

7 For a detailed analysis of the South African case see Mitchell Reiss, *Bridled Ambition: Why Countries Constrain Their Nuclear Capabilities* (Washington, DC: Woodrow Wilson Center Press, 1995), pp. 7–43.

8 A notable exception to this general pattern was Yugoslavia, whose brutal repression of the Albanian minority in Kosovo prompted the NATO bombing campaign of March–June 1999 to compel the withdrawal of Serbian forces from the province and permit the entry of a NATO-dominated peacekeeping force. A key factor in the decision to undertake this humanitarian intervention was the proximity of Kosovo to NATO countries. Although Yugoslav president Slobodan Milosevic was indicted as a war criminal, the Clinton administration, interestingly, did not designate Yugoslavia a rogue state.

9 The State Department's Office of the Coordinator for Counterterrorism publishes the "terrorist list" in its annual publication, *Patterns of Global Terrorism* (Washington, DC: U.S. Government Printing Office [GPO]).

10 *Public Papers of the Presidents: Ronald Reagan, 1985* (Washington, DC: U.S. Government Printing Office [GPO], 1986), p. 879.

11 George Shultz, "Terrorism and the Modern World," *Bulletin* (U.S. Department of State) 84 (December 1984), p. 13. Shultz, in the same speech, condemned the Soviet leadership for its "empty rhetoric" condemning "state terrorism" while "conniv[ing] with terrorist groups when they think it serves their own purposes."

12 Bruce Jentleson, *With Friends Like These: Reagan, Bush, and Saddam, 1982–1990* (New York: Norton, 1994), pp. 52–53.

13 Ambassador Richard Murphy's statement before the Subcommittee on Asian and Pacific Affairs of the House Foreign Affairs Committee on July 22, 1987, reprinted in U.S. Senate, Committee on Governmental Affairs, "Nuclear Proliferation Factbook" (103rd Cong., 2nd sess., 1994), p. 149.

14 The Pakistani case is examined in Reiss, *Bridled Ambition*, chapter 5. Pakistan was certified under the Pressler Amendment criteria in 1986–89 by the Reagan and Bush administrations. In 1990, the Bush administration could not provide this certification and aid was suspended.

15 Jentleson, *With Friends Like These*, p. 77.

16 Quoted in Michael Klare, *Rogue States and Nuclear Outlaws: America's Search for a New Foreign Policy* (New York: Hill and Wang, 1995), pp. 26–27.

17 Colin Powell with Joseph E. Persico, *My American Journey* (New York: Random House, 1995), p. 305.

18 Richard A. Melanson, *American Foreign Policy Since the Vietnam War: The Search for Consensus from Nixon to Clinton* (Armonk, NY: M. E. Sharpe, 1996), pp. 236, 245.

19 See, for example, the testimony of CIA Director Robert Gates before the Senate Governmental Affairs Committee on January 15, 1992, in U.S. Senate, Committee on Governmental Affairs, "Weapons Proliferation in the New World Order" (102nd Cong., 2nd sess., 1992), pp. 5–15. In addition to regional issues, Gates's testimony focused prominently on the implications for nonproliferation of the breakup of the Soviet Union. See also CIA Director James Woolsey's testimony of February 24,

1993, published in U.S. Senate, Committee on Governmental Affairs, "Proliferation Threats of the 1990s" (103rd Cong., 1st sess., 1993), pp. 8–18.

[20] See Jentleson, *With Friends Like These*, pp. 44–47.

[21] In the wake of the Gulf War, the *New York Times* ("Arms Policy: Dodges, Winks and Nods" [editorial], April 25, 1992, p. A22) criticized American policy that in the 1980s turned a blind eye to (and indeed encouraged) transfers of U.S. equipment to Iran (by Israel) and Iraq (by Saudi Arabia), depending on which regional power Washington was then cultivating: "The list of forbidden recipients of U.S.-made weapons during the Reagan and Bush Administrations reads like a roster of the world's chief troublemakers. U.S. law forbade sending them American arms. Yet for almost a decade, the two Administrations circumvented the law with covert transfers."

[22] Martin Indyk, "Challenges to U.S. Interests in the Middle East: Obstacles and Opportunities," *The Soref Symposium* (Washington, DC: Washington Institute for Near East Policy, May 18–19, 1993), p. 4. A month before the Indyk speech Elaine Sciolino, chief diplomatic correspondent of the *New York Times* wrote, "Past Administrations routinely looked at [Iran and Iraq] as players in a balancing act, historic rivals that could be . . . used against each other to insure that one did not become too strong at the expense of the other. . . . Now the Clinton Administration argues that neither regime should be strengthened and that each should be dealt with as a separate problem—a sort of parallel containment." See Sciolino, "Taking on Iran and Iraq, but Separately," *New York Times*, April 11, 1993, section 4, p. 4.

[23] Ibid., p. 5.

[24] Ibid.

[25] Ibid., p. 6.

[26] See Kenneth Katzman, *Iran: U.S. Containment Policy*, Congressional Research Service (CRS) Report for Congress no. 94-652F (August 11, 1994), pp. 5–6, for a discussion of the development of the dual containment policy.

[27] Anthony Lake, "Confronting Backlash States," *Foreign Affairs* 73, no. 2 (March/April 1994), pp. 45–46.

[28] F. Gregory Gause III, "The Illogic of Dual Containment," *Foreign Affairs* 73, no. 2 (March/April 1994), p. 60. The Lake-Gause exchange is discussed in Katzman, *Iran: U.S. Containment Strategy*, p. 5.

[29] Gause, "The Illogic of Dual Containment," p. 64.

[30] Lake, "Confronting Backlash States," p. 52.

[31] Bill Clinton, "Remarks to Future Leaders of Europe in Brussels," January 9, 1994, in *Public Papers of the Presidents: William J. Clinton, 1994* (Washington, DC: GPO, 1995), p. 11.

[32] Michael Nacht, letter to the editor, *Foreign Policy* 109 (Winter 1997–98), p. 181.

[33] Robert N. Bellah, "Civil Religion in America," *Daedalus* 96, no. 1 (Winter 1967), p. 7.

[34] International Institute for Strategic Studies, *Strategic Survey 1996/97* (London: Oxford University Press, 1997), p. 47.

[35] Although Cuba remains on the U.S. list of terrorist nations, the State Department's 1996 annual report said there was no evidence directly linking the Castro regime to terrorism; see Tim Weiner, "Terrorism's Worldwide Toll Was High in 1996, US Report Says," *New York Times*, May 1, 1997, p. A9.

[36] George Moffett, "To Befriend or Not Befriend Cuba? US Takes Up a Loaded Question," *Christian Science Monitor*, May 19, 1995, p. 5.

[37] The key provisions of the Helms-Burton Act would sanction foreign firms for profiting from or otherwise using property expropriated by the Castro regime following the 1959 revolution.

[38] As will be discussed in Chapter 5, Iranian president Hashemi Rafsanjani asserted that the Clinton administration missed an opportunity to improve relations with Iran when it vetoed the Conoco deal. Most Western experts on Iran, however, question whether the Teheran regime would have been able to overcome its own formidable domestic impediments to such a shift.

[39] Robert S. Greenberger, "Iran Creates Fresh Problems for the White House with Sen. D'Amato Adding Pressure of His Own," *Wall Street Journal*, September 1, 1995, p. 8.

[40] Opposition to the inclusion of Libya in the sanctions bill vanished after the crash of TWA flight 800 in July 1996 and the widespread belief that a terrorist bomb had downed it. Representative Benjamin Gilman (R-N.Y.), chair of the House International Relations Committee, told his colleagues, "We should have in place the strongest possible deterrent to any future acts of terrorism supported by such rogue regimes as Iran and Libya." Quoted in "Airplane Crash Spurs Clearance of Iran, Libya Sanctions Bill," *Congressional Quarterly* 54, no. 30 (July 27, 1996), p. 2133.

[41] Zbigniew Brzezinski, Brent Scowcroft, and Richard Murphy, *Differentiated Containment: U.S. Policy toward Iran and Iraq—Report of an Independent Task Force* (New York: Council on Foreign Relations, 1997), p. 19.

3

U.S. Strategy toward Rogue States (2): Assessment and Alternatives

ASSESSING THE POLICY

The preceding chapters examined the evolution of the rogue state concept and policy and its emergence as a central element of American foreign policy in the post–Cold War era. Among other themes, that discussion highlighted how the criteria determining rogue state status shifted from domestic to foreign policy behavior after 1979. Another important contextual point is that in contrast to the Cold War period, when the United States faced a global superpower rival in the Soviet Union, countries on the current roster of rogue states are notable for their weak and marginalized status. This asymmetry of power is an important factor that conditions U.S. policy toward these regimes. This chapter, building on that preceding analysis, will focus on the central argument of this study—namely, that the rogue state approach distorts U.S. policy and undermines its effectiveness by lumping a disparate group of countries under this pejorative rubric. In so doing, it leads to a generic approach to policy-making that obscures the particularities of individual cases and reinforces the false dichotomy between "containment" and "engagement." The first half of this chapter will elaborate on this critique of the rogue state approach. The second half will focus on the elements of an alternative strategy—what former national security adviser Zbigniew Brzezinski and others refer to as "differentiated containment"—that better relates the means and ends of U.S. policy.[1] Shifting away from a problematic generic label will promote the development of a repertoire of targeted strategies that will be more effective in achieving the discrete U.S. policy objectives in each case (behavior change in Iran, regime change in Iraq, "soft landing" in North Korea).

74

By this utilitarian criterion for judging a strategy, the rogue state approach can be critiqued on three grounds. First, American policy-makers have been *politically selective* in their designation of certain regimes as rogue states. Second, the approach *limits strategic flexibility* when circumstances warrant a shift; the generic label (and the demonization that accompanies the rogue state designation) makes its very difficult politically for policy-makers to adapt U.S. strategy to changing conditions. And third, the generic rogue state policy incurs *high political costs* with U.S. allies that outweigh its utility. Proponents of the policy dispute these criticisms and further argue that it has been instrumental in *mobilizing political support*, both domestic and international, for tough action against these rogue states that would not have occurred otherwise.

Political Selectivity

The discussion in Chapter 2 of the evolution of the rogue state policy revealed it to be an American phenomenon—the product of a unique political culture that depicts international relations as a moral struggle between forces of good and evil. Although the term has gained wide currency among U.S. policy-makers to describe an apparent category of states, it has been criticized at home and overwhelmingly rejected abroad.[2] The primary basis of this criticism is that the rogue state rubric is an American political pejorative that has no standing in international law. As discussed above, the Clinton administration's designation of rogue status on a country is based on three key criteria rooted in that regime's external (i.e., foreign policy) behavior: the acquisition of weapons of mass destruction (WMD), the use of terrorism as an instrument of state policy, and efforts to threaten or destabilize neighboring states. Given its subjective nature and use as a malleable instrument, the rogue state policy is susceptible to charges of political selectivity.

The charge of political selectivity is not new to American policy. During the 1980s, the Reagan administration's policy of "constructive engagement" toward South Africa was condemned by critics who noted that the Pretoria regime had an active program to develop nuclear weapons and was destabilizing neighboring Mozambique and Tanzania through military intervention and terrorism. In short, South Africa shared the same characteristics that the administration used to justify a policy of containment and isolation toward other states. The factors accounting for this difference in approach between South Africa and the members of what President Reagan referred to as "Murder Incorporated" (Iran,

Libya, North Korea, Cuba, and Nicaragua) were the following: first, the assessment that South Africa did not threaten important American interests (indeed, the pressure it put on Angola was considered a plus), and second, the view that a positive domestic evolution within South Africa could be promoted through continued U.S. engagement.

In the post–Cold War debate about America's rogue state policy, the charge of political selectivity has revolved, in particular, around the cases of Cuba and Syria. The inclusion of Cuba in the roster of rogue states cannot be justified in terms of the Clinton administration's own criteria: Cuba neither possesses nor is attempting to acquire WMD;[3] the Castro regime does not actively support terrorism (though Cuba remains on the State Department's terrorist list for providing safe haven to some fugitives); and Cuba neither threatens nor is attempting to destabilize other Latin American countries.[4] As the leader of one of the world's few remaining Marxist regimes, Fidel Castro may indeed be a "dinosaur" (to quote Secretary of State Madeleine Albright), but that does not make Cuba a rogue state comparable to Iraq. Even if one accepts the rogue state designation as an analytically useful category in international relations, Cuba does not fit the Clinton administration's own criteria. Given this anomalous status, one must conclude that the inclusion of Cuba in the U.S. roster of rogue states is the product of American domestic politics (i.e., general antipathy toward Castro buttressed by the political clout of the Cuban-American émigré community).

The case of Syria strikingly illustrates the problem of political selectivity and inconsistency cutting the other way—that is, a state whose behavior fits the administration's criteria but that is excluded from the roster of rogue states. In contrast to Cuba, Syria *does* possess chemical weapons, along with ballistic missiles to deliver them, and is making a concerted effort to augment its WMD capability. Moreover, Syria remains on the State Department's terrorist list; the Assad regime has been implicated in providing significant support to Islamic groups that employ terrorism to derail the Israeli-Palestinian peace process. Finally, in terms of its regional role, Syria occupies Lebanon (which it claims is part of "greater Syria") and poses a potential threat to the pro-Western regimes in Jordan and Saudi Arabia through its indirect support of terrorist groups. And yet, because of Syria's pivotal importance in terms of the Middle East peace, the Clinton administration, like its predecessors, has sought to cultivate the Assad regime through a policy of diplomatic engagement. The perceived disjunction between the realities of Syrian behavior and this policy of political cultivation has led to congressional calls that the strict sanctions regime imposed on other rogue states (such as Iran and Iraq) be extended to Syria. A senior State Department official rejected the "characterization of U.S. policy toward Syria as a policy of appeasement" in a hearing of the House Committee on International Relations in July 1996: "It is a very firm policy of opposing Syrian support for terrorism. It is also a policy of diplomatic engagement with an important state in the Middle East, . . . a country which is an important element in the peace and stability of that region. It is in the interest of the United States to do everything within our power to engage with Syria to persuade it to change its policies with respect to terrorism and to promote the expansion of the peace process."[5] In the same congressional hearing, the efficacy of this approach was contested by Middle East policy analyst Patrick Clawson, who observed, "Syria is treated by the U.S. Government almost as if it were a friend. Many references have been made about how the Secretary of State has visited Damascus more often than he has visited any other capital, and, of course, President Clinton has met with Mr. Assad twice. . . . [W]e have to ask the question what does the United States gain from this policy of engagement with Syria? The answer, unfortunately, is that we have a Syria that engages in the same unacceptable behavior as the other rogue states."[6]

The Cuban and Syrian cases underscore the politically selective manner in which the rogue state policy has been implemented: while Cuba has been included in the administration's rogues' gallery even though it does not fit the criteria, Syria has been excluded from the listing on political grounds despite its behavior. In addition to these cases on the extremes, there are a number that fall into a middle group, countries that exhibit some but not all characteristics attributed to rogue states. India and Pakistan possess nuclear weapons, but neither uses terrorism as an instrument of state policy. Following the May 1998 nuclear tests on the subcontinent and the application of U.S. sanctions, Asia specialist Robert Manning noted that "in the eyes of U.S. law, India is now a 'rogue' democracy." Richard Haass of the Brookings Institution argued that "American policy has always placed India, Pakistan and Israel in an unstated special category—the de facto weapons state. So we need to continue distinguishing, in fact, if not in arms control theory, between them and rogue states."[7] In contrast to India and Pakistan, Sudan does not have a WMD program but is on the State Department's terrorism list and has supported insurgency movements in neighboring countries.[8] The Clinton administration has not included Sudan in its declaratory list of rogue states (e.g., it was not included in National Security Adviser Anthony Lake's 1994 *Foreign Affairs* article). The *Washington Post*, however, in a December 1996 editorial on "The Menace of Sudan" labeled the Khartoum regime an "authentic rogue state."[9] Until the sweeping expansion of U.S. economic sanctions in November 1997, the U.S. approach toward Sudan was more akin to its relations with Syria than with Iran.[10]

This group of regimes exhibiting some rogue characteristics is particularly problematic given the assertion that rogue states constitute a distinct category of countries in the post–Cold War international system. Either these cases are included in the rogue state roster, thus expanding it beyond the Clinton administration's core group, or they are excluded. From an analytical perspective, one would be hard-pressed to explain why Sudan is included in the roster (as many believe it should be) while Pakistan (toward which successive U.S. administrations have pursued engagement policies, even as it developed WMD capabilities) is omitted. This contradiction underscores the problem of selectivity and, again, reflects the fundamentally political, as opposed to legal, basis of the rogue state designation.

The preceding examples point to the inconsistent application of the rogue state policy even within its own terms—that is, criteria relating to objectionable external behavior. This is particularly striking in view of the neo-Wilsonian orientation of the administration's overall approach to foreign policy as manifested in its strategy of "engagement and enlargement." The discussion in Chapter 1 noted that within this liberal conception of international order, legitimacy is rooted in the states' internal character rather than the realist conception that emphasizes a stable distribution of power between states, regardless of their internal character, as the key to international stability. Thus, given the Clinton administration's overarching approach to international relations, one would expect its rogues' gallery to include those regimes with abhorrent records of behavior toward their own peoples. To be sure, states such as Nigeria and Burma have been sharply criticized for their abuse of human rights. Indeed, with respect to the latter, a State Department spokesperson said that because of the military regime's "perfidious and inhumane nature," Burma should not be treated "as a normal country."[11] And yet, the rogue state designation has been reserved only for those countries whose external behavior Washington finds objectionable. This tension between focusing on internal or external norms of behavior reflects the competing pulls of realism and liberalism (or idealism) in the formulation of American foreign policy. In so doing, it again highlights the problem of political selectivity and inconsistency that invariably accompanies an attempt to designate certain states rogue according to one set of criteria while ignoring the other. This recurrent criticism of the rogue state concept, in turn, calls into sharp question its utility as a basis for policy formulation.

Strategic Inflexibility

The political, as opposed to legal, basis on which the rogue state designation is made invariably opens the policy to charges of manipulation and inconsistency. Once a state is included in this demonized category, however, a different set of problems inhibits the ability of the administration to adjust U.S. policy to changing circumstances. The inability to pursue targeted policies toward these countries flows from the generic quality of the rogue state approach. The demonization of this group of countries through the use of this label invariably pushes U.S. policy toward a default strategy of comprehensive containment and isolation.[12] The problem of strategic inflexibility has been manifested in two distinct contexts: first, the development of differentiated strategies toward those states *within* the category, and second, the process by which a state, if successfully "resocialized" and ready to rejoin the "family of nations," can be moved *out* of it.

In the first instance, the difficulty in distinguishing between states in the rogue state category is exacerbated by the assertion that these countries constitute a distinct class of states in the post–Cold War international system, as well as the use of these emotive terms for political mobilization purposes. Although Lake's article asserted that policy would be tailored to particular cases, the political dynamic of the rogue state approach has pushed the Clinton administration toward a one-size-fits-all strategy of containment and isolation. The North Korean case, however, is the notable exception to this pattern and underscores the problem. Lacking a viable military option to deal with the threat posed by North Korea, the Clinton administration embarked on a new diplomatic approach that integrated an engagement component into its overarching containment strategy. The primary instrument of this revised policy has been the October 1994 U.S.–North Korean Agreed Framework.

The signing of the Agreed Framework was followed a month later by the 1994 elections that swept a Republican majority to power in both houses of Congress. The Republicans came to office not only with an ambitious domestic agenda (outlined in the "Contract with America"), but also with attitudes on foreign policy that challenged the Clinton administration's approach on key issues. In part, this was a reaction to the difficulties that the administration experienced in its first two years (see Chapter 1). That record shaped perceptions of the North Korean deal and the administration's negotiating strategy. As one analyst notes, "After setbacks in Bosnia, Somalia, and Haiti, Washington never had the tactical flexibility to make the type of productive unilateral concessions to the North that the Bush administration had offered; indeed the Clinton administration was crucified in the press and on Capitol Hill for doing less."[13]

In their critique of the Agreed Framework, Republican legislators accused the Clinton administration of "appeasement." An expert on Korea observed that "while working as planned in North Korea," the nuclear agreement "was on thin ice politically in the United States."[14] The administration had difficulty persuading Congress to appropriate the American share for the implementation of the agreement; this totaled some $20–30 million per year and constituted only 5 percent of the total costs (versus 75 percent for South Korea and 20 percent for Japan). Congress eventually relented when faced with the stark alternative—the breakdown of the Agreed Framework and the specter of a renewed nuclear crisis on the Korean Peninsula.

The domestic political debate over the North Korean nuclear agreement highlights the strategic inflexibility that stems from the designation of a country as a rogue state. Having effectively demonized the regime, how does an American administration then justify having relations with it? In such a politically charged context, any concession, even a reciprocated one, can be cast as an act of appeasement to a regime that is "beyond the pale." That is why the labeling of a state as a rogue pushes the U.S. administration toward a default strategy of containment and isolation. Even though American objectives toward this disparate group of states vary from the moderation of behavior to a regime change, the underlying issue remains the character of these regimes. The fact that the avowed U.S. objective toward Iran is to change the Teheran regime's behavior is less an endorsement of the acceptability of that regime than a realistic assessment of the American ability to effect a regime change. The issue of objectives—how they are set and their relation to the instruments of American policy—will be discussed further below. The salient point in this context is that the rogue state designation, and the use of this policy for purposes of political mobilization, does invariably raise the root question about the unacceptable character of these states' regimes. That, in turn, raises a major political hurdle that any American administration must overcome in entering into negotiations with these states. In the North Korean case, the clinching argument was the imminent danger posed by Pyongyang's nuclear program—and the absence of a better alternative course of action, including a military option. The political hurdles in other cases, such as Iran and Cuba, may be higher.

The preceding analysis points to one way in which the rogue state policy limits strategic flexibility: the demonization of this group of countries to mobilize political support for tough action makes it difficult to pursue differentiated policies toward those states *within* the category when circumstances warrant it. A related problem arises at a later stage. What happens if the strategy toward a particular rogue state begins to yield results, whether it be a change in behavior or the character of the regime? In the absence of a revolution or the collapse of the ruling regime, such changes will be incremental rather than wholesale. The process by which one of these radical regimes is "resocialized" and rejoins the "family of nations" will likely unfold over an extended period.

In dealing with rogue states and other countries of concern, American policy will be shaped as much by its own domestic politics as by external realities. Consider the case of Vietnam and the legacy of that traumatic and politically divisive war. Not until July 1995, more than twenty years after the collapse of South Vietnam, were Washington and Hanoi able to establish diplomatic relations. The domestic political resistance to a shift in policy—even when external changes and the national interest warrant it—can be formidable. The rogue state policy further exacerbates this problem. Once a country is branded an "outlaw" and placed in this category, it is very difficult politically to move that state out of it. Ever since the conclusion of the Agreed Framework, the Clinton administration has experienced this problem with respect to North Korea. From missile proliferation to food aid to a range of other issues, Washington has been negotiating with a regime that had been a charter member of its rogues' gallery. To indicate a change in policy, Secretary of State Warren Christopher quietly dropped North Korea from its listing of rogue states in a January 1996 speech.[15] But, after a prolonged period of demonization, a political residue of the former policy remains—and critics of the administration's new approach continue to view moves toward engagement as a form of appeasement.

The purpose of this study is not to endorse one particular policy or other, nor to rationalize a blanket policy of engagement toward those states currently labeled as rogues. Rather, it is to highlight and analyze the distortions that stem from a policy that lumps a disparate group of states under a generic rubric. It has been argued that the subjective nature of the rogue state rubric, and its use for the purposes of political mobilization, pushes policy-makers toward a generic containment and isolation approach. This is the case even when an alternative approach might be more effective in terms of affecting the internal evolution of the target state and attaining the U.S. policy objective. There may also be extreme cases (such as that of Iraq under Saddam Hussein) in which policy-makers will want to go beyond containment and isolation to an explicit strategy of rollback to change the regime.

Impact on Alliance Relations

A traditional source of tension between the United States and its major allies has been how to deal with security threats beyond the geographical bounds of formal treaty arrangements, such as the North Atlantic Treaty Organization (NATO). During the Cold War, differences between the United States and West Europeans arose over Vietnam and Suez, as well as the U.S. invasion of Grenada in 1983 and the bombing of Libya in 1986. The so-called out-of-area problem remains a major issue of alliance management in the transformed circumstances of the post–Cold War era. The security institutions forged during the Cold War are being pressed to redefine their roles in the absence of an overriding great power threat that was their original raison d'être. In the ongoing debate about NATO's future, some have argued that the alliance will go "out of business" if it does not go "out of area" to deal with clear threats to Western interests requiring collective action, such as Iraqi regional aggression.

The controversy between the United States and its allies, principally the Europeans, over policy toward rogue states has been less a dispute over ends than one over means. Indeed, there is broad agreement on the need for significant changes in Iranian behavior (especially with respect to terrorism and the Middle East peace process) and the need to check Iraqi expansionism (though views differ on whether Saddam's removal is necessary or feasible). The focus of this ongoing transatlantic debate has been primarily over the appropriate strategy and policy instruments to achieve these objectives. The divergent European and American approaches to dealing with rogue states have reinforced the false dichotomy between containment and engagement.

The European approach emphasizes the use of political dialogue and economic relations as positive inducements both to moderate the behavior of rogue states and, conceivably, to positively affect their evolution into responsible members of the international community. Trade and dialogue, it is argued by the Europeans, will give these problem states a tangible stake in a stable international order. Isolating them will only give recalcitrant leaders, like Castro and the Iranian mullahs, a foreign scapegoat on whom to blame their countries' economic problems. The American counter view is that the European engagement approach is all carrot and no stick. It removes any incentive these rogue regimes might otherwise have to change their behavior by providing the benefits of normal relations without an explicit quid pro quo. Such material support could even serve to prop up these regimes by strengthening their ability and political will to resist change.[16] The U.S. alternative to engagement is comprehensive containment and isolation so as to compel these states "beyond the pale" to alter their behavior and, ideally, to bring about the collapse of their ruling regimes.

The case in which this dichotomy between the European and American approaches has been most strikingly evident is that of Iran. The European Union's policy of engaging in "critical dialogue" with Iran was announced at its 1992 Edinburgh summit. French president Jacques Chirac characterized the policy as follows in a March 1996 interview: "Critical dialogue is . . . not open and friendly, as it would be with countries with whom we have normal trade, cultural, and political relations. It is a limited, organized dialogue through which the Europeans convey to Iran a certain number of ideas, notably in the area of human rights, a certain number of thoughts, not always pleasant to hear, but which nevertheless preserve the ability to talk."[17] Critical dialogue was the rubric under which the European Union's members, particularly France and Germany, continued their political contacts and economic relations with the Teheran regime.

The underlying rationale of "critical dialogue" was to use economic incentives (e.g., trade credits and debt rescheduling) to bolster the position of pragmatic elements within the theocratic regime and thereby promote the moderation of Iranian foreign policy behavior. Former Central Intelligence Agency (CIA) director James Woolsey offered a blunt assessment that reflected the widespread criticism of "critical dialogue" in the U.S. policy community: "The German-French approach [is to] wink at Teheran's support for terrorism and rationalize, in effect, appeasement of it."[18] Middle East expert Robert Satloff observed, "Whether this policy is driven by a sincere belief in the wisdom of 'engagement' as a means to affect Iranian behavior or merely as a cover for certain states to maintain trade links with Iran, to ensure access for Caspian oil pipelines transiting Iranian territory, or [to] insulate themselves against Iranian-backed terrorism is unclear."[19] The European Union's policy suffered a sharp setback in April 1997 when a German court found the Iranian leadership complicit in the assassination of Kurdish dissidents at a Berlin restaurant (the Mykonos) in September 1992. European Union (EU) officials were forced to concede that "critical dialogue" had yielded little discernible change in Iranian behavior. The "Mykonos affair" lent support to the American view that the Iranian regime would successfully resist any linkage of trade and politics. Even as the EU's critical dialogue with Iran faced a dead end, European policy-makers countered that the American policy of dual containment had been similarly unsuccessful.

The transatlantic dispute over policy toward rogue states—the latest manifestation of the traditional "out of area" problem—stems from a periodically heated debate over how best to achieve Western objectives. The debate has threatened to spill over into other issue areas. One manifestation of this acrimony can be seen in each side's occasional questioning of the motivations of the other. American critics of the European approach view it as a mercantilist policy driven by economic interests (whether they be offshore oil rights in Iran or construction projects in Baghdad). The Europeans, alternatively, see the American approach as overly militarized and powerfully influenced by domestic political interest groups (such as the Cuban émigré community and the American-Israel Public Affairs Committee [AIPAC]). They also view it as an illegal effort to export American law overseas (through the imposition of extraterritorial sanctions) and hypocritical (citing the Clinton administration's acquiescence to Iranian arms shipments to the Bosnian Muslims).

At the end of the first Clinton administration, the transatlantic dispute threatened to escalate further after the enactment of the Iran-Libya Sanctions Act (ILSA) and the Helms-Burton Act. As discussed in Chapter 2, these statutes, passed overwhelmingly by Congress and signed into law by President Clinton in mid-1996, would impose U.S. sanctions on foreign commercial entities trading with Iran, Libya, and Cuba. The EU responded to the American secondary boycott with a series of measures to aid European companies in their resistance to this unilateral U.S. policy. Castigating the EU's opposition to American sanctions on these "outlaw regimes," a former Bush administration official stated that "some Europeans have never lost faith in appeasement as a way of life."[20] One of the few congressional critics of the ILSA and Helms-Burton legislation was Representative Toby Roth (R-Wis.), chair of the House Subcommittee on International Economic Policy and Trade. He argued that in addition to being ineffective, a secondary boycott would politically isolate the United States from its closest allies: "No one disputes that Iran and

Libya are rogue states. . . . But what's the best way of toppling these regimes? . . . This sanctions law is necessary, its backers argue, to force Iran's and Libya's major trading partners to go along with our 'economic strangulation' strategy. But will this new U.S. law isolate Iran and Libya, or will it backfire, isolating us from other governments whose help we need to deal with this international problem?"[21] Speaking for the EU, British foreign secretary Robin Cook stated that ILSA "is wrong in principle and counterproductive in effect. It has unacceptable extraterritorial impact on legitimate business. A trade war ignited by this legislation will only harm US and European companies and benefit the hawks in Iran. The EU cannot forge a new partnership with the US on Iran while we are looking down the barrel of the Sanctions Act gun."[22]

Publicly the Clinton administration maintained its declaratory stance that the United States would act multilaterally if possible, unilaterally when necessary. But behind the scenes, U.S. policy-makers signaled a renewed interest in defusing the transatlantic dispute with the EU over secondary sanctions. In March 1998, during the preparations for the May meeting of the G-8, administration officials hinted that the President would waive the ILSA sanctions on a highly publicized natural-gas deal with Iran involving the French oil company Total, Russia's Gazprom, and Malaysia's Petronas.[23] On May 18, the president made the formal waiver announcement in Geneva on the heels of the G-8 summit. Putting the best face on this policy reversal, presidential press spokesperson Michael McCurry stated, "We receive[d] from the Europeans significant commitments with respect to our work together to counter the threat of terrorism and to work together to ameliorate the behavior of so-called *rogue nations*."[24] Albright stated that she remained opposed to the energy deal, but that it was in the U.S. national interest to waive the sanctions; the move might, for example, encourage Russian passage of the second Strategic Arms Reduction Treaty (START II). For their part, the Europeans, similarly seeking to defuse the sanctions showdown with Washington, dropped their plan to challenge the legality of the Helms-Burton legislation in the World Trade Organization and agreed to tighten further their export controls on weapons-related technology to Iran.[25] The shift in American approach can be attributed to two factors: first, the need to maintain alliance cohesion during the continuing impasse with Iraq during 1997–98 over United Nations Special Commission (UNSCOM) inspections, and second, the upset victory of Khatami in Iran's May 1997 presidential election.

Despite these developments, the Clinton administration's scope for diplomatic maneuver on the sanctions issue was significantly circumscribed by the very domestic political forces that had been instrumental in enacting the ILSA and Helms-Burton legislation.[26] The administration was also captive to its own tough, occasionally hyperbolic, rhetoric. Indeed, as discussed above, a major liability of the rogue state approach is the limitation of strategic flexibility that stems from the lumping and demonization of these target countries. In October 1997 congressional testimony, Undersecretary of State for Economic Affairs Stuart Eizenstat stated that the Clinton administration eschewed a "one-size-fits-all" approach and that the president "must have the flexibility to tailor our response to specific situations." But, in the case of rogue states, he argued, "In many instances, engagement can be preferable to isolation, although the choice is not always so stark. In some cases, a mixed policy approach that incorporates both carrots and sticks may be appropriate. Engagement, including engagement by the U.S. business community, may contribute a positive influence. In the case of some rogue regimes, however, engagement would simply feed the regime's appetite for inappropriate or dangerous behavior."[27]

Assessing the transatlantic dispute about rogue states, the International Institute for Strategic Studies' *Strategic Survey 1996/97* concluded,

Even more than in past crises, current transatlantic divisions undermine the effectiveness of either strategy—sanctions and containment are unlikely to bring down a regime when applied by the United States in isolation, but trade and dialogue are equally unlikely to foster change when the world's largest economy and political player is not involved. The result of a divided Western strategy toward rogue states, in other words, leads neither to the defeat of the unwanted regimes nor their integration into civilised behaviour, but rather to tensions within the Atlantic Alliance and an opportunity for rogue states to play the allies off against each other.[28]

The failure of either critical dialogue or comprehensive containment to yield the desired outcome underscored the need to move the policy debate beyond this false dichotomy. Notwithstanding the formidable domestic constraints on U.S. policy cited above, a low-key debate to bridge the gap between the European and American approaches has been taking place since 1998. On both sides of the Atlantic, policy-makers increasingly recognized that the two policies are indeed complementary, not competitive. This conclusion is consistent with the Western alliance's Cold War experience with the Soviet Union when it pursued a dual-track policy of political dialogue and trade along with military containment.

The elements of a third way—an approach that breaks out of the false containment-engagement dichotomy—will be addressed in the second half of this chapter. The U.S. rogue state approach has not yielded the desired policy outcomes and has led to the isolation of the United States in international forums (such as the G-8, the Organization of American States, and the United Nations). The policy has highlighted the limits of American unilateralism. The development of an alternative, differentiated approach would increase Washington's strategic flexibility and ease alliance tensions by offering a framework for multilateral action on a case-by-case basis.

Political Mobilization

The analysis to this point has highlighted the liabilities of the U.S. rogue state policy that emerged in the aftermath of the Cold War and the Gulf War. Notwithstanding the concerns addressed above, does the rogue state policy have any utility? The main argument that can be made in favor of the rogue state approach is its utility in mobilizing political support both at home and abroad for tough measures against these states. The underlying assumption of this view is that in a post–Cold War era of peace and prosperity, the American public will not meet the challenge posed by these states unless roused to action through demonizing political rhetoric from the top leadership.

This phenomenon, of course, is not new to American diplomacy. Policymakers have long used political hyperbole and expansive rhetoric for actions they believed the public would not otherwise support if cast more narrowly. Consider the early Cold War era. In enunciating the Truman Doctrine, the administration decided to publicly present the specific matter of military assistance to Greece and Turkey as a statement of global policy with explicit reference to the ideological challenge of communism. Following a crucial February 1947 meeting with congressional leaders, one of the participants reported that Secretary of State Dean Acheson had "discovered that he had to pull out all the stops and speak in the frankest, boldest, wildest terms to attract their support for a matter which in parliamentary democracies without a tradition of isolation would have been undertaken quietly and without fanfare."[29] Thus, the Truman Doctrine was depicted not as a necessary step to maintain a balance of power in the eastern Mediterranean region, but as a moral crusade between "alternative ways of life." Successive American administrations from Truman to Reagan relied on what the French political philosopher Raymond Aron called the "mobilization of moralism" to maintain the national consensus for a global containment strategy.

Strong rhetoric, such as President Reagan's characterization of the Soviet Union as the "evil empire" in the early 1980s, certainly helped mobilize public and congressional support for Cold War levels of defense expenditures. The demonization of an adversary state has been effective as a political tactic because it reflects, and indeed plays on, the traditional American impulse to view international relations as a struggle between forces of good and evil (see Chapter 2). Unless the executive branch circumvents the system of congressional and constitutional restraints (as happened during the Iran-Contra affair), the president must make the case for a policy to the public and Congress. But is political hyperbole necessary to mobilize domestic political support—and can such a tactic lead to unintended consequences? With respect to the early Cold War period, historian Warren Cohen concluded,

The president can tell the people the truth, as Jimmy Carter promised to do, or he can tell them something "clearer" than the truth, as Dean Acheson had Harry Truman do, and as he believed all good teachers do. In this context articulating something clearer than the truth meant magnifying the Soviet threat, and the Soviet role in events with undesirable outcomes—to the delight of anti-Communist ideologues who then argued, if the Soviet threat was so great, why had Truman not done more. The exaggerated view of the Soviet threat took root, came back to haunt Truman, Acheson, Kennan, et al., and seems to have been internalized by some of the mythmakers themselves.[30]

Presidents and their aides will, of course, be loath to admit that they engaged in "threat inflation" to win popular support for their policies. The Soviet Union was an expansionist totalitarian state that threatened the post–World War II international order, just as Iraq, Libya, and the other rogue states pose real threats to American and allied interests in the post–Cold War era. The issue for political leaders, however, is whether the case for action to meet foreign policy challenges can be made in their own terms without resort to hyperbole. Could the Truman Doctrine have been presented as a necessary step to maintain the balance of power in an important region rather than as a moral crusade? In the Cold War context, as Cohen reminds us, the hyperbole did come back to "haunt" policy-makers. If Greece and Turkey merited the Truman Doctrine, critics asked, what about the even bigger strategic prize, China: why did the administration not adopt an explicit policy to "roll back" communist power on the mainland? Magnifying the communist threat and casting the Cold War in apocalyptic terms did yield short-term political dividends in terms of winning domestic support for the Truman Doctrine. But it also transformed the stakes of the superpower rivalry and led to significant distortions in policy. This unintended consequence was most evident when the arena of competition shifted to the Third World in the 1960s and 1970s. From Vietnam to Angola, American policy-makers viewed regional conflicts in a global framework and consistently downgraded the importance of internal factors. It resulted in an approach that former secretary of state Henry Kissinger characterized as "undifferentiated globalism."

A similar political dynamic has emerged with respect to rogue states in the post–Cold War era. The Clinton administration has used the rogue state rubric to galvanize support for its policies. Just as Acheson had to "pull out all the stops" to sell the Truman Doctrine to a reluctant Congress, so too have the Bush and Clinton administrations employed hyperbolic rhetoric for political mobilization purposes. Hence, a Clinton administration official indicated privately that unless the United States was "completely maniacal" about Iran in multilateral forums, the Europeans would take no firm action. Senator John Glenn (D-Ohio) offered the following assessment of the utility of the rogue state policy for political mobilization: "By simplifying the problem, the rogue nation approach has been useful to bureaucracies: it establishes priorities for the intelligence and defense communities; . . . it assists diplomats in mobilizing international action; it is easy to sell to the public; and it risks little diplomatic fallout."[31] This use of the rogue state policy for political mobilization raises two questions: first, whether the magnification of threats through demonization and the lumping of a disparate group of states in the "rogue" category has been effective and necessary for the mobilization of political support, and second, whether the political strategy has had adverse, unintended consequences for U.S. foreign policy.

With respect to the first issue, the Clinton administration's strategy to mobilize political support for its policies by demonizing certain states as rogues has been far more successful at home than abroad. In large part, this success reflects the influence of domestic political interest groups that advocate strong action against these regimes. Another determining factor that relates to the general context of American policy formulation and accounts for the rise of the rogue state approach is the historical tendency to view international relations as a moral struggle between forces of good and evil. Outside the American political culture, the term "rogue state" is an alien concept that, as previously noted, has no standing in international law. In the continuing transatlantic debate over how to deal with these countries, the European allies have not been won over by Washington's political hyperbole or its artificial grouping of certain states under a pejorative rubric (while selectively omitting similar ones on political grounds). The international implications of this outcome call into question the utility of the rogue state approach as an instrument of political mobilization.

Having propounded the concept in order to mobilize political support against Iraq, Iran, and the other core rogue states, the Clinton administration found itself under increasing domestic political pressure to expand the list to encompass additional states that exhibited some of the rogue attributes. One conservative critic labeled China a rogue nation because of its human rights abuses and nuclear cooperation with Pakistan and urged President Clinton to cancel his June 1998 state visit to Beijing.[32] Defending the trip, a senior White House official responded, "Look, suddenly China becomes a *rogue state* and it becomes a challenge to the engagement policy again, and there's a lot of domestic politics involved here. Those who say how can you grace Tiananmen with your presence have to answer: 'Where would we be on human rights and proliferation if we embraced the isolation policy that you advocate?'"[33] Other prominent cases are India and Pakistan; the two countries' nuclear tests in May 1998 led to the imposition of comprehensive U.S. sanctions and prompted some observers to question whether those states too should be added to the rogues' gallery. Seeking to avoid this political stigma, former Pakistani prime minister Benazir Bhutto stated, "Since India has forced Pakistan's hand, Pakistan must also signal to the world community that it is not a *rogue state.*"[34]

Closely linked to the issue of political selectivity is strategic inflexibility. Once relegated to the "rogue" category, the political dynamic underlying the policy makes it difficult to take the target country off the list. In 1998, the Clinton administration continued to face criticism from Congress and other quarters that its limited engagement of North Korea through the Agreed Framework was a form of appeasement; likewise the administration was unable to exploit the possibilities in Iran raised by the election of President Khatami. In both instances, the administration's own rogue state policy severely circumscribed its scope of diplomatic maneuver. This strategic inflexibility, coupled with the significant political costs incurred by U.S. allies, underscored the liabilities of the rogue state approach and pointed to the need for an alternative that goes beyond political hyperbole and a generic strategy.

FORMULATING ALTERNATIVE STRATEGIES

The terms "containment" and "engagement" have become standard reference points in the American post–Cold War foreign policy debate. Officials and policy analysts often use them without precision, almost as shorthand to indicate their positive or negative attitude toward a particular state. Political scientist Alexander George has observed,

It should be recognized that "containment" and "engagement" are general *concepts* that require specific content in order to become *strategies*. Each of these concepts is capable of generating significantly different strategies. Policy planning and the development of policies for dealing with "rogue states" must develop a specific containment strategy and/or a specific engagement strategy. The question that must be addressed is "which type of containment strategy" and/or "which type of engagement strategy" and "which particular combination of containment and engagement strategy." Unless this question of how to transform these general concepts into specific strategies and tactics is adequately and clearly answered, they are likely to encourage inconsistent, even contradictory behavior toward the rogue state.[35]

The goal of these discrete, targeted strategies is to resocialize rogue states by fostering their compliance with international norms. This process of reintegrating them into the international community requires careful case-by-case consideration. It encompasses a spectrum of possible actions and outcomes ranging from the narrow (behavior change) to the expansive (regime change). The starting point of this analysis is, of course, the target state itself—the regime's intentions and capabilities, its perceptions of external actors, the nature of its leadership, the possibilities for domestic political evolution, etc. This analysis would provide the basis for translating the *concept* of "containment" into a specific *strategy* for dealing with a particular country of concern.

Understanding the Target State

An adequate understanding of the target state is a prerequisite for policy development. In its absence, decision-makers lack a sufficient basis to set objectives and determine the appropriate strategies to achieve them. The assessment process requires input from a variety of expert sources. Particularly relevant is the expertise of area specialists, whose knowledge of the target state's history and political culture can provide policy-makers a much-needed context within which to frame their decisions. This type of country analysis is as much art as science. Policy judgments are based on information that is invariably incomplete and often contradictory. Area specialists can sometimes be too close to their subject matter or simply extrapolate future behavior from the past.

Prior to the Iraqi invasion of Kuwait in August 1990, for example, the conventional wisdom among Persian Gulf specialists was that the Baghdad regime, exhausted after eight years of attritional war with Iran, would seek a quiescent international environment so that it could focus on internal reconstruction. U.S. military intelligence analysts, who were tracking Iraqi military movements to the south in preparation for the invasion, were the ones to raise the alarm in Washington, not the regional specialists. This cautionary episode points to the need to cross-check contending analyses of target state behavior against one another to gain a more accurate understanding. Following the CIA's failure to predict the Indian nuclear test in May 1998, Director George Tenet announced a series of reforms, including steps to better integrate the capabilities of the intelligence community and the increased use of outside experts to reduce the danger of groupthink.

Even with institutional reforms to improve the assessment process, however, target state analysis remains inherently problematic. Because it is not an exact science, different policy experts can review the same data and come to sharply divergent conclusions. The Bush administration's plausible, though incorrect, conclusion that Saddam Hussein's objectives were limited in mid-1990 was supported by a number of key facts: (1) Iraq was demonstrably in need of internal reconstruction after the Iran-Iraq War; (2) no Arab state had ever invaded another Arab state; and (3) Iraq had previously used coercive diplomacy to extract concessions from the Kuwaitis. With respect to the Indian nuclear test, retired admiral David Jeremiah, who headed the review panel investigating why the CIA had failed to predict it, stated, "We should have been more aggressive in thinking through how the other guy thought."[36] In charting policy, decision-makers must remain open to multiple viewpoints and foster a decision-making environment in which target state analyses can be openly vetted and their underlying assumptions challenged.[37] In the end, it comes down to public officials' making a judgment about a target state under a particular set of circumstances.

The development of an appropriate strategy is contingent on an accurate "image" of the target state. Such an assessment should take the following factors into account: historical background, the character of the regime and its leadership, the regime's declaratory policy and ideology, the target state's economic and military capabilities, recent foreign policy behavior, the impact of current U.S. policies and the policies of other states on the target state, and the domestic context within the target state and the potential (given those conditions) for a favorable political evolution.

Historical Background. The past does not dictate the future, but it is a logical starting point for thinking about it. The historical record explains a state's current circumstances and provides insight into the context shaping future decisions by its ruling regime. Is the state revisionist? Does it seek a change in the territorial status quo with neighboring states? Does the target state have a governing ideology or belief system that it attempts to "export" to other countries as a means of transforming its region? A historical perspective on these questions can shed light on the target state's intentions. In the case of Iraq, for example, an assessment of future foreign policy behavior must begin with the fact that the Saddam Hussein regime invaded *two* neighboring states in the course of a decade.

Character of the Regime/Leadership. Knowledge of the leadership and the decision-making process in the target state is essential to any projection of future foreign policy behavior. How are decisions reached? Are there formal or informal decision-making structures? Are decisions taken by a single individual or a collective leadership? What are the key interest groups (either within the regime or the society at large) that affect policy outcomes? Given the closed and isolated nature of the various countries lumped together under the rogue state rubric, information is often not easy to obtain. These states exhibit significant variance in their types of leadership: Iraq is an extreme example of autocracy; Iran has significant, though circumscribed, elements of pluralism (such as its parliament [the Majlis] and the 1997 presidential election that brought a dark-horse candidate to power); in North Korea, questions remain about the degree to which Kim Jong Il has consolidated power since the 1994 death of his father, Kim Il Sung, and the extent to which the military is a check on his authority.

Declaratory Policy and Ideology. What a state says is less important than what it does, but sometimes the former is an important key to predicting the latter. Content analysis of speeches by the leadership, as well as newspapers and other publications linked to important institutions or interest groups, can shed light on internal debates and provide clues to future policy. Equally important is an understanding of any ideology or belief system that underpins the regime and is a possible motivation for its actions (e.g., Shia Islam in Iran). During the Cold War era, the field of Sovietology revealed both the possibilities and limitations of this analytic tool. It remains an important device, but must be used in tandem with analyses of other pertinent factors. Again, consider the Iraqi case: the fact that the Saddam Hussein regime continues to declare periodically that the border demarcation with Kuwait remains an open question, despite a final determination by the United Nations, is highly relevant to any assessment of future policy. Although the regime may be using this declaratory policy to gain leverage on other issues, it is clear from Saddam Hussein's record that such statements cannot be dismissed as pure political posturing.[38]

Capabilities. A threat can be defined as hostility plus the capability to do something about it. An analysis of nontangible factors, such as declaratory policy and the character of the ruling regime, can indicate the possible intentions of a state. A key question, however, is whether that regime possesses the wherewithal to translate those intentions into action. Intentions are inherently difficult to discern because they relate directly to the leadership—its state of mind and the often idiosyncratic factors that affect decision-making. Capabilities, on the other hand, are measurable indices, such as military spending or economic performance. Iraq and Iran provide contrasting examples of the difficulty of assessing military capabilities, even with the sophisticated monitoring technologies available to Western governments. Following the Gulf War, American officials were stunned by the findings of UNSCOM that revealed the extent to which Iraq was able to covertly develop WMD capabilities. The Iraqi experience fueled subsequent concern about a possible Iranian rearmament program in 1992–93. Ominous extrapolations based on shaky data, however, have not been borne out. Indeed, data compiled by the International Institute for Strategic Studies indicate a 60 percent reduction in Iranian defense spending following the end of the Iran-Iraq War before leveling off: from $9.9 billion in 1988 to $3.77 billion in 1991.[39]

Foreign Policy Behavior. The preceding discussion of how to assess target state behavior has focused on its historical record, leadership and decision-making system, declaratory policy, and capabilities. The next consideration builds further on that analysis to focus on the target state's foreign policy. Some trends may be readily apparent, such as Iran's diplomatic strategy to improve relations with the monarchical regimes of the Persian Gulf region after Khomeini's death. Other behavior may be contradictory, perhaps indicating divergent tendencies within the ruling regime. In surveying the target state's recent foreign policy behavior, are any patterns or trends evident? For example, since the May 1997 election of President Khatami, widely viewed as a political moderate at odds with the Teheran regime's radical theocratic elements, have there been discernible changes in Iranian foreign policy? Are any such changes tactical, reflecting a short-term adjustment, or strategic, with long-term implications?

The International Environment. Proponents of the realist school argue that the primary determinant of a country's foreign policy is its leadership's perception of the external environment—and, in particular, the distribution of power between states. For example, India's Hindu nationalist government pointed to the threat posed by a nuclear-armed China and its nuclear assistance to Pakistan as the chief motivation underlying its decision to resume nuclear testing in May 1998. Given the influence of the international environment on the target state, external actors must carefully assess the impact of their policies on the country in question. This issue was at the heart of the transatlantic dispute over policy toward Iran during the 1990s (i.e., the Clinton administration's comprehensive containment versus the EU's "critical dialogue"). Did the U.S. hard-line approach create domestic pressures that led to the election of Khatami or, conversely, did American efforts to isolate and punish Iran have the unintended consequence of pushing Iranian nationalists toward the theocratic regime? The questions surrounding this specific case underscore the general need for external actors to evaluate the influence of the international environment and, in particular, the impact of their policies on the target state.

Domestic Politics. The goal of any strategy along the containment-engagement continuum is to influence the target state—whether the objective is to moderate its foreign policy or bring about a change in regime. The formulation of an appropriate strategy requires a clear understanding of the domestic political milieu within the target state. An important factor bearing on strategy development is the extent to which the target state's leadership and decision-making process are insulated from or influenced by political interest groups in the broader society. Punitive strategies, such as comprehensive containment, aim not only to keep a rogue leader "in [a] box" (as the Clinton administration says of Saddam Hussein), but also to up the ante domestically by creating pressures that could precipitate change, such as a coup. Incentive strategies, incorporating some degree of engagement, also seek to shape the domestic political milieu by giving interest groups within the target state a tangible stake in improved relations. But an external actor's choice of strategy and its likelihood of success strongly depend on that constellation of internal interest groups and their ability to influence the leadership.

One sees this debate playing out in the context of U.S. relations with Iraq and Iran following the acknowledged breakdown of the Clinton administration's "dual containment" policy. In Iraq, the Saddam Hussein regime has proved adept at insulating itself from domestic pressures through sheer brutality, payoffs to its key institutional supports (the Republican Guard and the secret police), and an evidently successful political strategy of blaming the United States and United Nations (UN) sanctions for the country's dire conditions. Domestic politics outside what is permitted by Saddam Hussein simply do not exist. In Iran, by contrast, there are clear signs of increased, albeit circumscribed, pluralism—a condition manifested in the power struggle between Khatami and radical theocratic elements within the ruling regime. These encouraging domestic developments in Iran prompted a number of prominent foreign policy specialists to call for a change in the U.S. approach that would integrate an engagement component into its containment strategy. The relevant point in this context is not to advocate a particular policy, but rather to highlight how one's reading of the domestic milieu in the target state affects the choice of strategy. This assessment of the "ripeness" of the domestic political environment will determine the appropriateness and timing of any policy initiative.

The analysis above has focused on key factors that should shape policy-makers' "image" of the target state. Inadequate analysis—not "thinking through how the other guy [thinks]" in Admiral Jeremiah's words—can lead to misperception and miscalculation. In the absence of good target state analysis, decision-makers will be prone either to extrapolate future behavior from the past, impute some form of rationality based on preconceived notions, or view the adversary state as essentially a mirror image.[40] In turn, it is also important that the target state have a proper "image" of the major external actors with which it is dealing. For example, during the Iraqi occupation of Kuwait, Saddam Hussein reportedly believed that the Bush administration would not initiate a ground war because of the continuing influence of the Vietnam debacle on American policy.

Relating Means and Ends

The group of countries under the rogue state rubric are notable for two general characteristics: their diversity and their marginal status in international affairs. The former is at the heart of this study's critique of the generic strategic approach that has been pursued toward these countries. The latter bears significantly on the formulation of tailored strategies to address the very real challenges that these states pose. The nature of these threats, however, is of a wholly different magnitude than that of the Cold War era, when the United States confronted a global superpower armed with a vast nuclear arsenal. In *A World Restored*, Kissinger, arguing from a realist perspective in his analysis of the Congress of Vienna system, distinguished between states that accept the legitimacy of international norms and "revolutionary" states that reject them.[41] Whereas Kissinger was writing about the major powers of post-Napoleonic Europe, the rogue states of the post–Cold War era are internationally marginal and weak. Consider the Clinton administration's core group of rogue states. North Korea, one of the few remaining communist states, is on the brink of collapse. Libya has been successfully contained and deterred since the U.S. bombing of Tripoli in the April 1986 response to a Libyan-sponsored terrorist act in Berlin and the imposition of UN sanctions following the implication of Libyan intelligence officers in the bombing of Pan Am flight 103 in December 1988. Iraq remains under UN sanctions and Saddam Hussein, although not unseated from power in the aftermath of the Gulf War, has been kept "in his box." Iran faces a serious economic crisis stemming from the downturn in oil revenues and exacerbated by the effects of U.S. sanctions.

All of the states designated as rogues by the Clinton administration are dissatisfied with the international status quo in one way or another. But none possesses the capabilities (even through a horrific act of state-sponsored terrorism) to threaten the fundamental stability of the international system on the order of a Stalin or a Hitler. The primary threat that the rogue states pose is in their own immediate region. Iraq may threaten Kuwait, Saudi Arabia, and Iran, but Saddam Hussein cannot bring down the entire international system. When he was poised to control a high percentage of the world's proven reserves of oil (through the occupation of Kuwait and political coercion of Saudi Arabia), the United States and other major powers were motivated into action to repulse and contain Iraqi power.

The rogue states are revisionist, but not, in Kissinger's conception of international relations, "revolutionary." A notable exception to this pattern was Iran following the overthrow of the Shah. Ayatollah Khomeini was swept to power on the force of a revolutionary, transnational ideology—political Islam. Indeed, after the February 1979 revolution, there was much talk within the new theocratic regime of "exporting the revolution" across the Middle East and other parts of the Islamic world. Iran was not territorially expansionist like Saddam Hussein's Iraq, but it did challenge the legitimacy of other Middle East governments by offering a new (or rather, traditional) vision of how states in the region should be organized. Over time, the Teheran regime moderated its revolutionary rhetoric and sought to normalize relations with its regional neighbors. Still, as discussed in Chapter 5, a political tension persists in Iran between those who wish for the country to become a working member of the international community (i.e., an "ordinary" state) and those who view this revolutionary élan as the core of the society's identity. That continuing tension between accepting and rejecting the existing system of states is reflected in the country's paradoxical name—the Islamic Republic of Iran.

The weak and marginal status of the rogue states in the international system strongly conditions the design and implementation of strategies to deal with them. In *Strategies of Containment*, historian John Lewis Gaddis examined the oscillations of American Cold War policy from the 1940s to the 1970s. He developed a typology that distinguished between "asymmetrical" and "symmetrical" approaches pursued toward the Soviet Union by successive presidents.[42] During the Truman administration, the debate between these competing strategies was played out between George Kennan (who headed the State Department's newly founded Policy Planning Staff) and Paul Nitze (who succeeded him). Kennan argued that the United States should pursue an asymmetrical strategy that applied American strengths against Soviet weaknesses, rather than attempting to match the Kremlin in all strengths. This approach called for the delineation and defense of American vital interests in the world, while yielding nonvital positions outside those geographic core areas (i.e., the Third World) that could not be sustained at an acceptable cost. Nitze, by contrast, argued for a vastly more expensive symmetrical strategy that would respond to Soviet activism across the board, even in areas of peripheral interest to the United States.

Gaddis's analytic framework—the standard for assessing U.S. strategy of the Cold War period—does not translate into the current era because of the gross disparities of power that exist between the United States and the rogue states. During the Cold War, the Soviet Union's economy may have lagged far behind that of the United States, but there was a rough parity in military power that gave reality to the image of the Soviet Union as a superpower. Given the extraordinary differentials in power between the United States and the currently designated rogue states, any U.S. strategy toward them will be asymmetrical in Gaddis's terms of reference. An important implication of this asymmetrical power relationship relates to the conditions under which an engagement component might be integrated into a containment strategy. This is a central issue that has been raised in connection to U.S. policy toward Iran after the

May 1997 election of Khatami. The debate has been between those who seek a political dialogue with the Teheran regime to explore the opportunities created by Iran's domestic evolution and those who advocate the continuation of a punitive policy of comprehensive containment and isolation. For the Clinton administration, there is no imperative to dialogue with Iran. Furthermore, given the historical legacy of the hostage crisis and the Iran-Contra scandal, the policy carries clear political risks.

In this ongoing debate about U.S.-Iranian relations, there is an interesting parallel to the Cold War period, as well as a significant point of historical divergence. During the early Cold War, views differed over whether to engage the Soviet Union in negotiation or to eschew contact and isolate it. The emergence of the Soviet Union as a nuclear power capable of destroying American society settled that debate. In defending the Nixon administration's détente policy from domestic critics, Secretary of State Kissinger argued that the overriding responsibility of the superpowers to prevent nuclear war made negotiation and engagement a moral imperative.[43] In the post–Cold War era, no such general imperative exists to engage the so-called rogue states. Indeed, the default position of containment and isolation is viewed as a conservative approach that avoids political risk (such as the fallout of the 1986 Iran-Contra scandal). Significantly, the one case in which the Clinton administration deviated from this generic strategy toward rogue states was North Korea. It did so in the face of the acute threat posed by Pyongyang's mature nuclear program and the absence of any viable military option to deal with it. Under these circumstances, the Clinton administration opted for a containment strategy that incorporated a limited engagement component through the Agreed Framework. The conditions under which the United States might pursue limited engagement with a rogue state as part of a containment strategy will be further examined below.

In his controversial *Foreign Affairs* article, Anthony Lake concluded that at the outset of the Cold War, "George Kennan . . . made the case for containment of an outlaw empire. . . . Today the United States faces a less formidable challenge in containing the band of outlaws we refer to as the 'backlash states.' It is still very much in our power to prevail."[44] But prevail to what end? Lake cites the two objectives of Cold War containment identified by Kennan in his seminal 1947 "X" article in *Foreign Affairs*: "to increase enormously the strains under which Soviet power must operate" and thereby generate either "the break-up or gradual mellowing of Soviet power." Kennan viewed a regime change ("break-up") or moderation of unacceptable foreign policy behavior ("mellowing") as alternative paths to the Soviet Union's transformation from a revolutionary totalitarian state into a traditional great power. These two policy objectives—regime change and behavior modification—continue to motivate U.S. strategies toward rogue states in the post–Cold War era.

As reflected in Kennan's formulation of a Cold War containment strategy in the "X" article, policy-makers often articulate multiple policy objectives of varying time horizons with respect to the target state. In the case of the Soviet Union, the Truman administration's immediate goal was to prevent the further extension of Soviet power westward in Europe—an objective embodied in the creation of NATO in 1949. Beyond the immediate post–World War II challenge, however, Kennan conceived of containment as essentially an indefinite holding operation by the United States and its allies to deter Soviet expansionism and to increase external pressures on Stalin while the internal contradictions of Soviet society demanded change from within over the long term. He argued that the "break-up" or "mellowing" of Soviet power required "a long-term, patient but firm and vigilant" policy.[45] Kennan's containment doctrine thus embodied multiple political objectives, both immediate and long term.

This pattern has been evident in the formulation of American policies toward rogue states in the post–Cold War era. Consider the recent history of U.S. policy objectives toward Iraq. During the Gulf War, the Bush administration's declared objective was the liberation of Kuwait from Iraqi occupation. The overthrow of the Saddam Hussein regime itself was not part of the UN Security Council mandate and the United States's coalition partners, particularly the Arab states, would not have agreed to an expansion of the Gulf War's aims to encompass it. Nonetheless, a regime change in Baghdad was an implicit U.S. war objective given the prevailing belief within the Bush administration that the Iraqi military debacle in Kuwait would precipitate a coup or internal upheaval against Saddam Hussein.[46] After the Gulf War, this implicit objective became explicit as the Bush administration declared its intention to maintain economic sanctions on Iraq until Saddam Hussein was toppled. The Clinton administration issued a revised formulation that the sanctions regime would remain in place until Iraq complied with all Security Council resolutions. Elaine Sciolino of the *New York Times* reported, "The Administration argues that the Bush emphasis on Mr. Hussein's ouster raised false hopes, created a gap between American goals and those laid out in tough Security Council sanctions and threatened to divide the American-led coalition formed to confront Iraq. It has a convoluted explanation for its own policy: Mr. Hussein must comply with United Nations sanctions so tough that he could not possibly comply and remain in power."[47]

As the years since the Gulf War passed, and with no signs that the U.S. strategy of comprehensive containment would generate a regime change in Baghdad, tension over objectives developed in the Clinton administration's policy toward Iraq. This clash of competing objectives was highlighted during the 1997–98 showdown between Iraq and the Security Council over unfettered access of UNSCOM inspectors to suspected WMD sites. In March 1997, months prior to the onset of the autumn 1997 crisis instigated by Saddam Hussein, Secretary of State Albright laid out a hard-line case for rollback—that is, explicitly seeking the removal of Saddam Hussein from power. In her speech, entitled "Preserving Principle and Safeguarding Stability," Albright stated that "a change in Iraq's government could lead to a change in U.S. policy" and that the Clinton administration stood ready "to enter rapidly into a dialogue with a successor regime."[48] When the autumn 1997 crisis began, the Clinton administration found itself under pressure from other Security Council members to back off this hard-line objective. To woo the support of France and the Arab states, the administration stopped asserting that sanctions would remain in place until Saddam Hussein was replaced by a "successor regime." The British government supported this softer line to maintain the last vestiges of the Gulf War coalition and to provide some incentive for Saddam Hussein to permit the resumption of UNSCOM inspections.[49] In a major address at the height of the showdown with Iraq in February 1998, President Clinton articulated this narrowing of the U.S. objective. He stated that "our purpose is clear. We want to seriously diminish the threat posed by Iraq's weapons-of-mass-destruction program. We want to seriously reduce his capacity to threaten his neighbors."[50] In this formulation of American policy, the emphasis was on disarming Iraq and "keeping Saddam in his box," not unseating him from power. The administration came under harsh criticism from the Republican leadership in Congress for its retreat from the hard-line position articulated by Albright in March 1997. In the aftermath of the 1997–98 crisis, the Clinton administration's Iraq policy continued to oscillate between objectives. The *Wall Street Journal* reported that the administration, again embracing the goal of a regime change in Baghdad, had sought "broad new authority from Congress to plan and mount covert operations against [the] Iraqi dictator."[51]

U.S. policy toward Iraq after the Gulf War will be examined in greater detail in Chapter 4. The pertinent point in the context of this chapter relates to the process by which policy-makers determine objectives—and then translate those goals into specific strategies tailored to the particularities of the target state. This discussion, which began with Kennan's original containment doctrine and ended with the post–Cold War challenge of Saddam Hussein's Iraq, has highlighted that policy-makers will often pursue multiple objectives of varying time frames. That condition, in turn, will require flexible strategies that themselves consist of multiple tracks to accommodate these short- and long-term goals.

At times, as evidenced in the U.S. experience with Iraq after the Gulf War, these multiple objectives (e.g., keeping Saddam Hussein "in his box" in the short term, toppling him from power in the long term) may be at odds. Political requirements, such as conditions within the target state or the attitudes of other key actors, may require an emphasis of one over another. The Clinton administration, muting its call for Saddam Hussein's overthrow and emphasizing the need for Iraq to comply with the UN weapons inspection regime, did this to maintain the anti-Iraq coalition during the UNSCOM crisis in late 1997. The downside of this type of tactical adjustment in declaratory policy is that it does raise questions about the policy-makers' commitment to their long-term objective. Thus, critics asked whether the administration was going "wobbly" (in British prime minister Margaret Thatcher's colorful phrase from 1990) and reconciling itself to Saddam Hussein's continued rule as long as he was contained within his borders. In August 1998, questions about U.S. objectives were raised when UN weapons inspector Scott Ritter resigned from UNSCOM, claiming that U.S. officials had intervened on two occasions to prevent inspections. Albright and Assistant Secretary of State Martin Indyk affirmed the U.S. commitment to the inspection regime and the continuation of sanctions. Senior officials argued that the administration was seeking to build broad support in the Security Council for the continuation of sanctions and wished to avoid a premature showdown over inspections.[52]

The Cold War experience with the Soviet Union and the Iraqi case highlight the challenge that decision-makers face in their pursuit of multiple policy objectives. This analysis has focused on the ends of American foreign policy. Attention will now shift to the question of means— that is, translating policy objectives into specific strategies. As argued throughout this study, this task requires policy-makers to move beyond the false containment-engagement dichotomy and to formulate a repertoire of targeted strategies across a continuum of choice. The spectrum of possible relationships between states ranges from military conflict to an alliance partnership. For the purposes of this study, the focus will be on that part of the continuum that relates to the variegated threats posed by those countries referred to as rogue states.

In *Strategies of Containment*, Gaddis developed the concepts of "symmetrical" and "asymmetrical" containment to explain the evolution of American strategy toward the Soviet Union from Truman to Carter. He persuasively argued that the oscillations in this Cold War containment policy stemmed as much from U.S. domestic political and economic considerations as from Soviet foreign policy behavior. This study argues that, in the post–Cold War era, the political typing inherent to the rogue state approach has had a major distorting impact on American policy. In the case of the U.S. "dual containment" policy toward Iran and Iraq, a Council on Foreign Relations task force led by former national security advisers Brzezinski and Brent Scowcroft, along with former ambassador Richard Murphy, called for the adoption of an alternative approach of "differentiated containment." Such an approach needs to be extended beyond these two Persian Gulf states to encompass the entire set of countries labeled as rogue states. In so doing, the generic rogue state approach would be supplanted by *strategies of differentiated containment* that are designed to address the particularities of each case. The purpose of this study is not to advance any particular policy option in relation to these states. Rather, the analysis presented here is to argue for the adoption of this analytical framework as the basis for determining specific policies. The pertinent strategies within such a typology can be clustered under three categories: (1) rollback (an overt strategy to change the regime); (2) comprehensive containment (politico-economic isolation and military deterrence); and (3) conditional containment (mixed strategies that integrate an engagement component into an overall containment approach). This discussion will not consider strategies oriented more toward engagement (e.g., conditional engagement), since such options, although theoretically possible, are not politically plausible given current conditions.[53] A brief description of each category of strategies follows.

Rollback. The objective of this strategy is to alter the status quo—either by reversing regional aggression (e.g., following the Soviet invasion of Afghanistan) or changing a rogue regime (e.g., Saddam Hussein). This term, whose political roots can be traced to the early Cold War era, was used by critics of the Truman administration's containment strategy during the 1952 presidential election campaign. These hard-line critics considered the policy too "static" and "passive." In its place, they advocated that the United States adopt an assertive policy to "liberate" East European states under Red Army occupation and roll back Soviet power. The political high point for rollback came in the wake of the East German uprising in June 1953. The Eisenhower administration, initially surprised by the extent of anticommunist civil disorder, quickly responded with the adoption of NSC-158. That document asserted that the June 1953 event had created "the greatest opportunity for initiating effective policies to help roll back Soviet power that has yet come to light."[54] NSC-158 specified measures (covert operations, "elimination of key puppet officials," etc.) to implement this rollback strategy. Within weeks, however, the Eisenhower administration backed away from this provocative psychological warfare plan in the face of strong reservations both within the U.S. government and among U.S. allies. President Eisenhower's reluctance to run the risks of rollback was again demonstrated during the 1956 Hungarian Revolution. Despite Secretary of State John Foster Dulles's excessive rhetoric, the administration refused to take any supportive action for the rebels in what was acknowledged to be the de facto Soviet sphere of influence.

Rollback rhetoric was revived in the early 1980s. Ronald Reagan assumed the presidency sharply critical of his predecessors' strategy toward the Soviet Union. Reagan condemned the détente policies of Nixon-Kissinger and Carter for their seeming acceptance of the status quo and failure to deter Soviet adventurism in the Third World. The Reagan administration's strong rhetoric was reflected in Secretary of State Alexander Haig's assertion that the United States was prepared to "go to the source" and blockade Cuba in order to halt Havana's support for Central American insurgency movements. Many questioned whether Reagan was embracing rollback as a hard-line alternative to containment. While radical in rhetoric, the Reagan administration was prudent in action. It continued to pursue core elements of the American policy toward the Soviet Union inherited from the 1970s, most notably in the area of arms control. The administration did, however, integrate a significant rollback component into its overall containment strategy in the form of the Reagan Doctrine.[55] This policy targeted vulnerable, pro-Soviet regimes in the Third World by providing military assistance to anticommunist insurgency movements to topple them. These groups included, most notably, the Nicaraguan Contras, the Afghan mujahideen, and Angola's UNITA.

Rollback strategies seek not merely to contain the target state within its borders, but to overthrow its ruling regime through a variety of mechanisms (ranging from covert intelligence operations to overt support for an external opposition group). The policy, in short, aims to assertively alter the status quo. With respect to the Clinton administration's roster of rogue states, the only case in which there has been substantial public discussion about the feasibility of a rollback strategy has been Iraq.

Comprehensive Containment. This strategy, alternatively referred to as "broad" or "hard" containment, has been the generic policy pursued by the Clinton administration toward rogue states (with the notable exception of North Korea). It employs economic, diplomatic, and military instruments to isolate the target state and deter its ruling regime from regional aggression. By levying tangible costs for unacceptable actions, the strategy aims to moderate the target state's behavior in the short run. Over a longer time period, comprehensive containment and isolation may generate domestic pressures leading either to the overthrow of the regime or a change in its ideology and foreign policy orientation. Comprehensive containment was the policy advanced by Kennan in his "X" article. Kennan held little hope for fruitful negotiations with Stalin's Soviet Union. His initial formulation of containment was essentially an indefinite holding operation to promote either the "mellowing" (i.e., moderation) of the Soviet regime or its "break-up." American strategy shifted from comprehensive to conditional containment following the death of Stalin and the recognition that the reality of the Soviet Union as a nuclear-armed superpower necessitated substantial engagement on issues of mutual interest (such as arms control).

A most extensive containment regime has been directed at Iraq in the wake of the Gulf War. The "four pillars" of this strategy have been UNSCOM inspections to monitor the destruction of Iraq's WMD capabilities, multilateral economic sanctions, no-drive and no-fly military exclusion zones in northern and southern Iraq, and the threatened use of force to deter Iraqi aggression and ensure Baghdad's compliance with Security Council resolutions.[56] While this strategy has met the minimum objective of keeping Saddam Hussein "in his box," it has not led to his ouster (contrary to the Bush administration's widely shared view that the Iraqi dictator would not survive the Gulf War debacle).

In pursuing the comprehensive containment of rogue states, the Clinton administration's primary policy instrument has been economic sanctions. Economic sanctions have been the cutting edge of American coercive diplomacy toward rogue states. During the post–Cold War era, the executive branch and Congress have had "the tendency to see economic sanctions as 'below' the use of military force on some imagined ladder of foreign policy escalation. . . ."[57] Military power has been exercised less demonstratively to deter aggression, but not to compel changes in behavior. The exception to this general pattern has been Iraq, where the United States and Britain have threatened air strikes to force Iraqi compliance with Security Council resolutions on weapons inspections. They are intended to ratchet up economic pressure on the target state's ruling regime and demonstrate that unacceptable rogue behavior carries a considerable economic price.

The United States employed sanctions multilaterally in the cases of Iraq and Libya, and unilaterally in the case of Iran. The Clinton administration struggled to maintain political support in the Security Council for the continuation of sanctions against Iraq and failed to win multilateral backing for sanctions against Iran. The record of success has been mixed. Sanctions failed to either coerce Saddam Hussein from withdrawing from Kuwait prior to the Gulf War or generate sufficient pressures in its aftermath to oust him from power. They have, however, significantly retarded the reconstitution of the Iraqi dictator's military machine and his ability to challenge neighboring states. Saddam Hussein's fitful cooperation with the UNSCOM weapons inspection regime has come only after the United States and Britain have credibly threatened the use of force. What success economic sanctions have had in affecting Iraqi behavior has stemmed from their multilateral character. With each passing year that Saddam Hussein ruthlessly clings to power (and, indeed, consolidates his domestic position, in the view of country specialists), international political support for the continuation of UN sanctions wanes. But the United States and Britain remain ready to veto any move to weaken full-scope sanctions in the Security Council until UNSCOM finds Iraq in full compliance with all Security Council resolutions, most notably those pertaining to the destruction of its WMD capabilities.[58]

In contrast to the Iraqi case, American sanctions targeted at Iran (as discussed above) have been the focal point of an ongoing transatlantic political dispute because of their unilateral and extraterritorial nature. The impact of the ILSA on Iran's behavior and foreign policy orientation remains a source of contention. ILSA proponents argue that U.S. sanctions generated economic pressures that contributed to the election of President Khatami, a political moderate. Critics counter that unilateral sanctions internationally isolated the United States, not Iran. During 1997–98, American oil companies protested their inability to invest in Iran because of U.S. statutes and the consequent loss of business to European firms. Administration officials maintained that oil revenues would prop up the

Teheran regime (thereby insulating it from the consequences of rogue behavior) and fuel the development of its WMD capabilities. Undersecretary Eizenstat stated, "This is a situation where the strategic interests of the United States are so great that they outweigh temporary advantages of American companies. . . . This seems to be a factor the Europeans discount. We don't have the luxury of discounting the strategic burden."[59]

The controversy over Iran is embedded in a broader policy debate, beyond the scope of this study, concerning Washington's widespread use of economic sanctions in the post–Cold War era. By mid-1998, the Clinton administration and the Republican leadership in Congress, under pressure from the American business community, began to reassess the reliance on economic sanctions as the foreign policy instrument of first choice and an alternative to the use of military force.[60] Debate focused on the scope of sanctions (comprehensive versus targeted) and whether the United States should employ them unilaterally or only in concert with others.[61]

The experience with Libya reveals a political tension between the scope of economic sanctions and the degree of multilateral participation. The United States imposed comprehensive unilateral sanctions on Libya in 1986 for its support of international terrorism. Partial multilateral sanctions were imposed in 1992 in response to Qaddafi's refusal to extradite for trial two Libyan intelligence officers implicated in the 1988 Pan Am bombing. These sanctions, which included an arms embargo and the cutoff of civilian air flights, had reduced impact on the Qaddafi regime because they excluded the sale of petroleum products (which provides Libya some $10 billion annually in revenues). During this political stalemate, the Clinton administration maintained international backing for limited sanctions on Libya but did not win support to broaden their scope.[62] In April 1999, the Security Council suspended sanctions after the Qaddafi regime, desiring to break out of its political pariah status and under increased economic pressure because of the downturn in world oil prices, surrendered the two suspects for trial by a special court in the Netherlands.[63] In July 1999, however, the Clinton administration threatened to veto a proposed Security Council resolution to formally lift sanctions, arguing that such a move could come only after Libya had compensated the victims' families and ended support for terrorist groups.[64]

In a recent study on sanctions, John Stremlau of the Carnegie Commission on Preventing Deadly Conflict concluded, "Washington . . . has learned important lessons about the efficacy of sanctions in the post–Cold War era. The most important is that the broader the international support the more likely the regime will be effective. . . . But the brief post–Gulf War surge in UN mandated sanctions . . . reconfirms that achieving multilateral consensus is rarely a simple process. Full scope sanctions, as used against Iraq and the former Yugoslavia, are the most difficult, especially if the goal is to change a regime or a government's national security policies."[65] This conclusion underscores the dilemma of comprehensive containment. The success of this strategy relies on full-scope sanctions supported multilaterally. And yet, the broader the sanctions regime the more difficult it is politically to win multilateral support.

The difficulty in obtaining and then sustaining multilateral support for broad sanctions, even in the case of rogue states like Iraq and Libya, has prompted calls for an alternative approach that would feature targeted sanctions linked to narrower foreign policy objectives. In the case of Iran, for example, critics of the ILSA argued that narrower sanctions aimed at specific areas of concern, such as WMD proliferation, would enjoy broader international support and be more effective. Any such departure from full-scope sanctions on rogue states is likely to encounter stiff opposition in Congress because of their demonized status in American politics. As argued above, the process of demonization that mobilized support for comprehensive containment will make any change in policy highly problematic, even when altered political circumstances might warrant it. Comprehensive containment has been the default strategy pursued toward those countries designated by the Clinton administration as rogue states with the significant exception of North Korea.

Conditional Containment. This strategy is a hybrid combining the traditional elements of containment (such as the deterrence of expansionism) with limited engagement (i.e., positive incentives) to induce changes in the target state's behavior and foreign policy orientation. This strategy may utilize an approach described in the scholarly literature as "conditional reciprocity"—that is, linking meaningful changes in behavior to each concession or benefit.[66] The objective of the strategy is to use the enticement of "carrots," backed by the deterrent threat of "sticks," to motivate the target state to cease unacceptable, rogue foreign policy behavior. The process of limited engagement is intended (in Kennan's term) to "mellow" the regime and lead to an evolutionary change in its foreign policy orientation that will permit its resocialization into the international community. Again, it is important to distinguish between short-term objectives relating to specific behavioral changes and the longer-term goal of transforming the target state's ruling regime.

The Nixon-Kissinger détente policy toward the Soviet Union in the early 1970s is a prominent recent example of conditional containment. The essence of the Nixon-Kissinger strategy was to constrain Soviet behavior through the creation of linkages (or what Kissinger called a "web" of relations) between military, political, and economic issue areas. The underlying assumption was that positive inducements, such as favorable trade terms and access to Western technology, would give the Kremlin a tangible stake in what Nixon termed "the emerging structure of peace." The détente process would thereby promote more responsible Soviet foreign policy behavior, most notably in the Third World. The Nixon-Kissinger détente policy foundered, however, on the Soviet leadership's ability to compartmentalize relations and frustrate the Nixon administration's efforts to establish linkages. The mutuality of superpower interest in arms control made it impossible, in practice, for Washington to link progress on strategic nuclear arms limitation (e.g., the Strategic Arms Limitation Treaty [SALT I]) to Soviet support of Third World insurgency movements from Angola to Vietnam. Thus, the Nixon-Kissinger détente policy provided not an alternative to superpower competition, but a set of tacit understandings to govern it given the omnipresent danger of inadvertent military escalation to the nuclear level. Détente, in short, was revealed to be a condition, not a structure, of international relations.[67]

This strategy of conditional containment also encountered political difficulties on the U.S. domestic front. President Nixon's hyperbolic characterization of U.S.-Soviet détente mobilized political support for his policies but also raised false expectations. The continuing competitive quality of the relationship was dramatically evidenced during the October 1973 Arab-Israeli War. Soviet leader Leonid Brezhnev's threat to intervene in support of Egypt prompted Nixon to order a heightened alert status for U.S. nuclear forces as a signal of American resolve to forestall such a unilateral action. That crisis contributed to a public backlash against détente. Conservative critics argued that détente had become a "one-way street" and asked how the Nixon administration could "trust" the Kremlin to implement arms control agreements if it could not be trusted in the Middle East. Moreover, domestic interest groups began to push their own linkage policy. For example, congressional legislation championed by Senator Henry Jackson (D-Wash.), the 1974 Jackson-Vanik Amendment, explicitly linked the expansion of U.S.-Soviet trade to Jewish emigration from the Soviet Union.

Through détente, Nixon and Kissinger sought to transform the U.S.-Soviet relationship from "competitive" to "cooperative" coexistence.

This mixed strategy of containment and engagement sought to alter the overall superpower relationship by forging linkages across issue areas (e.g., Vietnam and arms control). This ambitious strategy, conceptually flawed in the eyes of many, failed primarily because of its inability to overcome the fundamentally contending Soviet and American conceptions of international order. Although the Nixon and Kissinger carrot-and-stick approach was not able to constrain Soviet adventurism in the Third World, the fact is that both superpowers sought unilateral political advantage at the expense of the other. The Soviet Union did this militarily at the outset of the Angolan civil war in 1975–76; the United States did it politically in the Middle East following the October 1973 war. Although the Brezhnev policies of the 1970s generated a political backlash against détente, the administrations that followed Nixon's maintained the principal elements of conditional containment (i.e., maintaining some degree of engagement with Moscow). Kissinger argued that the dangerous realities of the nuclear age necessitated continued dialogue. Even Ronald Reagan, the most vociferous critic of détente, who came to power in the wake of the Soviet invasion of Afghanistan, did not revert to a strategy of comprehensive containment.

In the post–Cold War era, the Clinton administration has pursued a strategy of conditional containment toward North Korea. This policy stands in sharp contrast to that adopted toward the other countries designated by it as rogue states. In those cases, the administration has implemented a generic approach—a strategy of comprehensive containment that seeks to isolate, deter, and punish the target states, that eschews any meaningful engagement, and that demonizes them to mobilize political support for this hard-line policy. The Clinton administration departed from this default strategy in the face of the imminent danger posed by North Korea's mature nuclear weapons program. Its recourse to a mixed strategy that included policy inducements was taken in the absence of any better alternative. The policy shift during the 1993–94 showdown with North Korea stemmed from the recognition that a purely punitive strategy to compel the Pyongyang regime to forego its nuclear option and resume its NPT obligations was unlikely to be successful. A military strike to destroy North Korea's nuclear infrastructure, advocated by some conservative newspaper columnists and Republican critics, carried unacceptable risks. Within the Clinton administration, most notably in the Pentagon, such an action was viewed as a probable catalyst for a general war on the Korean Peninsula. Beyond the military option, a punitive strategy based on economic sanctions was also highly problematic, given the Chinese government's cool attitude toward any such tough measures.

The Agreed Framework, with its "elaborately choreographed steps," in the words of nonproliferation specialist Leon Sigal stipulated that the dismantlement of North Korea's nuclear facilities and the construction of replacement light-water reactors were designed to proceed in tandem.[68] Satisfactory completion of mutual obligations at each stage would be required before the initiation of the next. But beyond the nuclear issue, the Agreed Framework also committed "the two sides [to] move toward full normalization of political and economic relations." The bilateral agreement thus provided a "framework" for expanding the scope of diplomatic engagement with the Pyongyang regime to address important collateral issues, such as the resumption of a North-South dialogue, North Korean ballistic missile transfers, and food aid to North Korea.

The U.S.–North Korean nuclear accord is a remarkably creative example of a negotiating approach referred to in the scholarly literature as "conditional reciprocity." In this case, however, congressional and other critics often denounce the use of positive inducements as being "appeasement." The "engagement" of an adversary under conditional reciprocity can be clearly distinguished from "appeasement" in three important respects. First, the inducement must be tied to specific changes in the target state's behavior, not general expectations of improved behavior. Second, the reward should come only after the specific change in behavior. If the reward is provided in advance of behavior modification or is not linked to a specific behavioral change, it may be legitimately criticized as a bribe. And third, such an approach depends on mutual adherence to the specific conditional reciprocal steps in the sequence. If the target state does not fulfill its obligations, the process can be halted and the benefit withdrawn.[69] The negotiation and implementation of the Agreed Framework will be examined in greater detail in Chapter 6.

The distinctive North Korean experience raises an important issue, with potentially broader implications, relating to the engagement of a target state. What are the conditions under which a target state would seek engagement with the United States, and vice versa? Recent historical experience both during and after the Cold War points to two factors that would prompt a diplomatically isolated target state to seek engagement with the outside world.

The first such condition is a state of economic crisis threatening the stability of the ruling regime. Although little is known about the inner workings of the Pyongyang regime, the country's deepening economic problems were a key determinant in North Korean leader Kim Il Sung's decision to initiate a limited opening to the West. In December 1993, the regime made the stunning public admission that the North Korean economy was in a "grave situation."[70] The economic gap with South Korea was becoming a chasm. Meanwhile, the Soviet Union and China, North Korea's great power patrons, were demanding hard currency payments for oil and other essential commodities. Neither continued autarky nor reliance on communist allies was an option for the Pyongyang regime. Under these conditions, Kim Il Sung reportedly sided with pragmatists inside the regime and approved limited engagement with the outside world. With no other bargaining assets, the Kim regime used the North Korean nuclear program to seize Washington's attention. While its nuclear program provided bargaining leverage, the factor underlying the Kim regime's decision to embark on a policy of engagement with the United States was its dire economic crisis—a continuing condition that has prompted references to North Korea as a "failed state."

A second factor that could precipitate a diplomatically isolated state to seek engagement with an outside power is an overriding national security threat. Consider the case of China during the period leading up to Kissinger's secret mission to Beijing in July 1971. China was a radical state then emerging from the traumas of the Cultural Revolution. Mao Zedong's communist government was virulently anti-American in rhetoric and was providing important military assistance to the North Vietnamese in their war against the U.S.-backed Saigon regime. U.S. strategy toward China was essentially one of comprehensive containment. A dramatic change in Beijing's foreign policy orientation, however, was precipitated by a sharp deterioration in relations with Moscow following the Soviet invasion of Czechoslovakia in August 1968. Clashes along the Sino-Soviet border in 1969, as well as rumors that the Soviet Union was sounding out Warsaw Pact diplomats about a preemptive strike on Chinese nuclear facilities, underscored China's vulnerability to external attack. This Soviet strategic threat prompted a diplomatic countermove by Mao that eventually yielded a Sino-American rapprochement. The opening to Washington, historian Roderick MacFarquhar observed, "undermine[d] the calculations of the Russians as to the impunity with which they could attack China."[71] A core threat to Chinese national security from its former communist ally thus led to the initiation of a strategic dialogue with Beijing's longtime adversary.

A more recent example of this phenomenon involves one of the countries designated by the United States as a rogue state. In 1985–86, Iran conducted secret negotiations with the United States over the supply of military hardware (anti-tank and air-defense missiles) in return for Teheran's assistance in obtaining the release of American hostages held in Lebanon. That Iran entered into these direct, if covert, talks with the "Great Satan" was a reflection of its dire military state in the war with Iraq. With the depletion of its U.S. military stocks (inherited from the Shah's era), the politically unthinkable became a military necessity for the Khomeini regime. After the "arms for hostages" scandal broke in 1986, relations between Teheran and Washington reverted to their prior state of enmity. But, as Middle East experts Shahram Chubin and Charles Tripp wrote, "Something important had been broached in the act of contact. Iran had survived the political revelations about the contacts and the even more embarrassing links with Israel. . . . [President Hashemi] Rafsanjani continued . . . to pose conditions for a renewal of formal relations, but he also referred with some regularity to the channels established and the eventual resumption of ties."[72] Whatever the flaws and illegalities of the "arms for hostages" deal, the salient point in this context is that Teheran's interest in limited engagement with the United States stemmed from the overriding Iraqi military threat.

For the United States, the conditions under which Washington has shifted from a strategy of comprehensive to conditional containment have also been tied to national security concerns. In the case of China cited above, Nixon and Kissinger shared Mao's motivation to initiate a strategic dialogue because they viewed China as an important counterweight to Soviet power during a period when the Kremlin was becoming increasingly assertive. Likewise, the Reagan administration's National Security Council considered the covert dialogue with Iran as a means of countering Moscow's influence in a geostrategically important country on the Soviet Union's southern border. Relative to national security motivations, economic factors have not played a discernible role in Washington's decision to undertake limited engagement with a pariah state.

This chapter has focused on the development of targeted strategies to address the varied threats posed by the countries grouped under the rogue state rubric. That process of differentiation requires a fuller understanding of the conditions, as in the North Korean case, under which policymakers would shift from a generic strategy of comprehensive containment to a mixed strategy of conditional containment incorporating a significant degree of engagement with the target state. For the foreign policy community, officials and academic analysts alike, this shift from a generic to a differentiated approach poses major challenges both of conceptualization and implementation. Moreover, it has implications that go beyond the small group of dangerous but politically marginalized rogue states.

U.S. policies toward other problematic countries, such as China and Pakistan, have also been caught up in the debate over containment and engagement. Differentiation would permit the formulation of mixed strategies that reflect the complex nature of American relations with these countries. The U.S. relationship with China, for example, combines deep economic engagement with official concern about Chinese behavior with respect to nonproliferation and Taiwan. The debate over China policy has now moved beyond the sterile containment-engagement dichotomy. Within the typology of strategies developed earlier in this chapter, the U.S. approach would fall under the category of "conditional engagement."[73] The focus in that discussion was on the range of strategies that might be pursued toward those countries under the rogue state rubric—rollback, comprehensive containment, and conditional containment. Conditional engagement is the next category of strategy along this continuum of policy choice. As indicated in the term, it is a strategy combining containment and engagement, but in which the engagement component is very substantial. This study's critique of the rogue state approach is by no means intended as an unqualified recommendation for engagement. Indeed, an extreme case of regime pathology, such as Iraq, might well warrant a shift from comprehensive containment (i.e., keeping Saddam Hussein "in his box") to an overt strategy of rollback. The selection of this or any strategy, however, is contingent on the amalgam of factors that go into target state analysis. In Part II, this topic—strategy formulation and differentiation—will be explored more fully in the context of case studies on U.S. policy toward Iraq, Iran, and North Korea.

NOTES

[1] "Differentiated containment" was advocated by Zbigniew Brzezinski, Brent Scowcroft, and Richard Murphy as an alternative to the U.S. "dual containment" strategy toward Iran and Iraq in *Differentiated Containment: U.S. Policy toward Iran and Iraq—Report of an Independent Task Force* (New York: Council on Foreign Relations, 1997). This book will apply the concept more broadly in addressing the full range of countries that the Clinton administration has designated as rogue states.

[2] Because of its usage by U.S. policy-makers, some foreign leaders have picked up the term, particularly when addressing an American audience. For example, British foreign secretary Robin Cook recently wrote, "The United States and Europe have together put in place an impressive net to prevent *rogue countries* from being able to build . . . weapons [of mass destruction]." See Robin Cook, "The Good Fight after the Cold War," *Washington Post*, March 29, 1998, p. C7 (emphasis added).

[3] Secretary of Defense William Cohen, in a letter attached to a threat assessment on Cuba requested by Congress, stated that he is concerned about the potential for

Cuba to develop biological weapons because of its civilian biotechnology industry. There is no indication, however, that Cuba is attempting to develop such weapons, and previous Department of Defense publications on weapons proliferation did not mention Cuba as a country of concern in this area. See Dana Priest, "Cuba Poses 'Negligible' Threat, Report Says: Potential to Develop Biological Agents Still Concerns Defense Secretary Cohen," *Washington Post*, May 7, 1998, p. A8.

[4] Indeed, Latin American states are openly defying U.S. efforts to isolate Cuba. See, for example, James Brooke, "Latin America Now Ignores U.S. Lead in Isolating Cuba," *New York Times*, July 8, 1995, pp. A1, 5.

[5] Testimony of Ambassador Philip Wilcox, State Department coordinator for counterterrorism, in U.S. House, Committee on International Relations, "Syria: Peace Partner or Rogue Regime?" (104th Cong., 2nd sess., 1996), pp. 15–16.

[6] Ibid., p. 23.

[7] Robert Manning, "India, the Rogue Democracy," *Los Angeles Times*, May 17, 1998; Richard Haass quoted in Judith Miller, "New Blasts Shake Foundation of Effort to Limit Nuclear Arms," *New York Times*, June 3, 1998, p. A8.

[8] Citing Sudan's support for Lord's Resistance Army in northern Sudan, an administration official characterized Sudan as the greatest threat to peace in sub-Saharan Africa. Secretary of State Albright met with Sudanese opposition leaders during her December 1997 trip to Africa to "ratchet up the pressure" on the Khartoum regime. See Thomas W. Lippmann, "Albright Vows New Pressure on Sudan," *Washington Post*, December 11, 1997, p. A29.

[9] "The Menace of Sudan" (editorial), *Washington Post*, December 4, 1996.

[10] David Ottaway reported that administration officials "have struggled to provide a consistent rationale" for Sudan's exemption from the 1996 Anti-Terrorism Act (Ottaway, "GOP Targets Sudan Loophole," *Washington Post*, February 7, 1997, p. A30). Some observers suggested that this exemption was made to permit Occidental Petroleum to pursue a lucrative oil exploration deal with Sudan. The reason for the collapse of the Occidental deal is unclear; it was alternately attributed to pressure from the Clinton administration on the U.S. firm to forego the exploration or the failure to reach satisfactory commercial terms. On November 4, 1997, Secretary Albright announced the extension of U.S. sanctions on Sudan. See Reuters, "Linking Sudan to Rights Abuses and Terror, U.S. Adds Penalties," *New York Times*, November 5, 1997, p. A7. The administration's action provided exceptions for certain activities "in the U.S. interest," such as imports of gum arabic, a key ingredient in candy and sodas.

[11] Reuters, "U.S. Raps Burma for Arrests," *Washington Post*, May 22, 1997, p. A26.

[12] An example of this effort to demonize rogue states can be found in Secretary of State Warren Christopher's March 1995 statement regarding Iranian behavior in the Middle East: "Wherever you look, you will find the evil hand of Iran in this region." Quoted in Elaine Sciolino, "Condemning Iranian Oil Deal, U.S. May Tighten Trade Ban," *New York Times*, March 10, 1995, p. A2.

[13] Mitchell Reiss, *Bridled Ambition: Why Countries Constrain Their Nuclear Capabilities* (Washington, DC: Woodrow Wilson Center Press, 1995), p. 284.

[14] Don Oberdorfer, *The Two Koreas: A Contemporary History* (Boston: Addison-Wesley, 1997), p. 364.

[15] Michael S. Lelyveld wrote, "While the change is still only rhetorical, it may mark a milestone in U.S. policy. Government officials and Korea experts say the United States has embarked on an initiative to influence and eventually open the mysterious Marxist nation, building on the nuclear accord. . . . The administration wants Pyongyang to become a 'more responsible member of the international community,' said one official." Donald Gregg, former U.S. ambassador to Seoul, added, "We wouldn't conduct liaison with a pariah." See "U.S. Removes North Korea from List of 'Pariah States,'" *Journal of Commerce*, February 2, 1996, p. 1.

[16] For an excellent discussion of this issue see "Secondary Boycotts and Allied Relations," in International Institute for Strategic Studies (IISS), *Strategic Survey 1996/97* (London: Oxford University Press, 1997), pp. 46–47ff.

[17] Televised interview on March 13, 1996, at the close of the multilateral summit on terrorism held in Egypt. Quoted in Simon Serfaty, "Europe and the United States in the Gulf," paper presented at the meeting of the U.S.-Iran Study Group, Nixon Center, Washington, DC, April 1997.

[18] James Woolsey, "Appeasement Will only Encourage Iran," *Survival* 38, no. 4 (Winter 1996/97), p. 18; cited in Serfaty, "Europe and the United States in the Gulf."

[19] Robert Satloff, "America, Europe, and the Middle East in the 1990s: Interests and Policies," in Robert D. Blackwill and Michael Stürmer, eds., *Allies Divided: Transatlantic Policies for the Greater Middle East* (Cambridge, MA: MIT Press, 1997), p. 27. See also Phebe Marr, "The United States, Europe and the Middle East: Cooperation, Co-optation or Confrontation," in B. A. Roberson, ed., *The Middle East and Europe: The Power Deficit* (London: Routledge, 1998), pp. 74–103.

[20] John R. Bolton, "Appeasement as a Way of Life," *New York Times*, July 28, 1996, section 4, p. 3.

[21] Toby Roth, "New Iranian-Libyan Sanctions Will only Hurt U.S.," *Wall Street Journal*, August 6, 1996, p. A14.

[22] "Speech by British Foreign Secretary, Mr. Robin Cook, to the European Institute, Washington, DC," press release, EU, January 15, 1998.

[23] In September 1997, these foreign firms concluded a five-year deal to invest $2 billion to develop one of Iran's largest offshore gas fields, South Pars.

[24] "White House Press Release: Press Briefing by Mike McCurry," White House, Office of the Press Secretary, May 20, 1998.

[25] James Bennet, "To Clear Air with Europe, U.S. Waives Some Sanctions," *New York Times*, May 19, 1998, p. A6.

[26] Senator D'Amato expressed outrage at the waiver decision: "The decision is a mistake. It will send a signal to others that they can do business as usual with Iran at a time when Iran continues to pursue weapons of mass destruction and continues to support terrorism." Quoted in ibid.

[27] Testimony of Stuart Eizenstat, undersecretary of state for economic, business, and agricultural affairs, before the U.S. House Ways and Means Committee, Subcommittee on Trade, October 23, 1997, text available at www.state.gov/www/policy_remarks/971023_eizen_house.html.

[28] IISS, Strategic Survey 1996/97, p. 42.

[29] Joseph Jones, *The Fifteen Weeks* (New York: Viking, 1955), p. 143.

[30] Warren I. Cohen, *The Cambridge History of American Foreign Relations*, vol. 4, *America in the Age of Soviet Power, 1945–1991* (Cambridge: Cambridge University Press, 1993), pp. 254–55.

[31] John Glenn, "Revenge of the Rogues," in U.S. Senate, Committee on Governmental Affairs, *Proliferation Watch* 4, no. 2 (March–April 1993), p. 1.

[32] Gary Bauer, President of the Family Research Council, on *Meet the Press*, June 14, 1998, transcript obtained at www.msnbc.com.

[33] Steven Erlanger, "Citing Gains Clinton Says He Will Make China Visit," *New York Times*, May 27, 1998, p. A5 (emphasis added).

[34] Her comment was made on the *NewsHour with Jim Lehrer*, May 26, 1998, transcript obtained from the "Online NewsHour" site at http://www.pbs.org.

[35] Alexander George made this comment at a workshop on "U.S. Strategies toward 'Rogue States': Strategies, Instruments, and Objectives," Woodrow Wilson International Center for Scholars, Washington, D.C., May 13, 1997. This section draws heavily on Alexander L. George, *Bridging the Gap: Theory and Practice in Foreign*

Policy (Washington, DC: United States Institute of Peace Press, 1993), chapter 4, "Reforming Outlaw States and Rogue Leaders", pp. 45–60.

[36] CIA, Office of Public Affairs, "Jeremiah News Conference, June 2, 1998," transcript obtained at http://www.odci.gov/cia.

[37] At the press conference describing the findings of his review panel, Admiral Jeremiah stated that "you begin to fall into a pattern. You operate the way you expect things to happen and you have to recognize there is a difference and you could argue that you need to have a contrarian view that might be part of our warning process, ought to include some diversion thinkers who look at the same evidence and come to a different conclusion and then you test that different set of conclusions against other evidence to see if it could be valid." Ibid.

[38] To cite another pertinent example, prior to the May 1998 Indian nuclear test, CIA analysts discounted the public statements of the Hindu nationalist Bharatiya Janata Party (BJP) vowing to turn India into a nuclear power; most of the analysts believed that the BJP would moderate this position once in power. See James Risen, "India's A-Tests Prompt C.I.A. to Review Its Warning Systems," *New York Times*, July 4, 1998, p. A3.

[39] Cited in Shahram Chubin, *Iran's National Security Policy* (Washington, DC: Carnegie Endowment for International Peace, 1994), p. 38. Chubin concludes that "in comparison with either Saudi Arabia or Iraq, Iran's military expenditures and arms imports have been modest. . . . Compared with the baseline year of 1979 and the inventory inherited from the Shah, trends in military capability and balance have shifted against revolutionary Iran."

[40] George, *Bridging the Gap*, pp. 126–28.

[41] Cited in Ibid., pp. 48–49. For a more detailed discussion of this issue see Philip Windsor, "Henry Kissinger's Scholarly Contribution," *British Journal of International Studies* 1, no. 1 (April 1975), pp. 27–37.

[42] John Lewis Gaddis, *Strategies of Containment: A Critical Appraisal of Postwar American National Security Policy* (Oxford: Oxford University Press, 1982), pp. 352–57.

[43] President Nixon laid out the realist case for engaging the Soviet Union in a June 1974 speech on "Pragmatism and Moral Force in American Foreign Policy": "Not by our choice, but our capability, our primary concern in foreign policy must be to help influence the international conduct of nations in the world arena. . . . We cannot gear our foreign policy to the transformation of other societies. In the nuclear age, our first responsibility must be the prevention of a war that could destroy all societies: We must never lose sight of this fundamental truth of modern international life. Peace between nations with totally different systems is also a high moral objective." Richard Nixon, "Pragmatism and Moral Force in American Foreign Policy," *Bulletin* (U.S. Department of State) 71, no. 1827 (June 1974), pp. 4–5.

[44] Anthony Lake, "Confronting Backlash States," *Foreign Affairs* 73, no. 2 (March/April 1994), p. 14.

[45] See George F. Kennan ("X"), "The Sources of Soviet Conduct," *Foreign Affairs* 25, no. 4 (July 1947), pp. 572–82.

[46] For an analysis of the Bush administration's internal deliberations concerning the termination of the Gulf War see Michael R. Gordon and Bernard E. Trainor, *The General's War: The Inside Story of the Conflict in the Gulf* (Boston: Little, Brown, 1995), pp. 476–77. A major reason for this view was an inaccurate battlefield assessment of Iraqi military losses (in particular, a failure to trace the elite Republican Guard divisions that escaped back into southern Iraq from Kuwait).

[47] Elaine Sciolino, "Taking on Iran and Iraq, but Separately," *New York Times*, April 11, 1993, section 4, p. 4.

[48] U.S. Department of State, Office of the Spokesman, "Secretary of State Madeline Albright's Remarks at Georgetown University, 'Preserving Principle and Safeguarding Stability,' March 26, 1997."

[49] Reported in Jim Hoagland, "Crisis-Managing in a Fog," *Washington Post,* November 26, 1997, p. A19.

[50] President Clinton's remarks were made to the Joint Chiefs of Staff and Pentagon staff on February 17, 1998. See "In Clinton's Word: Containing the 'Predators of the 21st Century,' " *New York Times,* February 18, 1998, p. A9.

[51] David Rogers, "Clinton Seeking Support for Plan against Saddam," *Wall Street Journal,* July 17, 1998, p. A16.

[52] Thomas Lippman, "Albright Defends Handling of Iraq," *Washington Post,* September 10, 1998, p. A2.

[53] The next strategy along the containment-engagement continuum would be "conditional engagement," a mixed strategy in which the engagement component would be dominant (c.f. "conditional containment," in which the reverse is the case). U.S. policy toward China in the 1990s would fall under the category of "conditional engagement." Although the United States is heavily engaged with China economically, aspects of the Beijing regime's behavior raise serious concern (e.g., threats on Taiwan, transfers of dual-use technologies to rogue states). Strategies of "conditional containment" are not appropriate for the problem states under consideration in this book and are mentioned here for the purpose of illustration, not policy recommendation.

[54] This discussion of the "rollback" strategy articulated in NSC-158 is drawn from Christian F. Ostermann, "Operationalizing Roll-back: NSC 158," *American Historians of Foreign Relations Newsletter* 26, no. 3 (September 1996), pp. 1–7.

[55] See Fareed Zakaria, "The Reagan Strategy of Containment," *Political Science Quarterly* 105, no. 3 (1990), pp. 373–95, and Bruce W. Jentleson, "The Reagan Administration and Coercive Diplomacy: Restraining More Than Remaking Governments," *Political Science Quarterly* 106, no. 1 (1991), pp. 57–82.

[56] Patrick Clawson, ed., *Iraq Strategy Review: Options for U.S. Policy* (Washington, DC: Washington Institute for Near East Policy, 1998), p. 5.

[57] Richard Haass, "Sanctioning Madness," *Foreign Affairs* 76, no. 6 (November/December 1997), p. 78.

[58] See, for example, John M. Goshko, "Iraq Sanctions Stir Debate: New Approach Needed, Some Security Council Members Say," *Washington Post,* April 25, 1998, p. A13.

[59] Jane Perlez and Steve LeVine, "Curbs on Iran Anger American Firms," *New York Times,* August 9, 1998, p. A4.

[60] During 1993–96, U.S. sanctions were imposed 61 times—more than during the entire 1945–92 period. In January 1998, Undersecretary Eizenstat announced that the State Department would review the use of economic sanctions and announced guidelines for imposing such measures. Associated Press report in the *Washington Post,* January 8, 1998, p. A22.

[61] See, for example, Eric Schmitt, "U.S. Backs Off Sanctions, Seeing Poor Effect Abroad," *New York Times,* July 31, 1998, pp. A1, 6; Gary Hufbauer, "The Snake Oil of Diplomacy: When Tensions Rise, the U.S. Peddles Sanctions," *Washington Post,* July 12, 1998, p. C1.

[62] In August 1998, the United States and the United Kingdom proposed that the two Libyan suspects be tried before a panel of Scottish judges in a special court in the Netherlands. Qaddafi, who had earlier argued for a trial in a third country, balked at this proposal, declaring that further "negotiation" was required. Barbara Crossette, "Qaddafi Says 'Negotiation' Is Needed on Lockerbie Suspects," *New York Times,* August 28, 1998, p. A3.

⁶³ Anne Swardson, "Lockerbie Suspects Delivered for Trial," *Washington Post,* April 6, 1999, pp. A1, 16. This arrangement was criticized by some victims' families for limiting the judicial inquiry to the role of these low-level operatives and not exposing the possible involvement of the Libyan leadership in authorizing the bombing.

⁶⁴ Colum Lynch, "U.S. Threatens to Veto Libyan Sanctions," *Washington Post,* July 8, 1999, p. A18. This move coincided with the announcement that the United Kingdom had restored diplomatic relations with Libya.

⁶⁵ John Stremlau, *Sharpening International Sanctions: Toward a Stronger Role for the United Nations—A Report to the Carnegie Commission on Preventing Deadly Conflict* (Washington, DC: Carnegie Corporation, November 1996), pp. 18–19.

⁶⁶ George, *Bridging the Gap,* pp. 50–51ff.

⁶⁷ For a sustained analysis of the Nixon-Kissinger détente policy see Litwak, *Détente and the Nixon Doctrine.*

⁶⁸ Leon Sigal, *Disarming Strangers: Nuclear Diplomacy with North Korea* (Princeton, NJ: Princeton University Press, 1998), pp. 190–91.

⁶⁹ George, *Bridging the Gap,* pp. 55–56. For an extended discussion of the use of positive incentives in strategies of conflict prevention see David Cortright, "Incentive Strategies for Preventing Conflict," in David Cortright, ed., *The Price of Peace: Incentives and International Conflict Prevention* (New York: Rowman and Littlefield, 1997), pp. 267–301.

⁷⁰ Oberdorfer, *The Two Koreas,* p. 297. Oberdorfer reports that the North Korean economy, once roughly equal in size to that of the Republic of Korea (ROK), was then estimated to have a GNP equal to only one-sixteenth that of the ROK.

⁷¹ Roderick MacFarquhar, "The Succession of Mao and the End of Maoism, 1969–82," in Roderick MacFarquhar, ed., *The Politics of China, 1949–1989* (Cambridge: Cambridge University Press, 1994), p. 263.

⁷² Shahram Chubin and Charles Tripp, *Iran and Iraq at War* (London: I. B. Tauris, 1988), pp. 212–13.

⁷³ For an elaboration of this strategy as a U.S. policy option see James Shinn, ed., *Weaving the Net: Conditional Engagement with China* (New York: Council on Foreign Relations Press, 1996). See also David Shambaugh, "Containment or Engagement of China? Calculating Beijing's Responses," *International Security* 21, no. 2 (Fall 1996), pp. 180–209.

II

Case Studies

4

Iraq: Containing Saddam Hussein
after the Gulf War

U.S. POLICY DEVELOPMENT

Since the Gulf War, the United States has simultaneously pursued two
policy objectives toward Iraq—in the near term, containing Saddam
Hussein by keeping him "in his box," while, in the long term, working
for his overthrow. These twin goals were evident during the December
1998 bombing campaign by U.S. and British aircraft, when Clinton administration officials alternately described the mission as "degrading"
Saddam Hussein's weapons of mass destruction (WMD) capabilities and
attacking key elements of his domestic power base to hasten a regime
change in Baghdad. This chapter will trace the development of U.S. strategy toward Iraq since the Gulf War and show how these twin goals have
produced a continuing tension in Washington's approach.

Immediately following the hundred-hour ground war to liberate
Kuwait from Iraqi occupation in February 1991, President Bush
recorded in his personal diary that he had "no feeling of euphoria" over
the outcome: "It hasn't been a clean end; there is no battleship *Missouri*
surrender. This is what's missing to make this akin to WWII, to separate
Kuwait from Korea and Vietnam."[1] Bush's comments highlighted this
underlying tension that existed in U.S policy objectives throughout Operation Desert Storm and has persisted since its conclusion. The United
Nations (UN) Security Council resolutions authorizing the use of force
by the U.S.-led coalition were linked to a specific goal—the liberation of
Kuwait, not the overthrow of the Saddam Hussein regime. The latter,
however, was an implicit American war objective.

But removing the Iraqi dictator was not to be achieved by a "march
on Baghdad" by the U.S.-led coalition. The Bush administration rejected

such a move on both political and military grounds. First, such an expansion of war aims would have led to the defection of Syria, Egypt, and other Arab states from the coalition. Second, the U.S. military, having attained the war's designated objective in an action that was widely hailed and contrasted with Vietnam, was reluctant to take on an ambiguous mission that might lead to the indefinite occupation of Iraq. Instead of continuing the war into Iraq, administration officials hoped that the decisive defeat of Iraqi forces in Kuwait would generate enough political pressure within the Baathist regime in Baghdad to lead to a coup d'état. Without directly calling on the Iraqi military to do so, Bush stated "that the Iraqi people should put him aside and that would facilitate the resolution of all these problems that exist, and certainly would facilitate the acceptance of Iraq back into the family of peace-loving nations."[2] But rather than triggering a military coup within the regime, the Gulf War precipitated two popular uprisings—one ethnic, by the Kurds in northern Iraq; the other sectarian, by the Shiite Muslims in southern Iraq. These revolts highlighted the underlying fragility of the Iraqi state, in general, and the minority status of Saddam Hussein's Sunni Muslim regime, in particular. (Recent Central Intelligence Agency [CIA] estimates place the Kurdish population at 15–20 percent of Iraq's total 22 million, and Shiite Muslims at 60–65 percent.)[3]

The simultaneous Kurdish and Shiite uprisings caught the Bush administration by surprise. They also posed a major policy dilemma. For while the Bush administration sought the removal of Saddam Hussein from power, it also wanted to ensure Iraq's continuation as a unitary state. National Security Adviser Brent Scowcroft viewed Iraq as a regional counterweight to a potentially resurgent Iran. Policy-makers were also concerned that an autonomous Shiite political entity in southern Iraq, although ethnically Arab, would invariably be drawn into the Iranian political orbit. The Kurdish and Shiite uprisings posed the greatest threat both to Saddam Hussein's personal survival and to the cohesion of the Iraqi state since the Baath Party seized power in 1968. But, in the absence of military support from the allied coalition for the Kurds and the Shiites, the Iraqi dictator, defying predictions of his imminent downfall, was able to overcome the uprisings. Two military factors contributed to his unlikely success. First, because of the Bush administration's desire to promptly terminate hostilities once Iraqi forces were expelled from Kuwait, some of Saddam Hussein's politically loyal Republican Guard divisions escaped unscathed from the Basra region in southern Iraq and moved north toward Baghdad to save the Iraqi dictator. And second, the cease-fire agreement concluded by General Norman Schwarzkopf with an Iraqi military delegation failed to include a ban on Iraqi helicopter flights. With these elite armored units and helicopter gunships, Saddam Hussein was able to ruthlessly put down the revolts of March 1991.

The flow of Kurdish refugees into Turkey, a North Atlantic Treaty Organization ally, prompted the U.S.-led coalition to create a "safe haven" for them in northern Iraq. The allies barred Iraqi aircraft and mechanized ground forces from this zone. In the south, the Shiites, who suffered an estimated 50,000 dead, were provided less protection. That region was declared a "no-fly zone" but not a "safe haven," thereby permitting Iraqi ground forces to assert fuller control. The Bush administration reportedly considered the creation of a demilitarized zone in southern Iraq to monitor the cease-fire and put added pressure on the Saddam Hussein regime. This option, which the Security Council likely would have approved, was opposed by General Colin Powell and General Schwarzkopf, who considered their primary mission completed and wanted to avoid any long-term entanglement inside Iraq through the rapid extrication of U.S. ground forces from Kuwait.[4] In announcing the establishment of the no-fly zone in southern Iraq—designated "Operation Southern Watch"—President Bush declared that "we seek Iraq's compliance, not its partition. The United States continues to support Iraq's territorial unity and bears no ill will toward its people."

UN Security Council Resolution (UNSCR) 687 codified the cease-fire terms of the Gulf War in early April 1991 (see Appendix). Among its provisions, the resolution required Iraq to formally recognize its border with Kuwait and to compensate Kuwait for losses. It also created the UN Special Commission (UNSCOM), headed by Ambassador Rolf Ekeus of Sweden, to oversee the destruction of any WMD that survived the Gulf War and to establish a verification system to ensure long-term compliance. Iraq would be permitted to resume unrestricted oil exports once the Baghdad regime had complied with the provisions relating to the destruction of Iraq's WMD capabilities.[5] But this resolution, as well as the companion UNSCR 688, relating to human rights abuses, did not impose any specific penalties on the Iraqi regime for its aggression against Kuwait. Saddam Hussein was not charged with war crimes and no change in the character of the Baghdad regime was mandated by the Security Council, again reflecting that body's reluctance to intervene in a member state's internal politics.

UNSCR 687 exposed an underlying tension—one that would become more pronounced as the years passed—between the American and the

Security Council positions on the basic objective of the sanctions and weapons inspection regime. UNSCRs 687 and 688 outlined the specific actions and behavioral changes that would lead the existing Iraqi regime to international rehabilitation, whereas the United States made no secret of its desire to see Saddam Hussein out of office. In May 1991, when it was evident that the Iraqi military was not going to move against Saddam Hussein, the Bush administration declared that sanctions would remain in place until the Iraqi dictator was removed from power. Toward this end, it authorized a $15 million program (later increased by Congress to $40 million) to oust him. Since the end of the Gulf War, CIA analysts have consistently maintained that economic sanctions on their own are unlikely to accomplish this objective.

Questions about whether the incoming Clinton administration would continue the Bush policy were raised by an interview with the president-elect in mid-January 1993 by Thomas Friedman of the *New York Times*. Clinton said that he was not "obsessed" with Saddam Hussein and that as a religious man, Clinton "believe[d] in deathbed conversions." He further stated that if Saddam Hussein "wants a different relationship with the United States and the United Nations, all he has to do is change his behavior." When the interview triggered a barrage of criticism, Clinton denied that he was signaling a willingness to establish normal relations with the Saddam Hussein regime.[6] Likewise Vice President–elect Albert Gore stated that there would be "no fundamental difference" between Bush and Clinton administration policies toward Iraq and that the new White House would not "do business" with Saddam Hussein.[7]

In a significant shift in the Clinton administration's declaratory policy toward Iraq during a Security Council review of economic sanctions in March 1993, senior U.S. officials purposely omitted the call for Saddam Hussein's removal from power. They said that the administration's aim was to "depersonalize" the question of Iraqi behavior by dropping a demand that was not supported by other Security Council members (particularly Russia and France), as well as U.S. allies in the Arab world. These states, several of which had been part of the Gulf War coalition, said that the American objective to change the regime in Baghdad went well beyond the pertinent Security Council resolutions and had no basis in international law.

The Clinton administration's new declaratory policy was deliberately ambiguous. To maintain Security Council support for continued sanctions, it shifted the focus in that forum from Saddam Hussein to compliance with UNSCRs 687 and 688. To the American domestic audience, the official line was that the U.S. attitude toward the Baghdad regime was unchanged. Presidential spokesperson Dee Dee Myers, seeking to downplay the significance of this shift in declaratory policy, stated that the Clinton administration did not believe that Iraq could come into full compliance with Security Council resolutions while Saddam Hussein remained in power. "Therefore," she stated, "there's no practical difference" between the Bush and Clinton policies.[8] This ambiguity was intended to bridge the gap between the contending objectives of the Security Council majority (France and Russia, aligned with China) and the United States (supported by Britain). Within the Clinton administration, two schools of thought emerged over strategy toward Iraq: one advocating an immediate rollback and the other promoting a form of long-term comprehensive containment.

The first, which enjoyed strong congressional support, was to keep the focus on Saddam Hussein and make a concerted effort to oust him from power through covert action and support for Iraqi opposition groups in Turkey and Europe. The primary drawback of this rollback approach was that it enjoyed scant support from the other members of the Gulf War coalition. Iraq's neighbors feared that such a drive could lead to the country's dismemberment into separate Kurdish, Sunni, and Shiite zones. Many in the region privately preferred a weak but unified Iraq to the uncertainties of any alternative. Boutros Boutros-Ghali, then serving as Egypt's foreign minister, commented that, despite the Kuwait crisis, Egypt could coexist, and even cooperate, with the Saddam Hussein regime.[9] Other critics of a rollback strategy argued that it was unlikely to yield success, went beyond the terms of UNSCR 687, and removed any incentive for Saddam Hussein to cooperate with UNSCOM on the destruction of Iraq's WMD capabilities. In November 1994, for example, the *New York Times*, in an editorial describing the Clinton approach as "Half a Policy on Iraq," stated, "Three and a half years after the end of the Persian Gulf war, it is time to acknowledge that Washington is not about to overthrow Saddam Hussein. . . . U.N. inspectors are now satisfied that Iraq's most dangerous weapons have been located and destroyed. . . . The U.S., supported by Britain, will not agree. Washington though it never says so directly has made it plain that it will not consider relief so long as Saddam Hussein remains in power. That is no way to encourage Iraqi cooperation on arms control, or to encourage allies to maintain sanctions."[10] Although the *Times*'s editorial line changed after Saddam Hussein's son-in-law, Hussein Kamel defected to Jordan in August 1995, criticism of the rollback option has remained a persistent theme in the U.S. policy debate about Iraq.

The second approach considered by the Clinton administration was aimed not at ousting Saddam Hussein, but at keeping him "in his box." General Powell, who continued his term as chair of the Joint Chiefs of Staff under President Clinton, reportedly supported this variant. His emphasis was on the deterrence of regional aggression, as well as denying the Iraqi dictator the means to threaten the Gulf region. In characterizing this strategy, one Pentagon official familiar with General Powell's thinking said, "You treat Saddam like a toothache. There are periods when it doesn't hurt as much as other times, but it just doesn't go away and you never quite forget about it."[11] While keeping Saddam Hussein "in his box" in the near and intermediate term, the long-term aim of this application of comprehensive containment would be to erode Saddam Hussein's domestic power base and lead to his overthrow. The major liability of this strategy was that it relied on multilateral cooperation during a period when U.S. allies, as well as Iraq's regional neighbors, were suffering from "sanctions fatigue."

Since the end of the Gulf War in 1991, the U.S. policy debate about Iraq has revolved around these contending approaches. Like the Bush administration before it, the Clinton administration has struggled to reconcile the inherent tension between the two strategies—rollback to change the Baghdad regime versus comprehensive containment to "keep Saddam Hussein in his box." The primary policy arena in which this tension has been evident is in the ongoing struggle between Iraq and the Security Council over the implementation of UNSCR 687. Although Baghdad has claimed full compliance to win sanctions relief, UNSCOM has revealed a pattern of deception and obstruction that underscores the overriding priority that the Iraqi dictator places on the retention of his WMD capabilities. To maintain Security Council support for sanctions, the Clinton administration has focused on Iraqi compliance with UNSCR 687. Deliberate ambiguity between the two approaches was defended as a political necessity given the lack of international support for ousting Saddam Hussein. But that tactic generated confusion and raised a fundamental question, most assertively in Congress, about the ultimate objective of the administration's Iraq policy.

Multilateral economic sanctions may have proved insufficient in generating internal dissension to oust Saddam Hussein, but he would never have permitted UNSCOM inspections in Iraq without their coercive influence. To get the sanctions lifted, Saddam Hussein has pursued a political strategy that combines assertions of compliance with brazen acts of defiance. Since the Gulf War cease-fire and the codification of its terms under UNSCR 687, the Iraqi dictator has initiated periodic crises and exercises in brinkmanship to pressure the international community into ending the sanctions regime. These crises have ended only after the exercise of force, or the credible threat of force, by the United States and Britain. In December 1992–January 1993, Iraq activated air defenses in southern Iraq to challenge the "no-fly" zone and interfered with UNSCOM inspections of suspected WMD sites. Just before leaving office, President Bush ordered air strikes on those Iraqi military capabilities, as well as a cruise missile attack on a nuclear weapons facility at Za'afraniyah.[12] The Clinton administration's first significant use of force against Iraq was taken in June 1993, when cruise missiles struck Iraq's intelligence headquarters in Baghdad in retaliation for an April 1993 plot to assassinate President Bush during a visit to Kuwait.[13] (This episode demonstrated Saddam Hussein's own ability to "personalize" policy.) The next major showdown came in October 1994, when Saddam Hussein deployed 60,000 troops and 1,000 tanks along the Kuwaiti border. The United States responded with the regional deployment of an additional aircraft carrier and two ships with cruise missiles, along with 2,000 marines. Given the threat that coalition forces posed to his elite Republican Guard units, Saddam Hussein backed down and the Security Council passed a resolution that forbade the forward deployment of Iraqi troops along its southern border with Kuwait and Saudi Arabia.

In mid-1995, Iraq precipitated yet another crisis over UNSCOM inspections. Since its creation in 1991, UNSCOM, under the determined leadership of Ekeus, had documented a sustained pattern of Iraqi deception and concealment in defiance of UNSCR 687 (as well as UNSCRs 707 and 715, which also dealt with the destruction of Iraq's WMD capabilities). In February 1995, UNSCOM reported that Iraq was concealing its biological weapons (BW) program and had never accounted for seventeen tons of biological cultures that could produce BW capabilities. Iraqi representatives denied the charge and said that it was a "political fabrication" to maintain sanctions. In May 1995, Deputy Prime Minister Tariq Aziz signaled the start of another round of defiance and confrontation when he announced that future Iraqi cooperation concerning its BW program would be contingent on UNSCOM's certification that the conditions of UNSCR 687 had been met. UNSCOM rejected this ultimatum and, in turn, Saddam Hussein raised the political stakes by declaring in his Revolution Day speech on July 17 that Iraq would cease cooperation with the United Nations if sanctions were not lifted by August 31.[14]

With the Security Council poised for a renewed showdown with Iraq, Jordanian officials made the stunning announcement that Lt. General Hussein Kamel, the husband of Saddam Hussein's eldest daughter and czar of Iraq's WMD programs, had defected to Amman on August 8, 1995.[15] The defection broke the summer 1995 crisis and led to the uncovering of approximately 1.2 million pages of documents that Iraqi officials preposterously claimed Hussein Kamel had unilaterally withheld from UNSCOM. The documents dealt primarily with Iraq's clandestine nuclear program, but also covered its biological, chemical, and missile programs. UNSCOM declared that this additional documentation revealed Iraq's WMD procurement efforts to be "larger and more advanced in every dimension than previously declared."[16] Perhaps most ominous among the startling revelations was confirmation that Iraq had an offensive biological warfare program which had progressed to the deployment of missile warheads and aerial bombs loaded with botulinum toxin and anthrax spores. The new materials also documented a major smuggling effort by Iraq after the Gulf War cease-fire to covertly procure nonconventional weapons and missile components. In addition, UNSCOM's discoveries undercut the position of France and Russia, who had argued since 1994 that Iraq was on the verge of complying with the pertinent Security Council resolutions to eliminate its nonconventional weapons and should therefore be permitted to resume unfettered oil exports. The grim record of deception that emerged after the Hussein Kamel defection was testimony to the overriding priority that Saddam Hussein personally places on the retention of his regime's WMD capabilities. Ekeus underscored this crucial point in a 1997 interview at the end of his six-year tenure as UNSCOM's chief executive:

The systematic pursuit of the proscribed weapons and the huge funds thrown into their development point to a singular mind and extraordinary insistence. The present leader of Iraq has demonstrated that he has ambitions for his country reaching far outside the borders of Iraq. These grand designs of extended influence presuppose access to weapons of mass destruction and the means for their delivery. Even if there appears to be a commonly held view in the country's military and political circles that Iraq, because of its geopolitical situation, needs a special military capability to balance the presumed extension of Iran's sphere of influence, it is highly doubtful that any alternative Iraqi leadership would continue to pursue a weapons of mass destruction program, considering that the consequences of such a policy would be sanctions, political isolation and loss of huge financial revenues from blocked oil exports.[17]

The defection of Hussein Kamel revealed a deep rift within Saddam Hussein's ruling clique. The Clinton administration, hoping to use the crisis to revive the Gulf War coalition, suggested additional measures to ratchet up the economic pressure on Iraq. The goal was to undermine Saddam Hussein's power base and thereby create internal pressures that could lead to his ouster. But, as with previous threats to his personal survival, the Iraqi dictator was able to survive through the brutal efficiency of his internal security apparatus and luck. Equally important, Arab states were unwilling to move beyond comprehensive containment to an explicit rollback strategy. Despite increased American pressure after the Hussein Kamel defection, King Hussein declared that Jordan would not close its border with Iraq to tighten the sanctions regime.[18] A senior Saudi official acknowledged, "Nobody is interested right now in any serious change in Iraq. For [Saudi Arabia] the status quo is best. . . . [T]here is no alternative to Saddam except chaos on our borders, with Iranians, Turks and others playing a role that leads to the unknown."[19]

Although Hussein Kamel's defection yielded an intelligence windfall for UNSCOM and forced Baghdad to address the serious charges of noncompliance, Iraqi behavior rapidly reverted to what Secretary of State Madeleine Albright characterized as "denial, delay, and deceit." Throughout 1996, Iraq blocked UNSCOM inspectors from suspected WMD sites. Ekeus revealed that Iraq retained an operational Scud force, probably capable of delivering warheads with chemical or biological agents.[20] He further reported that Iraqi scientists were under orders to maintain readiness to rapidly reconstitute WMD capabilities, even if UNSCOM destroyed existing stocks: "We have documentary evidence about orders from the leadership to preserve a strategic capability. . . . That means to keep the production equipment ready to produce at any given moment."[21] American declaratory policy stiffened in response to Iraqi intransigence toward UNSCOM, as well as troop movements into the Kurdish "safe haven" in September 1996 that prompted a retaliatory U.S. cruise missile strike against air-defense targets in southern Iraq.

In March 1997, Albright declared a hard-line policy toward Iraq reminiscent of President Bush's May 1991 statement that sanctions would remain in place until Saddam Hussein was removed from power:

We do not agree with the nations who argue that if Iraq complies with its obligations concerning weapons of mass destruction, sanctions should be lifted. Our view, which is unshakable, is that Iraq must prove its peaceful intentions. It can only do that by complying with all of the Security Council Resolutions to which it is subject. . . . Is it possible to conceive of such a government under Saddam Hussein? . . . [T]he evidence is overwhelming that Saddam Hussein's intentions will never be peaceful. . . . Clearly, a change in Iraq's government could lead to a change in U.S. policy. Should that occur, we would stand ready, in coordination with our allies and friends, to enter rapidly into a dialogue with the successor regime.[22]

The most significant aspect of the March 1997 Albright speech (see Appendix) is that it reaffirmed an American policy that went beyond UNSCR 687. The resolution's key provision had stipulated that Iraq would be permitted to export oil freely if it complied with UN requirements relating to the dismantling of its WMD capabilities. Because it linked the lifting of economic sanctions to Iraqi compliance with *all* Security Council resolutions, many viewed the Albright speech as "moving the goalposts." The *Washington Post* offered the following editorial assessment: "Secretary of State Madeleine Albright . . . has said for the first time the American intent is to see President Hussein out and that the United States will not give up on the economic sanctions binding him until he is replaced. This has been implicit, or at least hoped-for, in anti-Hussein circles. Now it is explicit. . . . To suggest the United States is pursuing not just Iraq's compliance with UN resolutions but also Saddam Hussein's departure is a bold step in a world of fragile states."[23] Albright's address was delivered against a political backdrop of increasing "sanctions fatigue" in the international community. After nearly seven years, the tension between the United States and other members of the Security Council (with the notable exception of Britain) threatened to become an open rift when the next, inevitable crisis over UNSCOM inspections began to unfold in mid-1997.

Middle East historian Amatzia Baram observes that the October 1997 showdown was a deferred crisis—one that Saddam Hussein had been building toward in 1995 before the defection of his son-in-law and the resulting revelations about Iraq's WMD programs. Baram argues that Saddam Hussein's decision to initiate the autumn 1997 crisis was influenced by developments in the Security Council, most notably, diminishing support to meet Iraqi intransigence with the credible use of force.[24] This trend had been evident in June 1997 when Iraq's obstruction of UNSCOM inspections had produced a flaccid Security Council response—a threatened ban on travel for all officials involved in Iraq's military-industrial complex.[25] The eroded political will of the Security Council to back up its diplomacy with force increasingly put the United States and Britain at odds with France and Russia. In December 1996, for example, France politically distanced itself from the United States by withdrawing its air forces from the enforcement of the no-fly zone in northern Iraq.[26] It was also reported that the two giant French energy companies, Total and Elf-Acquitaine, had completed negotiations to exploit some of Iraq's largest oil reserves once sanctions were lifted.[27] In addition to these two external factors shaping Saddam Hussein's actions, Baram observes that his risk-taking propensity must also be viewed within the context of Iraqi domestic politics and Saddam Hussein's moves to maintain his domestic power base.

Ambassador Richard Butler of Australia, who succeeded Ekeus as UNSCOM chief, reported to the Security Council in early October 1997 that the outstanding issues with Iraq were "numerous and grave." This came on the heels of a letter from Aziz to the United Nations claiming that Baghdad had made a "full, final and complete disclosure" on its biological weapons programs.[28] In response to the Butler report, Iraq instigated the autumn 1997 crisis by demanding the exclusion of Americans from UNSCOM inspection teams and threatening to shoot down American U-2 surveillance aircraft. Iraqi foreign minister Mohammed Said al-Sahaf said that American policy had "put [Baghdad] in a corner and there was no alternative to stop dealing or cooperating with the elements who are blocking the lifting of sanctions."[29] As in the previous crises over the implementation of UNSCR 687, Saddam Hussein's objective was clear: to gain an UNSCOM certification of compliance while retaining covert WMD capabilities or the production equipment to rapidly reconstitute them. In mid-November, the Security Council responded to Iraq's acts of defiance by implementing a travel ban on Iraqi officials (threatened in June) and raising the possibility of unspecified "further measures." But, in the debate over this resolution, France and Russia reaffirmed their opposition to military action and tighter sanctions. President Hosni Mubarak of Egypt, reflecting Arab empathy for Iraq and the erosion of the Gulf War coalition, publicly expressed the hope that "there will be no military operations against Iraq," while the semi-official newspaper *Al-Ahram* came out in editorial support for the Iraqi position.[30] A European official complained that the American policy of comprehensive containment offered no way out of indefinite sanctions: "we need an exit strategy, a road map for Iraq too."[31]

As President Clinton dispatched a second U.S. aircraft carrier to the Gulf region as "a demonstration of our resolve," Russian foreign minister Yevgeny Primakov attempted to convince his erstwhile Soviet clients in Baghdad that they should resume cooperation with UNSCOM to stave off a military confrontation. A Primakov-brokered deal, however, quickly fell apart when the Iraqis refused to grant UNSCOM access to "presidential" and other "sensitive" sites. At a mid-December 1997 press conference, President Clinton asserted that his administration was "[standing] strong against a rogue regime in Iraq." When asked for his assessment of Saddam Hussein's motivation and whether he was "simply crazy," Clinton stated,

Well, if he is, he's clever crazy on occasions. . . . I think there was a calculated decision here that other countries wanted to do business with him. . . . And that the burden of maintaining the sanctions had wearied many of those with responsibility for doing so, and there might be a way to split the alliance here. I also think he knew that the suffering of the Iraqi people is something which has touched the hearts of the whole world and he thought it was a card he could play. . . . Finally, I think that he felt probably that the United States would never vote to lift the sanctions on him no matter what he did. There are some people who believe that. Now I think he was dead wrong on virtually every point. But I don't think it was a decision of a crazy person. I just think he badly miscalculated. . . .

Administration officials were privately stunned by the Security Council's indifference to Saddam Hussein's bald-faced challenge to UNSCOM.

From mid-January 1998, the Clinton administration began to raise publicly the possibility of military action with or without Security Council authorization. British prime minister Tony Blair agreed on the need to "educate" the publics in both countries, but also insisted on a final effort by UN Secretary-General Kofi Annan to broker a deal.[32] President Clinton, describing the need to contain the "predators of the 21st century," articulated U.S. policy objectives toward Iraq in a major address at the Pentagon on February 17: "If Saddam rejects the peace and we have to use force, our purpose is clear. We want to seriously diminish the threat posed by Iraq's weapons-of-mass-destruction program. We want to seriously reduce his capacity to threaten his neighbors. . . . The economic sanctions will remain in place until Saddam complies fully with all UN resolutions. . . . [T]he only answer to aggression and illegal behavior is firmness, determination, and—when necessary—action."[33] President Clinton concluded with the dilemma facing American policy-makers: "What if [Saddam Hussein] fails to comply and we fail to act, or we take *some ambiguous third route* which gives him yet more opportunities to develop this program of weapons of mass destruction and continue to press for the release of the sanctions and continue to ignore the solemn promises he made?"[34]

Although polls indicated strong public support for the administration's positions, the White House was rattled by a highly contentious "town meeting" in Columbus, Ohio, featuring the administration's top national security team. It was also concerned that an Annan mission to Baghdad would break the momentum toward military action. Proponents of the "hard option" within the administration favored a "five minutes before midnight" ultimatum to Iraq to end unconditionally its obstruction of UNSCOM inspections.

The administration's public diplomacy in January–February 1998 gave rise to concerns and criticism. Senior officials were unable to answer the questions raised from Ohio to Moscow about its "post-strike strategy." The Joint Chiefs of Staff, painfully recalling the unsuccessful use of airpower as an instrument of coercive diplomacy in Vietnam, cautioned the administration not to oversell what air strikes alone could accomplish politically or militarily.[35] Meanwhile, congressional Republicans and others who favored an explicit rollback strategy to overthrow Saddam Hussein criticized the administration for not being bolder in its articulated goals. Columnist Charles Krauthammer argued, "The real objective of any air campaign against Iraq must be to depose Saddam. . . . Let's be clear: A return to the status quo would be a defeat. It makes no sense to resume this war aiming so low."[36] The Clinton administration's diplomatic strategy to build a Security Council consensus to meet Iraq's defiance of UNSCR 687 with the threat of force required the White House to mute its own preference for a change in regime. President Clinton indirectly acknowledged the tension between rollback and a less ambitious containment strategy: "Would the Iraqi people be better off if there were a change in leadership? I certainly think they would be. But that is not what the United Nations has authorized us to do; that is not what our immediate interest is about. . . ."[37]

The October 1997–February 1998 crisis ended when Annan returned from Baghdad with a memorandum of understanding (MOU), signed by Deputy Prime Minister Aziz and verbally endorsed by Saddam Hussein. At a UN press conference on February 24 explaining the MOU, Annan said, "I think I can do business" with Saddam Hussein. The Iraqi dictator failed to gain the removal of Americans from the UNSCOM inspection teams and the setting of a date certain for the end of sanctions. But he did win some concessions, including restrictions on inspections of "presidential" sites and greater involvement of the secretary-general's office in the appointment and oversight of inspection teams. Significantly, the agreement brokered by Annan referred to paragraph 22 of UNSCR 687, which stipulates that the ban on Iraqi oil exports will be lifted once UNSCOM finds Baghdad in compliance with its arms control requirements. Since the Gulf War, the Bush and Clinton administrations have consistently asserted that sanctions will remain in place until Iraq complies with *all* Security Council resolutions, not just the WMD provisions of UNSCR

687. Senate Majority Leader Trent Lott (R-Miss.) scoffed at Annan's willingness to establish "a 'human relationship' with a mass murderer" and urged President Clinton to reject the deal: "It is always possible to get a deal if you give enough away."[38] In addressing this criticism of the MOU, Butler denied that UNSCOM's authority had been undermined. The Clinton administration expressed reservations about the conditions governing the inspection of "presidential" sites but accepted a British-drafted Security Council resolution codifying the Annan-Aziz MOU that also warned Iraq of "the severest consequences" if it reneged on the deal.[39]

The 1997–98 crisis starkly underlined the extent to which the international consensus for a hard-line policy toward Iraq had eroded. In its aftermath, the Clinton administration initiated a major interagency review of U.S. policy toward Iraq. According to the *Washington Post*, this secret, high-level review acknowledged that the erosion of diplomatic support severely limited the U.S. ability to back intrusive UNSCOM inspections with the threat of force. Given this political reality, the policy review concluded that the administration's primary focus should be on maintaining international backing for economic sanctions.[40] This led to a marked change in policy during April–August 1998. Notwithstanding administration denials, American strategy shifted from one of compellence (i.e., to force Iraqi cooperation with UNSCOM) to deterrence (i.e., to keep Saddam Hussein "in his box" and deter him from regional aggression).

In early August 1998, Iraq, again charging that UNSCOM inspections were a front for U.S. intelligence, announced its cessation of cooperation with UNSCOM and demanded that sanctions be lifted immediately. The Cairo-based Arab League, whose spokesperson said, "Iraq has fulfilled all its commitments concerning weapons of mass destruction," supported the Iraqi action.[41] Albright, invoking Cold War phraseology, stated that the United States would respond to the Iraqi move with force "if necessary," "on our timetable," and "at a time and place of our choosing." But this threat rang hollow and one observer concluded that the United States had indeed embarked on the "ambiguous third route" between Iraqi compliance and American compellence that President Clinton had warned against.[42] In August, a senior American weapons inspector, Scott Ritter, resigned from UNSCOM, claiming that U.S. officials had interceded to prevent obtrusive searches for fear of provoking a confrontation with Baghdad. Ritter charged that this made a "farce" of the commission's work and was "a surrender to [the] Iraqi leadership."[43] Albright defended the administration's moves as a tactical adjustment "to shine the spotlight on the decision Saddam Hussein had made [not to comply with the terms of the Annan-Aziz MOU] and not on whether a particular inspection would go forward. . . ."[44] The administration, responding to stiff congressional criticism following the Ritter resignation, claimed that the Security Council's decision in September to maintain sanctions until Iraq resumed cooperation with UNSCOM vindicated its actions. Despite the increasing isolation of the United States in the Security Council on Iraq, support for an explicit rollback strategy remained strong on Capitol Hill. In October 1998, an exasperated Congress authorized the Pentagon and the State Department to transfer up to $97 million in military aid to the fractured Iraqi exile movement for the explicit purpose of ousting the Iraqi dictator. The administration declared its support for the objectives of the Iraq Liberation Act, but questioned its feasibility. The issue of Saddam Hussein's opposition and the ability of these external groups to effect a change of regime in Baghdad will be discussed in the section on the Iraqi domestic environment.

During autumn 1998, the impasse between Iraq and the Security Council over UNSCOM inspections persisted. Although the Security Council did extend sanctions in September, the threat of force to compel Iraqi compliance appeared lifted. This development was cast against continuing press reports concerning the detection of VX nerve gas on Iraqi warheads from missiles uncovered by UNSCOM. Aziz said the report was politically motivated and "timed to sow confusion and suspicion" in order to prevent the lifting of sanctions.[45] Meanwhile, the *Washington Post* reported that UNSCOM had credible evidence, not confirmed by U.S. intelligence or the International Atomic Energy Agency, that Iraq possesses the shells of 3–4 nuclear devices, lacking only their cores of enriched uranium.[46] Against this political backdrop, the Security Council and Iraq began to explore a proposal developed by Annan for the resumption of UNSCOM inspections in conjunction with a "comprehensive review" of Iraq's compliance with the WMD provisions of UNSCR 687. The United States, supported by Britain, asserted that any "comprehensive review" must encompass all pertinent resolutions, not just those dealing with Iraq's WMD capabilities that survived the Gulf War.

In a mid-October 1998 interview with the editors of the *Washington Post*, Annan provided an assessment that reflected the degree to which international support for the U.S. hard-line policy toward Iraq had eroded: "I personally believe, as I think a lot of the Security Council members believe with 100 percent certainty, that Iraq being fully disarmed is never going to be possible. At the end of the day, the Security Council must decide whether Iraq is disarmed to the extent that it is not a threat to its neighbors . . . [and] that will be a political judgment. . . . What do you do when the will [to use force] is not there, when the council is divided, when you don't have public support?" Annan further expressed his view that UNSCOM would have to take a more conciliatory and flexible approach because it has "a very intrusive mandate in a situation where the government is very nationalistic."[47] To critics, the Annan position amounted to phony inspections and a sharp retreat from the cease-fire terms specified UNSCR 687.

In late 1998, the Clinton administration increasingly found itself caught between the contending views of the Congress and the Security Council. In Washington, Capitol Hill was pushing for an explicit rollback strategy linked to substantial military assistance to the Iraqi opposition. In New York, the Security Council, consistent with Annan's comments, was moving toward the position that sanctions should be lifted if Iraq demonstrated "significant progress" in its compliance with the WMD provisions (paragraph 22) of UNSCR 687. The Clinton administration faced a policy dilemma: Congress's preference for a rollback strategy to change the Baghdad regime was considered unrealistic, while the Security Council's drift toward a loose interpretation of UNSCR 687 would allow Saddam Hussein to rapidly reconstitute his WMD capabilities.

In November 1998, the Clinton administration reacted to Saddam Hussein's defiance of UNSCOM. A major motivation underlying its moves in early November toward the use of force was the preservation of U.S. credibility after a succession of threats that were never acted on. One senior official made a self-mocking reference to the administration's image of conducting "diplomacy backed by meetings."[48] As the United States bolstered its military position in the Gulf region in anticipation of air strikes, Annan again interceded with the Baghdad regime to avert conflict. On November 14, the day of the planned air assault, Aziz sent Annan a letter pledging to resume cooperation with UNSCOM.[49] This last-minute backing down appeared a repeat of the February 1998 crisis. But the Clinton administration, which had assiduously worked to win international acquiescence (if not support) for its position, believed that it could not carry out air strikes while the UN secretary-general was proclaiming Iraq ready to resume compliance with UNSCR 687. The *Washington Post* reported that Clinton's decision to abort the raids had been opposed by some of his top national security advisers, including Albright and Secretary of Defense William Cohen.[50] Although military action was averted in mid-November 1998, President Clinton and Prime Minister Blair stated that there would be no future warning if Iraq reneged on its renewed commitment. In the wake of the November crisis, former secretary of state Henry Kissinger criticized the Clinton administration for allowing Saddam Hussein to control the subject and timing of the confrontation and for "becom[ing] captive to a fragile U.N. consensus"; he argued that any future U.S. military action against Baghdad should be substantial and aimed squarely at the institutions maintaining Saddam Hussein in power.[51]

On December 15, Butler reported that Iraq was violating its November commitment and again obstructing inspections. This "triggering authority" (in the words of a NSC spokesperson) led to four days of sustained air attacks by the United States and Britain.[52] The air campaign, code-named Operation Desert Fox, relied heavily on cruise missiles and was the most extensive use of force against Iraq since the Gulf War in 1991. Clinton administration officials vociferously denied that Butler had prepared the report to serve U.S. political objectives and that the timing of the raids had no connection to the ongoing impeachment proceedings in the House of Representatives. Senate Majority Leader Lott was not persuaded on the latter point: "I cannot support this military action in the Persian Gulf at this time. Both the timing and the policy are subject to question."[53]

During the four-day air campaign, Albright and Cohen and National Security Adviser Sandy Berger declared that the U.S. commitment to use force against Iraq was open-ended.[54] But to what end? At the outset of Operation Desert Fox, Cohen stated that the goal was to degrade Iraq's WMD capabilities and "not to destabilize the regime."[55] The Clinton administration was caught politically between domestic critics, who wanted more sustained air attacks aimed at undermining Saddam Hussein, and the Security Council, whose majority was reflexively opposed to the use of force and sought only Iraq's compliance with UNSCR 687. Addressing the tension between these twin objectives, Berger stated, "The strategy we can and will pursue is to contain Saddam in the short and medium term, by force if necessary, and to work toward a new government over the long term."[56]

When Operation Desert Fox concluded, U.S. and British forces had flown more than three hundred combat sorties and fired more than four hundred cruise missiles at Iraqi targets. In early January 1999, General Henry Shelton, chair of the Joint Chiefs of Staff, reported to Congress that the raids had inflicted more damage than originally estimated.[57] He said that the air attacks had killed "several key individuals" in the Iraqi hierarchy, as well as 600–1,600 troops of the Republican Guard, which Saddam Hussein relies on for internal security. Shelton also cited unconfirmed reports that the raids had triggered significant internal dissent, indicating that "[Saddam Hussein] was shaken and the regime was shaken."[58] In the United Nations, a majority of Security Council members opposed any further military action against Iraq without explicit approval and many favored the creation of a new arms inspection regime to succeed UNSCOM.[59] In addition, the United States was increasingly isolated, as France and Arab states lobbied for a lifting of economic sanctions to relieve the suffering of the Iraqi people.[60] This sympathy, however, did not extend to Saddam Hussein, who angered Arab governments by strongly castigating them as "accomplices" of the United States and "silent devils."[61] Egyptian president Mubarak shot back in an interview with a government newspaper: "We opposed the air attack because in the final reckoning, it is the people of Iraq who pay the price. . . . [T]he regime in power is the root of all problems."[62]

THE IRAQI DOMESTIC CONTEXT

Since the Saddam Hussein regime is the target of U.S. strategy, the success of American policy will be judged, in large part, on its ability to favorably influence the Iraqi domestic environment. The focus of this section is on the nature of that internal milieu—in particular, the institutional and familial underpinnings of Saddam Hussein's power base. A historical review of modern Iraq under Saddam Hussein reveals complex and important linkages between the regime's domestic and foreign policies. At times, domestic considerations have contributed to the Iraqi dictator's greatest strategic miscalculations. He has also proved strikingly adept at manipulating external actors to bolster his domestic power base.

Consider the following episodes. Saddam Hussein's decision to invade Iran in September 1980 was motivated by concern that the Teheran regime's Islamic revolutionary character might undermine his control over the Shia population in southern Iraq. Ten years later, Saddam Hussein's next act of external aggression—his unilateral decision to invade Kuwait—was occasioned by a severe domestic economic crisis following the Iran-Iraq War and the mistaken perception that the international community would acquiesce to it. In turn, the Gulf War, which resulted from his invasion of Kuwait, precipitated the gravest domestic crisis of his rule, simultaneous Kurdish and Shiite uprisings that threatened the unity of the Iraqi state. Following the Gulf War, economic hardship caused by the sanctions regime and runaway inflation prompted Saddam

Hussein to reluctantly accept the United Nations's "oil for food" proposal (UNSCR 986). That humiliation prompted the Iraqi leader to shore up his domestic power base by defying the international community through a military move into the Kurdish "safe haven" in September 1996. Finally, during the October 1997–February 1998 crisis, Saddam Hussein was able to exploit fissures within the international community in order to weaken the weapons inspections regime and thereby demonstrate to his domestic constituencies that he had a political strategy for the lifting of sanctions.[63] Political scientists Daniel Byman, Kenneth Pollack, and Matthew Waxman have persuasively argued that "the best way to coerce Saddam's regime is to target its 'centre of gravity' [Clausewitz's term]: the relationship between Saddam and his power base."[64]

Before returning to the issue of U.S. policy options toward Iraq, it is necessary to describe briefly the nature and political dynamics of Saddam Hussein's "power base." Middle East security specialists Anthony Cordesman and Ahmed Hashim characterize it as "a permeating *informal* political structure of power based on ethnicity and ties of kinship and long-standing friendships, and a vast *formal* structure of power based on state institutions."[65] In practice, these two spheres of power are interconnected, for Saddam Hussein has placed members of his family and tribe into key institutions, particularly those that make up the regime's military-industrial complex and internal security apparatus. The Iraqi political system revolves around Saddam Hussein and has become largely a reflection of his personality. His centrality gives new meaning to the phrase *l'état, c'est moi.* Saddam Hussein has been able effectively to exploit that centrality within the Iraqi system to maintain the fidelity of his core constituency groups by arguing that his demise would lead to collapse and chaos: *après moi, le déluge.* Apart from North Korea's Kim Jong Il (who has carried on the tradition of his late father, Kim Il Sung), no contemporary world leader has created a cult of personality to rival that of Saddam Hussein. Drawing on the nation's rich archeological legacy, the regime's efforts at political iconography have gone so far as to portray the Iraqi dictator in slogans and art as a modern-day Nebuchadnezzar.[66] This cult of personality complements his use of repression and economic incentives as a key instrument of political control.

Saddam Hussein has proven to be a master in the art of political survival. In the wake of the Gulf War, he survived simultaneous uprisings on Iraq's periphery—in the Kurdish north and the Shiite south. As noted above, the conventional wisdom, shared by the Bush administration, was that the trauma of the war and the humiliation of his expulsion from

Kuwait would lead to Saddam Hussein's ouster, most likely at the hands of the Iraqi military or some other element of his power base. To be sure, the post–Gulf War revolts in the north and south posed a grave threat to the regime. But some observers argued that these challenges on the Iraqi periphery, paradoxically, might have pushed the regime's officer corps toward Saddam Hussein in order to defend the country's Sunni heartland. This episode reveals the complex interrelationship between the politics of Iraq's "periphery" and that of its "center." The core of Saddam Hussein's power base is Iraq's Sunni Arab minority (augmented by a cadre of Shiite and Christian loyalists, such as Deputy Prime Minister Aziz). This Sunni "center" comprises four provinces, one of which, Saladin, includes Saddam Hussein's home city of Takrit. Saddam has been able to draw on the support of his own "Takriti" clans, as well as the loose confederation of other Sunni tribes inhabiting this core region. He has continued the process initiated by the Baath Party after it seized power in 1968 to use the traditional source of power and legitimacy vested in the tribes as an integral part of his informal political structure:

The Baath Party, with its pretensions of being a modern Arab socialist political organization, has long been ambivalent about its reliance on traditional authority structures rooted in the tribes. Indeed, as Amatzia Baram observes, "The presence of so many tribesmen within the elite military units and security services . . . gave them the access to Saddam and the levers of power needed to overthrow the regime, while their tribal loyalties occasionally took precedence over their loyalty to the regime and furnished a ready-made network to recruit coup plotters."[67] During the post–Gulf War period, Saddam Hussein has faced a severe challenge to maintain the loyalty of the key Sunni tribes.

The Sunni tribal confederation constitutes the outer circle of Saddam Hussein's informal power structure. His inner circle comprises those individuals whose bonds of loyalty are even tighter and more longstanding—his extended network of relatives and friends from Takrit. Saddam Hussein has placed this cadre of loyalists from his informal power structure into key positions in the country's formal institutional structure, especially the military and security services. During the post–Gulf War period, Saddam Hussein's rivaling sons, Uday and Qusay, rose to greater prominence. Uday became a leading profiteer from the sanctions regime and was given command over a praetorian security detail called Saddam's Feda'iyeen (Saddam's Commandos), as well as control of three newspapers and a television station. Qusay was made head of the dreaded Amn al-Khass (Special Security Organization, or SSO), with broad responsibility for the regime's security and intelligence apparatus. Members of Saddam Hussein's inner circle—a Takriti mafia ranging from cousins to half-brothers to members of his extended clan—were placed into other key institutional positions. These appointments continued the pattern established by Saddam Hussein since his assumption of the presidency in 1979. Just as he has faced challenges in the outer circle of his power base (i.e., the Sunni tribal confederation), so too has he been confronted with a grave crisis in his inner circle, the extended family. In August 1995, his son-in-law, Hussein Kamel al-Majid, defected to Jordan. The precipitant of Hussein Kamel's defection appears to have been a personal feud with Uday rather than a policy dispute with Saddam Hussein.

At the time, many observers viewed this defection of a key member of the inner circle, the father of Saddam Hussein's grandchildren, as portending the demise of the Iraqi dictator. In its aftermath, however, Saddam Hussein again proved skillful at managing what Middle East expert Charles Tripp refers to as the "politics of patrimonialism." Under Saddam Hussein's tacit direction, the defector's clan, the al-Majids, disavowed Hussein Kamel, who found himself increasingly isolated and dismissed as a serious Iraqi political figure in Amman. When he returned to Baghdad in February 1996 under the ostensible protection of Saddam Hussein and his puppet Revolutionary Command Council, the al-Majids extracted revenge for his dishonoring of the clan by murdering him and many in his immediate family. This was a dramatic exercise of the Iraqi dictator's informal structure of power: the challenge arose from Saddam Hussein's inner circle and, in turn, he used that circle (and in particular, the defector's clan) to eradicate the threat and assert his control.

Under Saddam Hussein's rule, the formal institutions of the Iraqi state—the Revolutionary Command Council (RCC), the Baath Party, the cabinet departments, and the military—have been transformed into instruments to maintain Saddam Hussein's domestic power base. To cite one prominent example, the Baath Party has been stripped of a pan-Arabist orientation that dated from the 1960s. Although some of the party's old guard remain on the political scene, their government positions are dependent on their obeisance to Saddam Hussein. Iraq's formal structures are little more than an institutional facade for Saddam Hussein's domestic power base. In describing what he refers to as the "family-tribe-state symbiosis," Baram writes, "At the helm in Baghdad is one man: the president, who imposes his will on the party luminaries, the army officers' corps, and the nation through his family, which controls the rural tribal praetorian guard."[68] Therefore, to understand the dynamics of political power in Saddam Hussein's Iraq, one must look at the kinship ties that underlie the formal institutional structure of state power. Tripp characterizes the nature of this "patrimonial" system and how it reinforces the bond between Saddam Hussein and his followers:

> It has been common knowledge that the present regime of Saddam Hussein has been heavily weighted in favor of his immediate and distant relatives in the inner circles of power. . . . This does not mean that all the people favored by Saddam Hussein come from this background; rather, it means that those who are placed in positions that give them a degree of unsupervised power have been largely from this "community." . . . [A]s the crises besetting Iraq have built up, this community consists of people so closely identified with Saddam Hussein that he can have some confidence that their fear that they may share his fate gives them a strong incentive to preserve his rule.[69]

The main theme of this section has been the complex linkages between Saddam Hussein's domestic and foreign policies—and the primacy of his drive to maintain his domestic power base. Attention will now turn to three key episodes during the post–Gulf War period in which these dimensions of Iraqi policy-making were evident: first, Saddam Hussein's reluctant acceptance of UNSCR 986 in May 1996, thereby permitting the resumption of monitored oil exports to finance Baghdad's purchase of food and medical supplies; second, his September 1996 military incursion into the Kurdish "safe haven" in defiance of the allied coalition; and third, his showdown with the United States and the Security Council over UNSCOM inspections in 1997–98.

Saddam Hussein's acceptance of the "oil for food" plan codified in UNSCR 987 was an action forced on the Iraqi dictator by a domestic economic crisis that became acute in late 1995. After the imposition of multilateral economic sanctions following the August 1990 invasion of Kuwait, Saddam Hussein strove to insulate Iraq's Sunni "center," in general, and his domestic power base (numbering approximately one million people, by Baram's estimate), in particular, from privation. Over time, however, even the country's Sunni heartland began to experience serious food shortages, as well as a wicked combination of price inflation and currency deflation. Saddam Hussein's domestic political strategy was to shift the blame for the country's economic crisis onto the United States and Britain because of their key role in the maintenance of the sanctions regime (which was reaffirmed by a Security Council vote every sixty days). He also claimed that the UN "oil for food" plan, in which the international organization would play a central role in the monitoring of Iraqi oil exports and the disbursement of humanitarian aid, was an unacceptable infringement on Iraqi sovereignty. This argument gained considerable political traction internationally; many Arab states argued that the sanctions appeared a vindictive act aimed at the Iraqi people. Given the absence of any mechanism to measure public opinion, it is difficult to assess the extent to which the Iraqi people indeed held the United States, rather than Saddam Hussein, responsible for their dire straits. The Clinton administration countered that Saddam Hussein, who was spending lavishly to rebuild his opulent network of presidential palaces, was squandering money that could otherwise be spent to improve his country's standard of living.

For Saddam Hussein, the Iraqi people's suffering (evidenced by increased infant mortality, declining caloric intake, etc.) became another policy instrument to further his objectives. While siphoning off resources to maintain living standards for the million people that made up his domestic power base, he cynically used human suffering for political leverage in the Security Council's sparring over sanctions. Saddam Hussein long resisted the "oil for food" plan because accepting UNSCR 986 would mean giving up this powerful propaganda tool in his struggle to have sanctions lifted on his terms. His decision in January–February 1996 to accept UNSCR 986 can be attributed to two major factors. First, after Hussein Kamel's revelations concerning Iraq's WMD capabilities, France and Russia advised Baghdad that sanctions would continue for the foreseeable future. Second, and perhaps most important, economic conditions were seriously deteriorating to the point of potentially threatening the stability of his domestic power base. The economic crisis, coupled with assurances that France and Russia would push for an early end to sanctions, were evidently sufficient to win Saddam Hussein's approval of an "oil for food" plan that he had long rejected. In May 1996, after several months of negotiation, Iraq and the United Nations signed the agreement that permits Baghdad to sell one billion dollars' worth of oil every ninety days under UN monitoring.[70] Iraqi haggling over issues such as the number of UN monitors permitted and U.S. insistence that the international community, not Baghdad, administer the distribution of food in Kurdish areas, however, stalled the implementation of the agreement.

The implementation of UNSCR 986 was further delayed by Saddam Hussein's military incursion into the Kurdish "safe haven" in August–September 1996. Indeed, Saddam Hussein's record supports the interpretation that his perceived humiliation in accepting UNSCR 986 under pressure was the likely precipitant of his counteraction in northern Iraq.[71] This conjunction of events again highlights the close linkages between

Saddam Hussein's domestic and foreign policies, as well as the politics of the "center" and the "periphery." Thus, while the international community was compelling his acceptance of the "oil for food" plan on its terms out of his need to economically stabilize the "center," he made a dramatic move to challenge the allied coalition's political authority over Iraq's northern "periphery." The occasion for the Iraqi attack on Irbil, the regional capital of the Kurdish enclave, was renewed infighting between the rival ethnic factions—the Kurdish Democratic Party (KDP), led by Massoud Barzani, and the Patriotic Union of Kurdistan (PUK), headed by Jalal Talabani. In response to Iranian support for PUK attacks on the KDP in spring 1996, Barzani entered into a tactical alliance with Iraq. In late August, three Republican Guard divisions and other Iraqi units (numbering some thirty thousand men and four hundred tanks) seized Irbil, expelling the PUK and turning control over to the KDP. During this brief occupation, Iraqi intelligence officers executed dozens of operatives of the Iraqi National Congress, the U.S.-created umbrella organization of the externally based Iraqi opposition. The Clinton administration retaliated for the Iraqi military incursion in southern Iraq (where U.S. cruise missiles struck Iraqi air defense units). The United States also announced the extension of the southern no-fly zone from the 32nd to the 33rd parallel (reaching the southern suburbs of Baghdad) and a further delay in the implementation of UNSCR 986, but no military steps were taken against the Iraqi units engaged in the Kurdish action. The American cruise missile attacks prompted Saddam Hussein to call off a threatened attack on the PUK stronghold at Sulaymaniyah and to withdraw his ground forces from the Kurdish zone. *New York Times* correspondent Elaine Sciolino noted that the Irbil crisis had embroiled the United States in Iraqi internal politics: "The irony is that the [PUK] faction that benefits from the American intervention . . . is currently supported by Iran, the world's leading 'rogue state' in Washington's view."[72]

Saddam Hussein was politically strengthened by his military incursion into northern Iraq in August–September 1996. The move bolstered his domestic power base by demonstrating his regime's ability to flex its military muscle anywhere in the country in defiance of the Security Council. In addition, the intervention reinforced the political wedge between the Kurdish factions, constituted a major setback for the U.S.-backed Iraqi resistance movement, and revived the morale of Saddam Hussein's military (purged earlier that summer following an abortive coup). Finally, Saddam Hussein, who is prone to major strategic miscalculation (witness his catastrophic decisions to invade Iran and Kuwait), did not overplay his hand.

When confronted with the credible threat of additional American military action after the initial round of cruise missile strikes, he withdrew across the cease-fire line and dispersed his Republican Guard units.

A year after the Kurdish crisis, Saddam Hussein provoked a major showdown with the United Nations over weapons inspections. The earlier discussion of the October 1997–February 1998 crisis identified the key external factors influencing the timing of Saddam Hussein's decision. Most notable among these were declining international support for the use of force in response to Iraqi noncompliance and a major political fissure in the Security Council, pitting the United States and Britain against France and Russia. Saddam Hussein's action must also be viewed, however, in the context of Iraqi domestic politics—in particular, his overriding political objective of maintaining his power base. The Iraqi dictator is evidently motivated by the belief that a perceived capitulation to UNSCOM and the total loss of high-prestige WMD capabilities will diminish his standing with the regime's security establishment.[73] Saddam Hussein has linked his own fate to the survivability of Iraq's WMD capabilities by placing them under the control of his presidential guard, the SSO, headed by his son Qusay. Thus, any U.S. military strike on Iraq's WMD capabilities is, in effect, an attack on Saddam Hussein personally. Indeed, UNSCOM officials believe that SSO units shuttled Iraq's WMD assets around Saddam Hussein's network of presidential palaces to defeat the UNSCOM inspection regime. A senior UNSCOM official refers to this tactic as Iraq's "philosophy of concealment through mobility."

The value that Saddam Hussein attaches to preserving his nonconventional weapons is underscored by his willingness to forego an estimated $120 billion in oil revenue since the end of the Gulf War—funds that could be financing Iraqi reconstruction. But, in accepting this steep price, Saddam Hussein needs to demonstrate to his domestic power base that that his unyielding political strategy is an instrumental defiance—specifically, that it will lead to the lifting or erosion of sanctions while preserving the regime's nonconventional capabilities.[74] The Iraqi dictator laid out his scenario for the ending of sanctions in his Revolution Day speech on July 17, 1998. In this major address to the Iraqi people, Saddam Hussein, acknowledging the Clinton administration's pledge to veto any Security Council move to end sanctions as long as he remained in power, asserted, "The blockade will not be lifted by unanimous Security Council resolution, as intended when it was first imposed. Rather, it will erode."[75]

With the decreasing likelihood that economic sanctions will lead to Saddam Hussein's ouster, what are the alternative paths to political change in

Iraq? The possibilities identified by Middle East policy analysts can be divided into two categories.[76] The first alternative, the one that the Bush administration believed would happen in the traumatic aftermath of the Gulf War, would be a move against Saddam Hussein from elements within his domestic power base, such as the military or the Sunni elite. The major concern about such a scenario is that someone deeply implicated in the crimes of his regime could replace Saddam Hussein (what some experts refer to as "Saddamism without Saddam"). This result would likely mean the continuation of a highly authoritarian system based on patrimony and tribal affiliation (as in Hafiz al-Assad's Syria), but one which is less menacing to Iraq's regional neighbors. Whatever its political lineage, any successor regime to Saddam Hussein could probably initiate Iraq's rapid reintegration into the international community. Given the Iraqi dictator's formidable internal security apparatus, it is impossible to predict if and when a disgruntled or ambitious member of the inner circle might attempt a coup d'état. Former Reagan defense official Richard Perle, among other critics of the Clinton administration's Iraq policy, faulted the CIA for devoting too much of its resources to ill-conceived covert operations rather than working with the externally based Iraqi opposition.[77]

This second alternative path to political change in Iraq has received increased attention since the October 1997–February 1998 crisis over weapon inspections. With strong congressional prodding, President Clinton signed the Iraq Liberation Act of 1998 in late October to provide up to $97 million in military aid to the Iraqi opposition. The primary recipient of this assistance program is the Iraqi National Congress (INC), favored by Congress to lead an overt military campaign against the Saddam Hussein regime. One proposal, advanced by retired Army general Wayne Downing on Capitol Hill, calls for the creation of an INC military force in the Kurdish zone under the protection of U.S. airpower. Proponents pointed to the April 1991 success of the Kurdish militias in pushing Saddam Hussein's forces from northern Iraq with U.S. military support as an example of how such a force could be used.[78] Critics argued that it could lead to a post–Cold War "Bay of Pigs" debacle. A *New York Times* editorial titled "Expensive Fantasies on Iraq" argued, "Instead of dreaming about military rebellions, Washington should devote its energy and resources to preventing Baghdad from rebuilding an arsenal of biological and chemical weapons."[79] With its explicit embrace of a rollback strategy, the Iraq Liberation Act of 1998 reflected Washington's most ambitious policy aspiration. And yet, even after the December 1998 air campaign had weakened Saddam Hussein's domestic power base, General Anthony Zinni told the Senate Armed Services Committee, "I don't see an opposition group that has the viability to overthrow Saddam at this point."[80] Given the weakness of the externally based political opposition, Saddam Hussein is unlikely to be dislodged from power, absent a coup d'état. Although such an event cannot be predicted, Washington could provide incentives to encourage internal dissent. Indeed, because of their fear about the possible fragmentation of Iraq if the challenge should come from external opposition groups on the periphery, most Arab governments would prefer a regime change originating from within the country's Sunni core.[81]

POLICY ASSESSMENT

The record of U.S. policy toward Iraq since the Gulf War is mixed. Assessing the relative success or failure of American efforts to contain Saddam Hussein is complicated by Washington's occasionally contradictory objectives. During the post–Gulf War period, the emphasis of U.S. policy has oscillated between rollback to change the Baghdad regime and comprehensive containment to "keep Saddam Hussein in his box." The inherent political tension between the two strategies has been evident, most prominently, in the Clinton administration's dealings with Congress over Iraq policy, as well as in U.S. efforts to maintain a multilateral policy in the Security Council. Managing these relationships, particularly in the United Nations, has led to ambiguity about the ends of U.S. policy—specifically, whether the ouster of Saddam Hussein should be an explicit objective or not. It is striking that shortly before President Clinton signed the Iraq Liberation Act, Marine Corps General Anthony Zinni, who heads the U.S. Central Command, criticized the legislation. In his assessment, because no "viable" opposition to Saddam Hussein currently exists, any effort to oust the Iraqi dictator could fragment the country and destabilize the region. He further argued that Iran, given its WMD programs and the continuing influence of radical anti-American forces within Teheran's ruling regime, poses a greater long-term threat to U.S. interests than Iraq.[82] The juxtaposition of the signing of the Iraq Liberation Act and Zinni's critique reflected the continuing tension within American policy: rollback or comprehensive containment? This tension continues to engender confusion and a potential drift toward what President Clinton himself warned of as "an ambiguous third route."

Although President Bush expressed personal disquiet over Saddam Hussein's political survival at the end of the Gulf War, his administration did not embrace an explicit rollback strategy that could have ousted him. The Bush administration did not support the Kurdish and Shiite uprisings that erupted in the wake of the February 1991 ground war, for an amalgam of politically plausible reasons: fear that these ethnic and sectarian insurrections could lead to a breakup of the country; belief that the extension of the war into Iraq would lead to the defection of Arab states from the Gulf War coalition; opposition in the U.S. military to being drawn into an Iraqi civil war and an open-ended occupation of the country; and the political assessment in Washington that Saddam Hussein was likely to be removed by elements of his own regime following the Kuwaiti debacle. In May 1991, when it was evident that the Gulf War trauma was not going to generate Saddam Hussein's immediate ouster, the Bush administration embraced a strategy of comprehensive containment and declared that sanctions would remain in place as long as the Iraqi dictator ruled in Baghdad.

Several members of the Gulf War coalition faulted the United States for making Saddam Hussein the issue. They have argued that the Bush and Clinton administrations' objective of ousting the Iraqi dictator goes beyond the pertinent Security Council resolutions and undercuts whatever incentive Saddam Hussein might have to cooperate with UNSCOM. An assessment reflective of this concern was made by President Mubarak's chief political adviser, Osama Baz: "The Iraqi regime seems to hold the view that no matter what they do, they will be targeted by the United States. So they say, 'If the game is to topple us, then we'd be crazy to cooperate any further.' "[83]

Notwithstanding this critique, the Bush and Clinton administrations viewed comprehensive containment as the most effective means of exacerbating Saddam Hussein's domestic problems and creating a tangible incentive for his ouster by potential coup-makers. In its initial formulation, this strategy would keep Saddam Hussein "in his box" and strip him of his WMD capabilities, while the corrosive power of economic sanctions eroded his domestic power base and led to a regime change. Saddam Hussein's ability to frustrate the American strategy of comprehensive containment can be attributed to two interconnected factors: first and foremost, his success in insulating his domestic power base from the consequences of economic sanctions; and second, the erosion of international support for the continuation of sanctions ("sanctions fatigue"), as well as for the use of force to compel Iraqi cooperation with UNSCOM (as mandated in UNSCR 687). As Baram puts it, Saddam Hussein was winning the "contest" between the erosion of the international coalition and that of his own domestic power base. That success, in turn, reduced the chances of a coup or any meaningful internal challenge to his rule.

In 1998–99, the failure of comprehensive containment to oust Saddam Hussein pushed the policy debate on Iraq in two directions. The first, strongly advocated by Congress, was the hard-line turn toward an explicit rollback approach, as manifested in the Iraq Liberation Act. This policy was a post–Cold War analogue to the Reagan Doctrine, which supported insurgency movements to overthrow pro-Soviet regimes in the Third World during the 1980s. The approach discussed in conjunction with the passage of the Iraq Liberation Act called, in essence, for the implementation of the strategy that the Bush administration had balked at in 1991. The plan would entail the use of the northern Kurdish zone (and, potentially, the southern Shiite zone) as "liberated" areas to which disaffected Iraqi military units could defect and from which the INC, backed by American airpower, could strike at Iraq's Sunni heartland. During the February 1998 showdown with Iraq over UNSCOM inspections, Middle East specialist Fouad Ajami argued that such an approach would require the Clinton administration "to accept a burden dodged by those who waged Desert Storm: the remaking of the Iraqi state and the unseating of Saddam. We should be rid of the fears that paralyzed us in the past—the rise of the Shia, the fragmentation of Iraq. These are scarecrows."[84] Critics of the rollback approach, however, continued to focus on the serious concerns that had dogged this strategic option since the end of the Gulf War. As discussed above, most notable among these were the military effectiveness of the Iraqi opposition and the lack of regional support for this objective.

While Congress pushed the Clinton administration (including a reluctant Pentagon) to implement an explicit rollback strategy, the Security Council and Arab states increasingly favored a shift from comprehensive to a more limited containment policy. The United States faced the choice of either pursuing a maximalist strategy unilaterally or developing a new approach with narrowed objectives to win multilateral support. Declining international support for comprehensive containment was manifested in the erosion of the sanctions regime and the lack of political will in the Security Council to compel Iraq's cooperation with UNSCOM through the use of force, if necessary. A strategy of limited containment would focus on deterring Saddam Hussein from regional aggression and denying him the means, both conventional and nonconventional, of threatening his neighbors. The goal would be to "keep Saddam Hussein in his box," not to change the Baghdad regime. The mechanisms to achieve this objective would include passive measures (e.g., an arms transfer ban and rigid export controls), but would retain the military option if Saddam Hussein were to threaten a breakout from his "box" (e.g., the mobilization of Iraqi forces on the Kuwaiti border).

Pollack characterizes such a strategy of "narrow containment" as follows: "The goals of a policy of narrow containment are to prevent Saddam Husayn's Iraq from making mischief beyond its borders and to limit the forces the Iraqi dictator would have for aggression. . . . Narrow containment is not intended to cause the collapse of Saddam Husayn's regime—only to prevent it from destabilizing the Gulf. It is not intended to bring about Saddam's overthrow. To the extent that it does try to exert pressure on Saddam (pressure that could, theoretically, lead to his overthrow) it does so to limit his freedom of action."[85] Pollack points to the successful containment of North Korea since 1953 as an example in which the United States was able to coordinate a small working coalition (with Japan and South Korea) that operates independently of the Security Council. Proponents of limited or "narrow" containment argue that this option would essentially make the best of a bad situation given the political reality of eroded international support for comprehensive containment. It would focus on the central concerns relating to Iraq's foreign policy behavior (e.g., development of WMD capabilities) and establish "red lines" that would trigger penalties for unacceptable behavior. After Operation Desert Fox, UNSCOM chief Butler reported to the Security Council that Iraq was still actively concealing its WMD programs and that Secretary-General Annan's main interlocutor during the February and November 1998 crises, Deputy Prime Minister Aziz, had a central role in this effort. In the Security Council, Russia and France push for the easing of sanctions, whereas a competing British and Dutch proposal (supported by the Clinton administration) would require Iraq to meet specific benchmarks set by inspectors before such a move would even be considered.[86]

A strategy of limited containment may reflect the political realities in the international community, but it is anathema to major constituencies in the United States, most notably in Congress. Thus, the duality of the American policy debate on Iraq—"keeping Saddam Hussein in his box" through limited containment versus ousting him through a rollback strategy—is likely to persist as long as the Iraqi dictator rules in Baghdad. Although there may be a political tension between containment and rollback strategies, they are not mutually exclusive. As National Security

Adviser Berger declared in the wake of the December 1998 air campaign, Washington seeks Saddam Hussein's containment in the short to medium term and his ouster from power in the longer term. Whatever one's position in this policy debate, however, all parties agree on the central role of Saddam Hussein. A decade after Desert Storm, the question remains whether he can hold onto power and, should he be ousted, what type of Iraq can emerge from his legacy of totalitarian, personalized rule.

NOTES

[1] Reported in Walter Pincus, "Bush Says He Hoped Saddam Would Flee Iraq," *Washington Post*, September 2, 1998, p. A2.

[2] Michael R. Gordon and Bernard E. Trainor, *The General's War: The Inside Story of the Conflict in the Gulf* (Boston: Little, Brown, 1995), p. 443. Pages 452–53 describe secret contingency plans developed by members of General Schwarzkopf's CENTCOM (Central Command) for an offensive to take Baghdad.

[3] Cited in Anthony H. Cordesman and Ahmed S. Hashim, *Iraq: Sanctions and Beyond* (Boulder, CO: Westview, 1997), p. 4.

[4] In *The General's War*, p. 456, Gordon and Trainor dispute the Bush administration's contention that a major factor underlying its decision not to support the Kurdish and Shiite uprisings was Saudi and Turkish opposition. They report that the Saudis were in favor of providing military aid to the Shiites on the model of U.S. support for the Afghan mujahideen and that Turkish president Turqut Ozal also wanted to continue efforts to topple Saddam Hussein.

[5] Kenneth Katzman, "Iraq: Current Sanctions, Long Term Threat, and U.S. Policy Options," Congressional Research Service (CRS) Report for Congress no. 94-465F, May 25, 1994, p. CRS-2. Resolution 687 is worded more generally to cover Iraqi exports, but that essentially means oil, as that commodity accounted for 98 percent of the country's exports prior to the imposition of the trade ban. If oil sales resume, 30 percent of the monies would be used to compensate Kuwaiti victims. Any recommendation to the Security Council to lift the export ban on the basis of Iraqi compliance with the WMD provisions of Resolution 687 would come from UNSCOM but would be subject to veto by any permanent member.

[6] Thomas L. Friedman, "The New Presidency: Clinton Backs Raid but Muses about a New Start," *New York Times*, January 14, 1993, p. A1.

[7] Gwen Ifill, "Gore Rules Out Regular Links with Iraq Chief," *New York Times*, January 18, 1993, p. A9. Gore stated, "The phrase 'do business' implies normal relations, and the answer to that is no. We will have trouble from Iraq so long as Saddam Hussein and his regime are in power."

[8] R. Jeffrey Smith, "U.S. Drops Demand for Saddam's Ouster," *Washington Post*, March 30, 1993, p. A17.

[9] Elaine Sciolino, "Clinton Steps in and the World Looks On," *New York Times*, January 24, 1993, section 4, p. 1.

[10] "Half a Policy on Iraq" (editorial), *New York Times*, November 28, 1994, p. 16.

[11] Sciolino, "Clinton Steps In."

[12] For an excellent analysis of the use of coercive instruments against Iraq see Daniel Byman, Kenneth Pollack, and Matthew Waxman, "Coercing Saddam Hussein: Lessons from the Past," *Survival* 40, no. 3 (Autumn 1998), pp. 137ff.

[13] Douglas Jehl, "Raid on Baghdad: The White House; Administration Just Finds Keeping a Secret Can Be a Triumph," *New York Times*, June 28, 1993, p. A6.

[14] For a detailed analysis of Saddam Hussein's decision-making with respect to UNSCOM and the sanctions regime see Amatzia Baram, *Building toward Crisis: Saddam Hussein's Strategy for Survival* (Washington, DC: Washington Institute for Near East Policy, 1998), pp. 74–83.

[15] Yossef M. Ibrahim, "Senior Army Aides to Iraq President Defect to Jordan," *New York Times*, August 10, 1995, p. A1. Another defector was Hussein Kamel's brother, Saddam Kamel, who was married to another daughter of Saddam Hussein and had been in charge of Iraq's special forces.

[16] Quoted in Cordesman and Hashim, *Iraq: Sanctions and Beyond*, p. 294; see chapter 15, pp. 290–339, for a comprehensive review and assessment of Iraq's WMD capabilities.

[17] "Leaving Behind the UNSCOM Legacy in Iraq: An Interview with Rolf Ekeus," *Arms Control Today* 27, no. 4 (June/July 1997), p. 5.

[18] A high-ranking U.S. delegation led by Assistant Secretary of State Robert Pelletreau was dispatched to the region after the Hussein Kamel defection. One American goal was to engineer a political reconciliation between Saudi Arabia and Jordan, whose relations had been strained since King Hussein's tilt toward Baghdad during the Kuwait crisis, to reduce Jordan's dependence on Iraqi oil. This, in turn, would have made it easier for Jordan to curtail its economic links with Iraq. See Eric Schmitt, "U.S. Action in Persian Gulf Is Said to Seek Iraqi's Ouster," *New York Times*, August 19, 1995, p. A6.

[19] Youssef M. Ibrahim, "U.S. Bid to Topple Iraqi Falters, Lacking Support in Arab World," *New York Times*, August 24, 1995, p. A1. A month after the Hussein Kamel defection, columnist Thomas L. Friedman observed, "While the Clinton Administration is working and praying for Saddam's demise, most of his fellow rulers like him just the way he is. That is, strong enough to hold Iraq together, weak enough not to threaten his neighbors, embargoed enough not to be able to sell too much oil and caged enough not to be a factor in inter-Arab politics. That is a Saddam that serves a lot of people's interests, and the Clinton Administration is fooling itself if it thinks otherwise." "Long Live Saddam Hussein," *New York Times*, September 17, 1995, section 4, p. 15.

[20] R. Jeffrey Smith, "Iraq Is Hiding 6 to 16 Scuds, U.N. Suspects: Warheads Can Deliver Germ, Nerve Agents," *Washington Post*, March 21, 1996, p. A1.

[21] Barbara Crossette, "Iraq Still Lies about Arms, Outgoing UN Inspector Says," *International Herald Tribune*, June 26, 1997, p. 6. Ekeus said that Iraq had been consistently noncooperative since the creation of UNSCOM: "They come up with a new explanation every time. They are very, very innovative. This is frustrating and irritating sometimes, but also . . . highly amusing. It is like the 'Thousand and One Nights,' where every night they tell a different story to save themselves." After leaving his UNSCOM post, the Swedish diplomat revealed that he had received credible intelligence of an Iraqi plot on his life, denied by Iraq's UN ambassador, Nizar Hamdoon.

[22] U.S. Department of State, Office of the Spokesman, "Preserving Principle and Safeguarding Stability: United States Policy Toward Iraq, March 27, 1997" (http://secretary.state.gov./www/statements/970326.html); Thomas Lippman, "Albright Says U.S. Adamant about Maintaining Sanctions against Saddam's Iraq," *Washington Post*, March 27, 1997, p. A28.

[23] "Undoing Saddam Hussein" (editorial), *Washington Post*, March 31, 1997, p. A20.

[24] See Baram, *Building toward Crisis*, pp. 79–83.

[25] John M. Goshko, "After Wooing Russia, U.S. Wins a Victory against Iraq at UN," *International Herald Tribune*, June 23, 1997, p. 2. For additional background information see Greg Saiontz, "A Chronology of Diminishing Response: UN Reac-

tions to Iraqi Provocations since the Gulf War," *Research Notes*, no. 1 (Washington, DC: Washington Institute for Near East Policy, June 3, 1997).

26 Craig R. Whitney, "France to Pull Its Planes Out of Patrols over Northern Iraq," *New York Times*, December 28, 1996, p. 5.

27 Youssef Ibrahim, "Iraq Said to Sell Oil in Secret Plan to Skirt UN Ban," *New York Times*, February 16, 1995, p. A1.

28 Barbara Crossette, "New UN Monitor Says Iraq Is Still Hiding Data on Weapons," *New York Times*, October 8, 1997, p. A7.

29 Barbara Crossette, "UN's Council Moves to Block Travel by Iraqis," *New York Times*, November 12, 1997, p. A1.

30 Douglas Jehl, "Gulf Alliance: A Falling Out," *New York Times*, November 13, 1997, p. A1.

31 Steven Erlanger, "Gulf War Alliance: 6 Years Later, Seams Fray," *New York Times*, November 5, 1997, p. A6.

32 For a detailed account of the Clinton administration's decision-making during the October 1997–February 1998 crisis see Barton Gellman, Dana Priest, and Bradley Graham, "Diplomacy and Doubts on the Road to War: U.S. Prepared to Bomb Iraq while Wondering If the Aftermath Would Be Worth It," *Washington Post*, March 1, 1998, pp. A1, 24.

33 Text of President Clinton's address to the Joint Chiefs of Staff and Pentagon staff in *New York Times*, February 18, 1998, p. A9.

34 Barton Gellman, "Shift on Iraq May Signify Trade-Off," *Washington Post*, August 17, 1998, p. A1 (emphasis added).

35 Ibid.

36 Charles Krauthammer, "To Bomb without Serious Intent," *Washington Post*, February 6, 1998, p. A25.

37 United States Information Agency, "President Clinton and British Prime Minister Blair in the White House Oval Office, February 5, 1998." Here and elsewhere in this manuscript, I would like to acknowledge Iraq expert Laurie Mylroie for her Internet newsletter, "Iraq News," a daily compilation of press clippings and government reports with her commentary.

38 Eric Schmitt, "Top GOP Senator Opposes UN Deal on Iraq Inspection," *New York Times*, February 26, 1998, p. A1.

39 John M. Goshko, "Chief Weapons Inspector Backs Annan against GOP Criticism of Iraq Accord," *Washington Post*, February 27, 1998, p. A29. The Annan-Hussein agreement was codified in UNSC Resolution 1154 on March 2, 1998.

40 Gellman, Priest, and Graham, "Diplomacy and Doubts on the Road to War," p. A17.

41 Reuters, August 9, 1998.

42 Gellman, Priest, and Graham, "Diplomacy and Doubts on the Road to War," p. 16.

43 Judith Miller, "American Inspector on Iraq Quits, Accusing UN and U.S. of Cave-In," *New York Times*, August 27, 1998, p. A1.

44 Secretary Albright defended the administration's actions at the Carnegie Endowment for International Peace on September 17, 1998. For the text of her remarks, including the question-and-answer period in which the Ritter epidode was raised, see http://www.ceip.org/new/albright.

45 Youssef M. Ibrahim, "U.S. and Iraq Fail to End Arms Impasse," *New York Times*, October 2, 1998, p. A5.

46 Barton Gellman, "Iraqi Work toward A-Bomb Reported," *Washington Post*, September 30, 1998, p. A1.

47 John M. Goshko, "Annan Says Iraq Will Never Be Fully Disarmed," *Washington Post*, October 17, 1998, p. A13.

[48] Barton Gellman and Bradley Graham, "U.S. Closer to Airstrikes against Iraq," *Washington Post*, November 7, 1998, pp. A1, 11.

[49] Steven Erlanger, "Clinton Accepts Iraq's Promise to Allow Weapons Inspections," *New York Times*, November 16, 1998, pp. A1, 10.

[50] Bradley Graham, "Senior Officials Split on Aborting Airstrikes," *Washington Post*, November 16, 1998, p. A1, 18.

[51] Henry Kissinger, "Bring Saddam Hussein Down," *Washington Post*, November 29, 1998, p. C7.

[52] Barton Gellman, "Why Now? U.S. Says Iraq Determined Timing," *Washington Post*, December 17, 1998, p. A29.

[53] Eric Schmitt, "G.O.P. Splits Bitterly over Timing of Assault," *New York Times*, December 17, 1998, p. A1.

[54] Thomas Lippman, "U.S. Warns Iraq of More Raids," *Washington Post*, December 21, 1998, p. A1.

[55] Bradley Graham and Dana Priest, "U.S. Details Strategy, Damage," *Washington Post*, December 18, 1998, p. A1.

[56] James Risen, "U.S. Stands Firm in Calling for U.N. Inspections in Iraq," *New York Times*, December 24, 1998, p. A6.

[57] The raids destroyed or severely damaged twelve missile production sites and eleven command-and-control facilities. Warren P. Stobel, "Sticking It to Saddam," *U.S. News and World Report*, January 11, 1999, p. 38. U.S. and British planners did not target chemical and biological weapons facilities reportedly out of fear that such attacks might release deadly toxins into the atmosphere.

[58] Steven Lee Myers, "Iraq Damage More Severe Than Reported, Pentagon Says," *New York Times*, January 9, 1999, p. A3.

[59] Russia called for the dismissal of UNSCOM chair Richard Butler on the heels of reports that the United States and the United Kingdom had used the inspections as cover for intelligence operations. UN Secretary-General Annan was reported to have convincing evidence of such claims, denied by the Clinton administration. Barton Gellman, "Annan Suspicious of UNSCOM Role," *Washington Post*, January 6, 1999, p. A1.

[60] To counter this pressure, the United States proposed to eliminate the ceiling on oil sales ($5.25 billion every six months) as long as the proceeds were used to purchase food and medicine. John M. Goshko, "U.S. Seeks to Alter Iraq 'Oil for Food' Program," *Washington Post*, January 15, 1999, p. A24.

[61] Amatzia Baram, "Saddam Husayn's Rage of Fury: Impact of the Bombing Campaign," *Policywatch*, no. 360 (Washington, DC: Washington Institute for Near East Policy, June 11, 1999).

[62] Barbara Crossette, "Iraqi Chief Finds New Enemies Even among Former Friends," *New York Times*, December 29, 1999, p. A4.

[63] Baram, *Building toward Crisis*, p. 79.

[64] Byman, Pollack, and Waxman, "Coercing Saddam Hussein," p. 127.

[65] Cordesman and Hashim, *Iraq: Sanctions and Beyond*, p. 11.

[66] See Amatzia Baram, *Culture, History and Ideology in the Formation of Ba'thist Iraq, 1968–89* (London: Macmillan, 1991), chapter 4.

[67] Baram, *Building toward Crisis*, p. 27. The Iraqi tribal system is a central underpinning of Saddam Hussein's power base. A detailed discussion of this highly articulated and complex system can be found in Ibid., chapter 2. Baram's volume contains the most complete family tree for Saddam Hussein that has been compiled.

[68] Amatzia Baram, "Between Impediment and Advantage: Saddam's Iraq," *USIP Special Report* (Washington, DC: United States Institute of Peace, June 1998), p. 14.

⁶⁹ Charles Tripp, "The Future of Iraq and of Regional Security," in Geoffrey Kemp and Janice Gross Stein, eds., *Powder Keg in the Middle East: The Struggle for Gulf Security* (London: Rowman and Littlefield, 1995), p. 135.

⁷⁰ Barbara Crossette, "Accord Reached by Iraq and UN for Oil Exports," *New York Times*, May 21, 1998, pp. A1, 8.

⁷¹ Amatzia Baram offers the following interpretation of the relationship between the stalled implementation of UNSCR 986 and Saddam's August–September 1996 move into the Kurdish region: "So frustrating had the process become that many began to speculate that Saddam . . . was simply proclaiming his acceptance of the resolution to restore confidence in the dinar [Iraq's currency] but he had no intent actually to proceed with the deal. . . . [N]othing could have been more erroneous. Saddam's attack on Irbil was a crucial aspect of his acceptance of Resolution 986." See Baram, *Building toward Crisis*, pp. 71–72.

⁷² Elaine Sciolino, "Taking Sides in Iraq," *New York Times*, September 4, 1996, p. A1.

⁷³ Baram, *Building toward Crisis*, pp. 80–82.

⁷⁴ Ibid.

⁷⁵ Barbara Crossette, "Iraqi President, Altering Tone, Predicts Slow End to Sanctions," *New York Times*, July 18, 1998, p. A5.

⁷⁶ See, for example, Tripp, "The Future of Iraq and of Regional Security," pp. 138–48; and Cordesman and Hashim, *Iraq: Sanctions and Beyond*, pp. 350–56.

⁷⁷ Richard Perle, "No More Halfway Measures," *Washington Post*, February 8, 1998, p. C1. See also Zalmay Khalilzad and Paul Wolfowitz, "We Must Lead the Way in Deposing Saddam," *Washington Post*, November 9, 1997, p. C9.

⁷⁸ Vernon Loeb, "Congress Stokes Visions of War to Oust Saddam," *Washington Post*, October 20, 1998, p. A1.

⁷⁹ "Expensive Fantasies on Iraq" (editorial), *New York Times*, October 19, 1998, p. A20.

⁸⁰ Philip Shenon, "U.S. General Warns of Dangers in Trying to Topple Iraqi," *New York Times*, January 29, 1999, p. A3.

⁸¹ Jane Perlez, "Albright Introduces a New Phrase to Promote Hussein's Ouster," *New York Times*, January 29, 1999, p. A3.

⁸² Bradley Graham, "U.S. General Attacks Aid for Groups Seeking to Topple Iraqi Leader," *Washington Post*, October 22, 1998, p. A32.

⁸³ John Lancaster, "Egypt Urges Diplomacy, Not Force, in U.S.-Iraq Dispute," *Washington Post*, November 14, 1997, p. A35.

⁸⁴ Fouad Ajami, "The Reckoning," *New Republic*, February 23, 1998, p. 21.

⁸⁵ Kenneth M. Pollack, "Contain Narrowly: Looking Beyond the Security Council," in Patrick L. Clawson, ed., *Iraq Strategy Review: Options for U.S. Policy* (Washington, DC: Washington Institute for Near East Policy, 1998), pp. 38–39. The Clawson volume surveys the broad range of policy options toward Iraq, ranging from narrow deterrence to invasion and occupation.

⁸⁶ Karen DeYoung, "Baghdad Weapons Program Dormant," *Washington Post*, July 15, 1999, p. A19. The British-Dutch proposal would create an UNSCOM successor agency called UNCIM (United Nations Commission on Inspection and Monitoring).

5

Iran: Revolutionary State or Ready to Rejoin the "Family of Nations"?

U.S. POLICY DEVELOPMENT

More than two decades after the Iranian Revolution of February 1979, U.S. relations with Iran remain powerfully influenced by its legacy. The revolution is a political prism through which the two countries view each other. American administrations from Carter to Clinton have grappled with the dual nature of postrevolutionary Iran—a duality reflected in its very name, the Islamic Republic of Iran. As a "republic," Iran exists as a sovereign state in an international system of like states. Its "Islamic" character, however, asserts a legitimacy derived from a higher authority that transcends manmade political demarcations. After the revolution, radical elements of the country's new theocratic leadership vowed that Iran would "export" its revolution to other Middle East countries to create a transnational Islamic community. Although this rhetoric has moderated over time, the political tension created by Iran's dual nature persists. In short, is Iran an "ordinary" state that accepts the legitimacy of the international system or a revolutionary state that rejects its norms and seeks to radically alter, if not overturn, that system?

The dilemma of postrevolutionary Iran is reminiscent of the early Soviet era, when Stalin developed his doctrine of "socialism in one country" while simultaneously continuing activities to extend socialism and, not coincidentally, Soviet power globally. Iran's leaders have likewise concentrated their efforts on the establishment of what one might call (to extend the Soviet analogy) "Islam in one country." Nonetheless, the Teheran regime continues to utilize foreign policy initiatives in support of Islam, such as assistance to Hizbollah in southern Lebanon or opposition to the Middle East peace process, for domestic political purposes.

For some radicals, revolutionary activism abroad remains an integral part of Iran's identity and a source of legitimacy at home. This political duality—the contending visions of Iran as an ordinary versus a revolutionary state—is a major cause of the political schism evident within the Teheran regime and Iranian society at large. In turn, this duality has been reflected in the American policy approach toward Iran.

Since the revolution, American administrations have periodically sought to engage "moderates" inside the regime who purportedly desire to normalize Iran's relations with the external world. The election of Mohammed Khatami as Iran's president in May 1997 was viewed by the Clinton administration within that context. A year later, the opportunity created by President Khatami's meteoric political rise prompted a major policy address by Secretary of State Madeleine Albright in which she called on Iran to join the United States to develop "a road map leading to normal relations."[1] This speech reflected the dominant strand of American policy in which the problem with Iran is defined with respect to its behavior, not the very nature of its ruling regime. This position, while widely supported, has been countered by those who argue that Iran's objectionable behavior is inextricably linked to the character of its revolutionary theocratic regime. Before the Khatami election, House Speaker Newt Gingrich (R-Ga.) and others in Congress called for a strategy to change the Teheran regime.

This question of "behavior" versus "regime" is not as pronounced as in the case of Iraq, where domestic U.S. political support for a rollback strategy to remove Saddam Hussein from power is substantial. In contrast to Iraq, the Teheran regime, which permits the only meaningfully contested elections in the entire Persian Gulf region, enjoys genuine domestic legitimacy. No significant political opposition exists that could lead to the ouster of the theocratic regime. Despite the minority position of those who continue to view the postrevolutionary regime itself as the core of the problem, the stated objective of U.S. policy is to moderate Iranian behavior and promote Iran's resocialization (to use political scientist Alexander George's term) into international society. The central question for American policy-makers is whether Iran's reformist president can negotiate such a transformation in the face of stiff domestic opposition from radical factions that want the Islamic Republic to remain true to its revolutionary roots. On the American side, domestic impediments to a changed relationship remain formidable given the legacy of the past (symbolized by the 1980–81 hostage crisis) and the demonization of Iran (as part of the rogue state policy's political mobilization strategy). To explore the implications of President Khatami's political ascendance for U.S. policy, it is necessary to place this development into historical context. In the case of U.S.-Iranian relations, the past is more than prologue. It continues to shape current and future possibilities.

The roots of American involvement in Iran can be traced to World War II, when the United States used the "Persian corridor" as a major military supply route to the Soviet Union.[2] In the aftermath of World War II, Soviet reluctance to withdraw from its occupation zone in northern Iran became the precipitant of the first Cold War crisis. Stalin, then providing support to the pro-Moscow Tudeh Party, backed down only in the face of Western pressure supported by the newly created United Nations (UN). A major turning point in U.S. policy toward Iran occurred in August 1953, when the United States and Britain helped to engineer the overthrow of Prime Minister Mohammed Mossadegh, who had nationalized Iran's oil industry, and to restore the Shah to a paramount political position. During the 1950s and 1960s, the Shah closely aligned Iran with the United States and the Western anti-Soviet alliance. In October 1955, Iran was a founding member of the Baghdad Pact (transformed into the Central Treaty Organization when Iraq withdrew after the July 1958 coup that overthrew the monarchy there).

The Kennedy administration, which emphasized economic development as a key instrument to counter the appeal of socialism in the Third World, pushed the Shah to focus on the challenges of modernization. The Shah embarked on his "White Revolution" of economic and social reform, but this program faced opposition from religious leaders and landlords that culminated in riots in June 1963. In putting down this opposition, the Shah was able to further consolidate his domestic power, which in turn gave him the confidence to pursue a more independent foreign policy line.[3] The British decision in 1968 to withdraw from military positions "East of Suez" became the occasion for another major shift in American policy toward the Persian Gulf region, in general, and Iran, in particular. The British move came at the height of the Vietnam War, when U.S. public opinion favored a scaling back of America's worldwide security commitments. Instead of supplanting the British role with a direct U.S. military presence, the Nixon administration adopted a policy, consistent with the Nixon Doctrine, to rely on the regional countries themselves to play a more active security role.[4] Thus the Shah undertook a major buildup of Iranian military capabilities. The ascendance of Iran as the dominant power in the Persian Gulf region was made possible financially by the sharp increase in oil prices in 1973–74.[5] American arms transfers became a symbol of the close U.S. relationship with Iran and, in turn, the Shah became even more closely identified with Washington in Iranian domestic politics. This close political identification accounts for the virulent anti-Americanism that accompanied the Iranian Revolution (although that historic event should be viewed as a more general popular reaction against the authoritarianism and Western secularism of the Shah's regime).

The seizure of the American embassy and the taking of American hostages by radical "students" in October 1979 was an outgrowth of the revolution and accelerated the deterioration in U.S. relations with Teheran's new clerical regime. The hostage crisis was shortly followed by the Soviet invasion of Afghanistan in December 1979. The twin Iranian and Afghan crises prompted the enunciation of the Carter Doctrine, which provided an explicit U.S. security guarantee to the Arab Gulf states against potential Soviet aggression and Iranian destabilization. This fear of Iran was accentuated by rhetoric about "exporting the revolution" that was being espoused by radical clerics. To meet a range of potential threats to regional security and the free flow of oil, the Carter administration created the Rapid Deployment Force that was the precursor to the U.S. military's contemporary Central Command. In January 1981, the Iranian government, preoccupied with its war with Iraq and perhaps fearful of American military action under the newly elected Reagan administration, moved to end the hostage crisis. The resulting Algiers agreement, negotiated by President Carter's deputy secretary of state, Warren Christopher, established the U.S.-Iranian Claims Tribunal at the Hague to resolve outstanding financial matters.

U.S. economic sanctions against the Teheran regime were tightened in 1984 when the State Department designated Iran as a state sponsor of terrorism. This decision followed a series of terrorist acts in the Middle East (most notably, the October 1983 bombing of the U.S. military barracks in Beirut) in which Iran was directly or indirectly implicated. President Reagan identified Iran, along with Libya, North Korea, Cuba, and Nicaragua, as "outlaw governments" that constituted "a new international version of Murder Incorporated." This tougher line toward Teheran indicated a so-called tilt toward Iraq, conspicuously omitted from the State Department's terrorist list, in its war with Iran. One manifestation of this political tilt and Iran's pariah status was the jarring American silence occasioned by the Iraqi use of chemical weapons in the war that Saddam Hussein had initiated against Iran. To avert an Iraqi military defeat and further increase pressure on Teheran to accept a cease-fire, the Reagan administration pushed for an international embargo, "Operation Staunch," to deny U.S. military equipment to Iran. And yet, while maintaining this tough public line, the Reagan administration's own National Security Council (NSC) undertook a covert operation in 1985–86 that subverted that policy and led to the Iran-Contra scandal.

The backdrop to the Iran-Contra affair was the deterioration in Iran's military situation vis-à-vis Iraq by 1985. This change prompted the Teheran regime to accept what not long before would have been unthinkable—contact with the "Great Satan"—in order to obtain the military equipment necessary to continue the war against Iraq. In terms of the American policy debate, the Iran-Contra plan had both strategic and tactical rationales, and their relationship was never clear.[6] National Security Adviser Robert MacFarlane and NSC aide Oliver North viewed the Iranian need for U.S. military equipment (such as anti-tank munitions) as potential leverage to gain Teheran's assistance in the release of American hostages in Lebanon held by pro-Iranian radicals. The funds secured through these covert sales would then be used to circumvent congressional restrictions on U.S. assistance to the Contra guerrillas seeking to overthrow the pro-Moscow Sandinista regime in Nicaragua. Beyond this immediate arms-for-hostages rationale, arms sales to Iran (advocated by some in the Reagan administration who knew nothing of the MacFarlane-North covert operation) were viewed as a means of reviving bilateral relations with a pivotal regional actor on the Soviet Union's southern border.

In the aftermath of the Iran-Contra affair, American policy turned more confrontational with Iran, as Washington embarked on a policy of coercive diplomacy to win Teheran's acceptance of a cease-fire with Iraq. This foreign policy objective prompted Washington to accede to the 1987 Kuwaiti request for U.S. protection of its oil tanker fleet from the Iranian navy. U.S. military strikes against Iranian naval targets led the *Economist* to observe that "the Americans are now getting uncomfortably close to fighting Iraq's war for it."[7] In the UN Security Council, the Reagan administration won agreement to a resolution imposing mandatory sanctions on the party (namely, Iran) refusing to accept the cease-fire terms. Citing Iranian intransigence, President Reagan declared a ban on Iranian imports (notably exempting oil). After a U.S. naval vessel accidentally shot down an Iran Air jet in early July 1988, Iran announced its acceptance of the cease-fire. Although the decision (likened by Ayatollah Khomeini to taking poison) followed a string of demoralizing Iranian military defeats, political scientist Shahram Chubin argues that the U.S. Navy's downing of the Iranian airliner "gave Iran's leaders precisely the moral cover of martyrdom and suffering in the face of an unjust superior force they needed to camouflage the comprehensive defeat of their political goals."[8] Iranians viewed the indirect American support provided Iraq during the eight-year war—the "tilt"—as evidence of Washington's implacable hostility toward the Teheran regime. American policy during the Iran-Iraq War remains part of Iran's historical grievances toward the United States and continues to affect the Teheran regime's policy toward Washington.[9]

With the end of the Iran-Iraq War, the newly elected Bush administration appeared open to the possibility of improved relations with Teheran. In his January 1989 inaugural address, President Bush, making what aides described as an oblique reference to Iran, declared that "good will begets good will."[10] While Bush sought to moderate the tone of U.S. policy, the signals from Teheran were mixed—again reflecting the political tension between Iran's dual identities. In February 1989, Khomeini issued a religious edict (*fatwa*) that pronounced a death sentence on Salman Rushdie, a British resident, for the publication of his book *The Satanic Verses*. After Khomeini's death in June 1989, the last will and testament of the leader of Iran's revolution contained a final defiant call for "fierce animosity to the West, a militant assertion of Iran's Islamic identity." Two months later, Ali Akbar Hashemi Rafsanjani, viewed as a political pragmatist, became Iran's new president. Coupled with Bush's inaugural overture, Rafsanjani's election offered the possibility of a changed U.S.-Iranian relationship. Nonetheless, as examined in the following section on Iranian domestic politics, President Rafsanjani's scope for diplomatic maneuver on this core foreign policy issue was sharply limited by the schism within the theocratic regime. His own rhetoric was, on occasion, inflammatory—as when he called on Muslims to kill five Westerners for every Palestinian "killed by Israel."[11] Notwithstanding this catering to the regime's radical faction, President Rafsanjani also took two specific actions that Iranian officials characterized as a concerted effort to take up President Bush's inaugural address offer. First, he expended capital, both political and financial, to win the release of the last American hostages held in Lebanon by groups under Iran's influence. Second, during the 1990–91 Gulf War, the Rafsanjani government assumed a position of positive neutrality, thereby taking no action to complicate the U.S.-led coalition's campaign to oust Saddam Hussein's forces from Kuwait. Iranian Foreign Ministry officials claimed that both moves were intended to facilitate improved bilateral relations and expressed frustration that the Bush administration had failed to respond.

From the Bush administration's perspective, Iranian words and actions were contradictory. For example, in March 1991, immediately following the Gulf War, President Rafsanjani stated that a normal relationship was possible with the United States if it abandoned its "hostility toward Iran." Two months later, however, the Iranian leader backtracked, telling seminary students at Teheran University that "Iran is not thinking about restoring relations with the United States."[12] In terms of actions, the Teheran regime's strong hostility toward the Middle East peace process, one of Bush's top diplomatic priorities, militated against a changed American policy. Iran's official antipathy toward the Arab-Israeli negotiations was highlighted during the U.S.-sponsored Madrid conference in October 1991, when Teheran was the venue for a counter-meeting of radical states and political groups implacably opposed to the peace process. This stance toward the peace process was not motivated by a core Iranian national security interest; rather, it assumed symbolic importance to the regime's radical elements, who considered the Islamic Republic's external mission a key part of its political identity and legitimacy. U.S. concern focused on two additional areas of behavior linked to the emerging rogue state policy—support for international terrorism and the pursuit of weapons of mass destruction (WMD). In terms of the former, Iran was linked to the bombing of the Israeli embassy in Buenos Aires in March 1992 and the murder of Iranian Kurdish leaders in Berlin in September of the same year. With respect to the latter, Bush administration officials asserted that Iran was actively pursuing the development of WMD capabilities. Central Intelligence Agency (CIA) Director Robert Gates told a congressional committee in March 1992 that Iran could develop nuclear weapons by 2000.

The nuclear issue, however, was part of a broader debate within the Bush administration over Iran's foreign policy intentions in the post–Gulf War era. Official views, particularly within the intelligence community, were divided on this core question. One group, which included Gates, depicted Iran as an increasingly assertive local power that could threaten U.S. regional interests in the near future. Proponents pointed to other developments, such as Iran's conventional arms buildup (then estimated at $2 billion per year) and its occupation of Abu Musa Island (also claimed by the United Arab Emirates) at the mouth of the Persian Gulf, as supporting evidence for this ominous interpretation of Iranian intentions. They likened Iran in the early 1990s to Iraq in the 1980s—the decade in which Saddam Hussein's drive to acquire nuclear weapons went undetected by the International Atomic Energy Agency. Other intelligence analysts and officials questioned this view of Iran's regional intentions, arguing that it was an inaccurate extrapolation from the Gulf War experience with Iraq. This group noted that postrevolutionary Iran was devoting fewer resources to the military than under the Shah's government and only 40 percent of what Iraq had spent prior to its invasion of Kuwait. They further argued that the alarmist interpretation of Iranian interpretations failed to take into account Iran's legitimate security concerns—specifically, the continued rule in Iraq of the dictator who had launched a war against them in September 1980.[13]

The Bush administration's NSC undertook a review of U.S. policy toward Iran in early 1992 that included the consideration of "constructive engagement" through the lifting of selective sanctions. According to *New York Times* diplomatic correspondent Elaine Sciolino, the NSC review, completed in April 1992, concluded that any gesture that "might be politically meaningful in Teheran—lifting the ban on oil sales to America, for example—would have been politically impossible at home. On the other hand, a reward small enough to be painless in American political terms, such as lifting the ban on exports of carpets and pistachios, would have seemed too petty to Teheran." Sciolino reported that "even those analysts [in the Bush administration] who defend the use of incentives to moderate behavior are bewildered about how to treat Iran" because of the difficulty in assessing Teheran's contradictory behavior, which itself reflects the competing pulls of Iranian domestic politics. "What confuses the picture is that there is no answer to a fundamental question about Mr. Rafsanjani's moves to curb radical elements in his regime and expand ties with Western industrialized countries. Do his actions represent a strategic shift in the course of Iran's . . . revolution, or are they only a tactical maneuver that could be reversed once Iran succeeds in reconstructing its economy? Mr. Rafsanjani himself may not know the answer to the question. . . ."[14] Within this confused political context, even a conciliatory gesture by Teheran was discounted in Washington. When it was reported, for example, that President Rafsanjani had interceded to win the release of U.S. hostages in Lebanon, some American hard-liners argued that this merely proved Iran's complicity in their incarceration all along. The net effect was to maintain the default position against improved relations with Iran.

As discussed in Chapter 1, American foreign policy in the 1990s has been powerfully influenced by the twin events that began the decade—the end of the Cold War and the hot war to expel Saddam Hussein from Kuwait. With the demise of the Soviet threat and the Iraqi experience fresh in mind, U.S. officials viewed Iran as the type of security challenge that the United States would face in the post–Cold War era. At the time of the Iraqi invasion, President Bush had spoken of the need to prepare for the "Iraqs of the future." The CIA's 1992 National Intelligence Estimate on Iran's nuclear program was consistent with this archetype of what would later be characterized as a rogue state—a Third World regime armed with WMD and threatening a region of vital interest to the United States. This predisposition in the wake of the Gulf War affected American perceptions of Iran. The failure of the Bush administration's engagement strategy toward Iraq prior to 1990 reinforced the political rationale against pursuing a "constructive engagement" strategy toward Iran or offering any inducements to the Teheran regime for reformed behavior. It also led to a renewed focus on measures to strengthen the nonproliferation regime after the Gulf War. In October 1992, President Bush signed into law the Iran-Iraq Arms Nonproliferation Act prohibiting the transfer of any goods or technologies that might contribute to the development of destabilizing conventional weapons by either country. The act, subsequently extended by congressional amendments to encompass WMD capabilities, would impose sanctions on any government or commercial entity (foreign or domestic) that violates this U.S. statute.

The linking of U.S. policy toward Iran and Iraq under this nonproliferation legislation presaged the broader policy linkage under the Clinton administration's "dual containment" strategy in spring 1993. The Iran-Iraq Arms Nonproliferation Act was a unilateral measure with extraterritorial implications (since it threatened to sanction foreign firms found in violation). Its passage was complemented by the Bush administration's diplomatic push to win multilateral support for measures to forestall the development of Iranian WMD capabilities. This effort coincided with the imminent demise of the Coordinating Committee for Multilateral Export Controls (COCOM; see Chapter 1), which had served as the multilateral clearinghouse during the Cold War for Western export controls targeted at the Soviet bloc. In November 1992, the United States called on its G-7 partners to "harmonize export controls" to halt the sale of all militarily useful equipment to Iran—as well as Libya, Iraq, and North Korea.[15] Thus, beyond the agreed G-7 ban on arms transfers, the Bush administration was seeking to tightly regulate sales of dual-use technologies— commercially available equipment that might have military applications. In a dispute that would carry over into the Clinton administration, the European and Japanese governments balked at this limitation of trade with Iran.

This G-7 opposition to multilateral controls on dual-use transfers to Iran derived from two sources. The first was immediate and articulated. As detailed in Chapter 3, the other G-7 members, particularly the Europeans, favored a policy of engagement over comprehensive containment and isolation. They argued that an alternative approach, later adopted by the European Union (EU) under the rubric "critical dialogue," would use trade as a tangible incentive for improved Iranian behavior (vis-à-vis terrorism, etc.). This policy also reflected the Europeans' favorable assessment of the possibilities for change under President Rafsanjani. The second source of G-7 resistance to American pressure to curtail links with Iran was historical and largely unspoken. Throughout the Cold War era, the Europeans and Japanese had routinely acquiesced to U.S. demands to forego sales of dual-use technologies to East bloc states. American pressure tactics during these COCOM deliberations left a political residue that made the Europeans more assertively independent in the absence of the Soviet threat. The G-7 allies also pointed to the hypocrisy of U.S. government efforts to limit foreign economic contacts with Iran given the loophole in U.S. sanctions legislation that permitted American oil companies to purchase a quarter of total Iranian oil production for sale in non-American markets. U.S. manufacturers also opposed the Bush administration's unilateral export control policy to restrict the flow of dual-use goods and technologies to Iran, arguing that Teheran would simply turn to eager foreign suppliers. A prominent case in point was the Boeing Company's proposed billion-dollar deal in September 1992 with Iran Air for the sale of sixteen Boeing 737s.[16]

The Clinton administration initiated its own policy review vis-à-vis Iran on assuming office in January 1993. In the ensuing months, the elements of a tougher policy emerged that reversed the Bush administration's "good will begets good will" line. An early sign of the this new approach was Secretary of State Christopher's March 1993 characterization of Iran as "an international outlaw" for its support of international terrorism and its drive to acquire WMD. The Clinton administration did not formally eschew the possibility of dialogue with the Teheran regime, but did make clear that its objectionable behavior made normal relations impossible. Christopher's harsh rhetoric was a departure from the Bush administration policy, and some observers speculated that his hard-line attitude was shaped by his difficult experience negotiating the release of the U.S. embassy hostages in 1980–81. The Clinton administration's political demonization of Iran was intended to isolate it diplomatically and mobilize diplomatic support for what Christopher called a "collective

policy of containment." In May 1993, NSC official Martin Indyk enunciated the administration's "dual containment" strategy.[17] The linking
of U.S. policy toward Iran and Iraq was a major step in the development
of the Clinton administration's rogue state policy, with its central assertion that these countries, as well as Libya and North Korea, constitute a
distinct class of states in the post–Cold War international system.

In the 1993 policy review, national security concerns overrode significant economic interests. This was not a foregone conclusion, as President
Clinton had campaigned as a pro-business "new Democrat" and his economic team viewed export expansion as a major contributor to U.S. economic growth. Prominent among the seven key growth areas identified by
the administration was commercial aviation. Commenting on the aggressive marketing efforts by European governments to push for an increased
global market share for Airbus Industrie over Boeing and McDonnell
Douglas, President Clinton asserted, "I'm not going to roll over and play
dead."[18] In the interagency deliberations on Iran policy, the Commerce
Department advocated the lifting of export controls on civil aircraft (as
well as highway trucks and other nonmilitary goods), while the State and
Defense Departments opposed such a change in policy. Proponents of the
hard-line position argued that it would be diplomatically easier to convince
other countries to participate in multilateral containment if the United
States demonstrated a willingness to sacrifice its own economic interests.
At the end of the policy review in August 1993, President Clinton decided
to continue the policy of comprehensive containment, including the retention of export controls on dual-use goods and technologies. He took this
decision despite the opposition of the U.S. business community to unilateral sanctions and export controls, and despite lobbying by Boeing, Mack
Trucks, and other affected companies. This disappointing outcome for industry stood in contrast to President Clinton's active personal involvement
to win the extension of most-favored-nation trade status for China over
strong congressional opposition. These cases, however, differed in two important respects: first, Chinese behavior with respect to human rights and
nonproliferation, while objectionable (even rogue in the view of some), did
not approach that of Iran in degree; and second, the economic interests at
stake with China vis-à-vis Iran were exponentially larger.

The 1993 policy review was influenced by Iranian actions with respect
to terrorism and the acquisition of WMD capabilities—and the domestic
political backlash against Iran that they generated in the United States. An
additional major source of friction was the Teheran regime's hostility to
the Middle East peace process—specifically, the September 1993 Oslo

Accord between the Palestinians and the Israelis, negotiations in which the United States had invested much political capital.[19] This Iranian behavior raised questions about President Rafsanjani's intentions and power position within the ruling regime. Some Western diplomats in Teheran suggested that the failure of the United States to make any gesture toward Iran after the release of the American hostages in Lebanon had undermined the group associated with Rafsanjani who favored the development of relations with the West. This, in turn, had led to the adoption of more radical policies. A senior Clinton administration official rejected this interpretation and asserted, "We have never bought the distinction of others that somehow there are good guys and bad guys in the region and that we should be backing the good guys—the so-called pragmatic reformer Rafsanjani."[20] This continuing controversy again pointed to the complex interrelationship between Iran's domestic and foreign policies, a theme that will be addressed more fully in the next section.

The Clinton administration was unsuccessful in its efforts to win multilateral backing for its tougher line toward Iran. In March 1993, for example, the administration suffered a significant diplomatic setback when the World Bank overrode U.S. objections and approved a major loan to Iran for infrastructure development.[21] Even more damaging was the open breach that emerged between the United States and its allies over economic relations with Iran. As detailed in Chapter 3, the United States strongly opposed the EU's policy of "critical dialogue" that sought to foster more moderate Iranian behavior through the development of a web of relations. The Clinton administration argued that such an approach, rather than giving Iran a tangible stake in stability, would simply reward behavior that violated international norms and prop up the clerical regime.[22] Christopher stated, "Iran is an international outlaw, yet some nations still conduct preferential commercial relations with Iran and some take steps to appease that outlaw nation. They must understand that by doing so, they make it easier for Iran to use its resources to sponsor terrorism throughout the world."[23] And yet, the credibility of U.S. efforts to convince allies to curtail economic relations with Iran was undermined by the fact that the United States remained Iran's largest trading partner. German chancellor Helmut Kohl pointedly observed during a joint press conference with President Clinton in February 1995 that it was "American oil companies, not German oil companies" that "export [Iranian oil] into other countries."[24]

In March 1995, the Clinton administration moved to close this loophole in U.S. sanctions with the news that the American oil conglomerate

Conoco was on the verge of concluding a major deal with the National Iranian Oil Company to develop offshore oil. President Clinton issued an executive order prohibiting U.S. companies and their subsidiaries from investing in the Iranian energy sector, thus heading off the Conoco deal. In May 1995, this limited ban was followed by a broader executive order cutting off all U.S. trade and investment with Iran, including purchases of Iranian oil by American companies.[25] With these executive orders, U.S. sanctions on Iran and Iraq—"those two rogue states" in Christopher's words—were brought into line. A major difference, of course, was that the United States was pursuing comprehensive economic sanctions unilaterally in the case of Iran (whereas Iraq remained under multilateral sanctions authorized by the Security Council). Had the Clinton administration not acted in May 1995, it is likely that Congress would have passed legislation introduced by Senator Alfonse D'Amato (R-N.Y.) in January to impose a complete trade ban. The administration's decision, however, was not well received in the U.S. business community, which continued to oppose unilateral sanctions on the grounds that it unfairly disadvantaged American firms relative to their foreign competitors. Indeed, in July 1995, the Teheran government gave the French oil company Total the contract originally negotiated with Conoco to develop the Iranian oil fields off Sirri Island.

Some observers questioned why the Clinton administration was using "economic diplomacy" to deal with some authoritarian regimes, such as China and even North Korea, while eschewing it in the cases of Iran and Cuba. This attitude appeared at odds with the administration's overarching strategy of "engagement and enlargement," through which these authoritarian regimes were offered a post–Cold War social contract—access to the benefits of the global economy (i.e., capital and technology) in return for conformation with international norms. In explaining why Iran remained the target of comprehensive economic containment, a senior administration official stated, "We draw the line in countries with policies that are beyond the pale."[26] In his April 30, 1995, speech announcing the total trade ban on Iran, President Clinton argued, "Many people have argued passionately that the best route to changing Iranian behavior is by engaging the country. Unfortunately, there is no evidence to support that argument. Indeed, the evidence of the last two years suggests exactly the reverse." The important domestic political dimension of the administration's decision was highlighted by the *New York Times*, which reported that "Mr. Clinton's move was . . . heavy with political symbolism and appeal because he made the announcement at a dinner of the World Jewish Congress. . . ."[27]

U.S. allies rebuffed the Clinton administration's diplomatic campaign to transform the unilateral American sanctions on Iran into a comprehensive multilateral regime.[28] France and others did not even want the matter raised in G-7 meetings. During 1995–96, when Washington was seeking European support on other important foreign policy issues such as Bosnia, the administration had to gauge how hard it could push the allies on this particular issue. That task was complicated by pending congressional initiatives, such as the extraterritorial Iran Libya Sanctions Act (ILSA), that threatened to further escalate the transatlantic dispute over Iran policy. Unable to win multilateral support for broad economic containment, the administration focused its efforts on limiting Iranian access to foreign technologies that could contribute to its WMD capabilities. But even this sphere was contentious for the allies and other Western industrial states because of the administration's expansive definition of "dual use"—one that encompassed a wide range of high-technology goods. This issue was the major source of contention in the multilateral negotiations over the creation of a post–Cold War successor organization to COCOM to deal with export control policy.

The Clinton administration did win a pledge from the Europeans not to transfer nuclear technology to Iran. With no other supplier available, Iran turned to China and Russia, the latter of which was especially eager to secure business for its large nuclear establishment. In January 1995 the Iranian government announced a $940 million agreement with the Russian Ministry of Atomic Energy (Minatom) to complete the construction of two light-water nuclear reactors (LWRs) begun by the German firm Siemens during the Shah's rule. The announcement again raised questions about Iran's nuclear intentions given the country's vast fossil fuel reserves that obviated the domestic need for nuclear energy.[29] This concern was heightened by press reports that the agreement with Minatom included a secret protocol to provide a uranium-enrichment facility capable of producing weapons-grade material. Christopher declared that Iran was "engaged in a crash effort to develop nuclear weapons" and the Clinton administration embarked on an intense diplomatic lobbying campaign in Moscow to halt, or at least limit, Russian nuclear cooperation with Iran.[30] The American case was weakened by the fact that Iran was a signatory to the nuclear Nonproliferation Treaty (NPT), a core provision of which provides access to nuclear energy technology to those states that forego the weapons option.[31] Moreover, the Russians asked why Washington was transferring two LWRs to North Korea under the terms of the October 1994 Agreed Framework, while objecting to an analogous Russian sale to Iran. The *New York Times*, highlighting this precedent, editorially argued, "However distasteful the regime in Teheran may be, if the principal U.S. goal is a non-nuclear Iran, Washington would be better off trying to strike a bargain like the one it made with North Korea."[32] The Clinton administration forcefully argued that the cases were completely different. North Korea, with two active nuclear reactors and a uranium reprocessing plant, was on the verge of acquiring weapons; the Agreed Framework (as detailed in Chapter 6) offered two proliferation-resistant LWRs in return for the shutdown of those facilities. Iran, by contrast, did not have a developed nuclear infrastructure and the goal was to prevent them from acquiring one.[33] The administration further asserted that this policy did not violate the NPT's provisions regarding access of signatory states to nuclear energy technology because Iran was indeed intent on acquiring nuclear weapons.

Congress further pressured Moscow by threatening to cut off U.S. assistance to Russia if the nuclear deal with Iran went forward.[34] Under these circumstances, President Boris Yeltsin halted the transfer of reprocessing equipment in May 1995, but refused to cancel the sale of the two nuclear reactors. To further assuage American concerns, his government later agreed to return to Russia all spent fuel from the reactors in order to prevent any possible diversion of this fissile material into a weapons program. With respect to the other potential supplier of nuclear technology to Iran—China—the Clinton administration won Beijing's agreement to forego the sale of two nuclear reactors and a uranium-conversion plant.[35] Despite this success in limiting nuclear exports to Iran, the Teheran regime's intentions and compliance with its NPT commitment remain uncertain.[36] Some Middle East security specialists have observed that long-term efforts to deal with Iran's nuclear challenge must take into account the real threats to Iranian security (e.g., Saddam Hussein and the legacy of the Iran-Iraq War) that motivate the regime's drive to acquire nuclear and other WMD capabilities. The salient point in the context of this comparative case study is the difference between the Clinton administration's contrasting responses to the North Korean and Iranian nuclear challenges. In the North Korean case, the imminent threat of its mature nuclear program, and the absence of acceptable alternatives, created a political incentive in Washington for limited engagement through the Agreed Framework. As argued in Chapter 6, the Clinton administration's approach was limited engagement by necessity. By contrast, the Iranian nuclear program was at an incipient stage that posed no immediate military threat, and therefore the administration could pursue an alternative strategy of technology denial in lieu of limited engagement.

The administration's Iran policy also differed significantly from that toward Iraq, despite the linkage created through the "dual containment" strategy. The main theme of Chapter 4 was the policy confusion stemming from the twin objectives—ousting Saddam Hussein and behavior modification—that the Clinton administration has pursued simultaneously. In the case of Iran, this tension between political objectives has been evident but far less pronounced. From Reagan to Clinton, official U.S. policy toward Iran has been consistent: the stated aim has been to change rogue activities (with respect to terrorism and acquisition of WMD capabilities), not to change the theocratic regime. For example, in his important 1994 *Foreign Affairs* article, "National Security Adviser Anthony Lake stated, "More normal relations with the government in Teheran are conceivable, once it demonstrates its willingness to abide by international norms and abandons policies and actions inimical to regional peace and security."[37] Similarly, in November 1995 testimony before the House International Relations Committee, Undersecretary of State for Political Affairs Peter Tarnoff declared, "With respect to the government of Iran, we are not seeking to overthrow that government, but we are seeking to demonstrate as forcefully as possible that several key aspects of Iranian behavior are threats to peace in the region, and hostile to U.S. interests, and we are demanding and mobilizing support for change in the behavior of that government."[38]

While the Clinton administration focused on Iranian behavior, some in Congress argued that the problem was the regime itself. In February 1995, Gingrich called for an $18 million allocation in the U.S. intelligence community budget to support a strategy that "ultimately is designed to force the replacement of the current regime in Iran, which is the only long-range solution that makes any sense."[39] The Clinton administration eventually accepted congressional funding authority for covert operations against Iran, but said that such activities would be focused on changing the regime's behavior rather than its overthrow.[40] Thus, despite congressional pressure, the Clinton administration was not prepared to adopt a rollback strategy toward Iran. This political calculation reflected an amalgam of factors: the magnitude of the Iranian threat (as compared to Iraq, which had invaded two neighboring states in the course of a decade); the lack of international support for comprehensive containment, let alone a rollback strategy to change the clerical regime; the absence of a viable political opposition;[41] and the acknowledgement that the Teheran government (however objectionable its rogue behavior) enjoyed widespread domestic legitimacy.

From 1996 through mid-1997, the move toward a still harder-line American policy toward Iran continued to build momentum. This trend was fueled by a marked increase in Middle East terrorism that was abetted by the Teheran regime, according to U.S. officials. An Islamic militant convicted of terrorist bombings in Israel in February–March 1996, during the Israeli parliamentary campaign, said that he had been trained in Iran and Sudan. These bombings, which were hailed in Teheran, led to the convening of an international summit on terrorism in Egypt in March 1996—a meeting at which the United States sought to mobilize diplomatic support for its strategy to contain and isolate Iran.[42] In June 1996, the Palestinian Authority claimed that Iran was behind a plot to assassinate Yassir Arafat, its president.[43] That same month, nineteen American military personnel were killed in the bombing of the Khobar Towers in Dhahran, Saudi Arabia, and an Iranian-backed group of Shiite Muslims was suspected of the attack. These terrorist incidents, as well as Iran's continued support for Hizbollah attacks on Israel from southern Lebanon, provided a political backdrop to congressional approval of the ILSA, signed into law by President Clinton in August 1996. The serious transatlantic dispute precipitated by the ILSA's extraterritorial application of U.S. sanctions law on foreign firms engaged in commerce with Iran was examined in Chapter 3.

As official U.S. policy toward Iran further hardened with the enactment of the ILSA, some prominent commentators and policy experts outside government questioned the efficacy of the American approach. They noted that Iran had not emerged as the expansionist regional threat that some had feared in the wake of the Gulf War and that the Clinton administration had been unable to produce enough hard evidence of Iranian sponsorship of terrorism to win international support for sanctions. Moreover, unilateral U.S. economic sanctions were unlikely to generate sufficient domestic pressures to force Iran's acceptance of the Bush and Clinton administrations' proposal for an "authorized" dialogue. Some country specialists argued that the sanctions policy bolstered the position of hard-liners within the Teheran regime who used the image of America as an implacable enemy to justify the country's isolation and strict Islamic controls. To break the domestic political impasse on both sides, *New York Times* foreign affairs columnist Thomas Friedman suggested an alternative U.S. approach:

[The administration should] indicate to Iran that if it takes specific steps toward meeting [American] concerns [e.g., regarding terrorism and the acquisition of WMD capabilities], the U.S. will take specific steps toward lifting the economic and diplomatic isolation of Iran. Such an approach would help create more of a united front among the Western allies and, more important, would isolate Iran for spurning basic norms of international behavior rather than isolate the U.S. . . . [Iranian officials in favor of dialogue with the United States] will not risk pushing for a change in their policy if there is no assurance that the U.S. will respond. Let's keep Iran under sanctions, but let's also spell out what we'll do in response to changes in Iran's behavior. That might strengthen the pragmatists [in Teheran], exacerbate divisions within Iran's ruling system, and just maybe, over time, help tip the balance to those favoring a more normal relationship with the United States.[44]

In addition to this utilitarian argument, support for a changed U.S. policy came from those focused on traditional balance-of-power considerations and who questioned the continued appropriateness of "dual containment" as an overarching U.S. strategy in the Persian Gulf region. Former national security adviser Zbigniew Brzezinski argued that Iran should again be viewed as a counterweight to Iraq. The U.S. policy of isolating Iran made "it more difficult to isolate Iraq" and gain access to vast oil deposits in the Caspian Sea region and Central Asia.[45] An influential Council on Foreign Relations task force, co-chaired by Brzezinski and former Bush national security adviser Brent Scowcroft, argued that dual containment had become "more a slogan than a strategy" and advocated "a more nuanced and differentiated approach." Such a strategy, characterized as "differentiated containment," would promote targeted policies geared to the particular circumstances in each country. The report endorsed "the possibilities of creative trade-offs, such as the relaxation of opposition to the Iranian nuclear program in exchange for rigid and comprehensive inspection and control procedures."[46] Opponents of reconciliation maintained that there was no evidence that a shift in U.S. strategy from comprehensive containment would lead to a change in Iranian external behavior.[47]

Despite these calls for dialogue with Iran, the Clinton administration remained committed to its comprehensive containment. In April 1997, when a German court implicated the Teheran government in the 1992 assassination of Iranian dissidents, the administration renewed its appeal to the EU to end its policy of "critical dialogue" and participate in multilateral sanctions (see Chapter 3). In late May, however, the political environment was transformed by the unexpected landslide victory of Khatami, the moderate former minister of culture, over a virulently anti-American cleric in the Iranian presidential election. Calling the election "a very interesting development," President Clinton expressed the "hope that the estrangements [between the two countries] can be bridged."[48] With

Khatami's election, calls for the opening of a dialogue with Iran received new impetus and halted the momentum (manifested in the enactment of the ILSA) for a still stiffer American policy of containment and isolation. That development was based on the reading by many in the policy community of the domestic possibilities created by Khatami's election.

Because of the Iran-Contra legacy and the political dynamic of its own rogue state approach, the Clinton administration had refused to publicly draw any distinctions between contending "moderates" (also called "pragmatists" and "technocrats") and "radicals" inside the Teheran regime. The May 1997 presidential election had exposed the sharp cleavage in Iranian domestic politics. This split, again to highlight the major theme of this chapter, reflected the political tension between Iran's twin identities as a revolutionary and an ordinary state. This duality is symbolized by the two leadership positions created by the Islamic Republic's constitution— the "supreme leader," who is the country's head of state and highest religious authority (Ayatollah Seyyed Ali Khamenei, who succeeded Khomeini), and the president, who heads the government. As will be discussed in the following section, this bifurcation of authority is at the heart of the country's ongoing domestic political struggle, in which the issue of relations with the United States has been central.

While Ayatollah Khamenei and others continued their anti-Western pronouncements, President Khatami espoused a conciliatory approach. In mid-December 1997, at his first news conference since assuming the presidency, Khatami expressed his "great respect" for the American people and his desire "to have a dialogue of civilizations." Citing the participation of fifty-four countries in a recent meeting of the Islamic Conference in Teheran, he said that the U.S. strategy to isolate Iran had failed.[49] President Clinton said he "would like nothing better than to have a dialogue with Iran" but reaffirmed the administration's concerns regarding terrorism, etc., and its continuing commitment to the "dual containment" of Iran and Iraq.[50] On January 7, 1998, in an interview with CNN that received worldwide attention, the Iranian president repeated his call for a cultural dialogue between the two countries (through such measures as academic exchanges), which he carefully distinguished from "political relations" (see the Appendix for the text of this interview). Although the administration undertook no general review of U.S. policy toward Iran after the Khatami election, a contentious interagency debate developed over the implementation of the ILSA. The specific issue in question was whether the Clinton administration would apply or waive ILSA sanctions after a consortium of foreign firms (led by the

French energy giant Total) concluded a major agreement to develop Iranian natural gas fields. Following the May 1998 G-8 meeting, the administration, while maintaining its opposition to foreign participation in Iranian energy development, issued the sanctions waiver to avoid an open breach with the Europeans and the Russians.

In the wake of the ILSA sanctions decision, on June 17, 1998, Secretary Albright delivered a major policy address at the Asia Society in New York that was the administration's first comprehensive response to President Khatami's conciliatory statements. She welcomed the change in Iranian declaratory policy, citing President Khatami's denunciation of terrorism, and said that if his words "are translated into a rejection of terrorism as a tool of Iranian statecraft, it would do much to dispel the concerns of the international community. . . . " Albright said that U.S. economic policies (e.g., opposition to proposals for export pipelines through Iran for Caspian oil and gas) would "remain unchanged" as long as Iranian behavior of concern persisted. But, to dispel Iranian concerns about Washington's intentions, she stated, "[U.S.] policies are not, as some Iranians allege, anti-Islamic. . . . U.S. policy is directed at actions, not peoples or faiths. The standards we would like Iran to observe are not merely Western, but universal. We fully respect Iran's sovereignty. . . . We do not seek to overthrow its government. But we do ask that Iran live up to its commitments to the international community." After endorsing Khatami's call for cultural and academic exchanges and increased people-to-people contact, Albright stated, "We are ready to explore further ways to build mutual confidence and avoid misunderstandings. The Islamic Republic should consider parallel steps. If such a process can be initiated and sustained in a way that addresses the concerns of both sides, then we in the United States can see the prospect of a very different relationship. As the wall of mistrust comes down, we can develop with the Islamic Republic, when it is ready, *a road map leading to normal relations.*" In an implicit reference to criticism of the Clinton administration's generic approach toward those countries designated as rogue states, she concluded, "America cannot view every issue or nation through a single prism. We must take into account the full range of our interests. We must combine adherence to principle with a pragmatic sense of what works. . . . We must know when to engage and when to isolate, and we must always be flexible enough to respond to change and to seize historic opportunities when they arise."[51]

Albright reportedly negotiated the reformulation of U.S. policy toward Iran contained in her June 1998 speech without a major interagency battle. Given the highly contentious nature of the issue, President Clinton later congratulated her "for threading the needle."[52] The "road map" metaphor was apt. Although Washington could identify the destination—Iran's reintegration into the international community—the particular route remained unclear. Albright's pathbreaking speech embraced the differentiated policy that the critics of dual containment had advocated—a process of "parallel steps" that "addresses the concerns of both sides." (Such an approach is referred to in the political science literature as "conditional reciprocity.") The speech, with its assertion that "America cannot view every issue or nation through a single prism," also attempted to break with the administration's generic rogue state policy. And yet, the very success of that policy in mobilizing political support for a hard-line policy through demonization hindered the ability of the Clinton administration to navigate such a shift in response to changed circumstances in Iran. Formidable opposition in the Republican-led Congress and beyond hindered any change from the rogue state policy's default strategy of comprehensive containment and isolation. This continuing cleavage in American domestic politics over relations with Iran has been mirrored on the Iranian side. Attention will now turn to that pivotal question—the domestic political struggle in Teheran and its linkage to Iran's foreign policy.

THE IRANIAN DOMESTIC CONTEXT

A major theme of this chapter has been the contending visions of Iran as an ordinary versus a revolutionary state. That tension is at the heart of Iran's ongoing domestic political struggle. An inadequate understanding of the dynamics of change within Iran has hampered the ability of Washington and other foreign capitals to assess and respond to events since the 1979 revolution. The prior set of assumptions guiding Western policy was overturned with the revolution—thus creating an intellectual vacuum that still exists. Although revolutions are by their nature sui generis, they pass though broadly similar phases. Beginning more as a cause than a concrete program of action, successful revolutions are soon subject to the practical requirements of government. Revolutions radically alter perspectives within the society, but they cannot change the objective realities of the state. Those realities—geographic position, demography, natural resources, and the regional environment—define the possibilities of state action. Schisms within revolutionary leaderships often emerge over the degree of tactical accommodation that the regime must prudently make to realize its long-term revolutionary objectives. The continuing power struggle between radicals and pragmatists within the Teheran regime corresponds to this historical model. In the case of post-revolutionary Iran, one observer has characterized this as "the ideological conflict between the philosophy of the revolution . . . and the interests of the Iranian state."[53] The regime's radical faction is concerned that cumulative tactical shifts for the sake of pragmatism (such as ceasing efforts to "export" its revolution to neighboring states) will erode the legitimacy of the revolutionary vision. This concern about preserving the revolution's political legitimacy has resulted in a complex linkage between the clerical regime's domestic and foreign policies.

Political conflict is further fueled by the Islamic Republic's unique fusion of religion and politics. Eliminating the separation between mosque and state was the realization of Ayatollah Khomeini's revolutionary vision. Under Iran's 1979 Constitution, Khomeini was named "supreme leader" (*vali-ye faqih*), an unprecedented position with paramount religious and political authority. Khomeini invoked the Shiite legal concept of *velayat-i-faqih* ("rule of the supreme juris-consult") as the ideological underpinning for this new constitutional structure. The Assembly of Experts, a popularly elected body established in 1982 and dominated by the clergy, chooses the supreme leader from among the country's leading clerics. The supreme leader has ultimate authority over all state institutions, including the military, internal security services, judiciary, and broadcasting services, and also controls powerful "foundations" that are actually huge government-run companies with billions of dollars in assets confiscated after the 1979 revolution. In addition, the position exerts strong influence over the Council of Guardians, a body of twelve senior Islamic jurists and experts in Islamic law with power to void any legislation that it deems contrary to Islam or the 1979 Constitution. In striking contrast to the supreme leader, the powers of the president are quite circumscribed. The president is the chief executive with the power to appoint government ministers, subject to parliamentary (Majlis) approval, and run the government bureaucracy (particularly those parts dealing with social services and management of the economy). But, as Middle East historian Shaul Bakhash observes, the president's powers are often more notional than real since "the Supreme Leader is constitutionally empowered to set the broad policies of the Islamic Republic, and in practice he has acquired additional means of interfering in the running of the government."[54] In assessing the practical possibilities for President Khatami to alter Iranian foreign policy vis-à-vis the United States, this institutional context—and the relative distribution of political power that it reflects—is highly pertinent.

Khomeini's own personal stature was a pivotal factor in the unfolding of the revolution, and that charismatic leadership was institutionalized through the 1979 Constitution in the position of supreme leader. Mehdi Bazargan, a leading nonclerical Iranian political figure and the first prime minister of the Islamic Republic, observed that this constitutional arrangement was "a garment fit only for Mr. Khomeini."[55] After Khomeini's death in June 1989, a peaceful transfer of power occurred: Khamenei, a cleric known more for his political activism than his religious scholarship, was elevated to supreme leader, and Rafsanjani, another "religio-politician" (to use Iran expert David Menashri's term), was elected president. But with this transition, the challenge of the post-Khomeini era emerged: making a system institutionally centered on a supreme leader work in the absence of a charismatic political figure. Khomeini's unique standing had been such that his decisions never faced serious political challenge; certainly no one within the ruling regime questioned his authority (even if some of his fellow clerics were uncomfortable with his expansive interpretation of the *velayat-i-faqih* concept). That has not been the case for his successors—thus evidencing the dilemma identified by sociologist Max Weber of institutionalizing charismatic leadership. The post-Khomeini political struggle has revolved around the role of the supreme leader. The relative powers of the supreme leader and the president are connected vessels. To the extent that the supreme leader's authority is limited, the president has the potential to assert increased power over the instruments of government. This political competition was waged during Rafsanjani's eight-year tenure as president and has continued into the Khatami era.

Supreme Leader Khamenei and President Rafsanjani established an uneasy "diumvirate"—a mixed relationship that oscillated over time between competition and cooperation depending on the issue. Rafsanjani was identified with Iran's professional class, the so-called technocrats who sought to limit religious interference in economic and governmental affairs. As president, he initiated economic reforms to address the country's severe problems (declining oil revenues leading to budget deficits, decreased foreign investment, and an over-reliance on the oil economy). All of these were exacerbated by a rapidly rising population and by the eight-year war with Iraq that had sapped resources and destroyed infrastructure. The Rafsanjani economic reforms (such as increased privatization), as well as a limited liberalization in social and cultural affairs, generated a backlash from his political opponents and riots in major cities in spring 1992. As Menashri observes, "Rafsanjani's reforms . . . caused hardships for the poor and deviated from basic ideological convictions, which infuriated the radicals."[56] One political casualty of this political struggle was the future president, Khatami, who was forced to resign from his position as minister of culture for being too liberal. In a telling indicator of this radical backlash, Khatami's successor as minister for culture won a Majlis decision in September 1994 to ban satellite dishes throughout the country, arguing that foreign television programs amounted to "cultural occupation."[57] Opposition to the Rafsanjani reforms permitted Khamenei, who sided with the hard-liners, to increasingly dominate their political relationship.[58] And yet, it was within this increasingly radical political context that Rafsanjani made a striking decision in early 1995 to permit the U.S. oil conglomerate Conoco to develop one of Iran's major offshore oil fields.

The contending interpretations of Rafsanjani's initiative in the American policy community stemmed from differing assessments of Iranian intentions. The contradictory status of Rafsanjani himself, a member of the religious hierarchy not averse to playing the anti-Western card, contributed to this division of opinion. For example, in a rare press conference in January 1993, Rafsanjani vowed to fight "imperialism" anywhere, while stating that the resumption of relations with the United States "would not be in contradiction with Iran's objectives" if American policies were "truly corrected."[59] One interpretation of the Conoco overture was that it was a further effort by the Iranian president to reach out to the United States after his earlier involvement to win the release of American hostages in Lebanon. In this view, Rafsanjani was taking on powerful domestic political forces to begin a process of normalization. An alternative interpretation was that Rafsanjani was seeking a compartmentalized relationship—that is, gaining access to American capital and technology to assist the Iranian economy, while avoiding behavioral changes in areas of U.S. concern, such as terrorism.[60]

The Clinton administration, for reasons discussed above, not only nixed the Conoco deal, but also imposed comprehensive U.S. sanctions on Iran in May 1995. Rafsanjani denounced the administration's "extortionate policies" and claimed that they would have little impact on the country.[61] He was reportedly surprised by the administration's rejection of the Conoco deal, believing that the oil conglomerate's political clout would be sufficient to win approval. He asserted that Washington had missed an opportunity to improve relations with Teheran: "We invited an American firm and entered into a deal for $1 billion. This was a message to the United States, which was not correctly understood. We had a lot of difficulty in this country by inviting an American country to come here with such a project because of public opinion."[62] Said Rajai Khorassani, a member of the president's inner circle and head of the Majlis's foreign relations committee, lamented, "We don't have any counterparts in the Clinton administration and this has made it hard to promote a more lenient Iranian policy."[63] For his part, Khamenei welcomed the Clinton administration's announcement of a total trade embargo, arguing that it would encourage the country's self-sufficiency.[64] Assessing Rafsanjani's foreign policy initiatives within the context of Iran's ongoing domestic political struggle, Bakhash observed, "The reading of Rafsanjani as a pragmatist who wanted to re-engage Iran with the rest of the world was not wrong. But the circumstances have changed. Iranian behavior has become more inconsistent, incoherent, more radical, its foreign policy more sensitive to what the regime believes is necessary to be an international leader. To an extent, it's a reversion to the early years of the revolution."[65] Whatever one's reading of his underlying motivations, the Conoco episode marked Rafsanjani's final effort during his tenure as president to initiate an opening to Washington.

The issue of relations with Washington again emerged on the Iranian political agenda after the 1997 election that swept Khatami to power. His victory over Majlis Speaker Ali Akbar Nateq-Nuri, who had been endorsed by the regime's most conservative clerics, was a landmark political event reflecting a widespread popular desire for change. Postelection polling indicated that the electorate was primarily concerned with the economy and quality-of-life issues; only 15 percent, according to one poll printed in a pro-Khatami newspaper, felt that it was important for Iran's leaders to confront the West's "cultural onslaught" and resist accommodation with the United States.[66] The popular will expressed through the ballot box bestowed Khatami with the political legitimacy to act decisively.

After the election some referred to the new president as "Ayatollah Gorbachev." The analogy to the former Soviet leader was both misleading and apt. It failed to accurately portray Iran's domestic political struggle because of the fundamental difference between the structures of political power in the two countries. Gorbachev, as general secretary of the Communist Party in the Soviet Union, was the country's paramount leader with the political authority to carry out sweeping reforms. By contrast, under Iran's constitutional structure, the position of president remains subordinated to that of the supreme leader, who exercises direct control over key organs of state power (such as the military and the judiciary). So even though the 1997 election gave Khatami a mandate for change, his scope for action was severely constrained by this constitutional arrangement. But one attribute that Khatami shared with Gorbachev was that neither was a revolutionary. Like the former Soviet leader, Khatami entered office intending to make the Islamic Republic's system work better, not overthrow it.[67] He arose from the ruling clerical class, one of only 4 candidates out of nearly 240 that the Council of Guardians permitted to compete in the 1997 presidential election.[68] Khatami has not directly challenged the authority of the supreme leader based on the *velayat-i-faqih* principle enshrined in the constitution. He has, however, called for a "civil society ruled by law"—a phrase widely interpreted as a call for limiting clerical involvement, including that of the supreme leader, in politics. CIA Director George Tenet told the Senate Select Committee on Intelligence in January 1998 that Khatami is engaged in a "genuine struggle . . . with the hard-line conservatives."[69] This political struggle over the role of the clergy in society remains the central issue in Iranian politics. Its outcome, in turn, will determine the context within which the Teheran regime's policy toward Washington is made.

The sharp split between Khatami and Khamenei was evidenced at the December 1997 meeting of the Islamic Conference in Teheran, an international gathering of heads of state that marked Iran's emergence from pariah status. While Khamenei emphasized confrontation with the West, Khatami stated, "Our era is an era of preponderance of Western culture and civilization, whose understanding is imperative. . . . Undoubtedly, we will only succeed in moving forward . . . if we . . . utilize the positive scientific, technological and social accomplishments of Western civilization, a stage we must inevitably go through to reach the future."[70] A month later, in his CNN interview, Khatami expanded on his Islamic Conference speech and on a December 14 press conference in which he had expressed hopes for a "thoughtful dialogue" with "the great people of the United States." The centerpiece of the Iranian president's remarks was his proposal for a "dialogue between civilizations," a process that he carefully distinguished from "political relations" (see Appendix). *New York Times* correspondent Sciolino, reporting the claim by Khatami aides that Khamenei had been broadly apprised in advance of the initiative, concluded, "nowhere do the two men disagree more than on their view of the United States."[71] During a Friday prayer sermon at Teheran University following the CNN interview, Khamenei, while refraining from personal criticism of Khatami, rejected a rapprochement with the United States: "Talks with the

United States have no benefit for us and are harmful to us. We don't need any talks or relations with the United States. The regime of the United States is the enemy of the Islamic Republic. . . . You complain about us calling you the Great Satan while you do satanic acts."[72]

Following Secretary of State Albright's "road map" speech in June 1998 in response to Khatami's CNN interview, Iranian officials expressed irritation that it contained no specific proposal or incentive for a political dialogue going beyond expanded people-to-people contacts. In September, Khatami and Foreign Minister Kamal Kharrazi attended the opening of the UN General Assembly and used the occasion of their presence in New York to further address U.S.-Iranian relations. In a September 22 press conference, broadcast on Iranian television, Khatami stated that his proposal for a cultural dialogue had been misunderstood and precluded government-to-government talks for the time being.[73] Foreign Minister Kharrazi's speech at the Asia Society, billed by Iranian officials as the government's response to the Albright address, elaborated on Khatami's rebuff. While noting the "new tone" of American officials, Kharrazi said that Washington was still locked into a "cold war mentality."[74] In this speech, which former secretary of state Cyrus Vance characterized as "very tough," the Iranian foreign minister issued a stinging criticism of U.S. policies, including the imposition of unilateral U.S. sanctions on the grounds that they violated international law; Washington's opposition to the construction of a pipeline through Iran to transport oil and gas from Central Asia and the Caucasus, thereby "retarding [the] economic prosperity of Iran and the region"; the covert program authorized by Congress to destabilize Iran; the continued U.S. refusal to return Iranian assets frozen during the hostage crisis; and the U.S. "propaganda war" against Iran waged by the Prague-based Radio Free Iran.[75] During Khatami's highly publicized visit to New York, the political struggle between rivaling factions continued back in Iran. Judicial authorities, controlled by Khamenei, shut down several pro-Khatami publications for featuring articles by religious intellectuals that advocated restricting the authority of the supreme leader. This assault on the media was part of the broader backlash by conservative clerics and their radical supporters against Khatami's efforts to develop a new type of "civil society" and for adherence to the Islamic Republic's founding revolutionary principles. In July 1999, prodemocracy students mounted large public demonstrations against press restrictions and the arbitrary power of the conservative clerics. After the demonstrations turned violent, reportedly because of the infiltration of agents provocateurs into the students' ranks, Khatami issued a stern warning about the government's determination to maintain civil order, and the protests subsided.[76] But these dramatic six days of civil unrest point to the profound schism in Iran's domestic politics that continues to severely limit Khatami's scope for action, both domestically and in its relations with the United States.

The country's mounting economic problems have exacerbated the domestic political struggle between radical and moderate factions. The Iranian economy has remained beset by sluggish growth, high budget deficits and inflation, low foreign investment, and (until mid-1999) depressed oil prices. The low price of oil resulting from a global glut was of particular significance given the marginal size of Iran's non-oil economy and the consequent importance of these revenues for the regime to finance government services and subsidies. Given a population growth rate of over 2 percent per year, the Iranian economy must annually grow at 6 percent just to maintain the current standard of living; the economy must create seven hundred thousand jobs per year to meet the demand of the country's restive and increasingly assertive youth.[77] Experts differ over the impact of U.S. sanctions on the Iranian economy. Although these sanctions have been pursued unilaterally, the Clinton administration's drive to isolate Iran economically has had an undisputed impact on the extent of foreign investment in the country's energy sector. Economist Jahanagir Amuzegar offers a balanced assessment: "Since the early 1980s . . . the theocratic regime has moved forward on many economic fronts, but has been effectively held back in its efforts to reach [a] pre-revolution level of national prosperity. U.S. sanctions have had a part in the setback, but not a decisive role. While the regime may survive the enhanced sanctions [referring to the American total trade ban and the ILSA], the economy is not likely to prosper without American and Western support."[78] The domestic politics of Iran's economic crisis, and its implications with respect to relations with the United States and the West, are complex and often contradictory. As during Rafsanjani's presidency, it is clear that a major motivating factor behind Khatami's reconciliation policy was the need to gain access to American capital and technology. But that economic rationale has not been able to overcome the domestic political impediments to dealings with the United States discussed above. For the radicals, the United States has proved a useful scapegoat to shift blame for the theocratic regime's own economic mismanagement.[79]

Clinton administration officials have repeatedly stated that any change in the U.S. sanctions regime would be contingent on demonstrable changes in Iranian behavior in three key areas of concern. Those "red button" issues, as Middle East specialist Geoffrey Kemp calls them, include Iran's efforts to acquire WMD, its use of terrorism as an instrument of state policy, and its disruptive opposition to the Arab-Israeli peace process.[80] As these issues are key determinants of American policy, it is important to briefly consider Iranian attitudes and behavior with respect to each—and how they are affected by the ongoing political struggle between the moderate and radical factions.

Terrorism

Although Iran remained on the State Department's 1998 list of state sponsors of international terrorism, U.S. intelligence officials reported that President Khatami was sincerely working to end government support of terrorism and that the main impediment was his inability to consolidate control over the intelligence services.[81] Khatami has displayed political courage by taking on the powerful, shadowy, quasi-governmental foundations that have placed a bounty on Salman Rushdie and are a likely indirect source of funding for terrorist activities. The Iranian Intelligence Ministry made the extraordinary public admission in January 1999 that rogue intelligence officers had assassinated critics of the conservative clergy who opposed Khatami's policies.[82] As reflected in these developments, the issue of terrorism has become a major front in the ongoing domestic power struggle. Despite Khatami's commitment to curtail terrorism, there has been no discernible decline in such activities, according to U.S. officials. The Khatami camp recognizes the steep political price that Iran has paid with other Middle East states, the Europeans, and more broadly, the international community because of its sponsorship of terrorism. For this reason, Khatami's moderate faction pushed for the resignation of the minister of intelligence as a tangible symbol of change. And yet, radical elements within the theocratic regime and outside Khatami's direct control may continue to view terrorism as a useful instrument to defend and project the values of the revolution. Given the startling revelation of January 1999 regarding the Ministry of Intelligence's rogue operations, it is entirely plausible that the implacable opponents of reconciliation with the "Great Satan" might perpetrate terrorist acts to scuttle any nascent U.S.-Iranian rapprochement.

Weapons of Mass Destruction

During the Khatami era, the Teheran regime continued to deny any intention of developing WMD capabilities.[83] Iran is a signatory to the major nonproliferation agreements—the Nuclear Non-Proliferation Treaty (NPT), the Chemical Weapons Convention, and the Biological Weapons Convention. Iranian officials are quick to point out that Iran was the victim of Iraqi WMD attacks during the Iran-Iraq War while the international community stood by. Despite the regime's declarations to the contrary, Washington is suspicious of Iran's intentions. Clinton administration officials note that Iraq too was a signatory to the key nonproliferation treaties prior to the Gulf War and that it had taken advantage of a permissive export control regime to acquire Western, mainly European, dual-use technologies to mount a massive covert WMD program. Political scientists Chubin and Jerrold Green observe that the U.S. definition of "dual use" has now become so broad that it would bar Iran access to practically any modern technology. This broad technology-denial policy, as discussed above, has failed to win multilateral support. The Clinton administration was also pressed to explain why it opposed the transfer of Russian nuclear power reactors to Iran while it was in the process of providing the very same type of technology to North Korea under the Agreed Framework.

Iran remains a country of nonproliferation concern to American policymakers because of the country's two obvious motivations in obtaining WMD capabilities. The first is that these unconventional capabilities are an alternative to large conventional forces, which the regime has been unable to acquire owing to the country's sustained economic crisis. (Proponents of unilateral U.S. sanctions claim this crisis as a tangible indicator of success, although Iran's cash shortage can more obviously be attributed to the collapse in the price of oil.) The second is the nature of the regional security environment that Iran faces—particularly the potential threat from Iraq if Saddam Hussein should be able to overcome the UN sanctions regime and reconstitute his WMD capabilities. Like their American counterparts, Iranian officials also infer intentions from capabilities: they point to the large U.S. air and naval force in the Gulf region (that hitherto has been used only against Iraq) and Israel's undeclared, but widely acknowledged, nuclear weapons program. Given the political prism through which Iran's leaders view the world, this perception of threat is not implausible.

Developments during 1998–99 continued to raise questions about Iran's WMD intentions. These developments included the successful test of the Shabab-3 medium-range missile, described by a Teheran official as a defensive measure; the imposition of U.S. sanctions on more than a dozen Russian companies for transferring proscribed missile technology to Iran;[84] disturbing reports that China and Russia may renege on their 1995 commitments to the Clinton administration not to sell sensitive nuclear technologies (e.g., uranium enrichment equipment) to Iran;[85] and a *New York Times* report, denied in Teheran, that Iran had recruited Russian scientists to work in a covert biological weapons program.[86]

The WMD issue poses a dilemma for Iran's divided leadership. On the one hand, these weapons are an economical alternative to a conventional buildup, a potential source of regional influence, and a deterrent to the country's foes. On the other hand, acquiring WMD capabilities would be a violation of Iran's treaty commitments and would reinforce the international pariah status that Khatami seeks to overcome. Military analyst Michael Eisenstadt concludes, "President Khatami might find it difficult to reconcile the two goals, though the matter may not be his to decide."[87] Indeed, the WMD issue has become closely linked to that of relations with the United States in the internal power struggle. Consider the hardline stance articulated by the commander of the Iranian Revolutionary Guard Corps, Yahya Rahim Safavi, in April 1998: "Liberals . . . have taken over our universities and our youth are shouting slogans against despotism. We are seeking to root out counter-revolutionaries wherever they are. . . . Can we withstand American threats and domineering attitude with a policy of détente? Can we foil dangers coming from America through dialogue between civilizations? Will we be able to protect the Islamic Republic from international Zionism by signing the conventions to ban proliferation of chemical and nuclear weapons?"[88] This remark reflects the contentious domestic political context within which the WMD issue is rooted.

The Arab-Israeli Peace Process

Iran's attitude toward Israel and the peace process is a thorny issue whose status will significantly affect the prospects for reconciliation between Teheran and Washington. The United States has accused Iran of undermining the peace process through its indirect support of Palestinian opposition groups that rely on terrorism, such as Hamas, and its direct military assistance to the Lebanese Shiite group Hizbollah, which operates in southern Lebanon. Iranian leaders have staked out a political position on Israel and the peace process that is more extreme than the Palestinians'. In his January 1998 CNN interview, best known for its call for a "dialogue between civilizations," President Khatami reaffirmed Iran's opposition to the peace process and referred to Israel as a "racist terrorist regime."[89] Later that month, Arafat told U.S. officials that Khatami had privately assured him that Iran would accept any agreement that he negotiated.[90] And yet, Foreign Minister Kharrazi condemned the cancellation of clauses in the Palestinian Liberation Organization's charter calling for Israel's destruction, stating, "The recent move . . . to change the national charter is an act of meanness aimed at humiliating the Palestinian people."[91] Conservative clerics, such as Khamenei and Majlis Speaker Nateq-Nuri, have been even more extreme on Israel and the peace process. Nateq-Nuri told a Teheran University audience in January 1999, "Come out openly, like Iran, and say you don't accept such a country as Israel on the world map. We can make good use of our weapons, military equipment and all our forces."[92] The Palestinian Authority claimed in November 1998 that it had foiled a plot by Islamic militants, funded and trained by Iran, to assassinate Arafat and other Palestinian leaders.[93] In June 1999, the Iranian government announced that thirteen Jews had been arrested for "spying" for Israel and the United States.[94]

The issue of Israel and the Middle East peace process is particularly problematic for the Iranian leadership because it goes to the heart of the revolutionary principles on which the Islamic Republic was founded. This accounts for the contradictory public and private statements made by Khatami and others in the leadership. The regime draws on its external role as the ostensible leader of a worldwide Islamic movement as a source of political legitimacy at home. Although the Khatami election was striking evidence that the Iranian public is primarily concerned about domestic economic and social conditions, the clerical regime will find it difficult for ideological reasons to radically shift its policy. That said, a variety of proposals have been offered that would substantially defuse the issue in U.S.-Iranian relations by addressing objectionable Iranian behavior (e.g., ending military assistance to Hizbollah and links to Palestinian terrorist groups). As in other spheres of Iranian policy, a major impediment to change is the existence of independent power centers (such as the Revolutionary Guards, intelligence services, and foundations) that have the ability to circumvent Khatami's policies even if he should prevail in the domestic political struggle.

POLICY ASSESSMENT

This chapter has traced the evolution of the United States's strategy of comprehensive containment and isolation toward Iran since the 1979 revolution. In contrast to U.S. policy toward Iraq, the American objective is not to oust the Teheran regime, but to alter its objectionable behavior. Unlike in the Iraqi and Libyan cases, the United States has pursued this strategy unilaterally. In so doing, U.S. administrations from Reagan to Clinton have relied almost exclusively on punitive instruments, in particular economic sanctions, to affect the Teheran regime's behavior and bring Iran into compliance with international norms. The country's designation as a rogue or outlaw state by the Clinton administration was a political device to mobilize support, both at home and abroad, for tough measures to increase the pressure on the theocratic regime and thereby compel changes in its behavior. Even before Khatami's election, many in the American foreign policy community had concluded that the Clinton administration's "dual containment" policy was a strategic dead end that underscored the limits of American unilateralism. The administration, however, was moved to undertake such a reassessment only after the 1997 presidential election recast Iran's domestic political landscape. Secretary of State Albright's "road map" speech offered a possible shift from a hard-line strategy featuring only penalties to a mixed one incorporating incentives.

In January 1999, one year after President Khatami's CNN interview and seven months after the Albright speech, a senior State Department official stated that Albright's initiative was "basically moribund" because of pervasive hostility toward the United States in Iran's theocratic regime. The official concluded, "We continue to believe that Khatami is the best opportunity for change we have seen since 1979. . . . [He is] preoccupied . . . fighting a very difficult domestic battle."[95] Albright's "road map" metaphor suggests that the two parties share a common destination. In both countries, but particularly in Iran, there are those opposed to a normalization of relations because of the very character of the other state and society. Chubin and Green explain the symbolic importance of relations with the United States and why the issue is at the heart of the domestic power struggle:

Reconstituting normal relations will not be easy for either side, but the White House's formidable problems in changing course are minimal compared to those of its Iranian counterpart. Hostility to the US has been a central plank of the Revolutionary platform and sometimes appears to be the Revolution's *only* policy. Deprived of this, radicals would have to devise another enemy, another excuse, possibly even a programme. . . . Normalisation implies that Iran would be a country like any other, losing its Revolutionary mission. The more pragmatic Iran becomes, the less ideology will exercise a hold on its citizens. The clerical regime would lose its power over technocrats and its control over the country. . . . Apart from meeting US demands, Khatami will also have to fend off attacks from the conservatives. . . . His CNN interview . . . was aimed at least as much at Iranian public opinion as at the US. He sought to portray the US as an ordinary state with commendable values (as well as defects), and thereby undermine its image as the 'Great Satan', the fount of all oppression and vice.[96]

This assessment of Khatami's predicament again points to the profound conflict between the Islamic Republic's dual identities as a revolutionary and an ordinary state.

For Khatami, as with Rafsanjani in the early 1990s, a major motivation underlying the tentative policy of rapprochement with the United States has been Iran's continuing economic malaise. Along with major reforms (such as privatization), the Khatami faction views access to Western capital and technology as an important prerequisite for Iran's economic revival. But the economic pain associated with the unilateral U.S. sanctions has not been sufficient to bring change in Iran's political arena. As Amuzegar observes, American sanctions are unlikely to get the Teheran regime to "cry uncle" and are pushing the country toward greater self-sufficiency.[97] Iran may be economically stagnating, but it is not a "failed state." Unilateral sanctions (particularly the attempt under the ILSA to extend them extraterritorially) have diplomatically isolated Washington and, in Iran, are depicted by the opponents of normalization as evidence of implacable American hostility.

On the U.S side, the demonization of Iran as a rogue state has created a significant political impediment to normalization. Iran has been referred to as the "third rail" of American politics that contributed to the electoral defeat of one president (Carter, via the hostage crisis) and nearly brought down another (Reagan, via the Iran-Contra scandal). The United States may be a central defining issue for Iran, but Iran is not for the United States. There is an interest, but no overriding imperative—geostrategic or economic—for the normalization of relations with Teheran. As will be discussed in Chapter 6, this situation contrasts with that of North Korea, in which the imminent danger of the Pyongyang regime's nuclear program pushed the reluctant Clinton administration toward a strategy of limited engagement through the Agreed Framework. In the absence of such an imperative for engagement, the domestic political hurdles blocking normalization on the American side will likely remain formidable. One of this study's main critique's of the rogue state approach is that its demonization of the target state for the purposes of political mobilization makes any subsequent change in policy in response to altered circumstances (such as the election of Khatami) very difficult to negotiate. The Clinton administration has made some gestures in response to Khatami's call for dialogue and his willingness to take on the radicals: for example, it removed Iran from the government's list of major drug-producing countries in December 1998.[98] But the situation was reminiscent of that in 1993 when the Bush administration reviewed its Iran policy in the wake of the Gulf War and concluded that any American gesture that would make a real difference in Iran would be politically unpalatable in the United States.

Secretary Albright's important speech of June 1998 did not offer any specific incentive, but did propose a "road map" for normalization in which the two sides would undertake "parallel steps" to break down mutual distrust. This process of conditional reciprocity has not moved forward because of the domestic political impediments on both sides, particularly those in Iran. To break the impasse, some commentators have recommended that the Clinton administration be more explicit in articulating what concrete steps it would take with respect to sanctions if Iranian behavior changed in key spheres of U.S. concern, such as terrorism. In addition, although the scope of action is limited on the American side, some unilateral changes in current policy may be possible if they can be justified on humanitarian grounds or on the grounds that they needlessly penalize U.S. business. These would include U.S. sales to Iran of food and consumer goods that are readily available from foreign suppliers.

The key determinant of U.S.-Iranian normalization is the domestic political struggle in Teheran. In shaping U.S. policy, Chubin and Green have correctly observed that the American concern, articulated by senior officials, of "whether Khatami can deliver" should be reformulated as "what can the US do to see that Khatami can deliver?"[99] The challenge for U.S. policy-makers is to jettison the generic rogue state approach and develop a nuanced, targeted strategy toward Iran that will support the proponents of normalization inside the clerical regime and make possible Iran's reintegration into the international community. This process of normalization, given the gulf of mutual mistrust, is certain to be lengthy. The near-term issue is whether the reformers, including Khatami himself, will be able to survive the intensifying power struggle in Teheran—a process in which the United States has a clear stake and some ability to influence the outcome.

NOTES

[1]Barbara Crossette, "Albright, in Overture to Iran, Seeks a 'Road Map' to Amity," *New York Times*, June 18, 1998, p. A1.

[2] For a concise historical survey of U.S.-Iranian relations see Geoffrey Kemp, *Forever Enemies? American Policy and the Islamic Republic of Iran* (Washington, DC: Carnegie Endowment for International Peace, 1994), pp. 19–26.

[3] Ibid., p. 21.

[4] For a detailed examination of the Nixon Doctrine's regional strategy see Robert S. Litwak, *Détente and the Nixon Doctrine: American Foreign Policy and the Pursuit of Stability, 1969–1976* (Cambridge: Cambridge University Press, 1984), pp. 139–43.

[5] In deference to Arab sensibilities, the Nixon administration referred to its Persian Gulf strategy as a "twin pillar" policy, with Saudi Arabia as the other designated regional partner. Saudi Arabia was the dominant member of the then-powerful Organization of Petroleum Exporting Countries but was a negligible military power.

[6] See the excellent analysis of U.S. decision-making in Charles-Phillipe Davis, Nancy Ann Carol, and Zachary A. Selden, *Foreign Policy Failure in the White House* (Lanham, MD: University Press of America, 1993).

[7] *Economist*, September 5, 1987, p. 13, as cited in Shahram Chubin and Charles Tripp, *Iran and Iraq at War* (London: I. B. Tauris, 1988), p. 215. The Chubin-Tripp volume is the most comprehensive narrative history of the Iran-Iraq War.

[8] Shahram Chubin, "The Last Phase of the Iran-Iraq War: From Stalemate to Ceasefire," *Third World Quarterly* 11, no. 2 (April 1989), p. 13.

[9] Kemp, *Forever Enemies?* pp. 24–25.

[10] *Public Papers of the Presidents of the United States: George Bush, 1989*, vol. 1 (Washington, DC: U.S. Government Printing Office [GPO], 1990), pp. 1–4.

[11] The quotations from Khomeini's political will and Rafsanjani are cited in Bruce W. Jentleson, *With Friends Like These: Reagan, Bush, and Saddam, 1982–1990* (New York: Norton, 1994), pp. 96–97.

[12] Elaine Sciolino, "Distrust of U.S. Hinders Iran Chief," *New York Times*, April 10, 1992, p. A3.

[13] Elaine Sciolino, "CIA Says Iran Makes Progress on Atom Arms," *New York Times*, November 30, 1992, p. A1.

[14] Elaine Sciolino, "After a Fresh Look, U.S. Decides to Steer Clear of Iran," *New York Times*, June 7, 1992, section 4, p. 5; the spring 1992 policy review on Iran is discussed in Alexander L. George, *Bridging the Gap: Theory and Practice in Foreign Policy* (Washington, DC: United States Institute of Peace Press, 1993), p. 60.

[15] Elaine Sciolino, "U.S. Hopes to Broaden Ban on Arms Sales to Iran," New York Times, November 18, 1992, p. A5.

[16] Keith Bradsher, "Boeing Asks to Sell Jets to Iran Air," *New York Times*, September 30, 1992, p. D5.

[17] Elaine Sciolino, "Christopher Signals a Tougher U.S. Line toward Iran," *New York Times*, March 31, 1993, p. A3.

[18] Robert Keatley, "U.S., Hurting Boeing and Aiding Airbus, Is Likely to Keep Ban on Jet Sales to Iran," *Wall Street Journal*, April 9, 1993, p. A7.

[19] Ayatollah Khomeini's son, Ahmed Khomeini, called the PLO-Israel agreement "unprecedented treachery" and President Rafsanjani continued to refer to Israel as an "illegitimate state."

[20] Peter Waldman, "Turning Back: As Economy of Iran Worsens, Government Reverts to Hard Line; Radical Clerics Who Oppose Market Reforms Regain Control over Rafsanjani; Missed Chance for the U.S.?" *Wall Street Journal*, June 28, 1994, p. A1.

[21] Douglas Jehl, "U.S. Seeks Ways to Isolate Iran; Describes Leaders as Dangerous," *New York Times*, May 27, 1993, p. A1.

[22] Prior to a December 1993 meeting between U.S. and EU officials, a senior German official said, "The American position is not fair. The Americans are saying, 'These are the bad guys and be finished with them.' We are saying, 'These are the outcasts and isn't it better to have a dialogue with them.' We have a certain difference of

approach based on practicality." Quoted in Elaine Sciolino, "U.S. and Germany at Odds on Isolating Iran," *New York Times*, December 2, 1998, p. A13.

[23] Tim Weiner, "Iran and Allies Are Suspected in Bomb Wave," *New York Times*, July 29, 1994, p. A1.

[24] Cited in Geoffrey Kemp, *America and Iran: Road Maps and Realism* (Washington, DC: Nixon Center, 1998), p. 65.

[25] Todd S. Purdum, "Clinton to Order a Trade Embargo against Teheran," *New York Times*, May 1, 1995, p. A1.

[26] David E. Sanger, "The Iran Exception; U.S. Will Deal with Other Old Foes but Still Sees Teheran as an Outlaw," *New York Times*, March 15, 1995, p. D5.

[27] Purdum, "Clinton to Order a Trade Embargo against Teheran."

[28] In the lead-up to the June 1995 meeting of the G-7 and Russia in Halifax, Nova Scotia, the leading European nations voiced opposition to the U.S. trade ban and their commitment to "critical dialogue." German economics minister Gunter Rexrodt said, "We do not believe that a trade embargo is the appropriate instrument [for] influencing opinion in Iran and [bringing] Iran to behave responsibly. . . . Only political dialogue can bring Iran to behave responsibly." Alan Cowell, "U.S. Fails to Enlist European Allies in Iranian Trade Embargo," *New York Times*, May 3, 1995, p. A7.

[29] During the Shah's era, the Iranian rationale for pursuing nuclear energy was (a) oil reserves were limited; (b) by some date in the future, domestic consumption (for energy and raw materials purposes in chemical industries) would use up the bulk of Iranian oil production; and (c) oil and gas were more valuable as export products, especially if processed into petrochemicals, synthetic fibers, etc. This argument is not without merit. On this and other topics in this chapter, I gratefully acknowledge the help of Shaul Bakhash.

[30] Steven Greenhouse, "Russia and China Pressed Not to Sell A-Plants to Iran," *New York Times*, January 25, 1995, p. A6.

[31] For a more detailed analysis of Iran's nuclear program and intentions see Shahram Chubin, "Does Iran Want Nuclear Weapons?" *Survival* 37, no. 1 (Spring 1995), pp. 86–104; David Schwarzbach, "Iran's Nuclear Puzzle, *Scientific American* 276 (June 1997), pp. 62–65.

[32] "A Nuclear Deal with Iran" (editorial), *New York Times*, January 8, 1995, section 4, p. 18.

[33] In congressional testimony, Assistant Secretary of State for Near Eastern Affairs Robert Pelletreau stated: "We do believe that there are important distinctions between North Korea and Iran. Under our framework agreement with North Korea, they have agreed to abandon an existing nuclear weapons infrastructure, which is based on gas graphite reactors, in exchange for light-water reactor technology. That is less efficient for plutonium production. North Korea has agreed to limit its nuclear fuel cycle, and will neither reprocess spent fuel or plutonium, nor enrich uranium. Thus the North Korean nuclear agreement results in a large net nonproliferation gain. With respect to Iran, its nuclear infrastructure is now at a fairly rudimentary stage, and the provision of light-water power reactors to Iran would give Iran capabilities that they do not currently have. That would result in a large net nonproliferation loss. That is what we see as the essential difference. Acquisition of these reactors in the Iranian case would broaden Iran's nuclear infrastructure, and would provide training and potential technology that, over time, could form the foundation and be useful for a nuclear weapons program." U.S. House of Representatives, Committee on International Relations, "U.S. Policy Toward Iran and Iraq" (104th Cong., 1st sess., 1995), p. 31.

[34] The legislation included a presidential waiver provision, which the Clinton administration exercised in 1995 and 1996 because of its overriding commitment to

support the democratic transition in Russia and to resolve this matter with the Russian government diplomatically (e.g., through the periodic Gore-Chernomyrdin Commission meetings).

[35] Kemp, *America and Iran*, pp. 54–55. In foregoing these deals with Iran, Beijing was motivated by its desire to win certification under U.S. nonproliferation laws to qualify for nuclear commerce with the United States (i.e., the purchase of U.S. civil nuclear reactors).

[36] As noted in Chapter 1, one factor that profoundly changes the nonproliferation equation in the post–Cold War era is the potential availability of illicitly obtained fissile material from the former Soviet Union. The ability of Iran and other countries of proliferation concern to thus secure weapons-grade fissile material obviates their need to develop indigenous uranium-enrichment capabilities.

[37] Anthony Lake, "Confronting Backlash States," *Foreign Affairs* 73, no. 2 (March/April 1994), p. 52.

[38] U.S. House of Representatives, Committee on International Relations, "U.S. Policy Toward Iran," p. 23.

[39] David Rogers, "Gingrich Wants Funds Set Aside for Iran Action," *Wall Street Journal*, October 27, 1995, p. A16.

[40] Kenneth Katzman, "Iran: Current Developments and U.S. Policy," Congressional Research Service (CRS) Issue Brief no. 93-033 (January 2, 1997), p. 13.

[41] The United States has refused to have contact with the most active opposition group, the People's Mojahedin Organization of Iran, led by Maryam Rajavi, who is based in Paris. A 1994 State Department report concluded that the group is linked to Iraq, conducted terrorist attacks against Americans during the Shah's era, supported the 1979 takeover of the U.S. embassy, and does not have much support inside Iran. Ibid.

[42] At a press conference with President Mubarak at Sharm al-Shiekh, the site of the international conference, President Clinton declared, "I took far stronger steps against Iran than any of our European allies had taken up to that point. And many of them disagree with me honestly. They believe that it's better to maintain some dialogue, to have some engagement. I have continued to argue for the isolation of *rogue states*. I did it in the United Nations last year, and I continue to do that, and I will continue to do that based on the evidence we have at hand." White House, Office of the Press Secretary, "Press Conference by President Clinton and President Mubarak," March 13, 1996 (emphasis added).

[43] For more on the issue of Iran's links to international terrorism see Kemp, *America and Iran*, pp. 43–50.

[44] Thomas L. Friedman, "Rethinking Iran Policy," *New York Times*, September 11, 1996, p. A19.

[45] Elaine Sciolino, "Time to Shift Course on Iran?" *International Herald Tribune*, September 23, 1996, p. 5.

[46] Zbigniew Brzezinski, Brent Scowcroft, and Richard Murphy, *Differentiated Containment: U.S. Policy toward Iran and Iraq—Report of an Independent Task Force* (New York: Council on Foreign Relations, 1997), pp. 3, 12.

[47] See, for example, Peter W. Rodman, "Why Ease Up on Iran?" *Washington Post*, December 11, 1996, p. A25.

[48] Alison Mitchell, "Clinton Sees Hope in the Election of Moderate as President of Iran," *New York Times*, May 30, 1997, p. A10.

[49] Douglas Jehl, "Iranian President Calls for Opening Dialogue with U.S.," *New York Times*, December 15, 1997, p. A1.

[50] Elaine Sciolino, "Clinton Hails Iranian Overture but Isolation Policy Is Unchanged," *New York Times*, December 16, 1997, p. A1.

51 Department of State, Office of the Spokesman, "Secretary of State Madeleine K. Albright Remarks at the 1998 Asia Society Dinner, June 18, 1998" (http://secretary.state.gov/www/statements/1998/980617a; emphasis added).

52 Steven Erlanger, "Grading the Secretary: Albright, a Bold Voice Abroad Finds Her Role Limited at Home," *New York Times*, September 1, 1998, p. A1.

53 David Menashri, *Revolution at a Crossroads: Iran's Domestic Politics and Regional Ambitions* (Washington, DC: Washington Institute for Near East Policy, 1997), p. 7.

54 Shaul Bakhash, "Iran's Remarkable Election," *Journal of Democracy* 9, no. 1 (January 1998), pp. 80–81.

55 Cited in Menashri, *Revolution at a Crossroads*, p. 9.

56 Ibid., p. xv.

57 *Keesing's Record of World Events, 1994* (London: Longman, 1994), p. 40206.

58 Bakhash, "Iran's Remarkable Election," p. 83.

59 "Iran's Leader Challenges U.S. and Talks of Re-election Bid," *New York Times*, February 1, 1993, p. A2.

60 Kemp, *America and Iran*, pp. 65–66.

61 *Keesing's Record of World Events, 1995*, p. 40574.

62 Elaine Sciolino, "Iranian Leader Says U.S. Move on Oil Wrecked Chance to Improve Ties," *New York Times*, May 16, 1995, p. A6.

63 Peter Waldman, "Turning Back: As Economy of Iran Worsens, Government Reverts to Hard Line; Radical Clerics Who Oppose Market Reforms Regain Control over Rafsanjani; Missed Chance for the U.S.?" *Wall Street Journal*, June 28, 1994, p. A1.

64 *Keesing's Record of World Events, 1995*, p. 40574.

65 Elaine Sciolino, "Iran, the Sequel: New Actors, but the Same Lines," *New York Times*, January 23, 1994, section 4, p. 4.

66 Stephen C. Fairbanks, "Theocracy versus Democracy: Iran Considers Political Parties," *Middle East Journal* 52, no. 1 (Winter 1998), p. 18.

67 The Gorbachev analogy is examined in Shaul Bakhash, "Iran's Unlikely President," *New York Review of Books* 45, no. 17 (November 5, 1998), p. 51. See also David Menashri, "Whither Iranian Politics? The Khatami Factor," in Patrick Clawson, Michael Eisenstadt, Eliyahu Kanovsky, and David Menashri, *Iran under Khatami: A Political, Economic, and Military Assessment* (Washington, DC: Washington Institute for Near East Policy, 1998), pp. 20–21.

68 Fairbanks, "Theocracy versus Democracy," p. 17.

69 R. Jeffrey Smith, "Khatemi Wants to End Terrorism, Officials Say," *Washington Post*, May 5, 1998, p. A9.

70 John Lancaster, "Iran's Top Leaders Differ on Relations with West," *Washington Post*, December 9, 1997, p. A1.

71 Elaine Sciolino, "Mullah Who Charmed Iran Is Struggling to Change It," *New York Times*, February 1, 1998, pp. A1, 6.

72 John Lancaster, "Head Iranian Cleric Rejects Talks with U.S.," *Washington Post*, January 17, 1998, p. A18.

73 Elaine Sciolino, "Iranian Dismisses All Hope for Now of Political Thaw," *New York Times*, September 23, 1998, pp. A1, 7.

74 Elaine Sciolino, "A Top Iranian Aide Rejects U.S. Overture on New Ties," *New York Times*, September 28, 1998, p. A11.

75 Ibid.

76 Elaine Sciolino, "For Once, the Veil That Hides Conflict Slips," *New York Times*, July 18, 1999, section 4, p. 5. In the aftermath of the demonstrations, a number of the pro-Khatami student activists were arrested. In addition, some commanders of the Revolutionary Guards wrote an open letter in a hard-line newspaper to Presi-

dent Khatami indicating their opposition to his reformist agenda: "Our patience is at an end. We do not feel it is our duty to show any more tolerance . . ." (http://www.cnn.com/world/meast/9907/22/iran.protest/).

[77] Data cited in Shahram Chubin and Jerrold D. Green, "Engaging Iran: A US Strategy," *Survival* 40, no. 3 (Autumn 1998), p. 154.

[78] Jahangir Amuzegar, "Iran's Economy and the US Sanctions," *Middle East Journal* 51, no. 2 (Spring 1997), p. 185.

[79] Discussed in Chubin and Green, "Engaging Iran," pp. 154–55.

[80] Kemp, *America and Iran*, part 2.

[81] R. Jeffrey Smith, "Khatemi Wants to End Terrorism, Officials Say."

[82] Douglas Jehl, "Iranians Assert Rogue Officers Slew Dissidents," *New York Times*, January 6, 1999, p. A1.

[83] Chubin and Green, "Engaging Iran," p. 159.

[84] Kemp, *America and Iran*, p. 56.

[85] Michael Eisenstadt, "The Military Dimension," in Clawson et.al., *Iran under Khatami*, p. 82. For example, in January 1998, the United States obtained information that China was considering the sale of a uranium conversion plant to Iran and approached the Chinese government to head off the transaction.

[86] Judith Miller and William J. Broad, "Bio-Weapons in Mind, Iranians Lure Needy Ex-Soviet Scientists," *New York Times*, December 8, 1998, pp. A1, 12.

[87] Eisenstadt, "The Military Dimension," p. 86.

[88] Michael Eisenstadt, "Iran's Revolutionary Guard Commander Sends a Warning," *Policywatch* no. 314 (Washington, DC: Washington Institute for Near East Policy, May 7, 1998).

[89] Interview with Iranian President Khatami, CNN, January 7, 1998 (http://www.cnn.com/World/9801/07/iran/interview).

[90] Robin Wright, "Clinton Encourages More Exchanges, Better Ties with Iran," *Los Angeles Times*, January 30, 1998, p. A6, cited in "On the Record: Iran and the Middle East Peace Process," *Peacewatch* no. 196 (Washington, DC: Washington Institute for Near East Policy, January 20, 1999), pp. 1–2.

[91] *Reuters*, "Iran Slams Palestinian Charter Change," December 13, 1998.

[92] Agence France Press in "On the Record: Iran and the Middle East Peace Process," *Peacewatch* no. 196 (Washington, DC: Washington Institute for Near East Policy, January 20, 1999).

[93] *Jerusalem Post*, November 4, 1998; cited in ibid.

[94] Foreign diplomats in Teheran said that the arrests, which were strongly condemned by European governments and the Clinton administration, had been instigated by Khatami's conservative opponents to block a rapprochement with the United States. Douglas Jehl, "Arrest of 13 Iranian Jews as Spies Divides Factions in Teheran," *New York Times*, June 18, 1999, p. A12.

[95] Thomas W. Lippman and David Ottaway, "Iran Requests $500 Million in Food Items," *Washington Post*, January 19, 1999, p. A13.

[96] Chubin and Green, "Engaging Iran," pp. 163–64.

[97] Jahangir Amuzegar, "Adjusting to Sanctions," *Foreign Affairs* 76, no. 3 (May/June 1997), p. 37.

[98] Thomas W. Lippman, "U.S. Removes Iran from Its Drug List," *Washington Post*, December 8, 1998, p. A23.

[99] Chubin and Green, "Engaging Iran," p. 165. During the prodemocracy student demonstrations in July 1999, President Clinton wisely refrained from public comment at a White House press conference, arguing, "I'm reluctant to say anything for fear that it will be used in a way that's not helpful to the forces of openness and reform." White House, Office of the Spokesman, "Press Conference by the President, July 21, 1999."

6

<hr>

North Korea: Limited Engagement by Necessity

U.S. POLICY DEVELOPMENT

This study argues that the rogue state policy has promoted a generic approach to strategy. The lumping and political demonization of a disparate group of problem countries by U.S. policy-makers has yielded a default strategy of comprehensive containment (and, in the case of Iraq, rollback to change the regime). As explored in the preceding chapters, the American strategy toward rogue states has eschewed policy inducements and has been overwhelmingly, if not exclusively, punitive. This approach has continued even in instances when significant developments within the target state, such as those occasioned by the May 1997 election of President Mohammed Khatami in Iran, would warrant change.

The notable exception to this pattern has been the Democratic Republic of Korea (DPRK). In this case, the Clinton administration deviated from its generic rogue state policy of comprehensive containment and isolation in favor of limited engagement. The instrument of that significant policy departure was the U.S.–North Korean Agreed Framework, concluded in Geneva in October 1994 after fifteen months of intensive negotiations.[1] The main provision of the agreement commits North Korea to freeze activity at and eventually dismantle its existing graphite-moderated nuclear reactors and related facilities in return for two proliferation-resistant light-water reactors (LWRs), which are being provided by a U.S.-led international consortium, the Korean Peninsula Energy Development Organization (KEDO), whose other original members are South Korea and Japan. Beyond the nuclear question, the Agreed Framework committed Washington and Pyongyang to "move toward full normalization of political and economic relations," as well as engage in dialogue on other "issues of concern," such as North Korea's ballistic missile exports (see Appendix).[2]

Why did the Clinton administration depart from the generic rogue state policy in the case of North Korea—and what have been the results of this alternative approach? These questions are the central focus of this chapter. The aim is to examine the North Korean case within the context of the overall policy toward that group of countries that U.S. officials have designated as rogue states. This chapter characterizes the Clinton administration's policy toward North Korea as one of "limited engagement by necessity." Faced with the imminent danger posed by the DPRK's mature nuclear program, the administration integrated this significant engagement component into its overall containment strategy. The U.S. chief negotiator, State Department veteran and nonproliferation expert Robert Gallucci, later acknowledged that "everyone was reluctant about the Agreed Framework."[3] Administration officials argued that it was the best of a bad set of options to deal with this thorny issue inherited from the Bush administration. The primary alternatives to limited engagement through the Agreed Framework were military strikes on North Korea's nuclear facilities or United Nations (UN) sanctions, either of which, according to Joseph Nye, then assistant secretary of defense for international security affairs, "might have caused a large conventional war" and neither of which could guarantee North Korea's nuclear disarmament.[4]

The U.S. nuclear diplomacy with North Korea has been significantly affected by American domestic politics. The October 1994 accord met with strong criticism from Congress, which shifted from Democratic to Republican Party control after the November 1994 elections. Republican critics on Capitol Hill charged the administration with appeasement and castigated the Agreed Framework as a "giveaway" of Western nuclear technology with no assurance against North Korean cheating. Clinton administration officials countered that the deal was phased over time and that each step in the implementation process required demonstrable North Korean action before initiation of the next by the United States and its allies. (Such a strategy is referred to as "conditional reciprocity" in the political science literature.)

The contentious debate between the Clinton administration and the Republican-led Congress over the U.S.–North Korean nuclear accord was captured in the title of a 1995 Council on Foreign Relations task force report, *Success or Sellout?* That study, while pointing to some perceived shortcomings, was supportive of the Agreed Framework and concluded, presciently, "This agreement cannot prosper or possibly even survive in isolation. North Korea must understand that . . . tensions and incidents caused by its behavior—even if they do not directly violate the

terms of the agreement—will make it far more difficult to sustain political support in the United States, South Korea, and Japan to deliver on
their commitments or follow through on additional normalization measures the North wants."[5]

North Korean actions both within and beyond the terms of the bilateral
agreement threatened the fragile political support for the nuclear accord
in Washington. Notable among these were two developments in August
1998: press reports that U.S. intelligence agencies had detected a secret
underground nuclear facility, and the testing of a medium-range ballistic
missile across Japanese territory.[6] The missile firing revived interest in ballistic missile defense to meet the threat posed by rogue states, and the report of an underground facility fueled concern that the North Koreans
were attempting to break out of the Agreed Framework. U.S. policy analysts debated whether the suspect underground facility signified North
Korea's intent to keep the nuclear option open or whether it was simply
an attempt to gain increased negotiating leverage with Washington. The
renewed controversy about the nuclear accord coincided with continued
famine in North Korea and the manifestation of other socio-economic
indicators of a "failed state" that called into question the survivability of
the Kim Jong Il regime. This combination of economic collapse, political
uncertainty, and capabilities to produce weapons of mass destruction
(WMD) prompted Central Intelligence Agency (CIA) Director George
Tenet to tell the Senate Armed Services Committee in February 1999, "I
can hardly overstate my concern about North Korea. In nearly all respects, the situation there has become more volatile and unpredictable."[7]

In the face of intensified congressional criticism and the temporary sus-
pension of Japanese aid, North Korea denied any violation of the nuclear
agreement and claimed that its missile test (not covered by the Agreed
Framework in any case) was actually a satellite launch. The Pyongyang
government has also voiced its own concerns about the implementation of
the Agreed Framework, arguing (among other things) that the United
States has not abided by the provision dealing with the normalization
of diplomatic and economic relations. South Korean political scientist
Chung-in Moon has argued that the Agreed Framework is the linchpin of
the broader strategy toward Pyongyang that has been pursued more or
less in concert by Washington, Seoul, and Tokyo. The collapse of the nuclear accord would make it politically impossible to continue the Four
Party Talks (involving the two Koreas, the United States, and China) and
South Korean president Kim Dae Jung's "sunshine policy." Professor
Moon's assessment points to the complex and subtle linkages between dif-

ferent issues in the North-South Korean context.[8] Those broader policy questions, such as the viability of the Pyongyang regime and eventual reunification, are beyond the scope of this chapter. And yet, given these important policy linkages, North Korea's domestic evolution is pertinent to this discussion to the extent that it affects the outcome of the Agreed Framework, and is itself affected by the success or failure of the nuclear accord. Attention will now turn to a more detailed consideration of the Agreed Framework negotiations with North Korea—and why the Clinton administration deviated from its own generic rogue state approach through this instrument of limited engagement.

The roots of U.S. policy toward North Korea can be traced to the immediate aftermath of World War II, which resulted in the political division of the Korean Peninsula along the thirty-eighth parallel line separating Soviet and American occupation forces.[9] In the southern zone, UN-supervised elections led to the establishment of the Republic of Korea (ROK) in August 1948. In the northern zone, the DPRK was created the following month, with Kim Il Sung as premier. With these rival pro-Soviet and pro-American governments both claiming sovereignty over the entire Korean Peninsula, the structure of this Cold War conflict was set in place. The withdrawal of U.S. forces from the South in 1949, along with Soviet materiel support that tipped the military balance in the North's favor, emboldened Kim Il Sung to press Stalin for authorization to "liberate" the South. Although wary of the danger that an attack on South Korea might trigger a general war with the United States, the Soviet leader eventually acquiesced and Kim Il Sung's forces launched an offensive in June 1950.[10] Nuclear weapons were an omnipresent and controversial part of the political backdrop to the Korean War. President Truman indicated that the United States had given "active consideration" to employment of atomic weapons. Many diplomatic historians credit President-elect Eisenhower's ominous ambiguity about nuclear weapons' use as a significant factor (albeit secondary to the death of Stalin) affecting the Soviet and North Korean decision to accept a cease-fire along the thirty-eighth parallel in mid-1953.

In the aftermath of the Korean War, nuclear deterrence, based on theater nuclear forces, became a central component of U.S. strategy to avert renewed conflict on the Korean Peninsula. During the 1950s and 1960s, North Korea provided uranium ore to both the Soviet Union and China, signed nuclear cooperation agreements with both communist powers, and launched its own modest nuclear research program. A nuclear facility, the primary focus of the nuclear showdown with the United States in the

1990s, was established in 1964, the same year as China's first nuclear test, and was expanded in 1965 with the arrival of a small Soviet-supplied research reactor.[11] Although the deterrent power of U.S. nuclear and conventional capabilities was sufficient to avert renewed fighting, Kim Il Sung continued to press for reunification through subversion and covert operations. In January 1968, North Korea seized the U.S. intelligence-gathering ship *Pueblo* in international waters off its coast. Two days earlier, a North Korean commando team had attempted to assassinate South Korean president Park Chung Hee in Seoul. In April 1969, a North Korean MiG aircraft shot down an unarmed U.S. EC-121 reconnaissance plane in international airspace flying along the North Korean periphery. The *Pueblo* and EC-121 incidents presented the United States with the most serious crises on the Korean peninsula since the cessation of hostilities. Fearful of a second war in Asia at a time when the American public was clamoring for an end to the Vietnam War, the Johnson and Nixon administrations refrained from a strong retaliatory response. Indeed, this increased North Korean risk-taking did not forestall a twenty-thousand-troop reduction in U.S. forces in South Korea under the terms of the Nixon Doctrine, part of a strategy of post-Vietnam retrenchment stressing reliance on local partners in lieu of direct American involvement. These trends, as well as the 1974 Indian nuclear test and the collapse of South Vietnam, reportedly led President Park to explore a South Korean nuclear option. A combination of U.S. reassurance and pressure, however, helped persuade the Seoul government to renounce this unconventional military capability by ratifying the nuclear Nonproliferation Treaty (NPT) in 1975.[12] As part of this U.S. strategy to dissuade South Korea from "going nuclear," President Carter reaffirmed that American tactical nuclear weapons could be used to defend the ROK against a DPRK attack. A further planned reduction in U.S. ground forces was only partially implemented, then deferred in 1979 by Carter in the face of new, higher estimates of North Korea's military capabilities.[13]

The Reagan administration's concern about North Korea's nuclear intentions was heightened in the early 1980s by the construction of an indigenously engineered five-megawatt electric (MW(e)) nuclear reactor at Yongbyon (sixty miles from Pyongyang), which began operation in January 1986. From U.S. reconnaissance photographs, the facility was determined to be a natural uranium, graphite-moderated reactor. This relatively simple engineering design was well suited to North Korea, as it depended only on locally obtainable graphite and uranium, rather than imported heavy water and enriched uranium. The operation of the reactor also yielded a high proportion of plutonium in its spent fuel that could be used in a nuclear weapons program. Having earlier negotiated the Seoul government's accession to the NPT, Washington now sought Moscow's support in accomplishing the same diplomatic goal in Pyongyang. NPT members are required to declare their nuclear materials and facilities and to negotiate a safeguards agreement to verify this declaration through periodic inspections (including of undisclosed sites) conducted by the Vienna-based International Atomic Energy Agency (IAEA). North Korea signed the NPT in December 1985, reportedly in response to pressure from the Soviet Union and Moscow's promise of four additional nuclear power reactors.[14] Afterwards, however, the Kim Il Sung regime pursued dilatory tactics to block implementation, taking nearly seven years to provide the required inventory of its nuclear materials and facilities.

While the negotiations over the DPRK's implementation of the NPT unfolded, North Korea began construction of two larger graphite reactors (estimated at 50 MW(e) and 200 MW(e)). More ominously, however, U.S. intelligence detected a new facility at Yongbyon in 1988 to chemically extract weapons-grade plutonium from spent nuclear reactor fuel. Such a reprocessing facility served no purpose outside the context of a nuclear weapons program. According to the IAEA, North Korea shut down its one operational reactor on three occasions (for periods ranging from 30 to 71 days) in 1989–91. Expert opinion is divided over how much plutonium North Korea was able to reprocess during this period before the IAEA safeguards agreement finally came into force in 1992. But, for the Reagan and Bush administrations, the development of these capabilities led to an ominous reading of Kim Il Sung's nuclear intentions—and the dangerous challenge that North Korea posed to the international nonproliferation regime.

These nuclear developments occurred against the backdrop of the end of the Cold War and North Korea's deepening economic crisis (exacerbated by the collapse of the Soviet Union and the end of Moscow's subvention). Observers differed over the impact of these radically altered geostrategic and economic conditions on Pyongyang's foreign policy—specifically, whether it would lead to more conciliatory or aggressive behavior toward South Korea. Notwithstanding North Korea's continued hostile rhetoric and pursuit of a nuclear option, two veteran State Department analysts, Robert Carlin and John Merrill, pointed to North Korea's acceptance of a UN seat and its move to establish diplomatic relations with Japan as "major shifts with long-term implications, not just tactical maneuvering."[15] The juxtaposition of these apparently contradictory developments in the late 1980s and early 1990s (i.e., reprocess-

ing plutonium for a nuclear weapons program while diplomatically wooing Japan) highlighted the enduring ambiguity that has confounded efforts by Washington to discern Pyongyang's intentions throughout the
nuclear crisis. Nonproliferation specialist Mitchell Reiss characterizes
this dilemma confronting American policy-makers:

> Did North Korea believe that nuclear weapons were of no lasting benefit to the
> regime and that the nuclear program should be traded for diplomatic recognition
> and financial assistance? Was the country's nuclear program designed to gener-
> ate this bargaining leverage by deliberately arousing the concern of South Korea,
> the United States, and the international community so that Pyongyang could dic-
> tate the terms on which it entered the world? Or was the North Korean nuclear
> program a serious, dedicated effort to acquire a nuclear arsenal to counter the
> South's booming economy and growing conventional military strength so that
> the North Korean regime might be preserved? . . . The dilemma for the world
> was that much of the North's behavior could be used to satisfy both sets of ques-
> tions. . . . North Korea was either trying to build a bomb or trying to gain in-
> ternational legitimacy through a dangerous game of brinkmanship, or *both*—but
> who could tell?[16]

As the Cold War was ending, North Korea posed a clear danger and a
possible opportunity. The Reagan administration, long urged by the Chinese to talk directly with the Kim Il Sung regime, began a low-key dialogue with the North Koreans in Beijing in December 1988. This dialogue
was endorsed by South Korean president Roh Tae Woo, who hoped to
pursue his own policy of rapprochement toward the North (informally
dubbed *Nordpolitik* by a Seoul official, after West Germany's *Ostpolitik*
toward East Germany). The Reagan administration announced several
modest unilateral measures facilitating travel by academic, cultural, and
athletic groups and permitting limited exports of American humanitarian
goods. But it also articulated preconditions for improved government-to-
government relations, including the cessation of North Korean sponsorship of terrorism and implementation of its NPT obligations. According
to Leon Sigal, author of a detailed study of U.S.–North Korean nuclear
diplomacy, "Washington's message to Pyongyang was you go first."[17]
Former *Washington Post* diplomatic correspondent Don Oberdorfer, noting that North Korea had achieved its goal of direct talks with the United
States, argues that these talks were "fundamentally the result of Seoul's
policy reversal rather than a reflection of new thinking in Washington."[18]
With the opening of this bilateral channel, Pyongyang reduced its anti-
American rhetoric, proclaimed its opposition to terrorism, and offered
some cooperation in recovering the remains of missing U.S. soldiers from
the Korean War. But no progress was made on the nuclear issue. The Kim

Il Sung regime linked its NPT obligations (i.e., concluding a safeguards agreement with the IAEA) to the presence of U.S. nuclear forces in South Korea. Pyongyang demanded their withdrawal from the ROK and a "negative security assurance" from Washington that it would not use nuclear weapons against the DPRK.[19] Japan, then being courted by North Korea, diplomatically supported the United States and South Korea by affirming to Pyongyang that political normalization was contingent on IAEA inspections and direct North-South negotiations.

In spring 1991, a Bush administration interagency committee, chaired by Richard Solomon, assistant secretary of state for East Asian and Pacific affairs, addressed the impasse over IAEA inspections of North Korea's nuclear facilities. The committee framed three policy options for presidential review: (1) continuation of the existing policy with additional modest inducements; (2) diplomatic engagement coupled with the removal of nuclear warheads from South Korea and a reduction in joint U.S.-ROK military exercises; and (3) coercive diplomacy to compel DPRK compliance. While agreeing that the current policy was inadequate and coercion was premature, officials differed over the scope of engagement.[20] This debate occurred in the aftermath of the Gulf War, when the IAEA was the target of widespread criticism for having failed to detect Iraq's covert nuclear weapons program. Even if the Kim Il Sung regime agreed to the IAEA safeguards regime, many questioned the ability of the IAEA to guard against North Korean cheating given the Iraqi experience. The stalemate with North Korea over IAEA inspections was broken as a derivative consequence of a Bush administration initiative designed to aid the process of democratic transition in the Soviet Union. In September 1991, a month after Russian president Boris Yeltsin had overcome a failed coup and supplanted Mikhail Gorbachev as the country's dominant political figure, President Bush announced the worldwide withdrawal of tactical nuclear weapons from all U.S. naval and ground forces. This decision, which was accompanied by Bush's assurance to South Korean president Roh of continued protection under the U.S. nuclear umbrella, included the withdrawal of nuclear artillery and sixty air-delivered gravity bombs based in South Korea. Solomon, who had advocated such a move within the administration, stated, "We were able to hook a ride on a Soviet-related decision."[21]

The Bush announcement led to a period of heightened diplomatic activity between the United States and the DPRK, as well as between the two Koreas. In late October 1991, the South Korean prime minister visited the North Korean capital for a meeting with his counterpart. Shortly thereafter, Pyongyang responded to the Bush initiative by announcing that it would sign an IAEA safeguards agreement when the withdrawal of U.S. nuclear forces began. Although these promising moves were consistent with President Roh's own *Nordpolitik* strategy, he rejected the Bush administration's insistence that a satisfactory resolution of the nuclear dispute be linked to the broadening of economic and diplomatic contacts between North and South. The South Korean president also wanted to ensure that Seoul, not Washington, was the primary negotiating partner with Pyongyang. A follow-on visit by the North Korean prime minister to Seoul in December yielded a statement of general principles governing relations between the two countries that was of greater symbolic than practical significance. On December 31, 1991, the ROK and the DPRK concluded a "Joint Declaration on the Denuclearization of the Korean Peninsula," which committed the two sides to forego the production of nuclear weapons and the possession of nuclear reprocessing and uranium-enrichment facilities. The agreement deferred the issue of bilateral inspections to a subsequent round of negotiations by a Joint Nuclear Control Committee.[22]

Amid these developments in the last quarter of 1991, the Bush administration also sought to maintain the option for coercive diplomacy, including the use of force, should negotiations with Pyongyang over the suspect nuclear facilities break down. The underlying issue was the relationship between incentives and penalties within a strategy toward the DPRK. This question was contentious both within the Bush administration and between it and the other key actors (South Korea, China, and Japan), whose cooperation Washington would need to implement any strategy. Although the threat of force and economic sanctions was viewed as the prerequisite for diplomacy, it also offered an alternative to dialogue. This political tension was evidenced in late 1991 and would become a recurring issue in the development of U.S. policy toward North Korea. Consider the mixed signals that emerged from the U.S.-ROK Security Consultative Meeting in November 1991. The meeting between U.S. Defense Secretary Dick Cheney and South Korean Defense Minister Lee Jong Koo was accompanied by public speculation about a possible military response to the DPRK's nuclear program. At that meeting Minister Lee reportedly endorsed the option of attacking the Yongbyon site if the North Koreans again shut down the reactor and began to remove spent fuel for reprocessing.[23] Publicly, however, he discounted the military option: "If the United Nations Security Council . . . decide[s] on military sanctions against North Korea and if it means war on the Korean peninsula, the government will oppose it."[24] While the South Koreans were, at best, ambivalent about the threat of force, the Chinese made clear their opposition to any prospective U.S. effort to mobilize international support for economic sanctions or other punitive measures aimed at the Kim Il Sung regime. While Beijing had no interest in a nuclear (potentially reunified) Korea, it was also sensitive to Pyongyang's need to save face in its dealings with outsiders.

During President Bush's visit to Seoul in early January 1992, he and President Roh agreed to cancel the annual U.S.-ROK military exercise ("Team Spirit") for 1992. Coming in the wake of the bilateral ROK-DPRK denuclearization agreement, this move was another inducement to gain North Korean compliance with its NPT obligations. Despite South Korean qualms about direct U.S.-DPRK negotiations, the Bush-Roh meeting also led to the announcement that an unprecedented senior-level meeting between the Washington and Pyongyang governments would be held later that month to discuss the nuclear issue. The decision to agree to the meeting, a longstanding North Korean political objective, had been more contentious in Washington than in Seoul. The State Department's proposed direct dialogue with the Kim Il Sung regime encountered stiff opposition from senior officials at the Defense Department, the National Security Council, and the CIA, who were profoundly skeptical of Pyongyang's intentions and viewed U.S-DPRK talks as a potential political wedge between Washington and Seoul. U.S. officials stated emphatically that the purpose of the meeting was not to enter into a negotiating give-and-take, but to communicate simply and directly Washington's position to the Pyongyang regime. The bilateral meeting took place in New York on January 22, 1992, with U.S. and North Korean delegations headed, respectively, by Arnold Kanter, undersecretary of state for political affairs (the State Department's third-highest official), and Kim Young Sun, the secretary for international relations of the Korean Workers Party (KWP). Both sides stuck to long formalistic recitations of position, and Kanter subsequently affirmed that no further talks with the North Koreans were planned. The issue of meetings with the North Koreans became an issue of contention between Seoul and Washington. As noted above, the Roh government had been resistant to a U.S.-DPRK meeting on the nuclear issue, believing that the ROK should be the primary negotiator with Pyongyang on issues affecting the stability of the Korean Peninsula. Indeed, desiring to maintain the momentum of the December 1991 accords and notwithstanding opposition from hard-liners in Seoul, President Roh wanted to lay the groundwork during the early months of 1992 for the first meeting between the two Korean heads of state. The Bush administration, however, opposed such a move, insisting that the nuclear impasse had to be resolved before a summit.

In May 1992, IAEA Director-General Hans Blix visited North Korea after the Kim Il Sung regime had finally signed and ratified the IAEA safeguards agreement. The North Korean case was viewed by the IAEA as an opportunity for this international watchdog agency to redeem itself in light of public criticisms about its disastrous experience in Iraq. Prior to leaving for Pyongyang, Blix and his team, in a significant departure from past IAEA practice, had received a detailed briefing from U.S. intelligence officials on the DPRK's nuclear infrastructure. The visit did confirm that the suspect Yongbyon installation was indeed a reprocessing facility, contrary to North Korean assertions. Moreover, the size of this installation led IAEA experts to conclude that the North Koreans must have built a prototype at an undeclared site. There was also broad agreement that the North Koreans had reprocessed more plutonium than they had acknowledged in their official declaration to the IAEA (though estimates of the precise amount varied). One startling revelation to emerge later from the Blix visit was that the North Koreans had broached the possibility of replacing their outmoded graphite-moderated reactors with more advanced LWRs (which are much less useful for a nuclear weapons program). In an interview with Leon Sigal, Charles Kartman, director of Korean affairs at the State Department, stated that the "LWR gambit" was received with "enormous skepticism" in Washington and was never seriously considered "because we didn't have enough knowledge about North Korea and because it flew against everyone's prejudice." This LWR transfer proposal would be revived in July 1993 and became the central element of the Agreed Framework in October 1994.[25]

At the conclusion of the Blix visit, the Kim Il Sung regime agreed to additional routine inspections, as called for in the IAEA safeguards agreement. While Pyongyang tentatively moved toward cooperation with the IAEA, it blocked progress in the bilateral negotiations with Seoul to implement the December 1991 denuclearization agreement through the initiation of mutual inspections of nuclear facilities (which were intended as a confidence-building complement to IAEA inspections). As the talks over bilateral inspections bogged down, relations were further complicated by two developments in September–October 1992—the uncovering of a large North Korean spy ring operating in the South and the announcement by the U.S. and ROK defense ministers that the Team Spirit joint military exercise would be resumed in 1993.

The South Korean military reportedly led the drive to resume the Team Spirit exercises to improve military readiness and to put pressure on North Korea. U.S. Ambassador Donald Gregg called this unexpected decision, taken almost routinely in Washington, as "one of the biggest mistakes" of Korea policy during his tenure in Seoul.[26] Team Spirit prompted a sharp North Korean reaction, threatening to overturn the December 1991 reconciliation accord. U.S. and South Korean officials offered to suspend Team Spirit in return for progress on bilateral inspections in the ROK-DPRK denuclearization talks. Pyongyang responded that the cancellation of the Team Spirit series beyond 1992 had been a condition of its acceptance of IAEA inspections—a claim strenuously denied by American officials.

On November 1, 1992, Ronald Lehman, director of the U.S. Arms Control and Disarmament Agency, stated that the IAEA inspections had "stopped" the North Korean nuclear weapons program. That sanguine (and, as will be seen, short-lived) assessment again raised a basic and recurring question in the nuclear negotiations with North Korea: how to define success? With respect to North Korea, nonproliferation expert Michael Mazarr observes, "For most in Washington and Seoul, that definition did not merely include stopping the North Korean program. . . . [I]t included fully rolling back and gaining near-absolute certainty about the status of all disputed plutonium and other elements of risk very rapidly."[27] The relatively optimistic Lehman assessment was followed later in November by an IAEA revelation that the agency had evidence of two undeclared nuclear facilities in North Korea. In January 1993, the IAEA took the unprecedented step of requesting a "special inspection" of these suspect sites over the objection of the target state. Having been embarrassed in Iraq, the IAEA was determined to make North Korea the test case of the post–Gulf War nonproliferation regime. This move toward a renewed showdown with Pyongyang coincided with the transfer of presidential power in both Washington and Seoul with the twin inaugurations of President Clinton and South Korean president Kim Young Sam. With the arrival of these new and untested leaders, the Kim Il Sung regime diplomatically escalated its resistance to the IAEA's demand. On March 12, 1993, North Korea announced its intention to withdraw from the NPT, citing the treaty article permitting such an action if the "supreme interests" of the member state are jeopardized.[28] On April 1, 1993, the IAEA's Board of Governors declared to the United Nations that it could not "verify that there has been no diversion of nuclear material [to] nuclear weapons . . ." and that North Korea had refused to permit the inspection of suspect sites.[29] China's vote against this IAEA move again signaled the Beijing government's opposition to the use of coercive diplomacy (such as economic sanctions) against North Korea.

After North Korea raised the stakes in March 1993 by announcing its intention to withdraw from the NPT, there were some calls on Capitol Hill and by press commentators for a tough American counter-action, including the consideration of military options. The Clinton administration responded in April by signaling to Pyongyang its willingness to resume the high-level direct talks suspended since January 1992. That decision placed the United States in the lead negotiating role with North Korea vis-à-vis the Seoul government and the IAEA. The U.S.-DPRK talks resumed in New York in early June 1993, with the U.S. delegation led by Gallucci, then the assistant secretary of state for political-military affairs, and the North Korean side headed by First Vice Foreign Minister Kang Sok Ju. The meeting concluded on June 11, the day before North Korea's threatened withdrawal from the NPT was due to take effect, with the signing of a joint statement. The joint statement "suspended" the North Korean NPT withdrawal threat and committed the two sides to continued dialogue. The North Koreans viewed the document as an important political symbol because it accorded them political legitimacy as a negotiating partner with the United States. For that very reason, the precedent of a joint U.S.-DPRK statement was critically received by hard-liners in South Korea. That response reflected the general pattern that was to emerge from Seoul during the negotiations. When events were moving toward a showdown (and the exercise of punitive instruments), the South Koreans would press for a resumption of dialogue to avert a possible conflict. Likewise, when the U.S.-DPRK dialogue was proceeding and making some headway, Seoul expressed concern that Washington was cutting a deal that made too many concessions.

At a follow-on meeting in July 1993 in Geneva, the North Koreans revived the proposal they had reportedly made to Blix during his May 1992 visit. Kang announced to the American delegation that the DPRK was willing to trade its existing graphite-moderated reactors for more modern, proliferation-resistant LWRs provided by the international community to meet its energy needs. Gallucci was initially skeptical as to whether the DPRK would indeed give up its indigenously produced reactors and associated facilities, but he saw that this proposal could contribute to the resolution of the nuclear impasse with Pyongyang. One immediate question raised by the North Korean proposal was who would finance the replacement LWRs.[30]

No progress was made at the July 1993 meeting on the key issue that had led to the diplomatic confrontation with the IAEA and Pyongyang's resulting threat to withdraw from the NPT—inspections of two nuclear waste sites that could reveal information about North Korea's nuclear history. The Americans continued to press the North Koreans on what they termed the "continuity of safeguards" (meaning assurance that nuclear materials had not been diverted into a weapons program). Amid this continuing impasse over inspections, Secretary of Defense Les Aspin gave a briefing to reporters in early November that inadvertently fueled concern about a possible military showdown. Conservative columnist Charles Krauthammer wrote in the *Washington Post* that the Clinton administration "should stop talking to the North Koreans—it is time for an economic blockade—and start talking to the American people" about the military crisis on the Korean Peninsula.[31] In this charged political atmosphere, the North Koreans made public a proposal they had privately broached with an American diplomat. On November 11, 1993, First Vice Foreign Minister Kang called on the United States to negotiate a "package solution" that would address the nuclear question in the context of other military, political, and economic issues.

Such a comprehensive approach (as opposed to a narrowly focused negotiation on the nuclear question) had been raised periodically in the U.S. government since the Bush administration's policy review in spring 1991. The Clinton national security team was receptive to a two-track policy combining carrots and sticks, but officials differed over the particular economic and political inducements to be integrated into a mixed approach. The signals from Seoul were characteristically mixed. On the one hand, hard-liners argued that such an approach would reward North Korea's bad behavior by offering inducements for the Kim Il Sung regime simply to comply with its international obligations under the NPT. On the other hand, South Korean officials spoke of the need to "gradually bring the North back to the world community." This shorthand phrase was a political remedy to their nightmare scenario—the violent implosion of the DPRK, and the profound social and economic consequences such an event would produce for the ROK.[32] When President Kim Young Sam met with President Clinton in Washington in late November 1993, the administration had to carefully address this political tension in the South Korean government's attitude toward the U.S. negotiations with the North. As Senator Richard Lugar (R-Ind.) put it, "They're saying to us: be firm but not too firm."[33] The reportedly contentious meeting between Presidents Clinton and Kim produced general language to describe their strategy, but no agreement on a package of inducements (e.g., cancellation of U.S.-ROK military exercises) to offer the Kim Il Sung regime in return for IAEA inspections of the suspect nuclear sites. In a strained joint press conference, President Clinton stated that the United States and South Korea were "prepared to discuss with North Korea a thorough, broad approach to the issues that divide us, and once and for all resolve the nuclear issue, but we cannot do that in the absence of a dialogue between North and South Korea, and while there is still growing doubt about the continuity of safeguards." Alluding to the positive benefits of changed behavior for Pyongyang, President Clinton added, "the door will [then] be open on a wide range of issues, not only with the United States but with the rest of the world."[34]

In negotiating with North Korea, the Clinton administration faced a tactically adept adversary able to gain maximum leverage from the danger it posed *and* the weakness it manifested. This combination presented a state on the verge both of becoming a nuclear power and of collapsing economically. While the administration's immediate focus was on the inspection issue and the resumption of high-level talks, the long-term strategy is to manage a "soft landing" for North Korea as this process of collapse unfolds. In late 1993, General Gary Luck, the commander of U.S. forces in South Korea, said of the DPRK, "The place is going to implode or explode. I hope it's an implosion. Because I don't think the world would like to see what an explosion looks like."[35] For the Clinton administration, however, the question of managing North Korea's decline was more complicated than that of implosion versus explosion. Concern focused on the possible link between these alternative futures—that is, whether an implosion (a "hard landing") could lead to an explosion in the form of an attack on South Korea. This potential linkage between the Pyongyang regime's domestic plight and its foreign policy behavior toward the South was (and remains) at the heart of the dilemma confronting U.S. policy-makers with respect to North Korea.

In the aftermath of the November 1993 Clinton–Kim Young Sam meeting, wrangling between North Korea and the United States continued over the issue of inspections. Frustrated with the lack of progress in resolving the issue and moving on to the third round of high-level U.S.-DPRK talks, Washington announced in late January 1994 its intention to resume the Team Spirit joint military exercise with the South Koreans if the Pyongyang regime did not permit inspections. The North Koreans responded with a veiled threat to withdraw from the NPT and unfreeze their nuclear program.[36] The renewed sense of crisis was reinforced by leaked information to the press about North Korean nuclear weapons capabilities. A CIA National Intelligence Estimate reportedly concluded that North Koreans could have extracted as much as twelve kilograms of plutonium from fuel rods, enough for two bombs, when the Yongbyon reactor was shut down for one hundred days in 1989. But a senior Clinton administration spokesperson explained that this estimate represented a "worst case" analysis based on incomplete data.[37] For the administration, this press leak further complicated the already contentious domestic politics of the North Korean issue. A Defense Department official referred to the nuclear material that might have been extracted during the 1989 shutdown as "Bush's plutonium."[38] Some questioned the extent to which an accord with the Kim Il Sung regime would address North Korea's nuclear history (notably, the disputed amount of plutonium)— and whether the United States would tolerate any ambiguity relating to the DPRK's weapons capabilities. Notwithstanding this skepticism, the Clinton administration's declared objective was to freeze and then roll-back North Korea's nuclear program.

In spring 1994, a renewed crisis erupted. Gallucci, who during that period was appointed ambassador-at-large with primary responsibility for North Korea, later acknowledged that "this had an escalatory quality that could deteriorate not only into a war but into a big war."[39] The precipitant of the spring 1994 crisis was the North Korean announcement in April that their major reactor at Yongbyon would be shut down so that spent fuel from its core could be removed. This move raised alarm bells in Washington, Vienna, and Seoul because of estimates that these fuel rods contained sufficient plutonium to produce four or five nuclear bombs. The Kim Il Sung regime offered to permit IAEA inspectors to observe the process, but not test samples. Such testing of spent fuel rods was a priority because they held evidence of North Korea's nuclear history—specifically, whether the nuclear fuel was part of the original load (as claimed by Pyongyang) or had been replaced since the reactor began operation in 1987 (as suspected by the Clinton administration). This examination would reveal whether plutonium had been extracted and possibly diverted into a weapons program.[40] The North Korean announcement was sharply criticized in Washington and coincided with the arrival of Patriot antimissile batteries and other U.S. military reinforcements in the South. An IAEA team arrived in Pyongyang in late May to monitor the defueling of the Yongbyon reactor. Because of the rapid and chaotic manner in which the North Koreans were proceeding, however, as well as the fact that the process was halfway completed by the time they arrived on the scene, the IAEA officials could not garner the necessary data to reveal North Korea's nuclear history.[41] This action was consistent with the Kim Il Sung regime's desire to maintain the uncertainty about its nuclear capabilities—an ambiguity that was the primary source of its political leverage with the United States, South Korea, and Japan.

On June 2, Blix referred the matter to the UN Security Council and the United States moved to strengthen its defenses in South Korea in anticipation of a diplomatic campaign to impose economic sanctions on the North. The Kim Il Sung regime responded with defiance, declaring that sanctions would be tantamount to a declaration of war. The Clinton administration adopted the sanctions strategy after considering—and rejecting—the alternative of military preemption. William Perry, then serving as secretary of defense, explained the rationale behind this decision to forego the option that hard-liners outside the administration, including some senior Bush administration officials, were advocating: "By May [1994] the negotiations between North Korea and the IAEA had broken down . . . [and] we were faced with the highly dangerous prospect that North Korea could, within months, have five or six nuclear bombs. . . . I asked General Shalikashvili [chair of the Joint Chiefs of Staff] and General Luck . . . for an update of a contingency plan, which I had requested earlier, for destroying key components at the reactor site with a military attack. . . . The plan was impressive. . . . However, both General Shalikashvili and I had concluded that such an attack was very likely to incite the North Koreans to launch a military attack on South Korea."[42] The significant possibility that a preemptive attack on the Yongbyon nuclear facilities would have a "catalytic" effect triggering a general war on the Korean Peninsula effectively removed the military option from further consideration. Some observers drew a misleading analogy to the Israeli strike on the Iraqi nuclear reactor at Osirak in 1981, but that facility, unlike the one in North Korea, had been under construction, not fully functional and producing plutonium. In addition to the danger of inadvertent escalation, U.S. policy-makers had no assurance that air strikes would hit all the pertinent targets in and around Yongbyon, or that they would eliminate the North Korean nuclear threat if some illicit reprocessing of spent fuel to extract plutonium had occurred during the 1989–91 shutdowns.

In the first half of June 1994, the Clinton administration mounted a diplomatic offensive to win multilateral support for sanctions against North Korea (as had been done in the case of Iraq). The U.S. plan, formally unveiled by UN Ambassador Madeleine Albright on June 15, was to implement sanctions in phases. This approach was motivated, in part, by the lukewarm support that the sanctions option enjoyed among key members of the Security Council. In the first phase of the U.S.-proposed sanctions, states would end their arms trade with North Korea, a move estimated to cost the Pyongyang regime $50–100 million per year). The second phase would ban all financial transactions with the North (including the some $1 billion in remittance payments from North Korean citizens residing in Japan). If necessary, that would be followed by a third phase of sanctions entailing a total trade ban, on the Iraqi model.[43] U.S. officials claimed that South Korea and Japan would support the U.S. sanctions plan, although both countries remained concerned about a violent North Korean counter-response (and the Japanese claimed that a remittance ban would be difficult, in practice, to implement). The Russians were, at best, ambivalent about the use of sanctions against North Korea, but the political assessment in Washington was that they would not veto such a move by the Security Council. Most problematic, in terms of the sanctions option, was the position of China. During 1993–94, senior Chinese diplomats had expressed their opposition to "pressure" tactics against the North, such as economic sanctions. And yet, senior Clinton administration officials said that the Chinese had been "tacitly helpful" in dealing with the North Korean nuclear crisis. On June 10, Chinese diplomats circulated a report to their Western counterparts that the Beijing government had delivered a stern message to the Pyongyang regime urging it to end its defiant stand against the international community.[44] Given the mixed signals, it remains a matter of speculation how China would have voted on a sanctions resolution in the Security Council, or even if it did not veto the measure, whether Beijing would have rigorously enforced a sanctions regime.

In tandem with the diplomatic campaign for sanctions, the Clinton administration further bolstered U.S. defense forces in the ROK. This move was taken to provide an added deterrent to North Korean aggression, given its past pattern of behavior that had dangerously combined both risk-taking and miscalculation. From the North Korean perspective, however, such "defensive" deployments may have appeared similar to the military buildup during Desert Storm. Although the Defense Department had rejected the preemption option (at least for the time being), the Kim Il Sung regime, viewing the world through its own prism of paranoia and isolation, did not know that. Indeed, in Washington, influential voices outside the government (including some former Bush administration officials) were calling for possible military action, particularly if North Korea began to reprocess the spent fuel removed in May.[45] In response to U.S. reinforcement moves in the South (as well as Seoul's de-

cision to mobilize 6.6 million military reservists for a defense drill),
North Korea began military maneuvers that used up scarce fuel and that
were qualitatively different from its typical response to U.S.-ROK joint
maneuvers.[46] Given the mutual mistrust and the absence of regular contact between North Korea and the United States, the May–June 1994 crisis carried a significant risk of inadvertent military escalation through
misperception and miscalculation.

On June 15, the day that the Clinton administration made public its
sanctions proposal at the United Nations, a development occurred that
transformed the crisis—former U.S. president Jimmy Carter arrived in
Pyongyang to meet with Kim Il Sung. In contrast to the Bush administration, which had vetoed a proposed Carter visit, President Clinton reluctantly agreed to permit the former president to go to North Korea in
response to a standing invitation. After meeting with Kim Il Sung, Carter
stunned the White House with news that the North Korean leader had
agreed to "freeze" the DPRK's nuclear facilities under IAEA inspections
and resume high-level talks with the United States. He also persuaded
Kim Il Sung to extend an invitation without preconditions to meet with
South Korean president Kim Yong Sam in summer 1994. Those positive
developments notwithstanding, Carter greatly irritated U.S. officials by
announcing on CNN that the United States had ceased its sanctions campaign at the United Nations—a claim the White House publicly disavowed. The general nature of the Carter-Kim agreement, specifically the
meaning of the word "freeze," permitted the White House to interpret
the terms to its advantage—or, as Vice President Gore put it, to "make
lemonade out of this lemon." President Clinton recalled that the
Kennedy administration had used such a ploy during the Cuban missile
crisis when it ignored a hard-line Soviet letter demanding the withdrawal
of U.S. missiles from Turkey, choosing instead to respond to a more
moderate letter simply requesting an American commitment not to attack Cuba. Likewise, when presented with the Carter-Kim agreement,
the Clinton administration chose to "raise the bar" by interpreting
"freeze" to mean that North Korea would not refuel the Yongbyon reactor that had been shut down in April 1994—a requirement that, in
fact, went beyond North Korea's NPT obligations.[47] A senior official argued that the administration had reworked the deal Carter said he made
into the deal it could accept.

Former president Carter, just back from Pyongyang, told a White
House press conference on June 19 "the crisis is over," but questions re-
mained about the precise terms of his agreement with Kim Il Sung.[48]
Some of the outstanding issues were addressed in a letter from First Vice

Foreign Minister Kang, responding to one from Ambassador Gallucci detailing the Clinton administration's understanding. The Kang letter contained assurances that the North Koreans would neither reprocess plutonium from the recently removed nuclear fuel rods nor reload the idle reactor with new fuel rods. One key issue that the Carter-Kim agreement left unresolved was North Korea's nuclear history. The freeze proposal would keep the eight thousand fuel rods withdrawn from the Yongbyon reactor in cooling ponds under IAEA monitoring, but did not address the potential amount of plutonium extracted during the 1989 shutdown. President Clinton said that the Kim-Carter agreement "certainly gives us the basis of seeking a solution" and announced that high-level talks would resume in Geneva in July.[49] Senate Majority Leader Robert Dole (R-Kans.), a prospective electoral challenger to President Clinton, condemned the administration for an "apparent willingness to throw in the towel. There is no basis in history or experience to believe more talk and more delays will limit North Korea's nuclear ambitions."[50]

The role of the Carter mission to North Korea in defusing the June 1994 crisis was, and remains, a controversial issue. At the time, the Clinton administration's handling of the nuclear impasse was criticized from opposite directions—by critics (including many prominent Republicans) who advocated a tougher line toward Pyongyang, as well as by a contending group of outside specialists who supported an approach incorporating inducements. The hard-liners castigated the administration for accepting the elements of a deal that did not, in former secretary of state Henry Kissinger's word, "rollback" the North Korean program (i.e., deal with the plutonium that might have been previously diverted). They criticized a perceived willingness to give in to Pyongyang's stonewalling and to subcontract a major foreign policy issue to a former president all too willing to read benign intentions into an adversary's actions. Those who opposed the use of coercive diplomacy against North Korea criticized the Clinton administration for bringing the parties to the brink of conflict when the outline of an agreement was evident and Kim Il Sung was, indeed, ready to deal. The Clinton administration was criticized as being too soft *and* too tough. For its part, the administration characterized the Carter mission as fortuitous and maintained that the "makings of a deal" were already in place. As one State Department official put it, "We already had that, at least in outline form, by late 1993. Carter's intervention was crucial, not because of what it added to the deal, but because it let both sides step back long enough to get back to the deal they were already working on."[51] In other words, according to the Clinton administration, the tangible symbol of a former U.S. president courting the North Korean president had provided the Kim Il Sung regime a face-saving mechanism to end the crisis. That assessment, however, begs the question of how events would have unfolded in the absence of Carter's unanticipated intervention in the delicate nuclear diplomacy with North Korea, and whether such a break in the escalatory spiral toward conflict would have occurred otherwise.

The Carter-Kim meeting was followed by several rounds of intensive negotiations culminating in the Agreed Framework. The initial U.S.-DPRK meeting in Geneva was suspended on July 9, 1994, with the news that Kim Il Sung, North Korea's "Great Leader," had died of a heart attack. The bilateral talks resumed the following month and yielded a joint statement on August 12 incorporating the core element of a deal—trading North Korea's three graphite-moderated reactors and reprocessing facility for proliferation-resistant LWRs, along with a pledge by Pyongyang to cease reprocessing and remain an NPT party. After two more months of intensive negotiation, Ambassador Gallucci and First Vice Foreign Minister Kang announced the conclusion of an "Agreed Framework" on October 17 and formally signed the four-page document on behalf of their governments on October 21. The agreement outlined a series of carefully calibrated, reciprocal steps that would be implemented over a decade-long period. Gallucci stated that the agreement would address concerns "about the problems of the past, present and future" of the DPRK nuclear program.[52] A State Department "Fact Sheet" declared that "when fully implemented, the Agreed Framework will terminate the existing North Korean nuclear program. For now, the program will be frozen under IAEA supervision, and eventually it will be dismantled."[53]

Under the October 1994 accord, North Korea agreed to not restart its 5MW(e) graphite-moderated research reactor, to seal its reprocessing facility, and to freeze construction on and dismantle the 50MW(e) and 200MW(e) reactors. The spent fuel removed in May 1994 from the 5MW(e) reactor would remain in the cooling pond and eventually be shipped out of the country. All these provisions would be monitored by the IAEA. A confidential minute to the Agreed Framework banned construction of identical installations—graphite-moderated reactors and reprocessing facilities—at any other site in North Korea.[54] In return for the freezing and dismantling of the DPRK's nuclear facilities at or near Yongbyon, the United States agreed to create an international consortium, KEDO, to "oversee construction of two 1,000 MW(e) light water reactors of proliferation-resistant design in the DPRK over the next decade."[55] The total reactor replacement project was estimated at $4 billion, with the South Koreans offering to provide the two LWRs, accounting for approximately 70 percent of the total cost, and Japan agreeing to finance 25 percent of the deal.[56] The United States guaranteed the annual supply of some 500,000 tons of heavy fuel oil (estimated at $20–30 million) to compensate the DPRK for foregone energy production before the first LWR began operation. To assuage South Korean concerns, the accord obligated the Pyongyang regime to engage in a North-South dialogue and to implement the 1991 ROK-DPRK denuclearization agreement. In addition, the United States offered the DPRK a "negative security assurance" pledging that it would not use nuclear weapons against North Korea while it remained an NPT party.

Beyond the nuclear question, the Agreed Framework committed the United States and North Korea to opening diplomatic liaison offices as a first step toward "full normalization" of political and economic relations. The State Department "Fact Sheet" declared that the bilateral accord "will help integrate Pyongyang into the economic and political mainstream of East Asia."[57] One administration official cited Vietnam as a model for the phased normalization of relations between Washington and Pyongyang.[58] *New York Times* diplomatic correspondent Elaine Sciolino wrote,

> In its rush to strike a nuclear agreement with North Korea, President Clinton is gambling that the promise of $4 billion in energy aid can turn what he has labeled a "rogue state" into a responsible member of the global community. The agreement . . . reflects the Administration's conviction that offering the Communist Government in Pyongyang a way out of its economic difficulties will induce it to give up its nuclear ambition. . . . The complicated accord means that . . . those Administration officials who prefer to engage enemies have won out over those who want to isolate them. But the strategy represents a major leap of faith.[59]

As discussed below, North Korea's motivation for pursuing the diplomatic option with the United States can be explained by Pyongyang's deepening economic crisis and geostrategic isolation. But why did the United States, having branded North Korea a rogue state, deviate from the generic policy of comprehensive containment and isolation that Washington had adopted toward the other countries in that pariah category?

The reason lies in the imminent threat posed by North Korea's nuclear program and in the absence of viable alternatives. That acute danger led to what this study refers to as "limited engagement by necessity" through the instrument of the Agreed Framework. As discussed above, the two alternatives to limited engagement were a military strike on North Korea's nuclear facilities (which carried the significant risk of triggering a general war on the Korean Peninsula) and economic sanctions. With respect to the latter, even if China did not veto sanctions in the Security Council, it was highly questionable whether the Beijing regime would have supported them in practice, or if the imposition of sanctions would have had the desired effect on North Korea in terms of compelling Pyongyang to remain in the NPT and resume NPT inspections.

In a December 1994 briefing to State Department employees, Gallucci stated that U.S. negotiators focused on "the real threats to our national security and to regional stability," meaning, in short, "North Korean access to plutonium."[60] Achieving that key objective entailed, first, keeping the spent fuel (containing enough plutonium for an estimated 4–5 nuclear weapons) removed from the 5MW(e) reactor in the cooling pond with a plan for it eventually to be shipped out of the county; and second, preventing the completion of the 50 and 200MW(e) reactors capable of producing (along with the 5MW(e) reactor) 175 kilograms of plutonium a year. Gallucci noted that the Agreed Framework would be implemented in "parallel steps" with the North Koreans discontinuing their activities of greatest concern to the United States before the transfer of the key LWR components toward the end of the decade-long process. One issue that was deferred for at least five years under the agreement was the full accounting of the DPRK's nuclear history (specifically, the quantity of plutonium, estimated from gram quantities to a few kilograms, which was accumulated during the shutdowns of the 5MW(e) reactor during 1989–91).[61] Administration officials argued that it was better to promptly halt further North Korean production and reprocessing of plutonium, even if that meant deferring IAEA special inspections to clarify North Korea's past activities and, as Reiss puts it, "living with uncertainty."

Having negotiated the Agreed Framework and won its acceptance by key allies, the Clinton administration faced the challenge of selling the deal to a skeptical Republican Congress and the public at large. When the accord was announced in October 1994, those outside critics who had advocated a hard-line approach (including the possible use of force against North Korean nuclear facilities) condemned it as a sellout and an act of appeasement. Congressional Republicans joined in this criticism, but did not move to kill the agreement. Senator John McCain (R-Ariz.), a leading critic, stated, "What the Administration has done is put us into a box that is very difficult to get out of because if we refuse now to fund portions of this agreement, then of course we can be held responsible for the whole thing coming apart."[62] This view notwithstanding, the Clinton administration faced an annual struggle to win congressional approval for funds to pay for the heavy fuel oil shipments to North Korea that the United States was committed to make under the terms of the Agreed Framework. That appropriation became linked to North Korean behavior outside the bounds of the nuclear accord. In this way, it served as a barometer for the U.S. relationship with North Korea—a tangible symbol (because it required an affirmative vote by Congress) to express displeasure or residual skepticism. Proponents of the accord, including prominent congressional Democrats, argued that the administration, which had invested so much to conclude the agreement with Pyongyang, was strangely passive in defending it on Capitol Hill. In Seoul, the linkage of the Agreed Framework to broader developments affecting the Korean Peninsula was also a political reality. For example, South Korea temporarily halted its activities in KEDO after the September 1996 incursion of a North Korean submarine.

Following the conclusion of the Agreed Framework, the Clinton administration took some modest steps to ease economic sanctions on North Korea (e.g., allowing direct telecommunication links between the two countries and permitting the import of magnesite from the DPRK), but said it would "consider further sanctions-easing as North Korea makes progress on issues of concern to us."[63] In other words, Pyongyang's compliance with the nuclear aspects of the Agreed Framework would not be sufficient to gain a general normalization of economic relations with the United States. That development would be contingent on progress on a wider set of issues, such as the further improvement of ROK-DPRK relations. The Clinton administration did, however, adjust its rhetoric to the policy of limited engagement embodied in the Agreed Framework. Secretary of State Warren Christopher, for example, signaled a shift by dropping North Korea from the State Department's roster of rogue states in a January 1996 speech: "It is critical that North Korea's nuclear program stays shut down and on the way to the scrap heap. And pariah states like Iraq, Iran and Libya must be stopped in their efforts to acquire weapons of mass destruction."[64] Former ambassador Gregg similarly observed, "We wouldn't conduct liaison with a pariah."[65]

Despite the September 1996 submarine incursion and incidents along the demilitarized zone (DMZ), KEDO moved forward on the implementation of the Agreed Framework. It concluded a series of protocols with the DPRK that led to a ground-breaking ceremony in August 1997 at the LWR construction site at Sinpo on North Korea's east coast. U.S. and South Korean officials agreed that North Korea was fulfilling its commitments under these agreements with KEDO to implement the nuclear accord. The Clinton administration, however, annually struggled to overcome congressional skepticism to win approval for the heavy fuel oil appropriation. This congressional attitude reflected qualms about dealing with a state that many members continued to regard as rogue and lingering questions about North Korea's nuclear intentions. Those suspicions were fueled by the startling report in August 1998 that U.S. intelligence had discovered a huge secret underground facility in North Korea that might be part of a covert plan to circumvent the Agreed Framework.

Some critics of the October 1994 accord had earlier raised the possibility of a covert North Korean program, perhaps using the nuclear materials extracted following the 1989–91 shutdowns. A 1995 Congressional Research Service report alluded to this possibility: "The freeze will not prevent North Korea from producing a few nuclear weapons if . . . it has enough plutonium, sufficient technology to manufacture them, and hidden facilities."[66] Congress responded to the revelation of the underground site by linking future appropriations of funds to implement the Agreed Framework to a certification by the president that the Pyongyang regime was abiding by the terms of the agreement. It also required the administration to appoint a "North Korea policy coordinator" to oversee a policy review process and address the outstanding issues of concern. Former secretary of defense William Perry was subsequently named to this position.[67] In Washington, views on the meaning of the underground site vis-à-vis North Korea's nuclear intentions were divided. Joseph Nye stated, "Is this a nuclear breakout, a hedge, a bargaining chip? It's hard to know." All agreed, however, that the revelation threatened to void the Agreed Framework or permanently undermine political support for it in Washington and Seoul. (Japan, meanwhile, had temporarily suspended its activities in KEDO in response to the August 1998 North Korean ballistic missile test that passed over its northern island.) This major challenge to the nuclear accord and the policy of limited engagement with Pyongyang occurred against the backdrop of deepening crisis within North Korea. Reports of widespread famine and declining economic activity confirmed perceptions of the DPRK as a "failed state." This confluence of events again underscored the status of the Agreed Framework as a strategy designed to meet the imminent danger of the DPRK nuclear program, but one embedded in a broader policy to manage the demise of North Korea. Using Secretary of Defense Perry's analogy to a crashing airplane, policy-makers and outside experts debated how a "soft landing" leading to the DPRK's reunification with the ROK might be achieved, whether a "hard landing" was inevitable, and even whether the plane was indeed crashing. Attention will now turn to domestic political developments in North Korea with a particular emphasis on the motivations underlying Pyongyang regime's nuclear program and its own strategy of controlled engagement with the United States and the outside world.

THE NORTH KOREAN DOMESTIC CONTEXT

North Korea is commonly referred to as the most closed-off society in the world. Information on domestic conditions is indeed severely limited and often anecdotal. Former CIA director Robert Gates described the DPRK as a "black hole" and "without parallel the toughest intelligence target in the world."[68] The communist regime's unique strategy of national self-reliance (*juche*) reinforces this isolation and facilitates its tight political control over the population. North Korea is also a country in profound crisis. Many policy analysts characterize it as a "failed state." Economists estimate that the economy has contracted by 50 percent during the 1990s. Widespread famine, with reports of as many as two million deaths since the mid-1990s, prompted a *Washington Post* editorial in February 1999 entitled "23 Million Inmates in One Jail."[69] North Korea poses such a vexing foreign policy challenge because it combines such profound economic weakness with a major military threat stemming from its mature nuclear program and its large deployment of conventional forces deployed along the DMZ. In assessing North Korea's domestic state, economist Marcus Noland offers a cautionary reminder that "there is really no reliable theory linking economic distress or deprivation to political change."[70] How economic conditions will affect the Pyongyang regime's durability and foreign policy behavior remains a matter of debate. Despite the dearth of hard data on the DPRK, however, U.S. policies have not been formulated completely in the dark. After the conclusion of the Agreed Framework negotiations, for example, State Department expert Carlin observed that Washington had the lessons of the prior fifteen years to draw on in shaping a policy.[71]

Indicators of North Korea's economic decline are, of course, more readily observable than its current political state. Refugees reaching China report widespread famine. Satellite imagery of nighttime conditions in the North reveal—literally—that lights are out across the country with only a flicker emanating from Pyongyang. The acceleration of the DPRK's economic collapse coincided with the political crisis triggered by the death of Kim Il Sung in 1994 and the uncertain succession of his son and designated heir, Kim Jong Il. The "Great Leader" had ruled the country with an iron fist for nearly fifty years. He established the institutions of a totalitarian state, as well as a pervasive cult of personality (rivaled only by that of Saddam Hussein in Iraq). Kim Il Sung served both as president of the DPRK and secretary-general of the KWP. As in the Soviet Union and other communist states, the party thoroughly dominated the formal government institutions. For example, the Supreme People's Assembly, a legislative organ that was ostensibly the state's highest authority, has functioned, in practice, merely as a rubber stamp for the ruling KWP. Another key institutional actor has been the Korean People's Army, which has emerged over time as a key interest group affecting the ruling regime's foreign policy decision-making. In 1955, Kim Il Sung proclaimed his *juche* policy to assert his country's autonomy within the socialist camp at a time when the Kremlin was turning away from hard-line Stalinism.[72] This ideological line tapped into the powerful traditional force of Korean nationalism.

The division of the Korean Peninsula resulted in an imbalance of resources: the North inherited the bulk of the country's industrial base and natural resources, while the South had some two-thirds of the population. During the 1950s and 1960s, the DPRK's economic output exceeded that of the ROK because of that disparity. By the 1970s, however, the South Korean economy surged ahead as the North's began to stagnate and eventually collapse. The DPRK economy suffered from the combined impact of economic mismanagement, drought, and the decline of its modest export market (due to global recession resulting from the 1974–75 oil crisis). A key indicator of this emerging economic crisis was evidenced when North Korea became the first communist country to default on loans from free-market countries.[73] In the 1980s, the North Korean economy stagnated even as the regime continued to devote an estimated 25 percent of the nation's gross domestic product (GDP) to the military. As its economic plight deepened, the DPRK also faced a profound geostrategic challenge because of the end of the Cold War and the breakup of the Soviet Union. This epochal development, along with China's moves toward a market economy and the ROK's emerging international prominence (symbolized by its hosting of the 1988 Olympics), reinforced the Pyongyang regime's political isolation. The demise of the Soviet Union and its East European allies not only transformed the international environment to the North's detriment, but also had significant negative economic consequences, namely the termination of subsidized supplies of Russian oil and other goods. China also terminated concessionary trade agreements and moved to normalize relations with South Korea.

In response to the DPRK's deepening economic crisis and geostrategic isolation in the 1980s, the "Great Leader" reportedly initiated a major policy shift. By 1990, North Korean officials were telling American visitors that Kim Il Sung had approved a limited opening to the West for trade and investment, desired to improve relations with the United States, and was prepared to coexist with the South.[74] The initiation of a dialogue with Washington was the centerpiece of this political strategy. As Sigal observes, "The hope was that the United States would become a broker and guarantor of peace on the Korean peninsula and encourage investment and trade from South Korea and Japan."[75] According to one report, Kim Il Sung sided with "pragmatists" at the December 1991 party plenum to compromise on nuclear issues in return for economic engagement and diplomatic normalization with the United States and Japan. The military and other hard-liners agreed to suspend, but not terminate, its nuclear weapons program at that time.[76]

By the early 1990s, Pyongyang's nuclear program was an impediment to improved relations with the United States, but was also the main source of its negotiating leverage. As Oberdorfer observes, "The more the world feared it, the more its nuclear program was a valuable asset to North Korea. . . . There is no evidence that Pyongyang saw the nuclear program as a bargaining chip at its inception, but the record is clear that by the 1990s it had learned the program's value in relations with the outside world."[77] Following the conclusion of the Agreed Framework, Ambassador Gallucci stated that the North Koreans regard their nuclear program as "their bargaining chip and they want to make sure they get something for it."[78] For the Pyongyang regime, maximizing its leverage from this "bargaining chip" meant perpetuating the ambiguity surrounding its nuclear program—hence, for example, its desire to defer the IAEA special inspections at Yongbyon to resolve the issue regarding the possible diversion of nuclear materials during the 1989–91 shutdowns. Maintaining this ambiguity, however, has invariably revived the long-standing questions about North Korea's nuclear intentions and undercut political support in Washington, Tokyo, and Seoul for the Agreed Framework. This political dynamic was again evidenced with the August 1998 revelation of a suspected North Korean underground nuclear site. Views in the American policy community differed over whether this development constituted an effort to break out of the nuclear accord or to gain bargaining leverage. As the *New York Times* editorialized, "At best, North Korea's actions are an attempt to extort new money and concessions from the West. At worst they signal an intention to break the nuclear agreement or even to threaten South Korea and Japan."[79]

A detailed consideration of North Korea's domestic crisis is beyond the scope of this study. The salient issue in this context is the extent to which its nuclear diplomacy with the United States has been motivated and shaped by those domestic economic and political forces. Although questions persist about North Korea's nuclear intentions, the predominant view among Korea experts is that the country's rapidly deteriorating economic situation was a key determinant of Kim Il Sung's decision to put the DPRK's nuclear weapons program on the negotiating table and initiate a limited opening to the West. In December 1993, the Pyongyang regime made the stunning public admission that the DPRK economy was in a "grave situation," with a GDP only one-sixteenth that of the ROK.[80] Relations with the outside world, particularly the United States, offered the possibility of alleviating that crisis, but at a potentially steep political price to the extent that such an opening eroded the regime's totalitarian hold over North Korean society. Analyst David Reese aptly characterizes this central tension in North Korean policy in a recent study:

The regime clearly fears that reforming the economy will bring an influx of new ideas and cultural influences that will erode its authority; South Korea, with its stronger economy, is seen as posing the greatest threat. There is thus a tension at the heart of the North's policies. On the one hand, it sees its best chance of survival in keeping the country sealed off from outside influences; on the other, it recognizes the need for external assistance. The North's main challenge is striking a balance between these two demands so that it receives the aid it needs, while minimizing external influences, particularly from the South.[81]

In practice, the fear of political contagion has overridden economic necessity. The Kim Jong Il regime has been unwilling to implement economic reforms based on the Chinese model for fear of their political impact. A high-ranking defector, Hwang Jang Yop, who had been the leading theoretician of North Korea's ideology of *juche*, affirmed that for the Pyongyang regime "politics dominates economics." Nonetheless, he stated, the economic crisis and famine have narrowed the regime's options since it "cannot live without international aid [as] in the past. . . ."[82] This combination of dire need and an unwillingness to implement meaningful economic reform has led the North Koreans to utilize their sole source of negotiating leverage—their WMD and ballistic missile programs. Hwang ominously concludes, "I am sure [they] understand that there is no alternative to brinkmanship."[83] But engaging in brinkmanship revives questions about Pyongyang's intentions and creates the danger of miscalculation and inadvertent action. At minimum, provocative actions (such as the missile test over Japan) undermine political support in the

United States, Japan, and South Korea for assistance and resources to implement the Agreed Framework. Such incidents have made Washington reluctant to more fully implement the Agreed Framework's generally worded provision regarding the expansion of economic relations. North Korean officials have bitterly protested the Clinton administration's unwillingness to lift economic sanctions in return for their asserted compliance with the nuclear accord. This political dynamic highlights the linkage in North Korean policy between the Agreed Framework and the country's domestic crisis.

This linkage has also been evident in U.S. policy-making. Although the primary motivation underlying the Clinton administration's limited engagement strategy was the imminent danger posed by the DPRK's mature nuclear program, U.S. nuclear diplomacy was conducted with clear reference to North Korea's internal situation. Indeed, when the Agreed Framework was concluded, some Clinton administration officials did not believe that North Korea would survive long enough to reap the accord's benefits. According to Jeffrey Smith of the *Washington Post*, "U.S. officials crafted the Agreed Framework 'with the eventual dissolution of the present North Korean regime in mind.' The officials dismissed concerns that North Korea could restart its nuclear weapons program . . . after it received its promised light water reactors; the long implementation period of the Agreed Framework is almost certainly a sufficient period of time for their regime to have collapsed."[84]

Since the conclusion of the nuclear accord, U.S. officials have refrained from publicly predicting the demise of the Pyongyang regime. Even as the North Korean economic crisis deepened, Ambassador Kartman told the House International Relations Committee in February 1997, "We do not believe that the collapse of the DPRK is imminent. . . ."[85] The Clinton administration's decision in 1996 to provide food aid to North Korea signified a change in its "operational assumptions" about the DPRK, according to Congressional Research Service expert Larry Niksch.[86] Foremost among these revised assumptions was the assessment that the sudden collapse of North Korea—a "hard landing"—carried the significant possibility of war on the Korean Peninsula by triggering a final desperate act on the part of the Kim Jong Il regime. The South Korean government shared this view and was additionally concerned, in light of the German experience, about the staggering economic costs of rapid reunification, as well as the uncontrolled movement of refugees to the South. For similar reasons, the Chinese government provided the Pyongyang regime with food and other aid to forestall a collapse. Although some

U.S. analysts and public officials continue to believe that a "hard land-ing" for North Korea is inevitable and should not be forestalled, the major governments engaged with North Korea in Seoul, Washington, Tokyo, and Beijing have rejected promoting that course because of its profound dangers and uncertainties. Both President Clinton and Presi-dent Kim Dae Jung, a former political dissident who became the ROK's chief executive in February 1998, have sought to reassure the North Ko-reans of their commitment to peaceful reunification—or what analysts called a "soft landing."

The Agreed Framework was viewed as an important instrument to fa-cilitate the negotiation of that political transition. When ground was bro-ken at the LWR construction site in the North, South Korean and Amer-ican officials said that the project would help open up the DPRK to the outside world as workers from both North and South worked collabo-ratively.[87] Because of this potential societal impact on North Korea, some referred to the KEDO-provided nuclear reactors as "poison car-rots." From the American side, the nuclear accord has thus been im-plemented within the broader political context of the DPRK's future. (Again, the salient point in relation to this discussion is to acknowledge the linkage, not to thoroughly assess North Korea's alternative futures.) For the North Koreans, the Agreed Framework has meant extracting maximum economic benefit at minimum political cost, while maintain-ing ambiguity about their nuclear intentions for bargaining leverage or a possible breakout from the agreement. To meet this challenge, James Laney, then U.S. ambassador in Seoul, made the case for a strategy of de-terrence and engagement in a 1996 speech:

In order to maintain stability on the peninsula, we need to begin now to build an edifice of positive relationships that can complement and take us beyond deter-rence. One part of this edifice, the Agreed Framework, is being implemented. . . . If this process is to succeed, we in the ROK and U.S. will need to be willing to re-think the approach we have historically taken toward the DPRK. We should tone down our rhetoric and the lurid language we have used to characterize the North. . . . DPRK leaders are unlikely to play the negotiating game seriously as long as they see no way to survive except by repeatedly playing their military card. . . .

In evaluating policy options, when one is unquestionably strong, one should judge them not on the basis of whether they are "tough" or "soft," the conven-tional cliches, but whether they are "smart" or "dumb." If a policy is in U.S. and South Korean interests, we should pursue it; if it also accords with North Korea's interests so much the better. This should no longer be a "zero-sum game." It is not in our interests for the DPRK to lash out militarily, or to descend into chaos. . . .

[T]he implications for our policy are clear: we should focus our efforts on per-suading North Korea not only that its current path is a dead end, but also that there is a better alternative. We should foster its confidence that it can survive, compete, and even prosper if it picks up the offer now on the table. We should strive to demonstrate that we . . . have no interest in unification through any means other than negotiation and agreement between the South and the North.[88]

In November 1998, President Clinton visited South Korea against the political backdrop of two developments that framed the choices for the Pyongyang regime. The first was the revelation the previous August of the suspect underground site in the North, which the North Koreans offered to open to U.S. inspectors for $300 million. The second was the inaugural visit of South Korean tourists to the North under President Kim Dae Jung's "sunshine policy" of engagement. At a joint press conference with President Kim, President Clinton defended the Agreed Framework, noting that without the accord "North Korea already would have produced a sizable amount of weapons-grade plutonium." He also warned, "There will be great reluctance" in Congress to support the deal without a satisfactory resolution of the dispute over the underground facility. With respect to the Kim Jong Il regime's motivations, he stated, "No one can be absolutely sure of whether the North Korean position is simply a product of economic difficulties, so they're attempting to get more money out of various countries for doing what they should be doing anyway, or whether they really are moving toward a more aggressive posture."[89] Finally, President Clinton made a direct appeal to North Korea to abide by the nuclear accord and react positively to the South's "sunshine policy." Referring to the "very beautiful picture" of a South Korean cruise ship returning from the North, President Clinton observed, "Nothing could ever be put in that hole in the ground that would give the North Koreans as much advantage, as much power, as much wealth, as much happiness as more of those ships going up there full of people from [the South]."[90] National Security Adviser Sandy Berger similarly argued that North Korea was at a "crossroads," facing the choice either to "rejoin the international community" by "re-engaging with the South" or "continue to be a totally isolated, self-contained entity which . . . seeks to preserve its place in the world only through military means."[91]

This choice again highlights the profound tension in North Korean policy. On the one hand, the regime has clearly sought engagement with the outside world in response to the country's economic collapse. On the other hand, such engagement carries the political risk of undermining the ruling regime. In other words, a "soft landing" for North Korean society could lead to a "hard landing" for the current ruling regime. This concern about political survival accounts for Pyongyang's restrained response to President Kim Dae Jung's "sunshine policy" and its continued efforts to seek advantage or bargaining leverage from the DPRK's nuclear and ballistic missile programs. The economic crisis has evidently not led to an internal regime crisis. One major trend has been the decline of the KWP as a political force and the concomitant rise of the military. U.S. negotiators report splits between the Foreign Ministry and the military, but whether this signifies a significant fissure within the regime or is a political tactic in the negotiations remains unclear. As for Kim Jong Il, after an extended hiatus that raised questions about his status, his dynastic succession of Kim Il Sung was finalized in September 1998 when he assumed the position of "Great Leader" and chair of the National Defense Commission (described as "the highest post of the state").[92] In assessing regime dynamics in North Korea, a 1998 Council on Foreign Relations task force report noted various signs of breakdown, including discontent among elites, but concluded that "the regime's ideological and political control of the country seems complete."[93]

POLICY ASSESSMENT

This chapter has characterized the U.S. nuclear diplomacy culminating in the conclusion of the Agreed Framework as a case of "limited engagement by necessity." The Clinton administration deviated from the generic rogue state approach of comprehensive containment in its policy toward North Korea because of the imminent threat posed by the DPRK's mature nuclear program. That point of departure, which highlights the strategic liabilities of the rogue state policy, has been the particular focus of this discussion. During the 1993–94 negotiations, the administration reluctantly integrated a limited engagement component into its containment strategy, in the absence of any better policy alternative. A preemptive military strike on North Korea's nuclear facilities at Yongbyon carried the significant risk of triggering a general war on the Korean Peninsula (with no certainty of destroying whatever fissile material North Korea had squirreled away since 1989). Likewise, the administration's proposed economic sanctions, which the Pyongyang regime proclaimed would constitute an act of war, faced an uncertain fate in the Security Council—and China likely would not have enforced them even if it had not vetoed them.

The Agreed Framework was structured around a series of phased, reciprocal steps that KEDO could halt or break off in the event of North Korean noncompliance. Moreover, under the accord, North Korea was obliged to freeze activity immediately at the facilities of greatest concern to the United States and the ROK, while KEDO was not committed to provide key components for the LWR project until the latter years of the decade-long process. The accord did forestall the construction of the DPRK's planned gas graphite-moderated reactors that U.S. officials described as a plutonium factory because they could have provided nuclear material for dozens of weapons. But, as noted by critics, the agreement did not fully resolve questions relating to the North Korean nuclear program's history (in particular, the possible accumulation of weapons-grade materials during the 1989–91 reactor shutdowns). To address the immediate danger, the nuclear accord permits the Pyongyang regime to maintain a degree of ambiguity about its nuclear capabilities and, through that ambiguity, some continuing negotiating leverage with the United States. But it also keeps alive the issue of North Korea's nuclear intentions— whether the Pyongyang regime is maintaining a covert weapons program and intends to break out of the nuclear agreement and wed weapons with a developing long-range ballistic missile capability.

Given the historical record of North Korea's provocative actions and its consequent political demonization by Washington (including the designation as a rogue state), the Republican-led Congress was reflexively hostile to any incentive-based agreement with the North. Key Republican leaders grudgingly agreed not to scuttle the nuclear accord, but the negative attitude has persisted. The Clinton administration devoted enormous energy to the conclusion of the Agreed Framework, but, surprisingly, was lackluster in its promotion on Capitol Hill once concluded. Proponents of the accord outside government have charged that the administration never created a constituency for it in Congress, particularly with moderate Republican members who might have been coopted into support.

This political dynamic between North Korea and the United States has created a cycle. North Korea's actions that call into question its compliance with the Agreed Framework (e.g., the underground site), or other provocative actions (e.g., the submarine incursion and ballistic missile test over Japan), have undermined political support in Washington for the limited engagement strategy. These actions have made it politically difficult to ease U.S. sanctions and expand economic relations with North Korea as called for in the Agreed Framework. That outcome, in turn, has generated persistent complaints from the Pyongyang regime that the United States has not itself fully abided by the accord and may indeed promote further bad behavior by the North to get Washington's attention.[94]

An additional layer of complexity to the relationship between North Korea and the outside world has stemmed from the linkage between the nuclear agreement and the broader question of the DPRK's continued existence as a state. Western experts agree that, for North Korea, economic necessity was the key determinant of its decision to put its nuclear program on the negotiating table. For the Pyongyang regime, a profound policy tension exists between the imperative of economic engagement with the outside world and its fears that such economic relations will undermine its political survival. During the 1990s, political considerations have overridden economic ones. That may signify the Kim Jong Il regime's belief that it can withstand even economic calamity by insulating itself from the crisis (e.g., by diverting scarce food and resources to the leadership class and the military). Indeed, some U.S. analysts believe that the analogy to a crashing airplane (and the resultant "hard" versus "soft landing") is incorrect and that this regime's durability is underestimated. For the United States, the primary impetus behind its diplomacy was the major threat to international stability posed by the North Korean nuclear program. But the nuclear accord was also embedded in the broader issue of North Korea's future and whether the United States and its allies could facilitate a peaceful transition leading to reunification (with South Korea in the role of West Germany). The nuclear accord was thus viewed not only as a response to an imminent national security threat, but also as part of a process to promote a "soft landing."

The Agreed Framework remains the centerpiece of a U.S. strategy toward North Korea that Clinton administration officials characterize as "deterrence and engagement." The implementation of the nuclear accord has created a political context within which other negotiations and avenues of engagement can be pursued. Conversely, if the Agreed Framework collapsed, the Four Party Talks (involving the U.S., China and the two Koreas) and Kim Dae Jung's "sunshine policy" would be politically difficult, if not impossible, to sustain. During 1998–99, the revelation of a suspected underground facility threatened to derail the nuclear accord. Negotiations with the North Koreans led to an agreement in March 1999 to permit U.S. experts to inspect the suspect site. Countering congressional criticism, the Clinton administration maintained that six hundred thousand tons of additional food aid was a humanitarian gesture and not compensation for this access. U.S. experts, depending on their reading of North Korean intentions, were divided over whether this site signified a serious effort to break out of the nuclear accord or whether it was designed to gain additional bargaining leverage and economic benefits, or both. This episode of brinkmanship by the Pyongyang regime again highlighted the continuing problem of North Korea's nuclear ambiguity. Mitchell Reiss's authoritative account of U.S. nuclear diplomacy was aptly titled, "Living with Uncertainty." Although that remains the case, at some point that ambiguity will have to be satisfactorily resolved, as the eventual transfer of key LWR components will require IAEA certification of North Korea's non-nuclear status and a U.S.–North Korean nuclear cooperation agreement.

Through the appointment of former secretary of defense Perry as policy coordinator for the DPRK and the negotiation of an access agreement to the underground site, the Clinton administration struggled to maintain its limited engagement policy. But as that process was playing out, the administration's new ballistic missile defense posture pushed in the opposite direction. In January 1999, Secretary of Defense William Cohen announced an accelerated research and development program to address the growing long-range ballistic missile threat from rogue states. The impetus for this change was the tests of the Iranian Shahab-3 and North Korean Taepodong-1 missiles in summer 1998. The revived designation of North Korea as a rogue state by the Clinton administration in the context of ballistic missile defense was politically at odds with its efforts to maintain an engagement track with the Pyongyang regime that was already under heavy political attack in Congress. In May 1999, Perry visited Pyongyang after an interagency review of U.S. policy toward North Korea. This high-level meeting also came on the heels of the visit of a U.S. delegation to the suspect underground site at Kumang-ni and that expert team's determination that the site is not suitable for plutonium production or reprocessing and, therefore, does not violate the Agreed Framework. Perry reportedly held out to the Pyongyang regime the possibility of a "package deal" that would broaden U.S. economic engagement with the North (including the lifting of the trade embargo) in return for full DPRK compliance with the Agreed Framework and restraints on ballistic missile production and exports.[95] As in the past, the key question is whether the Kim Jong Il regime governing the "hermit state" would accept such a "package deal" to address the country's profound economic crisis, or whether it would view such a deal as a threat to its political survival.

NOTES

[1] This chapter relies heavily on the following works that trace the United States's nuclear diplomacy with North Korea leading to the conclusion of the Agreed Framework in October 1994: Mitchell Reiss, *Bridled Ambition: Why Countries Constrain Their Nuclear Capabilities* (Washington, DC: Woodrow Wilson Center Press; distributed by Johns Hopkins University Press, 1995), chapter 6, "North Korea: Living with Uncertainty," pp. 231–319; Michael Mazarr, *North Korea and the Bomb: A Case Study in Nonproliferation* (New York: St. Martin's, 1995); Leon V. Sigal, *Disarming Strangers: Nuclear Diplomacy with North Korea* (Princeton, NJ: Princeton

University Press, 1998); and Don Oberdorfer, *The Two Koreas: A Contemporary History* (Reading, MA: Addison Wesley, 1997), chapters 11–14. These detailed studies, providing almost a day-to-day account of the U.S.-DPRK negotiations, are based on extensive interviews with key U.S. and foreign officials involved in the negotiations. An additional, unpublished study is Gregory D. Koblentz, "Resocializing 'Rogue' States: The Case of North Korea" (B.A. thesis, Department of Political Science, Brown University, April 1996).

[2] The Agreed Framework was a bilateral accord between the Washington and Pyongyang governments, not a formal international treaty, and hence was not submitted by the Clinton administration to the Senate for ratification, much to the displeasure of many Republicans on Capitol Hill.

[3] Remarks of former ambassador Robert Gallucci at the seminar, "North Korea in U.S.-Japan Relations," Woodrow Wilson International Center for Scholars, January 15, 1999.

[4] "The North Korean Precedent," *New Perspectives Quarterly* 12, no. 3 (Summer 1995), p. 24.

[5] Richard Haass, *Success or Sellout? The U.S.-North Korean Nuclear Accord—Report of an Independent Task Force* (New York: Council on Foreign Relations and Seoul Forum for International Affairs, 1995), p. 15.

[6] David E. Sanger, "North Korea Site an A-Bomb Plant, U.S. Agencies Say," *New York Times*, August 17, 1998, pp. A1, 4.; Sheryl WuDunn, "North Korea Fires Missile over Japanese Territory," *New York Times*, September 1, 1998, p. A6.

[7] James Risen, "C.I.A. Sees a North Korean Missile Threat," *New York Times*, February 3, 1999, p. A6.

[8] Interview with the author, March 19, 1999.

[9] For historical background see Leonard S. Spector, *Nuclear Ambitions: The Spread of Nuclear Weapons 1989–1990* (Boulder, CO: Westview, 1990), pp. 118–27.

[10] For seminal research on the origins of the Korean War, documenting Kim Il Sung's primary role vis-à-vis Stalin in the initiation of conflict, see Kathryn Weathersby, "New Findings on the Korean War," *Cold War International History Project Bulletin* no. 3 (Washington, DC: Woodrow Wilson International Center for Scholars, Fall 1993), pp. 1, 14–18.

[11] Spector, *Nuclear Ambitions*, p. 121.

[12] See Joo-Hong Nam, *America's Commitment to South Korea: The First Decade of the Nixon Doctrine* (Cambridge: Cambridge University Press, 1986), pp. 102–6. Despite South Korea's accession to the NPT, questions about Seoul's nuclear intentions persisted into the late 1970s, when South Korea began to operate a nuclear reactor similar to one from which India had obtained the fissile material for its nuclear test.

[13] Spector, *Nuclear Ambitions*, p. 122–23.

[14] Reiss, *Bridled Ambition*, p. 233. See also Larry Niksch and Zachary Davis, "North Korean Nuclear Controversy: Defining Treaties, Agreements, and Terms," Congressional Research Service [CRS] Report for Congress no. 94-752 F (September 16, 1994), pp. 2–3ff.

[15] Sigal, *Disarming Strangers*, p. 25.

[16] Reiss, *Bridled Ambition*, p. 232.

[17] Sigal, *Disarming Strangers*, p. 26.

[18] Oberdorfer, *The Two Koreas*, p. 196.

[19] Reiss, *Bridled Ambition*, p. 236.

[20] The spring 1991 interagency review is detailed in Sigal, *Disarming Strangers*, p. 27.

[21] Oberdorfer, *The Two Koreas*, p. 261.

[22] Niksch and Davis, "North Korean Nuclear Controversy: Defining Treaties, Agreements, and Terms," p. 5.

[23] Sigal, *Disarming Strangers*, p. 33.

[24] Mazarr, *North Korea and the Bomb*, p. 63.

[25] In his study of U.S.–North Korean nuclear diplomacy, Leon Sigal considers the Bush administration's unwillingness to explore the seriousness of this North Korean trial balloon during the May 1992 Blix visit as a significant missed opportunity. See Sigal, *Disarming Strangers*, p. 40. This episode is also briefly discussed in Mazarr, *North Korea and the Bomb*, p. 84.

[26] Oberdorfer, *The Two Koreas*, p. 273.

[27] Mazarr, *North Korea and the Bomb*, p. 93.

[28] David E. Sanger, "North Korea, Fighting Inspection, Renounces Nuclear Arms Treaty," *New York Times*, March 12, 1993, p. A1.

[29] David E. Sanger, "Atomic Energy Asks U.N. to Move against North Koreans," *New York Times*, April 2, 1993, p. A2.

[30] Oberdorfer, *The Two Koreas*, pp. 289–90; Niksch and Davis, "North Korean Nuclear Controversy: Defining Treaties, Agreements, and Terms," pp. 6–7.

[31] Oberdorfer, *The Two Koreas*, p. 294–95.

[32] David E. Sanger, "U.S. Revising North Korea Strategy," *New York Times*, November 22, 1993, p. A5.

[33] Thomas L. Friedman, "U.S. and Seoul Differ on Appeal to North Korea on Nuclear Sites," *New York Times*, November 24, 1993, p. A16.

[34] Ibid.

[35] David E. Sanger, "North Korea's Game Looks a Lot Like Nuclear Blackmail," *New York Times*, December 12, 1993, section 4, p. 6.

[36] Reiss, *Bridled Ambition*, p. 265.

[37] Stephen Engelberg with Michael R. Gordon, "Intelligence Study Says North Korea Has Nuclear Bomb," *New York Times*, December 26, 1993, section 1, p. 1.

[38] Sigal, *Disarming Strangers*, p. 110.

[39] Oberdorfer, *The Two Koreas*, p. 306.

[40] Reiss, *Bridled Ambition*, p. 268.

[41] During the May 1994 defueling crisis, some tension emerged between the United States government and the IAEA. Clinton administration officials considered the IAEA overly legalistic. They emphasized the need to freeze North Korea's program and, if necessary, defer "special inspections" to ascertain North Korea's nuclear history (i.e., whether fuel rods had been removed during the 1989 shutdown). The United States offered some technical suggestions, resisted by IAEA experts, regarding methods to salvage useful data from the extracted fuel rods (which the North Koreans had placed in nearby cooling ponds). See Ashton B. Carter and William J. Perry, *Preventive Defense: A New Security Strategy for America* (Washington, DC: Brookings Institution Press, 1999), p. 126; Sigal, *Disarming Strangers*, p. 119.

[42] Carter and Perry, *Preventive Defense*, pp. 128–29.

[43] Paul Lewis, "U.S. Offers a Plan for U.N. Sanctions on North Korea," *New York Times*, June 16, 1994, p. A1.

[44] Reported in Oberdorfer, *The Two Koreas*, p. 320.

[45] See, for example, the op-ed by Bush national security adviser Brent Scowcroft and former undersecretary of state Arnold Kanter, "Korea: Time for Action," *Washington Post*, June 15, 1994, p. A25.

[46] Reiss, *Bridled Ambition*, p. 271.

[47] This episode is detailed in Sigal, *Disarming Strangers*, pp. 158–59.

[48] Michael R. Gordon, "Back from Korea, Carter Declares the Crisis Over," *New York Times*, June 20, 1994, p. A1.

[49] Doug Jehl, "Clinton Says the North Koreans Really May Be Ready for Talks," *New York Times*, June 23, 1994, p. A1.

[50] Ibid.

[51] Sigal, *Disarming Strangers*, p. 166.

[52] Quoted in Mazaar, *North Korea and the Bomb*, p. 173.

[53] U.S. Arms Control and Disarmament Agency, Office of Public Affairs, "Fact Sheet: U.S.–Democratic People's Republic of Korea Agreed Framework," October 21, 1994, p. 1.

[54] Joel Wit, "Dealing with North Korea's Nuclear Weapons Program," (mimeograph) Henry L. Stimson Center, November 16, 1998.

[55] Ibid., p. 2.

[56] The North Koreans resisted the offer of the South Koreans to provide the two LWRs. An imaginative diplomatic device was used to resolve this lingering issue from the autumn 1994 negotiations. In June 1995, after months of wrangling, parallel announcements were made—one by the U.S. and the DPRK stating that KEDO, the U.S.-led international consortium, would select the reactors, and another by KEDO designating the South Korean standard model reactors for the project. Andrew Pollack, "North Korea to Get Plants from Rival," *New York Times*, June 14, 1995, p. A5.

[57] Ibid., p. 4.

[58] David E. Sanger, "Clinton Administration Reports a Breakthrough in North Korea Nuclear Arms Talks," *New York Times*, October 15, 1994, p. A8.

[59] Elaine Sciolino, "Clinton Ups Atom Stakes," *New York Times*, October 20, 1994, p. A7.

[60] Federal News Reuter Transcript Service, "Ambassador-at-Large Robert Gallucci at the Secretary's Open Forum, 'North Korea and National Security,'" December 12, 1994.

[61] Ibid.

[62] Steven Greenhouse, "GOP's Strategy: Attack Accord, But Don't Kill It," *New York Times*, January 20, 1995, p. A8.

[63] Testimony of Acting Assistant Secretary for East Asian and Pacific Affairs Charles Kartman before the House International Relations Committee, Subcommittee on Asian and Pacific Affairs, February 26, 1997 (http://www.state.gov/www/regions/eap/970226_kartman_north_korea).

[64] Michael S. Lelyveld, "U.S. Removes North Korea from List of 'Pariah States,' " *Journal of Commerce*, February 2, 1996, p. 1.

[65] Ibid.

[66] Larry A. Niksch, "U.S.–North Korea: Agreed Framework and Other Aspects of U.S.–North Korean Relations," Congressional Research Service monograph, January 9, 1995; cited in Chuck Downs, *Over the Line: North Korea's Negotiating Strategy* (Washington, DC: American Enterprise Institute, 1999), p. 249. The Downs volume is a sustained critique of the Agreed Framework and of the Clinton administration's negotiating approach toward North Korea.

[67] See Richard P. Cronin, "North Korea: The U.S.-DPRK Agreed Framework and KEDO," Congressional Research Service monograph, January 4, 1999.

[68] Oberdorfer, *The Two Koreas*, p. 60.

[69] "23 Million Inmates in One Jail" (editorial), *Washington Post*, February 14, 1999, p. B6.

[70] Marcus Noland, "Why North Korea Will Muddle Through," *Foreign Affairs* 76, no. 4 (July/August 1997), p. 106.

[71] Remarks at a seminar on North Korea at the United States Institute of Peace, July 17, 1996.

[72] Mazarr, *North Korea and the Bomb*, p. 22.

[73] U.S. Department of State, Bureau of East Asian and Pacific Affairs, "Country Report: North Korea," October 1995, pp. 8–9.

[74] Sigal, *Disarming Strangers*, p. 24.

[75] Ibid.

[76] Oberdorfer, *The Two Koreas*, p. 263.

[77] Ibid, pp. 249–50.

[78] Federal News Reuter Transcript Service, "Ambassador-at-Large Robert Gallucci at the Secretary's Open Forum, 'North Korea and National Security,' " December 12, 1994.

[79] "A Frayed Deal with North Korea" (editorial), *New York Times*, January 12, 1999, p. A22.

[80] Oberdorfer, *The Two Koreas*, p. 297.

[81] David Reese, "The Prospects for North Korea's Survival," Adelphi Papers no. 323 (London: Oxford University Press, 1998), p. 10.

[82] Don Oberdorfer, "A Nation with an Iron Fist and an Outstretched Hand," *Washington Post*, March 14, 1999, p. B5.

[83] Ibid.

[84] R. Jeffrey Smith, "U.S. Accord with North Korea May Open Country to Change," *Washington Post*, October 23, 1994, p. A36, cited in B. C. Koh, "American Perspectives on Regime Dynamics in North Korea," in Chung-in Moon, ed., *Understanding Regime Dynamics in North Korea* (Seoul: Yonsei University Press, 1998), p. 100. The Koh chapter provides an excellent overview of U.S. official and academic thinking about the DPRK regime.

[85] Kartman testimony.

[86] Cited in Koh, "American Perspectives on Regime Dynamics in North Korea," p. 101.

[87] Kevin Sullivan and Mary Jordan, "N. Korea Initiates Huge Energy Project: Venture Viewed as Aid to Stability," *Washington Post*, August 20, 1997, p. A18.

[88] U.S. Ambassador to the Republic of Korea James T. Laney, "North and South Korea: Beyond Deterrence," speech delivered to the Asia Society Corporate Conference, Seoul, May 11, 1996.

[89] Kevin Sullivan and John F. Harris, "Clinton Defends 'Wise' Policy of Engaging Defiant N. Korea," *Washington Post*, November 21, 1998, p. A12.

[90] James Bennet, "Clinton Appeals to North Korea for Closer Ties," *New York Times*, November 22, 1998, section 1, p. 1.

[91] White House, Office of the Press Secretary, "White House Press Release: Press Briefing by National Security Advisor Sandy Berger, Seoul, Korea, November 21, 1998."

[92] Nicholas D. Kristof, "North Koreans Officially Inherit Another 'Great Leader,' " *New York Times*, September 6, 1998, p. A16.

[93] Morton I. Abramowitz, James T. Laney, and Michael J. Green, *Managing Change on the Korean Peninsula–Report of an Independent Task Force* (New York: Council on Foreign Relations, 1998), p. 11.

[94] In addition to Washington's refusal to ease sanctions, North Korean complaints about U.S. compliance with the Agreed Framework include the failure to deliver heavy oil on time and delays at the LWR construction site.

[95] Programme for Promoting Nuclear Non-Proliferation, *Newsbrief*, no. 45 (2nd quarter 1999), p. 16; Howard Diamond, "U.S. Says N. Korea Site Nuclear Free; Perry Visits Pyongyang," *Arms Control Today* 29, no. 3 (April/May 1999), pp. 39, 46. In September 1999, North Korea agreed to a temporary halt in its long-range missile tests. In a reciprocal action, the Clinton administration eased sanctions on consumer goods and lifted the ban on direct air links between the United States and North Korea. A Republican member of Congress criticized the administration's action as continuing the "cycle of extortion" with North Korea. David E. Sanger, "Trade Sanctions on North Korea Are Eased by U.S.," *New York Times*, September 18, 1999, pp. A1, 4.

Conclusion

"When I got to my first Clinton Administration job [as UN ambassador], being a professor, I tried to make some sense out of what I was seeing and to try to group the countries in some way. So I saw it basically as a room that was divided into four kinds of national groups. . . . [One] group [is] . . . the outsiders. We have called them the 'rogue states' at certain stages, but basically what they are are states that feel that they not only have no stake in the system, but, on the contrary, that their very being revolves around the fact that they want to undo the system, literally throw hand grenades into it to destroy it."

—Secretary of State Madeleine Albright, April 1998[1]

"We have changed the tone of our language. We no longer call Iran a rogue state and we no longer say things such as 'Iranian behavior.' Such is the language of tutelage not statesmanship. The use of the term 'rogue state' may make for a good sound bite, but it doesn't make for good policy."

—John Limbert, State Department official, January 1999[2]

American foreign-policy makers continue to identify rogue states as a significant threat to U.S. national security and international stability in the post–Cold War era. Secretary of State Madeleine Albright told a December 1998 meeting of North American Treaty Organization (NATO) foreign ministers that "a ballistic missile attack using a weapon of mass destruction from a *rogue state*" represents the type of security challenge that the alliance will face in the future.[3] The following month, at the time of President Clinton's 1999 State of the Union address, Defense Secretary William Cohen announced additional funding to develop a "national missile defense program to provide a limited defense for the 50 states against a long-range missile threat posed by *rogue nations*."[4] The major impetus behind this announcement was the ballistic missile tests conducted by Iran and North Korea in summer 1998. It is striking that, during this same period, the Clinton administration both attempted to maintain its limited engagement with North Korea through the implementation of the Agreed

Framework and explored the possibilities of expanded dialogue with Iran (given the significant domestic political changes under President Mohammed Khatami). Thus, while invoking the rogue state threat to mobilize political support for ballistic missile defense, the United States simultaneously sought to engage one (and potentially two) of the core group of countries that it included under the rogue state rubric. In so doing, the Clinton administration was working at cross purposes. The administration's mobilization of domestic support for ballistic missile defense through the continued political demonization of rogue states frustrated its ability to pursue differentiated policies toward these countries as circumstances dictated. Moreover, while this debate about ballistic missile defense was unfolding, NATO was waging an air war against Yugoslavia for the suppression of its Albanian minority in Kosovo. Although Serbian president Slobodan Milosevic was widely condemned as a war criminal, Yugoslavia was not included in the Clinton administration's roster of rogue states.

These contradictory developments again point to the key questions that were the starting point of this book. What is a rogue state? Is it a useful category of international relations—or, as argued here, a politically motivated concept that leads to counterproductive policies? This concluding chapter will briefly summarize the main themes of this study, outline the findings of the three case studies of Part II, and finally, explore the implications of this study for the development of containment strategies in the post–Cold War era.

MAIN THEMES OF THE STUDY

This study sought to refute the contention, made by senior U.S. policymakers and gaining widespread currency, that rogue states constitute a distinct category of countries in the post–Cold War international system. Its central argument is that the artificial lumping and demonizing of this disparate group of states significantly distorts policy. The rogue state approach has been used as a political instrument to mobilize support for hard-line policies (comprehensive containment and isolation, and even rollback). But in so doing, it sharply circumscribes policy-makers' ability to switch gears and adjust policy to meet the changing circumstances of the target state. The rogue state strategy, in short, is the antithesis of the differentiated approach to foreign policy-making necessitated by what former secretary of state Henry Kissinger has characterized as the "infinite complexity" of post–Cold War international relations.

ORIGINS AND DEVELOPMENT
OF THE ROGUE STATE STRATEGY

The contemporary emergence of the rogue state concept and policy can be traced back to the Cold War era. Prior to 1980, when the term "pariah state" was invoked by U.S. policy-makers, the regimes cited were Uganda under Idi Amin, Cambodia under Pol Pot, and South Africa under the apartheid system. This stigmatized status derived from the objectionable internal behavior of these ruling regimes toward their own people, not their international conduct. An important change in the conception of an "outlaw state" began in 1979, when the State Department inaugurated its annual listing of state sponsors of terrorism. With that development, the criteria used to designate a rogue state shifted from internal to external behavior. Terrorism supported by Third World states, such as Libya and Iran, became a central foreign policy focus of the Reagan administration. The proliferation of ballistic missile programs in the Third World and the Saddam Hussein regime's use of chemical weapons against Iran highlighted a second key criterion: the acquisition by a Third World power of weapons of mass destruction (WMD) or the means of their delivery. A Third World country that exhibited these characteristics became the archetype of the rogue state concept and policy that emerged during the 1980s.

The change in thinking about rogue states was further reinforced by the fact that the end of the Cold War coincided with a hot war in the Persian Gulf. Defense Secretary Dick Cheney spoke of the need to prepare for "Iraqs of the future." This mission assumed added urgency following the dramatic disclosures of the United Nations Special Commission (UNSCOM) about Iraq's nuclear, chemical, and biological weapons programs. The Bush and Clinton administrations developed plans for a U.S. force structure roughly three-quarters the size of that during the Cold War. That post-Soviet force structure was explicitly designed to meet two major regional contingencies (for example, simultaneous crises on the Korean Peninsula and in the Persian Gulf region).

The Clinton administration's rogue state policy was laid out by National Security Adviser Anthony Lake in a controversial article, "Confronting Backlash States," published in the Spring 1994 issue of *Foreign Affairs*. Although best known for its elaboration of the "dual containment" policy toward Iran and Iraq, the article more generally addressed the rogue state issue. In addition to Iran and Iraq, Libya, North Korea, and Cuba were cited as members of this rogues' gallery. Lake argued that these states shared a "recalcitrant commitment to remain on the wrong side of history." His article identified three key characteristics underlying the rogue state designation: first, the pursuit of WMD; second, the use of terrorism as an instrument of state policy; and third and most nebulously, constitution of a regional threat to important U.S. interests. Rogue status thus derives from realist criteria relating to these states' external behavior, not their domestic policies (e.g., compliance with human rights norms). By contrast, the Clinton administration's overarching foreign policy strategy of "engagement and enlargement"—expanding the community of democratic states to achieve international peace—is grounded in the liberal Wilsonian tradition.

Lake concluded his important article with an enunciation of a post–Cold War doctrine of containment: "As the sole superpower, the United States has a special responsibility for developing a strategy to neutralize, contain, and through selective pressure, perhaps eventually transform these backlash states into constructive members of the international community." Using political, economic, and military instruments, this strategy of comprehensive containment and isolation seeks to change either the target state's behavior or its ruling regime. The Bush and Clinton administrations have pursued this policy multilaterally in the cases of Iraq and Libya, unilaterally in the cases of Iran and Cuba. The notable exception to this pattern has been the case of North Korea, in which the United States has pursued a mixed strategy that integrates incentives and penalties.

The question of strategy highlights the polarized U.S. foreign policy debate between containment and engagement. The rogue state policy is essentially a political mobilization strategy that lumps a disparate set of countries under this generic rubric and demonizes them. It reflects a traditional impulse arising from the American political culture to view international relations as a moral struggle between forces of good and evil. Although the military may have invoked the rogue state threat to justify its post–Cold War force structure, the main impetus behind the policy came from the country's civilian leadership and U.S. domestic interest groups. The political clout of the Cuban émigré community was essential in winning passage of the Helms-Burton sanctions legislation on Cuba in 1995. Likewise, a year later, the American-Israel Public Affairs Committee was a driving force behind the passage of the Iran-Libya Sanctions Act (ILSA). Given its targets—Castro, Qaddafi, and the Iranian mullahs—this lobbying often goes unopposed. Nevertheless, the effort to extend U.S. law internationally through so-called secondary sanctions (as in the Helms-Burton and ILSA legislation) led to a major showdown with the United States's closest allies in NATO and Japan.

As discussed below, the political dynamic of the rogue state policy pushes the administration into a one-size-fits-all strategy despite significant differences in U.S. objectives toward and political circumstances within this disparate group of states. The rogue state policy regained prominence in 1998–99 when the Clinton administration cited the incipient long-range missile threat from Iran and North Korea (two of the four core countries grouped under the rogue state rubric) as the rationale for accelerated research on ballistic missile defense. Some have argued that such a defensive system is necessary because rogue states may be "undeterrable" (see Chapter 1). Paradoxically, the heightened focus on the rogue state menace coincided with efforts to continue diplomatic engagement with North Korea through the Agreed Framework and to explore the possibilities for dialogue with Iran under President Khatami. This confluence of events again highlighted the contradictions and flawed nature of the rogue state approach.

CRITIQUE OF THE ROGUE STATE STRATEGY

The term "rogue state" is an American political rubric without standing in international law. The policy critique presented in Chapter 3 focused on three strategic liabilities. First and foremost is the rogue state policy's political selectivity and inconsistency. This issue points to the problem of rogue behavior by states outside the United States's designated roster of rogue states. The case of Syria is perhaps the most glaring omission: the Damascus regime has active WMD programs and is on the State Department's terrorist list. The United States remains committed to a policy of engagement and seems reluctant to take punitive action in response to rogue behavior because of Syria's potentially central role in the Middle East peace process. Furthermore, if the pursuit of a WMD capability is a key criterion of rogue state status, how were India and Pakistan to be categorized after their May 1998 nuclear tests? Cuba, on the other hand, meets none of the criteria, but is included in the roster of rogue states for largely domestic political reasons. This political selectivity and inconsistency underscore the rogue state policy's political, as opposed to legal, basis, which accounts for its nearly universal rejection outside the United States.

The second major problem with the rogue state policy is that it limits strategic flexibility. The assertion that these countries constitute a distinct class of states and the use of the ambiguous term "rogue" for purposes of political mobilization pushes policy-makers toward a one-size-fits-all strategy. Because these states are called rogues and outlaws, critics view any shift from hard-line containment as tantamount to appeasement. Once a country is branded a rogue or outlaw state and placed in this category, it becomes very difficult politically to pursue any strategy other than comprehensive containment and isolation. This pattern has been evidenced with respect to North Korea, where the Clinton administration has been accused of appeasement for its policy of limited engagement through the Agreed Framework, and Iran, where the potential for a changed relationship following the election of President Khatami has led to calls for dialogue. The intensifying power struggle in Iran (in which Khatami's conservative clerical opponents invoke anti-Americanism as a source of political mobilization and legitimacy) and continuing Iranian behavior of concern (e.g., ballistic missile tests) have sharply limited the ability of the Clinton administration to alter U.S. policy toward that state. In the case of North Korea, a state that had been a charter member of the rogues' gallery, the Clinton administration remains significantly engaged with the Pyongyang regime on a range of issues. To indicate a change in U.S. policy, Secretary of State Warren Christopher quietly dropped North Korea from the State Department's listing of rogue states in a January 1996 speech. After such a prolonged period of demonization, however, a political residue of the former policy remains—and critics of the administration's policy continue to view moves toward engagement as a form of appeasement. The political consequence of the generic rogue state approach reflects its strategic inflexibility. In short, lumping and demonizing a disparate group of states frustrates the ability to pursue targeted, differentiated policies that reflect the individual circumstances of each country. This strategic inflexibility points to the absence of what Clinton administration officials refer to as an "end game": how will the strategy achieve its objective, and what is the ultimate goal?

A third and final liability of the rogue state approach is its significant political costs. During the late 1990s, the policy has emerged as a major source of contention with America's closest allies—Europe, Japan, and Canada. The focal point of this dispute is the use of extraterritorial sanctions against foreign firms doing business with rogue states. These so-called secondary sanctions, a policy instrument that other key international actors regard as illegal, were incorporated into both the Helms-Burton Act and the ILSA. By threatening the use of secondary sanctions against non-American firms, the United States turned the arguments it used against the Arab boycott of Israel on their head. The passage of the ILSA, one observer noted, changed the political dynamic from "the US and the world versus

Iran" to "Iran and the world versus the United States." European Union
(EU) leaders sharply protested the Helms-Burton and ILSA legislation, arguing that these extraterritorial measures were wrong in principle and
counterproductive in effect. To mitigate the adverse political impact of the
ILSA and Helms-Burton statutes on allied relations, the Clinton administration liberally exercised its waiver option under the sanctions legislation
and has argued for broadened presidential flexibility from Congress in the
conduct of U.S. economic policy. The State Department asserted that the
threat of secondary sanctions and the possibility of a waiver "helped encourage the European Union to strengthen and Russia to institute export
controls relating to Iran."[5] Critics question whether the Clinton administration could have achieved this objective without incurring such significant political costs.

This study argues that the strategic liabilities of the rogue state approach, highlighted in this three-part critique, outweigh whatever utility
the policy might have as an instrument of political mobilization. An alternative to this generic approach would be to develop a repertoire of
targeted strategies designed to address the particular circumstances of
each case. These strategies range across the policy spectrum: from a rollback strategy designed to completely alter the nature of the regime to
comprehensive containment and isolation without any engagement, to
mixed strategies that link incentives and penalties.

DEVELOPING STRATEGIES
OF "DIFFERENTIATED CONTAINMENT"

In *Strategies of Containment*, historian John Lewis Gaddis traced the development of American grand strategy to meet the global challenge posed
by Soviet power after World War II. In the post–Cold War era, the threats
posed by the diverse countries under the rogue state rubric call for the development of strategies of differentiated containment. Such an approach
would eschew the lumping and demonization inherent to the rogue state
policy in favor of targeted strategies addressed to the particularities of each
case. Political scientist Alexander George has observed that "containment"
and "engagement" are general concepts that require specific content in
order to become strategies. The goal of these discrete, targeted strategies is
to "resocialize" so-called rogue states either through behavior modification or a change in regime. The process of reintegrating them into the international community requires careful case-by-case analysis.

The prerequisite for such policy development is an adequate understanding of the target state. As argued in Chapter 3, effective target state

analysis depends on input from a variety of sources. Particularly relevant is the expertise of area specialists, whose knowledge of the target state's history and political culture can provide policy-makers with a much-needed context in which to frame their decisions. This type of country analysis is as much art as science. Policy judgments are based on information that is invariably incomplete and often contradictory. Area specialists can sometimes be too close to their subject matter or simply extrapolate future behavior from the past. Different policy experts can assess the same data and come to sharply divergent conclusions. A review panel created after the failure of the Central Intelligence Agency to predict the May 1998 Indian nuclear tests concluded that policy-makers should foster a decision-making environment in which target state analysis can be openly vetted and underlying assumptions readily challenged.

The development of an appropriate strategy is contingent on an accurate "image" of the target state. This type of assessment (aimed toward the development of what George refers to as an "actor-specific behavioral model") should encompass an amalgam of factors affecting target state behavior across domestic, regional, and international "levels of analysis." Among the key determinants identified in this study are the following: the target state's historical background, the character of the regime and its leadership, the regime's declaratory policy and ideology, its recent foreign policy behavior, the international environment within which the target state exists, and the domestic context within the target state and the potential (given those conditions) for a favorable political evolution. Effective target state analysis requires the shift from what George terms "generic knowledge" (e.g., an understanding of deterrence theory based on historical experience) to specific application (e.g., deterring Saddam Hussein from further regional aggression). Such analysis is not formulaic because there are multiple, often idiosyncratic, forces at work and the relative importance of any particular factor will vary from case to case. Although academic scholars can contribute to the development of an empirically grounded "actor-specific" behavioral model, in practice, public officials must make a judgment about a target state based on a particular set of circumstances.[6]

The preceding discussion has noted the diversity of the countries grouped under the rogue state rubric. This characteristic argues against a generic strategic approach, such as that embodied in the current rogue state policy, and in favor of a differentiated set of strategies that take the particularities of each case into account. Although the countries designated as rogues are noted for their diversity, they do share one key characteristic—a marginal status in the international system. This factor has significant bearing on the development of appropriate U.S. strategies to address the very real security challenges that these states pose. Although all of the rogue states are dissatisfied with the international status quo, none possesses the capabilities to threaten the stability of the international system on the order of a Stalin or a Hitler. The primary threat that the rogue states pose is to their immediate region. Because of the disparity in power between the United States and these countries, the strategies developed to address them will be asymmetrical, according to the framework developed by Gaddis.

Chapter 3 explored the development of strategies of differentiated containment to supplant the generic rogue state policy. The purpose of that discussion was not to advance any particular policy option in relation to these states. Rather, it argued for the adoption of a differentiated approach as the basis for determining specific, targeted strategies toward each of these countries. The pertinent strategies within such a typology can be clustered under three categories: (1) rollback (i.e., an overt strategy to change the regime); (2) comprehensive containment (i.e., politico-economic isolation and military deterrence); and (3) conditional containment (i.e., mixed strategies that integrate an engagement component into an overall containment approach). The discussion in Chapter 3 did not consider strategies further along the policy spectrum toward engagement (i.e., conditional engagement), since such options, while theoretically possible, are not politically plausible under current conditions.

CASE STUDY FINDINGS

The context and analytical framework presented in Part I provided the basis for the case studies that followed in Part II. The focus of analysis was on the formulation and implementation of U.S. policy in three particular contexts: Iraq in the aftermath of the Gulf War; Iran during the period leading up to and following the 1997 election of President Khatami; and the U.S.–North Korean Agreed Framework of October 1994. The case studies were intended not as detailed histories, but to illustrate the themes developed in Part I—specifically, the strategic liabilities stemming from the generic rogue state approach. By addressing a common set of questions (detailed in the Introduction) and an analytical framework, the aim was to identify policy patterns across a cross-section of case studies. These findings can be clustered under four headings: (1) the need to clarify objectives and the dilemma of multiple policy aims; (2) conditions under which the United States would adopt mixed strategies and the target state would seek engagement with the United

States; (3) divergences with allies and other important actors over strategies and instruments in dealing with the countries lumped under the rogue state rubric; and (4) the influence of U.S. domestic politics on policy formulation and implementation.

Policy Objectives

Clarity of objective is a prerequisite for successful policy design and implementation. Without setting the desired ends of policy, no basis exists to determine the requisite means; policy-makers' actions will therefore be unfocused and prone to inconsistency. The case studies indicate that the countries grouped under the rogue state rubric pose a particular problem with respect to the question of policy objectives. The Clinton administration has stated that the goal of U.S. strategy toward rogue states is either to change their foreign policy behavior or to bring about a change in regime in order to reintegrate these countries into the "family of nations." The case studies revealed a significant tension between these twin objectives, most pronounced with respect to U.S. policy toward Iraq. Bush administration officials believed that Saddam Hussein would not survive the tumultuous aftermath of the Gulf War, even though United Nations Security Council resolutions had authorized only the expulsion of Iraqi forces from Kuwait, not the Iraqi leader's ouster. Since that conflict, the Bush and Clinton administrations have oscillated between comprehensive containment (keeping Saddam "in his box") and rollback (overthrowing his regime) as the stated goal of U.S. strategy. The Clinton administration has been caught in a political bind between the Security Council, which is formally committed only to the dismantling of Iraq's WMD capabilities, and Congress, which has authorized an overt program to assist the Iraqi opposition in order to change the Baghdad regime.

The Clinton administration has sought to reconcile these contending objectives by asserting its commitment to the strict implementation of the Security Council resolutions, but with the caveat that Washington does not believe that Iraq can come into full compliance as long as Saddam Hussein rules in Baghdad. U.S. policy toward Iraq thus remains caught between the twin goals of containing and ousting the Saddam Hussein regime. Although this tension has generated considerable confusion about U.S. policy, the two objectives are not mutually exclusive. That is, the United States can seek to keep Saddam Hussein "in his box" in the short term while laying the basis for his ouster in the long run. The Iraqi case points to the possibility of a state pursuing multiple policy objectives over different time horizons.

The tension between behavior modification and regime change was also evident in U.S. policies toward Iran and North Korea. In the case of Iran, the avowed U.S. goal has been to moderate the Teheran regime's behavior, not to change the regime. This declaratory position reflected the U.S. government's political isolation vis-à-vis its Iran policy, its inability to forge a hard-line multilateral policy toward Iran (notably with the EU), and the Iranian regime's perceived domestic legitimacy (however odious Washington considers its behavior). While the Clinton administration has focused on objectionable Iranian behavior, some have argued that the magnitude of change Washington seeks would require a change in the Teheran regime's basic character. Thus, the issues of behavior change and the nature of the ruling regime have been tacitly linked. Likewise, in the case of North Korea, U.S. policy has addressed not only the Pyongyang regime's behavior in contravention of the nonproliferation regime, but the broader issue of North Korea's future as a state. The Agreed Framework has been part of an ambitious strategy to facilitate peaceful unification of the two Koreas through a "soft landing" for the North. The Pyongyang regime fears that engagement with South Korea and the United States, while an economic necessity, may promote its political downfall. With both Iran and North Korea, the United States has pursued a near-term strategy to deter objectionable behavior (e.g., terrorism or acquisition of WMD capabilities) within the context of a longer-term, tacit strategy to alter the character of the regime.

Conditions of Engagement

The sole exception to the generic rogue state policy has been North Korea, a case in which the Clinton administration integrated a limited engagement component into a containment strategy through the Agreed Framework. The accord, which provided for a U.S.-led consortium to construct two light-water reactors in return for the freezing and dismantling of North Korea's mature nuclear program, was undertaken in the absence of a viable alternative (either a preemptive military strike or economic sanctions). The impetus behind that policy departure was an immediate and overriding national security interest.

When the Agreed Framework was concluded in October 1994, some observers argued that the accord offered a model, or at least a process, for addressing the nuclear challenge in Iran. The Clinton administration, however, rejected that approach and pressed Russia and China to enforce strict export controls on nuclear technology in order to prevent

Iran from acquiring a nuclear infrastructure. Because of the comparatively undeveloped state of the Iranian nuclear program relative to that in North Korea, Washington was under no imperative to engage in negotiations with Teheran to freeze it. Neither was the magnitude of economic interests in Iran sufficient to prompt the U.S. government to alter its strategy of comprehensive containment and isolation. Hence the Clinton administration decided to veto the sale of Boeing aircraft to Iran in 1993, even though that permitted the European Airbus consortium to make a commercial inroad. The case studies in Part II support the conclusion that relative to national security considerations, economic considerations have not played a determining role in Washington's decision to undertake limited engagement with a rogue state. This study argues not for any specific policy, but for a differentiated approach in which strategies are tailored to the particularities of each case. The integration of an engagement component into a containment strategy may be appropriate in a specific context, but engagement is only a mechanism for achieving a policy objective, not an end in itself.

The obverse question relates to the conditions under which a rogue or otherwise politically isolated state would seek to engage the United States and the outside world. Two factors emerge from this analysis. First, the North Korean and Iranian cases point to the importance of economic considerations in decision-making. North Korea's deepening economic crisis in the 1980s was a key factor in the Kim Il Sung regime's decision to embark on negotiations with the United States over its nuclear program. Western specialists are in broad agreement that the Pyongyang regime, whose autarkic policies brought the country to disaster, accepted the development of trade relations with the outside world as an economic necessity. But that powerful motivation has been offset by an even more pronounced fear that such engagement could undermine the regime's political survival. This concern has led, in practice, to the primacy of political over economic considerations in North Korean policy. A similar process unfolded in post-Khomeini Iran, where pragmatists within the divided regime advocated an opening to the United States as a means of addressing Iran's economic problems. Clerical hard-liners, however, have strenuously opposed this line, fearing Western cultural and political contagion. Moreover, the clerical faction attempts to draw on anti-Americanism as a source of political legitimacy for the theocratic regime. This factional struggle, in which the issue of relations with the United States plays a central role, has intensified since the election of the more moderate President Khatami in 1997.

A second factor that could precipitate a diplomatically isolated state to seek engagement with an outside power is an overriding national security threat. Iran's secret negotiation with the Reagan administration to secure U.S. military hardware during the Iran-Iraq War is a case in point. Ayatollah Khomeini's approval of this "arms for hostages" relationship with the "Great Satan" in 1985–86 was a reflection of Iran's dire military state in the war with Saddam Hussein's Iraq. This overriding national security interest pushed the Teheran regime into accepting limited, albeit covert, engagement with the United States. Geopolitical considerations also weighed in the North Korean regime's decision to enter into negotiations with the United States over its nuclear program. The collapse of the Soviet Union deprived North Korea of its superpower patron. This development not only had enormous economic consequences (e.g., the end of concessionary oil sales), but also had significant national security implications for the Kim Il Sung regime by transforming the international environment.

Strategies, Instruments, and Allies

The term "rogue state" is a uniquely American political concept—one that has no standing in international law and that other countries have not adopted in the post–Cold War era. And yet, even if they reject the categorization, U.S. allies, as well as many other countries, agree that these rogue states do constitute a very real threat to international order. In addressing these challenges, the differences between the United States and its European and Japanese allies have been less over the ends of policy than over the means. On occasion, the U.S. government has acted unilaterally when unable to develop a multilateral consensus for its preferred course of action. This policy split was evident most prominently in the case of Iran, where the EU pursued an engagement strategy toward the Teheran government under the rubric of "critical dialogue." The Europeans argued that an expanding web of economic relations would create a positive incentive for more moderate Iranian behavior. Like the Bush administration before it, the Clinton administration advocated a strategy of comprehensive containment and isolation to both punish and prod the Teheran regime. The administration acquiesced to congressional passage of the ILSA, arguing that the legislation's sanctions-waiver provision provided an incentive for the Europeans and Russians to toughen their export control regimes relating to Iran.

In contrast to the case of Iran, where the United States adopted a tough unilateral line at significant political cost with its allies, Washington was somewhat more successful in orchestrating a multilateral approach toward Iraq. But, as discussed above, that political support went only so far as gaining Iraqi compliance with the pertinent Security Council resolutions vis-à-vis the destruction of Iraq's WMD capabilities. Fearful of creating a precedent, no state other than Britain supported a rollback policy to oust the Saddam Hussein regime. This attitude points to the conclusion that while states may support tough measures to address rogue behavior that contravenes important international norms, they will not support an overt policy to change a ruling regime. In other words, the principle of state sovereignty that united the Gulf War coalition against Iraq is the same principle on which states have based their opposition to U.S. efforts to change the Baghdad regime.

The competing pulls of unilateralism and multilateralism remains a persistent tension in U.S. post–Cold War foreign policy. A multilateral response through international institutions accords political legitimacy to the actions undertaken.[7] Moreover, the support of allies and other states for U.S. policies enhances the impact of sanctions or inducements. A Woodrow Wilson Center working group explored the possibility of a "grand bargain" in which the United States would employ sanctions more discriminatingly, after consultation with allies, if its allies pledged to adhere fully to such sanctions regimes. The working group further concluded that U.S. policy-makers must be cognizant of the trade-off in working through international institutions: the added legitimacy comes at the price of reduced policy independence, a cost that proponents of American unilateralism find excessive.[8]

Domestic Politics

U.S. domestic politics have strongly influenced the development of the rogue state policy. The Clinton administration has used the rogue state designation as a political instrument to mobilize support for hard-line policies toward these countries. The process of lumping and demonizing these states, however, significantly complicates the ability of policy-makers to shift from the default strategy of comprehensive containment to one that incorporates inducements if circumstances call for a change. The Clinton administration encountered this major strategic liability of the rogue state approach when it adopted a limited engagement policy toward North Korea through the Agreed Framework. Some congressional Republican critics and former Bush administration officials castigated the nuclear accord as a giveaway tantamount to an act of "appeasement." Other key Republicans on Capitol Hill, however, reluctantly consented to authorize funds for the agreement rather than take responsibility for scuttling it. Although the Clinton administration moderated its rhetoric after the signing of the Agreed Framework by dropping North Korea from the roster of rogue states, it did not vigorously court congressional support for the implementation phase. Some congressional proponents of the accord took the Clinton administration to task for failing to put as much effort into the mobilization of support for the Agreed Framework's implementation as it did for its negotiation. In sum, the rogue state approach sharply inhibits the ability of policy-makers to negotiate a shift in policy. But once an administration commits to such a change, as was done in the case of North Korea, it needs to mobilize and maintain political support for that change. That requires a willingness to invest political capital and prestige in the particular policy. This issue was raised in the context of the implementation of the Agreed Framework, but also pertains to the continuing debate about U.S. relations with Iran under President Khatami.

Change from the strategic straitjacket of the rogue state policy is possible if a president is prepared to make the political investment. But the impetus for change can also come from outside the administration. In the case of Iraq, for example, Congress passed the Iraq Liberation Act to push a wavering Clinton administration toward an explicit rollback strategy to oust Saddam Hussein from power. The Clinton administration was reluctant to openly embrace a rollback strategy for fear of losing the political support of those on the Security Council that rejected a regime change as the ultimate goal in Iraq. The same push from Congress, encouraged by domestic political interest groups, was also evident in the ILSA legislation stipulating the imposition of extraterritorial sanctions on foreign firms involved in the development of Iran's energy sector.

The case studies suggest the strong but unpredictable manner in which U.S. domestic politics affect strategy formulation and implementation. In the case of North Korea, the Clinton administration's effort to shift from comprehensive containment to conditional containment (incorporating a limited engagement component) encountered significant congressional resistance. In the cases of Iran and Iraq, Congress pushed the administration toward more hard-line positions.

IMPLICATIONS

This book concludes with a return to its starting point: the central challenge confronting policy-makers of relating means to ends—of selecting the strategies and instruments appropriate to one's political objectives. The fact that policy analysts can define the current "post–Cold War era" only with reference to the preceding forty-five-year period is testimony to what Kissinger called the "infinite complexity" of contemporary international relations. The challenge is profoundly different from the aftermath of World War II, when diplomat George Kennan developed the concept of "containment" to address the global challenge posed by Soviet power. The United States has experienced a decade of unprecedented prosperity since the end of the Cold War in an international system rife with horrific ethnic conflicts, but in which no power poses a politico-military challenge to the prevailing international order. It has been widely observed that not since the Roman Empire has a single power enjoyed such a hegemonic position relative to other states. Although Americans are inclined to view this paramount role as a benign hegemony, many foreigners express concern about a U.S. global primacy that is not only military but economic and cultural as well. Sounding a cautionary note with particular pertinence to this study, political scientist Samuel Huntington has written, "While the United States regularly denounces various countries as 'rogue states,' in the eyes of many countries it is becoming the rogue superpower."[9] This perception not only stems from the enormous disparity in power between the United States and other countries in the international system, it also reflects widespread anxiety about the sweeping socio-economic changes associated with the globalization that the United States is spearheading.

For many overseas, globalization, defined by *New York Times* foreign affairs columnist Thomas Friedman as the "the integration of capital, technology, and information across national borders," is considered synonymous with "Americanization."[10] In the post–Cold War era, states face the stark choice of either joining the community of democracies with market economies to participate in this process of globalization, or isolating and eventually marginalizing themselves. The Clinton administration has sought to promote a stable international milieu within which the ineluctable force of globalization can unfold through its strategy of "engagement and enlargement."[11] The challenge for the Clinton administration and its successors is to translate this slogan into a coherent overarching strategy to govern U.S. foreign policy. Will it require converting all states into democracies? Will it suffice if nondemocratic states adhere to the norms and practices of our preferred international order? These questions are pertinent to this study in that they suggest that the United States will want to induce changes in internal as well as external behavior in the states grouped under the "rogue" rubric.

The U.S. foreign policy debate remains notable for its polarization. As argued in the Introduction, however, it is a polarization less about the ends of foreign policy (though many have questioned the Clinton administration's priorities) than about the means. To contain or engage? That has been the recurring question across a range of foreign policy issues extending well beyond that of rogue states, notably with respect to relations with China. Foreign policy options, however, should be conceived not as a dichotomy, but as a continuum of choice. Within the post–Cold War context characterized above, the analysis presented in this study supports three conclusions.

First, the rogue state rubric is a political term that is analytically flawed and that therefore is not a useful category in international relations. The rogue state policy that flows from the concept is politically selective, limits strategic flexibility by creating a political dynamic that hinders the ability of policy-makers to change direction, and generates significant political costs with allies and other states opposed to American unilateralism. Whatever possible utility the policy has vis-à-vis the mobilization of political support for a hard-line approach is more than offset by these liabilities. Rather than artificially lumping and demonizing a disparate group of states, the focus should be on actions by regimes that contravene established international norms with respect to both external *and* internal behavior (e.g., human rights violations as well as efforts to acquire WMD capabilities). Those criteria, which enjoy broad international legitimacy that the unilateral American rogue state designation lacks, provide a basis for accountability (such as indicting individuals, including the top leaders of a regime, accused of war crimes or other crimes against humanity at the Hague).

Second, the alternative to the generic rogue state approach is the development of targeted strategies addressed to the particularities of each case. That change requires a conceptual breakout from the counterproductive, dichotomized containment-engagement debate to a more nuanced assessment of strategic options along a continuum of choice. Scholars can contribute to this process by assisting in the development of strategies that integrate "generic knowledge" about international relations (such as deterrence theory) with context-specific information about particular cases. The shift from a generic to a targeted approach would yield strategies of differentiated containment that would, for example, permit Washington to more freely explore the political opportunity for change created by the election of President Khatami in Iran. The applicability of this differentiated approach, however, would go well beyond the group of countries designated as rogue states. The most obvious case of a need to develop targeted strategies outside the persistent containment-engagement dichotomy is China. The United States has a complicated relationship with the People's Republic of China that is both cooperative and competitive and that therefore requires a mixed strategy combining elements of containment and engagement.

Third, and finally, the adoption of targeted strategies in lieu of the generic rogue state approach requires a different kind of foreign policy dialogue between the executive branch, Congress, and the general public. Most important, that entails making the case for action to meet a threat in its own terms, rather than relying on lumping and excessive demonizing. Such a targeted approach would make it easier to pursue discriminating policies toward Saddam Hussein's Iraq and Khatami's Iran that better relate the means and ends of American policy. A more focused and less rhetorical discussion between policy-makers and the public on the nature and response to threats would not supply any ready answers, but would improve the basis for choice.

NOTES

[1] Department of State, Office of the Spokesman, "Secretary of State Madeleine K. Albright Remarks at Howard University, April 14, 1998" (http://secretary.state.gov/www/statements/1998/980414).

[2] Nora Boustany, "Diplomatic Dispatches: A Rogue State No More," *Washington Post*, February 17, 1999, p. A14.

[3] William Drozdiak, "Albright Urges NATO to Take Broader Role," *Washington Post*, December 9, 1998, pp. A1, 30.

[4] Department of Defense, Office of Public Affairs, "Secretary of Defense William S. Cohen, DoD News Briefing, January 20, 1999" (http://www.defenselink.mil/news/Jan1999/t0120199_t0120md), emphasis added.

[5] Letter of Ambassador Stuart E. Eizenstat, Undersecretary of State for Economic, Business, and Agricultural Affairs, in *Foreign Affairs* 78, no. 3 (May/June 1999), p. 155.

[6] Alexander L. George, *Bridging the Gap: Theory and Practice in Foreign Policy* (Washington, DC: United States Institute of Peace Press, 1993), pp. 130–31, 137–38.

[7] Stephen Grand, rapporteur, "Beyond Containment-Engagement: A Workshop on Strategies Toward 'Rogue States' and Other Countries of Concern," Division of International Studies Working Paper (Washington, DC: Woodrow Wilson International Center for Scholars, 1999), p. 22.

[8] Ibid.

[9] Samuel F. Huntington, "Is American Hegemony Working?" *Foreign Affairs* 78, no. 2 (March/April 1999), p. 42.

[10] See Thomas L. Friedman, *The Lexus and the Olive Tree: Understanding Globalization* (New York: Farrar, Straus and Giroux, 1999).

[11] Political philosopher Arnold Wolfers coined the term "milieu goals" to describe the efforts of states "to shape conditions beyond their national boundaries." See his classic work, *Discord and Collaboration: Essays on International Politics* (Baltimore: Johns Hopkins University Press, 1962), pp. 73–75.

Appendix

ANTHONY LAKE, "CONFRONTING BACKLASH STATES"

A Group of Outlaws

The end of the Cold War and the emergence of newly independent states in eastern Europe have the potential to enlarge dramatically the family of nations now committed to the pursuit of democratic institutions, the expansion of free markets, the peaceful settlement of conflict and the promotion of collective security. For the sake of both its interests and its ideals, the United States has a special responsibility to nurture and promote these core values. As the president made clear in his State of the Union address, much of the Clinton administration's foreign policy is devoted to that effort.

At the same time, our policy must face the reality of recalcitrant and outlaw states that not only choose to remain outside the family but also assault its basic values. There are few "backlash" states: Cuba, North Korea, Iran, Iraq and Libya. For now they lack the resources of a superpower, which would enable them to seriously threaten the democratic order being created around them. Nevertheless, their behavior is often aggressive and defiant. The ties between them are growing as they seek to thwart or quarantine themselves from a global trend to which they seem incapable of adapting.

These backlash states have some common characteristics. Ruled by cliques that control power through coercion, they suppress basic human rights and promote radical ideologies. While their political systems vary, their leaders share a common antipathy toward popular participation that might undermine the existing regimes. These nations exhibit a chronic inability to engage constructively with the outside world, and they do not function effectively in alliances—even with those like-minded. They are often on the defensive, increasingly criticized and targeted with sanctions in international forums.

Finally, they share a siege mentality. Accordingly, they are embarked on ambitious and costly military programs—especially in weapons of

256

mass destruction (WMD) and missile delivery systems—in a misguided quest for a great equalizer to protect their regimes or advance their purposes abroad.

As the sole superpower, the United States has a special responsibility for developing a strategy to neutralize, contain and, through selective pressure, perhaps eventually transform these backlash states into constructive members of the international community. Each backlash state is unique in its history, culture and circumstances, and U.S. strategy has been tailored accordingly. But there are common denominators. In each case, we maintain alliances and deploy military capabilities sufficient to deter or respond to any aggressive act. We seek to contain the influence of these states, sometimes by isolation, sometimes through pressure, sometimes by diplomatic and economic measures. We encourage the rest of the international community to join us in a concerted effort. In the cases of Iraq and Libya, for example, we have already achieved a strong international consensus backed by U.N. resolutions.

The United States is also actively engaged in unilateral and multilateral efforts to restrict their military and technological capabilities. Intelligence, counterterrorism and multilateral export control policies, especially on weapons of mass destruction and their delivery systems, are all being employed. In the North Korean case, for example, its nuclear program is our most urgent concern. The prospect of a nuclear-armed North Korea poses extraordinary risks to our security interests in Asia and the integrity of the global nonproliferation regime. The U.S. military commitment to the security of South Korea is unshakable. America is leading an international effort to persuade North Korea to reverse course. At the same time, we have made it clear to Pyongyang that if it resolves international concerns over its nuclear program, doors will open to better relations. If it does not, however, North Korea will face increased isolation and hardship.

Like North Korea, Iraq and Iran pose serious challenges to our nonproliferation efforts. But because they are located adjacent to each other along the littoral of the vital Persian Gulf, where 65 percent of the world's oil reserves are located, these two backlash states also present a complex strategic puzzle that has confounded the policies of three previous American administrations.

The basic strategic principle in the Persian Gulf region is to establish a favorable balance of power, one that will protect critical American interests in the security of our friends and in the free flow of oil at stable prices. In previous administrations, this was pursued by relying on one regional power to balance the other. First the United States built up Iran under the shah as a supposed regional pillar of stability. Then it backed Saddam Hussein's Iraq in its war with revolutionary Iran to contain the influence of Khomeini's Islamic government. Both approaches proved disastrous. In the shah's case, the U.S. strategy for regional stability collapsed when he was overthrown. And in Saddam Hussein's case, American backing assisted him in acquiring a massive conventional arsenal which he used, first against his own people and then later Kuwait.

The Logic of Dual Containment

The Clinton administration's strategy toward these two backlash states begins from the premise that today both regimes pursue policies hostile to our interests. Building up one to counter the other is therefore rejected in favor of a policy of "dual containment." In adopting this approach, we are not oblivious to the need for a balance of power in this vital region. Rather, we seek with our regional allies to maintain a favorable balance without depending on either Iraq or Iran. We are able to do so because we have a number of advantages that previous administrations did not.

First, the end of the Cold War simply eliminated a major strategic consideration from our calculus. We no longer have to fear Soviet efforts to gain a foothold in the Persian Gulf by taking advantage of our support for one of these states to build relations with the other. The strategic importance of both Iraq and Iran has therefore been reduced dramatically, and their ability to play the superpowers off each other has been eliminated.

Second, over the last decade, a regional balance of power between Iran and Iraq has been established at a much lower level of military capability. Iraq's victory in the Iran-Iraq War substantially reduced Iran's conventional offensive capabilities. And Iraq's defeat in Desert Storm significantly diminished its offensive capabilities and brought its weapons of mass destruction under tight control. Without the backing of an alternate superpower, they now confront serious difficulties in challenging U.S. power.

Third, as a result of Iraq's invasion of Kuwait, the Gulf Cooperation Council (GCC) states are less reluctant to enter into security and prepositioning arrangements with Washington. These arrangements provide our military forces with an ability to deploy in the Persian Gulf against any threat that either Iraq or Iran might pose to these states.

Finally, broader trends in the region are positive. Washington enjoys strong relations with the region's other critical powers: Egypt, Israel, Turkey and Saudi Arabia. Progress in resolving the Arab-Israeli conflict solidifies our position in the Arab world and strengthens the ties between our regional allies. It increases the isolation of Iraq and Iran while reducing their ability to exploit the Arab-Israeli conflict to promote their regional ambitions. The comprehensive settlement that the United States seeks will cost Iraq the opportunity to manipulate the Palestinian cause and rob Iran of its ability to promote turmoil in Lebanon.

In sum, until circumstances change there is no longer a need to depend on either Iraq or Iran to maintain a favorable balance and protect U.S. friends and interests in the gulf. The Clinton administration is, nevertheless, confident that we can sustain this situation for some time, in large measure because we have an understanding with our regional friends about the common threats and how to deal with them. While working to consolidate these positive trends, we remain alert to the possibility of change.

"Dual containment" does not mean duplicate containment. The basic purpose is to counter the hostility of both Baghdad and Tehran, but the challenges posed by the two regimes are distinct and therefore require tailored approaches. Although neighbors, the two states are quite different in culture and historical experience. In Saddam Hussein's regime, Washington faces an aggressive, modernist, secular avarice; in Iran, it is challenged by a theocratic regime with a sense of cultural and political destiny and an abiding antagonism toward the United States.

In Iraq, the regime is responsible for both war crimes and crimes against humanity, a regime whose invasion of Kuwait and gassing of its own people have rendered it an international renegade. In post-Khomeini Iran, a revolutionary regime remains engaged in outlaw behavior. Nevertheless, the Clinton administration does not oppose Islamic government, nor does it seek the regime's overthrow. Indeed we remain ready for an authoritative dialogue in which we will raise aspects of Iranian behavior that cause us so much concern.

Containing Iraq presents a different kind of challenge than containing Iran. After the Gulf War, the United Nations established a far-reaching regime to ensure that Iraq never again threatens its neighbors or world peace and to deter Saddam Hussein's aggression against Iraqi citizens. Three years after the invasion of Kuwait, sanctions are still being sustained. The international community is sufficiently alarmed by Saddam's behavior and sufficiently suspicious of his intentions to support Washington's insistence on full compliance with all relevant U.N. Security Council (UNSC) resolutions. . . .

There is plenty of evidence to suggest that the only reason the Iraqi regime is beginning to cooperate with UNSCOM is to secure the lifting of oil sanctions. Once the oil starts flowing again, Washington must assume that Saddam will renege on long-term monitoring and begin re-building his WMD programs. Thus, before considering whether oil sanctions are to be lifted, there should be a high degree of confidence that Iraq has not only complied fully with the technical requirements of the WMD provisions but will continue to comply indefinitely. . . .

The U.N. resolutions also reflect the international consensus in support of an end to Saddam's repression of the Iraqi people. . . .

As a signal of our interest in a democratic Iraq, the Clinton administration . . . supports the objectives of the Iraqi National Congress, the exile organization that represents a broad spectrum of religious, secular and ethnic communities. The INC has recently broadened its base, established facilities in northern Iraq and deepened its ties with neighboring Arab governments that share the twin goals of maintaining Iraq's territorial integrity while promoting representative and benign governance in Baghdad.

Despite Saddam's efforts to buy loyalties, sanctions are taking their toll on the crucial inner circle on which the regime depends. There are now frequent reports of coup attempts and unrest among the relatively privileged Iraqi elite. These trends could lead to new conditions for the citizens of Iraq and new opportunities to build a more peaceful and normal relationship between Iraq and the outside world.

The Challenge From Tehran

Iran is both a lesser and a greater challenge. On the one hand, the Clinton administration is not confronting a blatantly aggressive state that invaded and occupied a weaker neighbor. More normal relations with the government in Tehran are conceivable, once it demonstrates its willingness to abide by international norms and abandon policies and actions inimical to regional peace and security. On the other hand, political differences with Iran will not easily be resolved. Iran is a revolutionary state whose leaders harbor a deep sense of grievance over the close ties between the United States and the shah. Its revolutionary and militant messages are openly hostile to the United States and its core interests. This basic political reality will shape relations for the foreseeable future. Reconciliation will be difficult, but the choice is Iran's to make.

The American quarrel with Iran should not be misconstrued as a "clash of civilizations" or opposition to Iran as a theocratic state. Washington does not take issue with the "Islamic" dimension of the Islamic Republic of Iran. As President Clinton has said, America has a deep respect for the religion and culture of Islam. It is extremism, whether religious or secular, that we oppose. The United States is concerned with the actions and policies of the Tehran government. Iran is actively engaged in clandestine efforts to acquire nuclear and other unconventional weapons and long-range missile-delivery systems. It is the foremost sponsor of terrorism and assassination worldwide. It is violently and vitriolically opposed to the Arab-Israeli peace process. It seeks to subvert friendly governments across the Middle East and in parts of Africa. It is attempting to acquire offensive conventional capabilities to threaten its smaller gulf neighbors. Its record on treatment of its own citizens—especially women and religious minorities—is deeply disturbing.

In confronting these manifold challenges, the Clinton administration faces an easier task than in the case of Iraq because Iran's weapons of mass destruction are at a relatively early stage of development. In that sense it has an opportunity now to prevent Iran from becoming in five years' time what Iraq was five years ago. But containment is also more difficult because the administration is not backed by an international consensus reflected in UNSC resolutions, as in Iraq's case. And it does not have broad sanctions in place to effect changes in Iran's unacceptable behavior. Previous administration have tried their hands at building up "moderates" in Iran. What we have learned from that experience is that these same "moderates" are responsible for the very policies we find so objectionable. However, Iran's economic mismanagement has combined with the downturn in the oil market to produce a desperate economic situation for the Iranian government. With 30 percent inflation, a $30 billion debt and $5 billion in arrears on its short-term repayments, Iran no longer looks like a good commercial proposition. This makes it easier to argue with U.S. allies against improving ties with Iran for purely commercial motives.

To counter Iran's quest for domination of the Persian Gulf, Washington works closely with friendly governments to prevent Iran from procuring needed imports for its nuclear and chemical programs, and is vigilant about the transfer of missiles and missile-related systems from Iran's current suppliers, including North Korea. This does not mean Washington intends to quarantine Iran or deny it all military-related goods. This administration tries to distinguish between defense items that do not affect the regional security environment and those items that have an offensive use and could destabilize the area.

Not a Crusade but a Commitment

The U.S. strategy depends heavily on active coordination and consultations with friendly countries. Iran needs to hear a steady and consistent message from the Western countries whose approval and trade it seeks. We have achieved some consensus among the European Union, Canada and Japan on those aspects of Iran's actions that we find unacceptable. Some of our allies believe, however, that the regional policy must rely largely on positive incentives for Iran. The record clearly shows, however, that positive inducements such as trade and aid concessions or rescheduling of loans do not lead to real changes in Iran's unacceptable behavior. The most effective message is a consistent one: no normal relations until these actions end. But we do not eschew an authoritative dialogue; dialogue and pressure are not mutually exclusive policy approaches.

There are some risks inherent in the coupling of our approaches to Iraq and Iran. To the extent they are pressured, they may be driven together in their efforts to resist the West. Indeed, Baghdad and Tehran seem to have engaged in limited cooperation over the past year, despite their differences. Ultimately, however, the prospects for reconciliation will remain limited for a simple reason: they mistrust each other more than they mistrust the United States. While they have a common interest in tactical cooperation, neither has a real interest in helping the other grow stronger; each knows that it will be the first target of a resurgent state on the other side of the Shatt-al-Arab. . . .

The Clinton administration has forged a realistic and sustainable policy that takes into account U.S. interests and the realities of the Persian Gulf region. Today the regimes in Baghdad and Tehran are weaker and increasingly on the defensive. Slowly but surely they are coming to understand that there is a price to pay for their recalcitrant commitment to remain on the wrong side of history. This is not a crusade, but a genuine and responsible effort, over time, to protect American strategic interests, stabilize the international system and enlarge the community of nations committed to democracy, free markets and peace.

Forty-seven years ago, George Kennan, writing under a pseudonym in this journal, made the case for containment of an outlaw empire. He argued that the United States had within its power the means to "to increase enormously the strains under which Soviet policy must operate" and thereby generate the "break-up or gradual mellowing of Soviet power." Today, the United States faces a less formidable challenge in containing the band of outlaws we refer to as "the backlash states." It is still very much within our power to prevail.

Source: Anthony Lake, "Confronting Backlash States," *Foreign Affairs* 73, no. 2 (March/April 1994).

SECRETARY OF STATE MADELEINE ALBRIGHT, "PRESERVING
PRINCIPLE AND SAFEGUARDING STABILITY:
UNITED STATES POLICY TOWARD IRAQ"

... My fundamental purpose is to reaffirm United States policy towards Iraq. That policy is part of a broad commitment to protect the security and territory of our friends and allies in the Gulf. We have a vital national interest in the security of the region's oil supplies, and we have forged strong friendships with countries in the area who agree with us that nations should respect international law, refrain from aggression and oppose those who commit or sponsor terror.

Here, as elsewhere, we recognize that stability is not an import; it must be home-grown. But we also know that circumstances may arise in which active American leadership and power are required. . . .

All this brings us to the present day. From the beginning of Operation Desert Storm until now, American policy towards Iraq has been consistent, principled and grounded in a realistic and hard-won understanding of the nature of the Iraqi regime. It has been bolstered by bipartisan support at home, and general approval in the region. And it has achieved a great deal.

Iraq's military threat to its neighbors is greatly diminished.
Most of its missiles have been destroyed.
Its biological and chemical warfare production facilities have been dismantled.
Nuclear materials have been removed and an international monitoring regime to prevent the construction of nuclear weapons is in place.
Iraq has been barred from importing weapons and weapons-related materials and technology.
And the area in which Iraqi military forces may operate freely has contracted.

To guard against further miscalculations on Baghdad's part, U.S. forces have been deployed to the region and we have demonstrated our ability to reinforce those troops rapidly if required.

Diplomatically, we have sustained an international consensus that Iraq should not be allowed again to threaten international peace. In statement after statement, and in 36 successive reviews, the Security Council has maintained its support for sanctions and its insistence on compliance.

Meanwhile, six years of sanctions and isolation have taken their toll on the regime in Baghdad. Saddam Hussein has become by far the most divisive force in Iraq, and several coup attempts have been made. Members of his own somewhat dysfunctional family have turned against him. His inner circle of advisers has been purged repeatedly. Today, his power rests on an increasingly narrow foundation of intimidation and terror.

So while Iraq's lawless policies are failing, our policies of law and firmness are working. As long as the apparatus of sanctions, enforcement, inspections and monitoring is in place, Iraq will remain trapped within a strategic box, unable to successfully threaten its neighbors and unable to realize the grandiose ambitions of its ignoble leader.

It is essential, however, that international resolve not weaken. Containment has worked, but—despite Iraq's present weakness—the future threat has not been erased. Iraq's behavior and intentions must change before our policies can change. Otherwise, we will allow the scorpion that bit us once to bite us again. That would be a folly impossible to explain to our children, or to the veterans of Desert Storm. . . .

To those who ask how long our determination will last; how long we will oppose Iraqi intransigence; how long we will insist that the international community's standards be met, our answer is—as long as it takes.

We do not agree with the nations who argue that if Iraq complies with its obligations concerning weapons of mass destruction, sanctions should be lifted. Our view, which is unshakable, is that Iraq must prove its peaceful intentions. It can only do that by complying with all of the Security Council Resolutions to which it is subject.

Is it possible to conceive of such a government under Saddam Hussein? When I was a professor, I taught that you have to consider all possibilities. As Secretary of State, I have to deal in the realm of reality and probability. And the evidence is overwhelming that Saddam Hussein's intentions will never be peaceful.

The United States looks forward, nevertheless, to the day when Iraq rejoins the family of nations as a responsible and law-abiding member. This is in our interests and in the interests of our allies and partners within the region.

Clearly, a change in Iraq's government could lead to a change in U.S. policy. Should that occur, we would stand ready, in coordination with our allies and friends, to enter rapidly into a dialogue with the successor regime. . . .

The rip in the fabric of Gulf stability that was created by Iraq's invasion of Kuwait has not fully mended. But the aggression has been rolled back. Iraq's military is contained. And the path for Iraq's re-entry into the community of nations is clearly laid out. This is not, to borrow Margaret Thatcher's phrase, the time to go wobbly towards Iraq.

The United States is committed—as are our friends—to the victory of principle over expediency; and to the evolution in Iraq of a society based on law, exemplified by pluralism and content to live at peace. . . .

We, as you know, have had a policy of dual containment. We believe that that policy is an appropriate one, and that it is important in fact for the stability of the region to make sure that Iran is also not involved in creation of weapons of mass destruction, . . . and does not support terrorism. Therefore, we consider that our policies as far as Iran and Iraq are concerned are the right policies, and we will pursue them in that vein. . . .

Source: Secretary of State Madeleine Albright, "Preserving Principle and Safeguarding Stability: United States Policy Toward Iraq," address at Georgetown University, Washington, D.C., March 26, 1997, transcript available at http://secretary.state.gov/www/statements/970326. html.

CNN CORRESPONDENT CHRISTIANE AMANPOUR, "INTERVIEW
WITH IRANIAN PRESIDENT MOHAMMAD KHATAMI"

PRESIDENT KHATAMI: . . . [W]e intend to benefit from the achievements and experiences of all civilizations, Western and non-Western, and to hold dialogue with them. The closer the pillars and essences of these two civilizations are, the easier the dialogue would become. With our revolution, we are experiencing a new phase of reconstruction of civilization. We feel that what we seek is what the founders of the American civilization were also pursuing four centuries ago. This is why we sense an intellectual affinity with the essence of the American civilization. . . .

But here I have to express pity over a tragedy which has occurred. Unfortunately, policies pursued by American politicians outside the United States over the past half a century since World War II are incompatible with the American civilization which is founded on democracy, freedom and human dignity. We ardently wished that those who enforced this foreign policy were representatives of the prominent American civilization; a civilization which was achieved at a heavy cost, and not the representatives of those adventurers who were defeated by the American people themselves.

This flawed policy of domination had three setbacks: One was severe damages that it incurred upon the deprived and oppressed nations, including our own. The other setback was that it dashed the hopes of the people of the colonized world, who had placed their trust in the U.S. tradition of struggle for independence. When the policies for domination were implemented in the name of the American people, the nations lost their trust in the Americans. This represents a grave damage done by the

U.S. policies on the American nation. The third and most important of these setbacks is that what was implemented was done in name of a great people that had risen for freedom. I feel that the American politicians should realize this fact and adjust themselves with the standards of Anglo-American and American civilization and at least apologize to their own people because of the approach they have adopted.

AMANPOUR: . . . [I]n all revolutions, the communist revolution in Russia, the French revolution, perhaps even the American revolution, the early years contain many excesses. Would you say that taking the American hostages, at the beginning of the Iranian Islamic revolution falls into the category of early revolutionary excesses?

PRESIDENT KHATAMI: . . . The image of Islam which has been presented, and I don't want to accuse anyone here, has been an erroneous one. Islam is a religion which calls all humanity, irrespective of religion or belief, to rationality and logic. . . . It seeks dialogue, understanding and peace with all nations. One of the major flaws in the U.S. foreign policy, which I recently construed as being behind times, is that they continue to live with cold war mentality and try to create a perceived enemy. . . . After the collapse of communism, there has been an attempt by certain circles to portray Islam as the new enemy, and regrettably they are targeting progressive Islam rather than certain regressive interpretations of Islam. They attack an Islam which seeks democracy, progress and development; an Islam which calls for utilization of achievements of human civilization including that of the west.

With regard to the hostage issue which you raised, I do know that the feelings of the great American people have been hurt, and of course I regret it. . . .

The feelings of our people were seriously hurt by U.S. policies. And as you said, in the heat of the revolutionary fervor, things happen which cannot be fully contained or judged according to usual norms. This was the crying out of the people against humiliations and inequities imposed upon them by the policies of the U.S. and others, particularly in the early days of the revolution. With the grace of God, today our new society has been institutionalized and we have a popularly elected powerful government, and there is no need for unconventional methods of expression of concerns and anxieties. And I believe when there is logic, especially when there are receptive ears, there is no need other than discourse, debate and dialogue. . . .

Today we are in the period of stability, and fully adhere to all norms of conduct regulating relations between nations and governments. . . .

AMANPOUR: . . . You talk about a new chapter in relations between the peoples of the world. What can you say to the Americans listening tonight, to show that person that your Iran is a new Iran or a different Iran?

PRESIDENT KHATAMI: I say that these issues should be examined with due consideration to their root causes and various dimensions. There are slogans being [chanted] in Iran. But, you as a journalist can ask all those chanting the slogans whether they are targeting the American people. And they would all say no. Not only we do not harbor any ill wishes for the American people, but in fact we consider them to be great nation. Our aim is not even to destroy or undermine the American government. These slogans symbolize a desire to terminate a mode of relations which existed between Iran and the United States. This is a response to that grave affront by a former U.S. defense secretary who said that the Iranian nation must be rooted out. It is also a response to the downing of the Iranian airliner that killed about 300 innocent people, mostly women and children. Even if we accept that the shooting was accidental, the decoration of the commander of the American naval vessel responsible for the tragedy was indeed adding insult to injury. There is also the recent allocation of $20 million by the U.S. Congress to topple the Iranian government. . . . No one has the intention of insulting the American nation. . . .

AMANPOUR: You say that you want to talk to the American people. Are you prepared to sit down eventually and talk to the American government about the issues that you have just mentioned tonight that separate and divide you?

PRESIDENT KHATAMI: Firstly, nothing should prevent dialogue and understanding between two nations, especially between their scholars and thinkers. Right now, I recommend the exchange of professors, writers, scholars, artists, journalists, and tourists. A large number of educated and noble Iranians now reside in the U.S. as representatives of the Iranian nation. This shows that there is no hostility between the two nations. But the dialogue between civilizations and nations is different from political relations. In regard to political relations, we have to consider the factors which lead to the severance of relations. If some day another situation is to emerge, we must definitely consider the roots and relevant factors and try to eliminate them.

Firstly, I have to state that U.S. foreign policy behavior toward Iran has inflicted damages upon us. But [it] also had a positive effect. It caused us to mainly focus on our domestic capabilities and resources to advance our objectives. Now, too, we feel no need for ties with the U.S., especially as the modern world is so diverse and plural that we can reach our objectives without U.S. assistance. I especially feel that many progressive countries—including the Europeans—are far more advanced in their foreign policies than the U.S. We are carrying out our own activities and have no need for political ties with the United States. . . .

The attitude of the U.S. after the victory of the revolution has not been a civilized one. They have adopted a hostile policy against Iran. They have tried to inflict economic damage upon us, a clear example of which is the D'Amato act which represents a continuation of cold war mentality and the lack of appreciation of realities to the point that they even want to impose their will upon other countries such as European countries and Japan or the allocation of . . . $20 million to topple the Iranian government.

The success of our revolution has come at a great cost to our nation. And the U.S. has a major share in the cost imposed upon the Iranian nation. There is a grave mistrust between us. If negotiations are not based on mutual respect, they will never lead to positive results. . . .

There must first be a crack in this wall of mistrust to prepare for a change and create an opportunity to study a new situation. Unfortunately, the behavior of American Government in the past up to this date has always exacerbated the climate of mistrust and we do not detect any sign of change of behavior.

We are looking for a world in which misunderstandings can be overcome, nations can understand one another and mutual respect and logic govern relations among states. It is the right of every nation to stand on its principles and values and have the expectation of respect and dignity from others. . . .

AMANPOUR: . . . As you know, many U.S experts say that the evidence is overwhelming, that elements of the Iranian authorities, Iranian officials, provide not only political and moral, but financial support to organizations that commit acts of terrorism, and result in the deaths of innocent women and children. If you were presented with proof and with evidence that any kind of Iranian was involved in that kind of financial support or act, what would you do about it?

PRESIDENT KHATAMI: . . . We believe in the holy Quran that says: slaying of one innocent person is tantamount to the slaying of all humanity. How could such a religion, and those who claim to be its followers get involved in the assassination of innocent individuals and the slaughter of innocent human beings? We categorically reject all these allegations.

Secondly, the logic of history has proven that violence is not the way to achieve desired end. I personally believe that only those who lack logic resort to violence. Terrorism should be condemned in all its forms and manifestations; assassins must be condemned. Terrorism is useless anyway and we condemn it categorically. Those who level these charges against us are best advised to provide accurate and objective evidence, which indeed does not exist. . . .

AMANPOUR: Regardless of the motive, do you believe that killing innocent women and children is terrorism, as for instance what happens on the streets of Israel?

PRESIDENT KHATAMI: It is definitely so. Any form of killing of innocent men and women who are not involved in confrontations is terrorism; it must be condemned, and we, in our term, condemn every form of it in the world. . . .

AMANPOUR: Iran has said that it doesn't agree with the Middle East peace process. Yasser Arafat was elected as a representative of the Palestinian legitimate aims. And he has entered into a peace process. Do you think that it is appropriate for any foreign power to engage in supporting the groups that are fighting against Yasser Arafat—the groups such as Hamas and others?

PRESIDENT KHATAMI: First of all, we have declared our opposition to the Middle East peace process because we believe it will not succeed. At the same time, we have clearly said that we don't intend to impose our views on others or to stand in their way. In our view all Palestinians have the right to express their views about their land, including the millions of Palestinians in Diaspora. They too have a right to self determination. Only then can there be a lasting peace. We seek a peace through which Jews, Muslims and Christians, and indeed each and every Palestinian, could freely determine their own destiny. And we are prepared to contribute towards the realization of that peace. . . .

AMANPOUR: Mr. President, you know another concern of the west is Iran's nuclear program. Would you consider entering a special agreement, a special sort of situation with the atomic energy agency, for special monitoring, if that would lessen the fears of the people you say you want to have a better dialogue with?

PRESIDENT KHATAMI: We are a party to the Nuclear Non-Proliferation Treaty. The official representatives of the International Atomic Energy Agency have inspected our facilities in Iran several times, and have publicly declared that we are not planning on building nuclear weapons and only aim to employ nuclear energy for peaceful purposes. It is ironic that those who are so concerned about saving humanity from nuclear weapons, fully support Israel which is a nuclear power and is unwilling to join the NPT or accept IAEA safeguards, while leveling allegations against Iran which has not even been able to complete its first nuclear power plant which began before the revolution. These are all pretexts for imposing certain policies on Iran and the region and to create panic and mistrust. We are not a nuclear power and do not intend to become one. We have accepted IAEA safeguards and our facilities are routinely inspected by that agency. . . .

Source: "Interview with Iranian President Mohammad Khatami," by CNN correspondent Christiane Amanpour, January 7, 1998, transcript available at http://cnn.com/WORLD/9801/07/iran/interview.html

SECRETARY OF STATE MADELEINE K. ALBRIGHT,
"REMARKS AT 1998 ASIA SOCIETY DINNER"

. . . One of the oldest continuous civilizations in the world, Iran is at the center of a region which includes countries that contain three-quarters of the world's population, three-quarters of the world's proven energy resources and sixty percent of global GNP. These facts of life, and the critical role that Iran plays in that region, make the question of US-Iranian relations a topic of great interest and importance to this Secretary of State.

The United States established relations with Iran, then Persia, in 1856. For decades, our ties were limited but cordial. After the Second World War, America supported Iran in a bitter territorial dispute with the Soviet Union. And through the first decades of the Cold War, as part of a strategy intended to counter Soviet expansionism, the US supported the Shah's regime and allocated to it large quantities of military and economic assistance.

We did so because of a common strategic interest. We were concerned with an effort to contain the spread of totalitarian influence across the globe. The exigencies of the Cold War also generated US policies and activities that were resented by many Iranians. In retrospect, it is possible to understand their reaction, but the Cold War is now over and it is time to put that period behind us.

After the forced departure of the Shah in 1979, Iran turned inward, in keeping with the Ayatollah Khomeini's slogan that "we must become isolated in order to become independent." This trend was manifested most extremely and unacceptably in the seizure of hostages at the US Embassy.

Neither country has forgotten the past, but most Iranians, like most Americans, are now focused on the future. And clearly, it is possible now—if Iran so chooses—for it to be both fully independent and fully open to the world.

Last May, Iran's people were given a chance to voice their support for a more open society, and did so. Nearly 70 percent supported the election of Mohammad Khatemi as President, providing him with a mandate for change, demanding from the Iranian Government greater freedoms, a more civil society based on the rule of law, and a more moderate foreign policy aimed at ending Iran's estrangement from the international community.

At the time, President Clinton welcomed this election, and as a former professor and lifelong student of history, I found the vote remarkable. The depth of the demand for change was obvious. So too was the evident desire of young Iranians and many Iranian women for greater openness and more personal liberty.

I was most impressed by the size of the mandate. Twenty million Iranians came forward to make themselves heard in the hope that, by so doing, they could effect real change in their government and in their daily lives.

Since taking office, President Khatemi has responded to the demands of the Iranian people by emphasizing the importance of dialogue among nations and cultures, and by acknowledging the world's growing interdependence. He has said that "a society intending to reach development cannot succeed without understanding Western civilization." I would say, in response, that the same can be said with respect to Eastern civilization and Islamic civilization.

President Khatemi has said that the American Government deserves respect because it is a reflection of the great American people. I would say that President Khatemi deserves respect because he is the choice of the Iranian people. In his interview with CNN in January, President Khatemi called for a dialogue between civilizations, something which President Clinton welcomed because of our strongly-held view that there is much common ground between Islam and the West, and much that we can do to enrich each other's societies.

In past years, Iran's opposition to the Middle East Peace Process and to those willing to negotiate with Israel has been vitriolic and violent. The Islamic Republic still refuses to recognize Israel, and its leaders continue to denounce Israel in inflammatory and unacceptable terms. But last December, Iranian officials welcomed Chairman Arafat to the Islamic Summit in Tehran and said that, although they did not agree with the logic of the peace process, they would not seek to impose their views and would accept what the Palestinians could accept.

In January, President Khatemi publicly denounced terrorism and condemned the killing of innocent Israelis. He argued that terrorism was not only against Islam but also counterproductive to Iran's purposes. Iran, after all, has also been a victim of terrorism.

If these views are translated into a rejection of terrorism as a tool of Iranian statecraft, it would do much to dispel the concerns of the international community from Germany to the Persian Gulf, and from Argentina to Algeria.

There are other signs of change, as well. For example, Iran's record in the war against drugs has greatly improved—at least within its own borders—and it has received high marks from the UN for its treatment of more than two million Iraqi and Afghan refugees. Iran is also participating in diplomatic efforts to bring peace and stability to Afghanistan and is making a welcome effort to improve relations with Saudi Arabia and other neighbors in the Gulf.

We view these developments with interest, both with regard to the possibility of Iran assuming its rightful place in the world community, and the chance for better bilateral ties. However, these hopes must be balanced against the reality that Iran's support for terrorism has not yet ceased; serious violations of human rights persist; and its efforts to develop long-range missiles and to acquire nuclear weapons continue.

The United States opposes, and will continue to oppose, any country selling or transferring to Iran materials and technologies that could be used to develop long-range missiles or weapons of mass destruction. Similarly, we oppose Iranian efforts to sponsor terror. Accordingly, our economic policies, including with respect to the export pipelines for Caspian oil and gas, remain unchanged.

But let me be clear. These policies are not, as some Iranians allege, anti-Islamic. Islam is the fastest-growing religious faith in the United States. We respect deeply its moral teachings and its role as a source of inspiration and instruction for hundreds of millions of people around the world. US policy is directed at actions, not peoples or faiths. The standards we would like Iran to observe are not merely Western, but universal. We fully respect Iran's sovereignty. We understand and respect its fierce desire to maintain its independence. We do not seek to overthrow its government. But we do ask that Iran live up to its commitments to the international community.

As in Indonesia, we hope Iran's leaders will carry out the people's mandate for a government that respects and protects the rule of law, both in its internal and external affairs. Certainly, Iranian voters last year were concerned primarily with domestic issues. But the Iranian people are also conscious of the critical role their country has long played in a region of global importance. What Iran must decide now is how its strength will be projected and to what ends. Much has changed in the almost twenty years Iran has been outside or on the fringes of the international system.

Nations have recognized, for example, that if they are to safeguard their own interests from the threat of terror, they cannot tolerate acts of indiscriminate violence against civilians, nor can they offer refuge to those who commit such acts.

Despite the recent South Asia [nuclear] tests, more and more nations have enlisted in the fight against the proliferation of weapons of mass destruction. Respected nations from South Korea to South Africa to South America have decided that it is best for their people to forgo developing such weapons. The tide of non-proliferation agreements reached in the last two decades is ample evidence of this trend.

What have proliferated are multilateral efforts to protect international security. The UN, regional organizations and coalitions have countered threats to peace during the Gulf War and in peacekeeping operations around the world. This global network has grown largely without Iranian participation. But Iran would be welcome if it is willing to make a constructive contribution.

We believe that President Khatemi expressed the sentiments of the Iranian people when he voiced the desire for "a world in which misunderstandings can be overcome and mutual respect and logic govern relations among states."

The United States shares that desire, and we are taking concrete steps in that direction. This month, we implemented a new, more streamlined procedure for issuing visas to Iranians who travel to the United States frequently. We also revised our Consular Travel Warning for Iran so that it better reflects attitudes in Iran towards American visitors.

We have supported cultural and academic exchanges, and facilitated travel to the United States by many Iranians.

We are ready to explore further ways to build mutual confidence and avoid misunderstandings. The Islamic Republic should consider parallel steps. If such a process can be initiated and sustained in a way that addresses the concerns of both sides, then we in the United States can see the prospect of a very different relationship. As the wall of mistrust comes down, we can develop with the Islamic Republic, when it is ready, a roadmap leading to normal relations.

Obviously, two decades of mistrust cannot be erased overnight. The gap between us remains wide. But it is time to test the possibilities for bridging this gap. Failure to do so would be irresponsible.

. . . America cannot view every issue or nation through a single prism. We must take into account the full range of our interests. We must combine adherence to principle with a pragmatic sense of what works. We must know when to raise our voices in public and when to work quietly behind the scenes. We must know when to engage and when to isolate, and we must always be flexible enough to respond to change and to seize historic opportunities when they arise. Above all, we must maintain our commitment to human freedom. For of all the ties that bind together the American and Asian peoples, this is the strongest. . . .

Source: Secretary of State Madeleine K. Albright, remarks at 1998 Asia Society Dinner, New York, N.Y., June 17, 1998, transcript available at http://www.asiasociety.org/speeches/albright.html.

AGREED FRAMEWORK BETWEEN THE UNITED STATES OF AMERICA AND THE DEMOCRATIC PEOPLE'S REPUBLIC OF KOREA

Geneva, October 21, 1994

Delegations of the Governments of the United States of America (U.S.) and the Democratic People's Republic of Korea (D.P.R.K.) held talks in Geneva from September 23 to October 21, 1994, to negotiate an overall resolution to the nuclear issue on the Korean Peninsula.

Both sides reaffirmed the importance of attaining the objectives contained in the August 12, 1994, Agreed Statement between the U.S. and the D.P.R.K. and upholding the principles of the June 11, 1993, Joint Statement of the U.S. and the D.P.R.K. to achieve peace and security on a nuclear-free Korean peninsula. The U.S. and the D.P.R.K. decided to take the following actions for the resolution of the nuclear issue:

I. Both sides will cooperate to replace the D.P.R.K.'s graphite-moderated reactors and related facilities with light-water reactor (LWR) power plants.

1) In accordance with the October 20, 1994, letter of assurance from the U.S. President, the U.S. will undertake to make arrangements for the provision to the D.P.R.K. of a LWR project with a total generating capacity of approximately 2,000 MW(e) by a target date of 2003.

—The U.S. will organize under its leadership an international consortium to finance and supply the LWR project to be provided to the D.P.R.K. The U.S., representing the international consortium, will serve as the principal point of contact with the D.P.R.K. for the LWR project.

—The U.S., representing the consortium, will make best efforts to secure the conclusion of a supply contract with the D.P.R.K. within six months of the date of this document for the provision of the LWR project. Contract talks will begin as soon as possible after the date of this Document.

—As necessary, the U.S. and the D.P.R.K. will conclude a bilateral agreement for cooperation in the field of peaceful uses of nuclear energy.

2) In accordance with the October 20, 1994, U.S. letter of assurance concerning interim energy alternatives, the U.S., representing the consortium, will make arrangements to offset the energy foregone due to the freeze of the D.P.R.K.'s graphite-moderated reactors and related facilities, pending completion of the first LWR unit.

—Alternative energy will be provided in the form of heavy oil for heating and electricity production.

—Deliveries of heavy oil will begin within three months of the date of this Document and will reach a rate of 500,000 tons annually, in accordance with an agreed schedule of deliveries.

3) Upon receipt of the U.S. assurances for the provision of LWR's and for arrangements for interim energy alternatives, the D.P.R.K. will freeze its graphite-moderated reactors and related facilities and will eventually dismantle these reactors and related facilities.

—The freeze on the D.P.R.K.'s graphite-moderated reactors and related facilities will be fully implemented within one month of the date of this document. During the one-month period, and throughout the freeze, the I.A.E.A. will be allowed to monitor this freeze and the D.P.R.K. will provide full access to the I.A.E.A. for this purpose.

—Dismantlement of the D.P.R.K.'s graphite-moderated reactors and related facilities will be completed when the LWR project is completed.

—The U.S. and the D.P.R.K. will cooperate fully in finding a method to store safely the spent fuel from the 5MW(e) experimental reactor during the construction of the LWR project, and to dispose of the fuel in a safe manner that does not involve reprocessing in the D.P.R.K.

4) As soon as possible after the date of this document U.S. and D.P.R.K. experts will hold two sets of experts talks.

—At one set of talks, experts will discuss issues related to alternative energy and the replacement of the graphite-moderated reactor program with the LWR project.

—At the other set of talks, experts will discuss specific arrangements for the spent fuel storage and ultimate disposition.

II. The two sides will move toward full normalization of political and economic relations.

1) Within three months of the date of this document, both sides will reduce barriers to trade and investment, including restrictions on telecom services and financial transactions.

2) Each side will open a liaison office in the other's capital following resolution of consular and other technical issues through expert-level discussions.

3) As progress is made on issues of concern to each side, the U.S. and D.P.R.K. will upgrade bilateral relations to the Ambassadorial level.

III. Both sides will work together for peace and security on a nuclear-free Korean Peninsula.

1) The U.S. will provide formal assurances to the D.P.R.K. against the threat or use of nuclear weapons by the U.S.

2) The D.P.R.K. will consistently take steps to implement the North-South Joint Declaration on the Denuclearization of the Korean Peninsula.

3) The D.P.R.K. will engage in North-South dialogue, as this Agreed Framework will help create an atmosphere that promotes such dialogue.

IV. Both sides will work together to strengthen the international nuclear non-proliferation regime.

1) The D.P.R.K. will remain a party to the Treaty on the Non-Proliferation of Nuclear Weapons (NPT) and will allow implementation of its safeguards agreement under the Treaty.

2) Upon conclusion of the supply contract for the provision of the LWR project, ad hoc and routine inspections will resume under the D.P.R.K.'s safeguards agreement with the I.A.E.A. with respect to the facilities not subject to the freeze. Pending conclusion of the supply contract, inspections required by the I.A.E.A. for the continuity of safeguards will continue at the facilities not subject to the freeze.

3) When a significant portion of the LWR project is completed, but before delivery of key nuclear components, the D.P.R.K. will come into full compliance with its safeguards agreement with the I.A.E.A. (INFCIRC/403), including taking all steps that may be deemed necessary by the I.A.E.A., following consultations with the Agency, with regard to verifying the accuracy and completeness of the D.P.R.K.'s initial report on all nuclear material in the D.P.R.K.

(signed)   Kang Sok Ju
              Robert L. Gallucci

Index

Abu Musa Island, 164
Abu Nidal, 54
Acheson, Dean, 88
Afghanistan, Soviet intervention, 27, 28, 161; Pakistan, 54, 55; Reagan administration, 104
Agreed Framework (U.S.-North Korea Agreed Framework, 1994), 5–6, 111; appeasement charged, 9, 10, 80, 251–52; as bilateral accord, 234n2; certification process, 222; congressional support, 231; Congress and public opinion, 220–21; covert circumvention, 222; described, 198, 230–31, 248; domestic crisis, 227; light-water reactors (LWRs), 172; negotiations leading to, 218; North Korean complaints about U.S. compliance, 237n94; North Korean concerns, 200, 228; North Korea's nuclear intentions, 225; origins, 38; as policy departure, 70; political transition, 228; Republican critique, 79–80; soft landing for North, 248; text of, 274–77
Ajami, Fouad, 151
Albright, Madeleine K.: air raids on Iraq, 138; assertive multilateralism, 32–33; categories of nations, 238; hard-line policy to Iraq, 131–32, 136–37, 263–65; Iran policy, 159, 177–78, 190, 270–74 (text); Iraq, 69, 131; Iraq regime change, 101; Khatami's conciliatory statements, 177, 270–74 (text); North Korea sanctions plan, 214; on rogue states, 3; sanctions against Iraq, 102; security challenges to NATO, 238; use of force in Kosovo, 32
Algiers agreement, 161

allies, relations with, 82–87, 243–44. *See also* Britain; Canada; Europe; Japan; Mexico
American-Israel Public Affairs Committee (AIPAC), 53, 241
Amin, Idi, 50
Amn al-Khass (Special Security Organization, SSO), 142–43
Angola, 51, 104, 110
Annan, Kofi, 134, 135, 137, 156n59
Anti-Ballistic Missile (ABM) Treaty, 41
appeasement: conditional reciprocity compared, 111; German-French, 83; of North Korea, 9, 10, 80, 81, 111, 243; strategic inflexibility and, 243; of Syria, 77
Arab-Israeli peace process. *See* Middle East peace process
Arab-Israeli War (1973), 109, 110
Arab states, Iraq and, 101, 124, 131, 140
Arafat, Yasir, 174, 188–89
arms control: ballistic missiles, 41; Clinton administration, 64; conditional containment, 105; détente, 109; end of the Cold War, 34; Reagan administration, 104
Aspin, Les, 29–30, 39, 211
Assembly of Experts, Iran, 179
assertive multilateralism, 32–33
asymmetrical containment, 98, 103, 246
Australia Group, 36
authoritarian regimes, 26, 44n17, 170
Aziz, Tariq, 129, 133, 135, 137

Baath Party, 124, 142, 143
backlash states, 2; characteristics, 60–61; Lake article on, 2–3, 7, 256–62 (text). *See also* rogue state concept
Baghdad Pact, 160